Sweden, the Swastika and Stalin

Titles available and forthcoming in the *Societies at War* series

War Damage in Western Europe
Nicola Lambourne

War Aims in the Second World War
Victor Rothwell

*The Battle of Britain on Screen:
'The Few' in British Film and Television Drama*
S. P. MacKenzie

British Children's Fiction in the Second World War
Owen Dudley Edwards

The Second World War and Forced Migration Movements in Europe
Rainer Schulze

Britain, Ireland and the Second World War
Ian S. Wood

*Sweden, the Swastika and Stalin:
The Swedish Experience in the Second World War*
John Gilmour

Sweden, the Swastika and Stalin

The Swedish Experience in the Second World War

John Gilmour

Edinburgh University Press

For Elspeth

© John Gilmour, 2010, 2011

First Published 2010 by
Edinburgh University Press Ltd
22 George Square, Edinburgh
www.euppublishing.com

This paperback edition 2011

Typeset in Melior by
Iolaire Typesetting, Newtonmore

A CIP record for this book is available from the British Library

ISBN 978 0 7486 2747 9 (paperback)

The right of John Gilmour
to be identified as author of this work
has been asserted in accordance with
the Copyright, Designs and Patents Act 1988.

Contents

List of Figures   vii
Acknowledgements   viii

Introduction   1

Part One

1. Shades of Neutrality? Political Challenges and Social Changes, 1900–1939   7
2. Wartime Power and Personalities   22
3. Isolation, 1939–1941   35
4. Towards the Turning Point, July 1941–July 1943   74
5. Eastern Approaches and Western Reproaches: Finland's Continuation War and the Collapse of Germany, June 1941–May 1945   92
6. Trading with Germany and the Allies – Blackmail and Brinksmanship   113

Part Two

7. Security, Subversion, Spies and Sabotage   133
8. The Battle for Sweden's Mind – Propaganda and Censorship   157
9. Race, Rejection, Reception, Rescue and Redemption – Swedish Humanitarian Endeavours   188

10.	Military Matters	209
11.	The Front at Home – *Beredskapstiden*	238
12.	Looking Back in Anger? The Assault on 'Small-State Realism'	270

Abbreviations and Glossary   291

Reference Sources and Bibliography   295

Index   309

Figures

1.	Map of strategic locations, 1939–45	x–xi
2.	Map of important rail and sea routes, 1939–45	xii–xiii
3.	Stockholm women's hunger march, 1918	9
4.	Gloster Gladiator fighter aircraft, 1939	13
5.	The wartime Coalition Government, 1939	26
6.	The oil tanker *Sveadrott*, 1940	119
7.	SOE sabotage at Krylbo Station, 1941	141
8.	Swedish newspapers, 1944	167
9.	The *Donau* loading for Auschwitz, Oslo, 1943	194
10.	Preparing for the *Luftwaffe*, 1940	255
11.	The transit myth, 1944	282
12.	The transit reality, 1941	283

Acknowledgements

The genesis of this book was in a Lund bookshop in 1967 when, as a history undergraduate at Edinburgh University, I bought Wahlbäck and Boberg's recently published collection of documents on Sweden and the war. The interest that this subject created remained with me for many years until, when teaching post-graduates on the Second World War MSc course at Edinburgh, I complained to my colleague, Jill Stephenson, about the paucity of material about wartime Sweden in English for students, particularly in relation to the Home Front. With her encouragement and that of the series editors, Paul Addison and Jeremy Crang, this book has been written.

Such an enterprise can only stand on the shoulders of others in the field and publications containing their research, findings and conclusions are listed in the Bibliography with admiration, appreciation and gratitude. In addition, the staff at the National Archives; Riksarkivet, Kungliga biblioteket, and Arbetsrörelsens arkivet in Stockholm; Edinburgh University Library and the National Library of Scotland have patiently and professionally supported my research.

Many friends and colleagues have also provided encouragement and advice. I want to thank particularly Paul Addison, Donald Bloxham, Gunilla Blom-Thomsen, Peter Graves, David Sugden and Neville Wylie for adding to their busy lives to provide feedback and comment without which this work would be much poorer. Encouragement, assistance and background information have also come from the late Lt Commander Dan Gibson-Harris in Ottawa, Ambassadors Leif Leifland and John Grant, and Philip Mallet who has also kindly allowed me to quote from his father's unpublished memoirs. I also wish to thank Curtis Brown Group Ltd, London on behalf of David Mitchell for permission to quote from *Cloud Atlas*, and Prospect Publishing Ltd on behalf of Walter Russel Mead for permission to quote from *Prospect* Magazine. For permission to reproduce photos, I would like to thank SVT Imagebank and PA Photos.

The generosity over the years of Jonas and Maja Frykman in Lund, Nils and Gun Peterson, the late Ingvar Tagtström and Ulla in Stockholm, Peter Bares and Eva Viktorsson in Göteborg, Brita and Torsten Nilsson and Lisa Andersson in Staffanstorp, and Britta Sugden in Edinburgh has allowed me to connect with Sweden in a way that has sustained my inner dialogue about this subject.

Finally, in preparing this book, I have depended on, and valued the unstinting support, tolerance, encouragement and advice from my wife Elspeth who has had to live with the intrusion of this demanding venture into our lives. Without her, this work would not have happened.

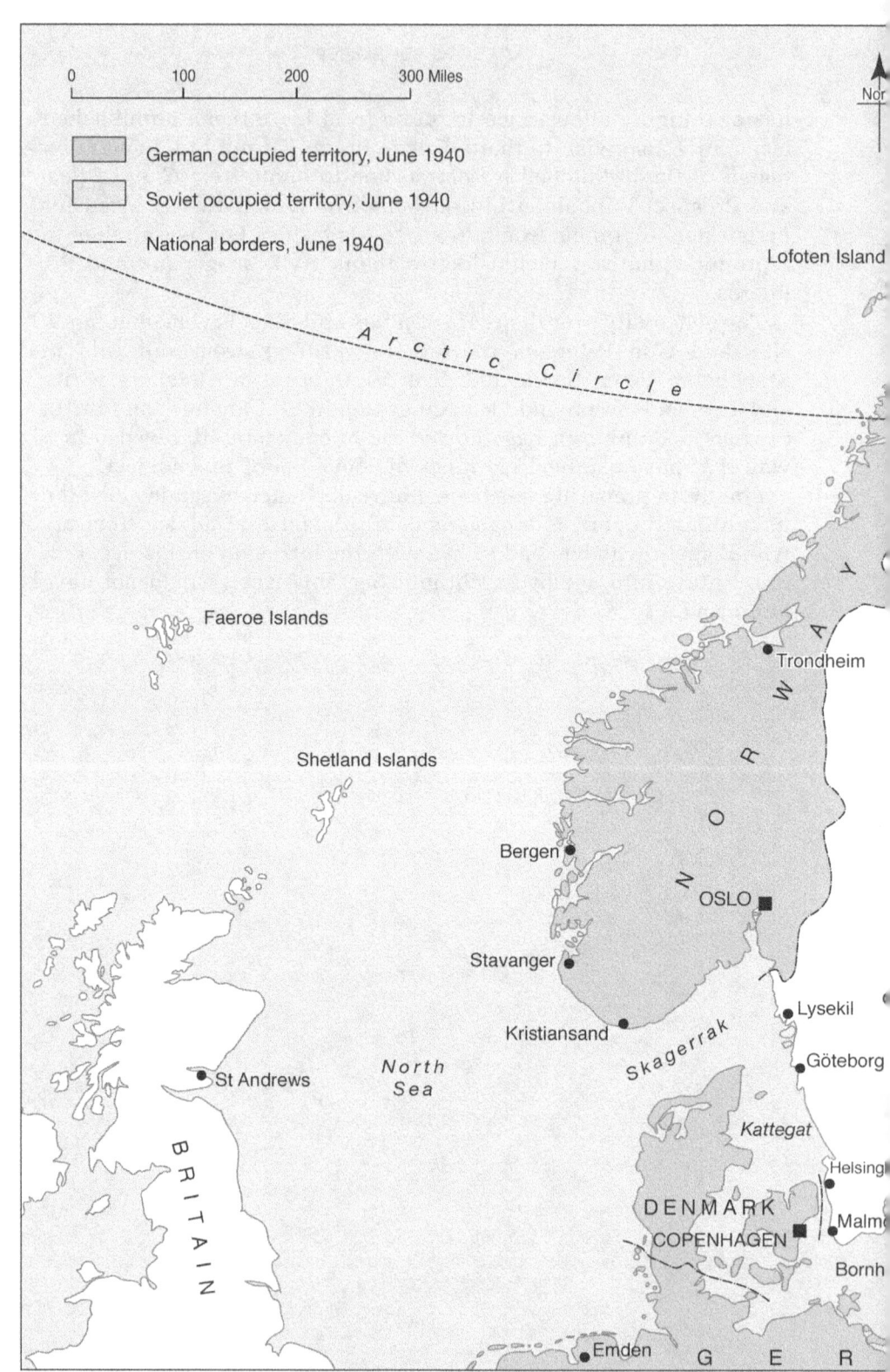

FIGURE 1 Map of strategic locations, 1939–45.

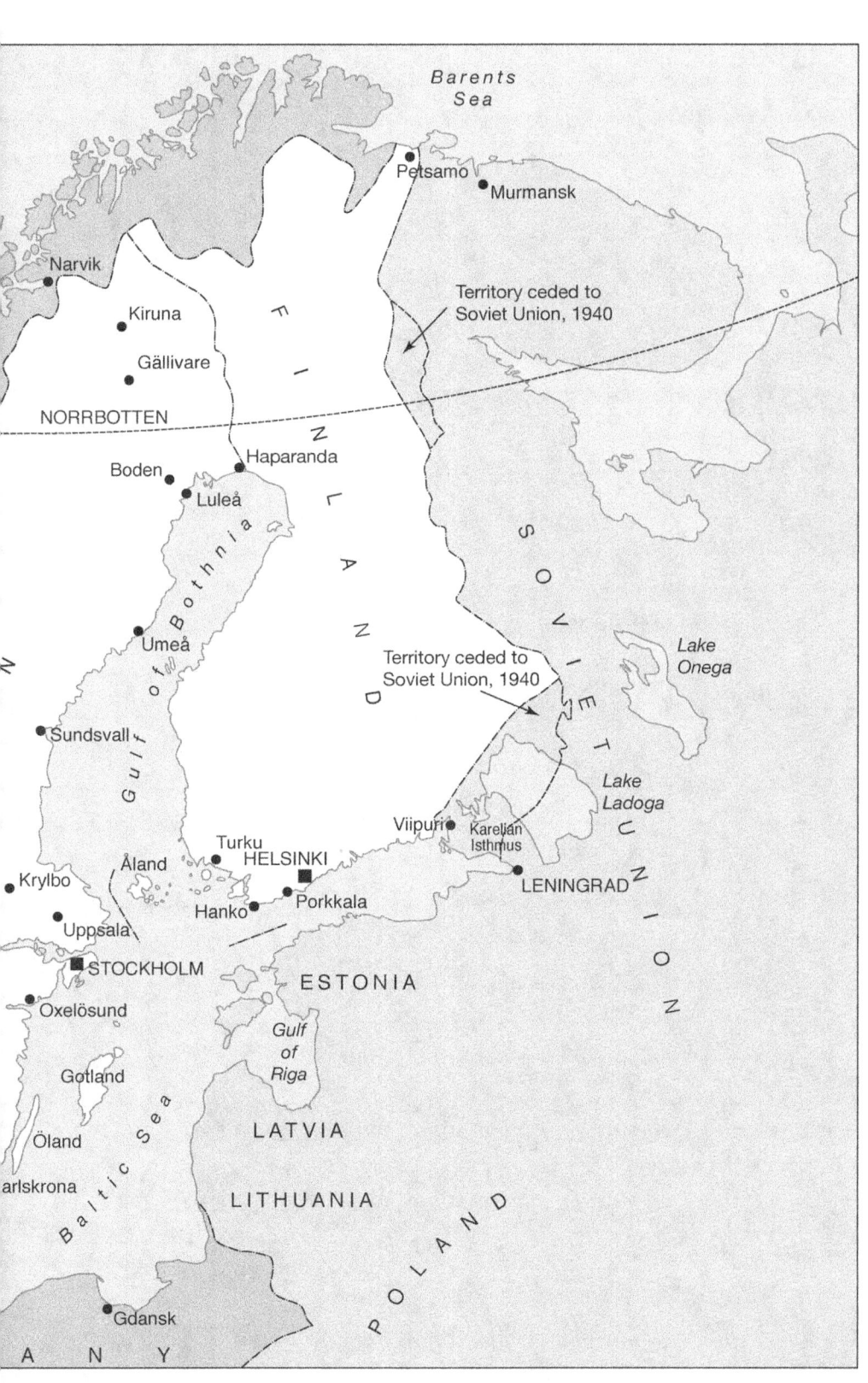

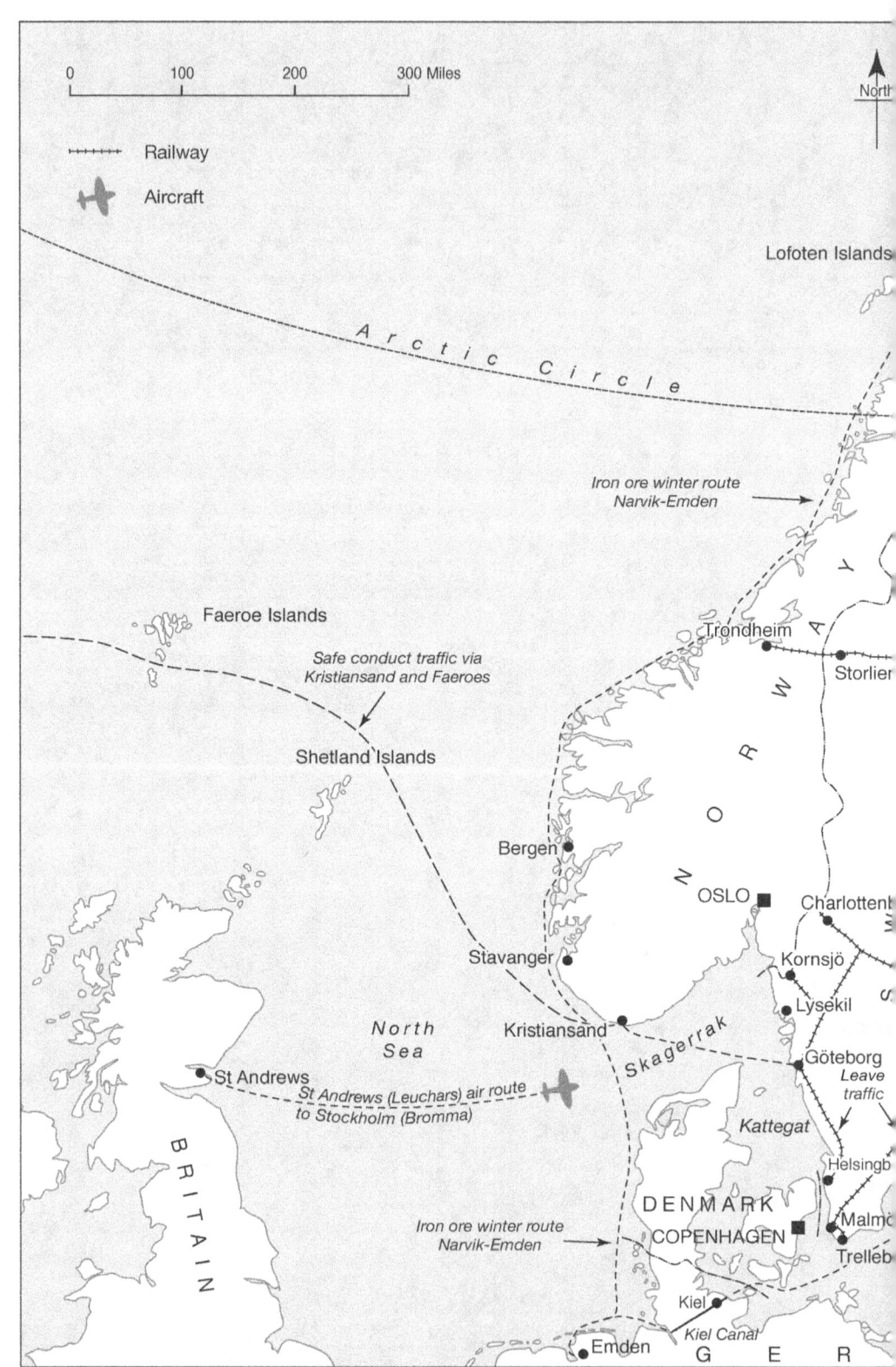

FIGURE 2 Map of important rail and sea routes, 1939–45.

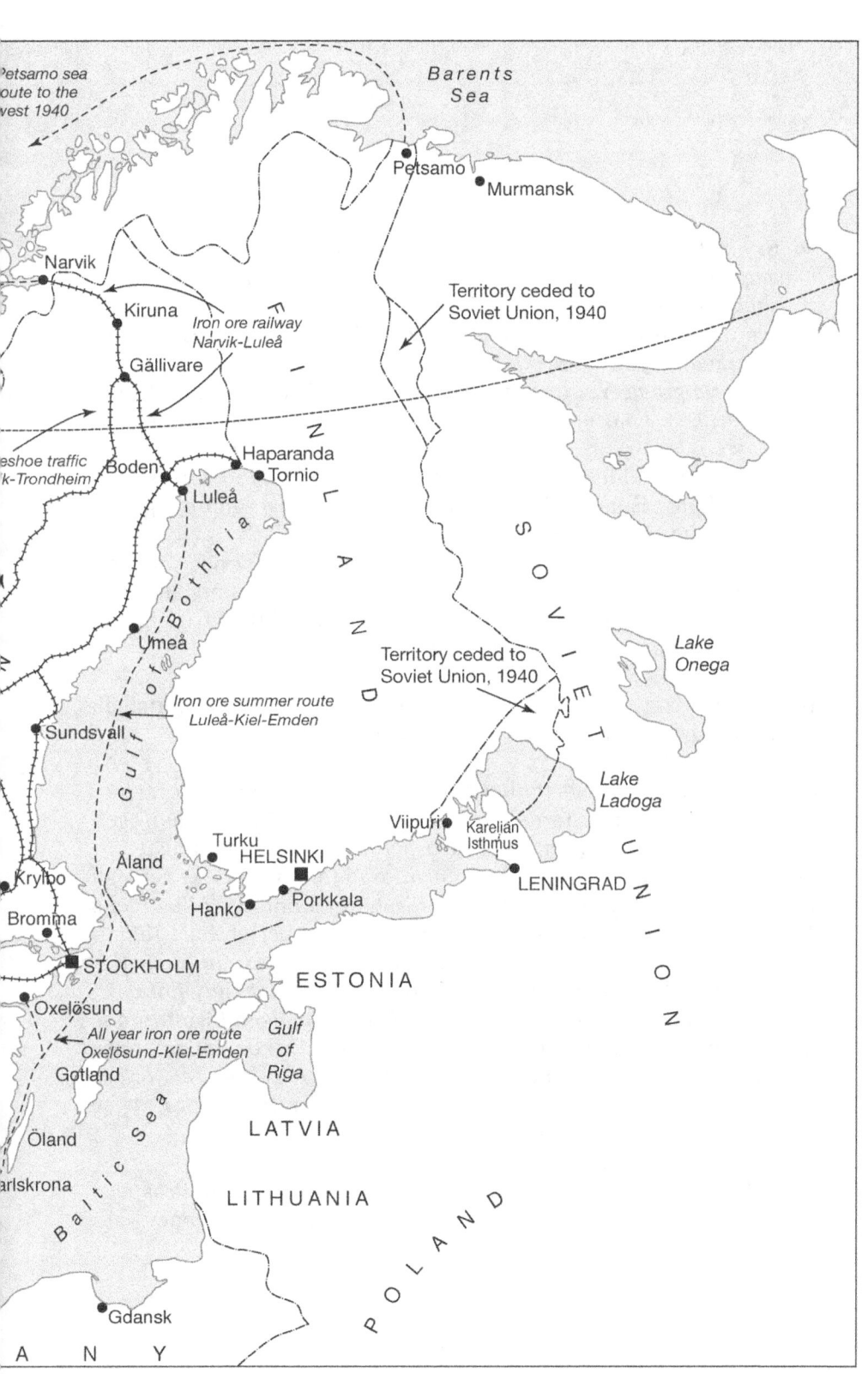

- Exposition: the workings of the actual past + the virtual past may be illustrated by an event well known to collective history such as the sinking of the Titanic. The disaster as it actually occurred descends into obscurity as its eyewitnesses die off, documents perish + the wreck of the ship dissolves in its Atlantic grave. Yet a virtual sinking of the Titanic created from reworked memories, papers, hearsay, fiction – in short, belief – grows ever 'truer'. The actual past is brittle, ever-dimming + ever more problematic to access + reconstruct: in contrast, the virtual past is malleable, ever-brightening + ever more difficult to circumvent/expose as fraudulent.
- The present presses the virtual past into its own service, to lend credence to its mythologies + legitimacy to the imposition of will. Power seeks + is the right to 'landscape' the virtual past. (He who pays the historian calls the tune.)

From Cloud Atlas by David Mitchell, pp. 408–9. © David Mitchell. Permission granted by Curtis Brown Group Ltd.

Att ta del av en främlings tankar om den egna nationens historia kan vara en omskakande erfarenhet. I ett sådant verk känner man igen många personer och situationer men perspektiven tycks något förskjutna. På vissa ställen förklarar författaren för mycket och ger sig i kast med det självklara medan han eller hon på andra ställen tycks förutsätta en mängd kunskaper som endast experter har. Ibland tycks skribenten utöva en finkänslig och helt onödig politisk försiktighet för att vid andra tillfällen åsidosätta de mest självklara och rimliga konventioner och tabun. Främlingar är ömsom förbluffande ogenomskinliga ömsom irriterande banala och lyckas sällan träffa helt rätt, men den ovanliga vinkel från vilken de betraktar den för oss så välbekanta terrängen gör det ofta möjligt för främlingar att se saker och ting som vi infödda missar.

From 'Tumultuous Britain', by Walter Russel Mead, in Prospect, November 2007, p. 40 [translated by Gunilla Blom-Thomsen].

Introduction

This history of Sweden during the Second World War is intended mainly for English-speaking readers in search of a key to the extensive Swedish-language historiography of the period. There are really two histories of wartime Sweden. One covers the outward-facing struggle to keep Sweden from being drawn into the war while maintaining the welfare and freedom of its citizens. The other covers the immense official and communal effort on the Home Front to mobilise the country's defences, resources and security.

The book is divided into two Parts to address both histories and provide the reader with insights into the key events and changes that shaped Swedish policies and experience. Many of the issues that arose during this period have a remarkable resonance with global issues of the twenty-first century which readers may find familiar. These include the overbearing use of military and economic power by large states to enforce their will on smaller countries; the treatment of refugees of other races fleeing from tyranny; the extent to which civil liberties should be limited in a democratic state to protect its citizens from external threat; the impotence of humanitarian criticism when directed at determined abusers of human rights; the extent to which relations should be maintained with regimes whose policies are abhorrent in order not to close off options; and the ability of a democratic society to express contradictory wishes and still expect its politicians to reconcile those wishes with implementable policies.

A large number of excellent Swedish-language secondary sources have informed the content of this book and these have been supplemented by memoirs and the results of my own researches in both Swedish and British archives. The intention has been to equip the reader with an understanding of Swedish perspectives, looking outwards, and the many unique characteristics of wartime Sweden, for example the fixation on Finland; the emphasis on national unity; the fear of Stalin's terror to the east; and the influence retained by the monarch in an electoral democracy.

The external account in Part I begins with an overview in Chapters 1 and 2 to provide an insight into the development of Swedish policies, institutions, society and culture, a process that did not of course begin – or end – in 1939. Chapters 3 to 5 offer a comprehensive narrative account of wartime events and Swedish responses that are necessarily focused on interactions with the great powers. Chapter 6 concerns Sweden's trading activity with the warring nations. This was also an integral part of foreign policy yet operated through the dynamics of international negotiation.

In Part II, Chapters 7 and 8 look at two areas of external incursion into Swedish life, espionage and propaganda, and how Sweden dealt with these. Chapter 9 concerns incursions of a different kind, by refugees, and Sweden's changing role as a haven in war-torn Europe. The military resources and deployments that underpinned Sweden's ability to defend herself from attack are described in Chapter 10. In Chapter 11, the deep impact of war and the consequential changes for Swedish society across a spectrum of activity from politics to literature are outlined. These serve to counter any view that neutral Sweden was untouched by the surrounding hostilities. Finally, the development of Swedish historiography for the period and subsequent controversies over Sweden's ambiguous role and actions are traced in Chapter 12 where some paradigms are suggested to assist the reader to make their own assessment.

Given constraints on length, it is inevitable that many relevant topics and issues concerning Sweden's war have had to be covered briefly or mentioned in passing. These include the story of Raoul Wallenberg's heroic mission to rescue Jews in Hungary in 1944, the Swedes who fought in the service of other countries, the merchant shipping fleet's role in supplying both sides, the activities of the Danish and Norwegian resistance groups in Sweden, the involvement of Swedes in official and unofficial peace initiatives, and the support given to the German resistance movement.

The focus instead is on Sweden's story, to explain how and why the war affected the country's leaders and people. For many English-speaking readers, this will be the first time that they are able to learn about and perhaps understand better the ambiguities surrounding Sweden and the Second World War. If so, then this book will have achieved its objective.

Part One

═══ 1 ═══

Shades of Neutrality? Political Challenges and Social Changes, 1900–1939

Ominously for neutral Sweden, the first shots of the Second World War were fired only 120 miles away on the opposite shore of the Baltic Sea at 4.45 a.m. on 1 September 1939. The Polish military fortification on Westerplatte overlooking the Gdańsk (Danzig) harbour channel was shelled by the German battleship *Schleswig-Holstein*, named after the Danish territory seized by the Prussians in 1863. Gdańsk lay to the south east of Sweden's largest Baltic naval base in Karlskrona, named in honour of Swedish seventeenth-century warrior-king Karl XI. The dockyard and town were about one hour's flying time away from Germany and well within range of the Ju87 bombers which had earlier attacked the Polish city of Wieluń at 4.40 a.m., killing eight per cent of the civilian population. German aggression again overshadowed Scandinavia, this time by air as well as land and sea. What was Sweden's position on the threshold of war and what had happened in the turbulent years leading up to 1939?

The first years of the twentieth century had been characterised by a bitter political debate over the state of the nation's defences triggered by right-wing fears of a resurgent Russia. The ruling Liberal party was reluctant to spend money on warships and military training and preferred to give priority to social reforms for the benefit of the working classes. This policy was challenged by an alliance of right-wingers whose fervour was due, in part, to renewed 'Russification' attempts after 1910 by the authorities in the neighbouring Russian Duchy of Finland. Finland had been a part of Sweden for six hundred years until its incorporation by Russia in

1810 and retained strong connections with the Swedish establishment. The writings of Sven Hedin, a world-famous explorer and great admirer of the Kaiser, helped to raise the popular anti-Russian temperature.

In 1914, the First World War found Sweden unprepared, divided and restless. King Gustav V was strongly influenced by his German wife Victoria, a granddaughter of Kaiser Wilhelm I, who actively sought a closer relationship with Berlin. A public declaration of support for arms spending by the King led to the fall of Liberal Prime Minister Staaf's administration in February 1914, and a major political crisis. The Social Democrats, the party which increasingly represented the working classes, had good reason to fear a military coup that could end almost a century of neutrality and promote an alliance with Germany. But the ensuing election of March 1914, which turned on the issue of 'people-power versus royal-power', increased the representation of the Social Democrats at the expense of the Liberals. Unable to persuade any of the professional politicians to head a government, the King offered the post of Prime Minister to Hjalmar Hammarskjöld (Dag Hammarskjöld's father), a law professor at the University of Uppsala. K. A. Wallenberg (Raoul Wallenberg's grandfather) became Foreign Minister.

When war broke out in 1914, the upper classes including the royal family, the military, and elements of the business community campaigned with various degrees of openness for Sweden to join Germany's struggle against Russia – and what were frequently portrayed as the Slavic hordes to the east. For his part Hammarskjöld pursued a policy of purist neutrality, but Sweden paid a high price for the tendentious and overbearing manner of his dealings with the Entente that was blockading Europe. The rights (and duties) of the neutral power and its nationals, as the authoritarian Hammarskjöld tirelessly and tediously reminded the Entente, were encapsulated in the Hague Conventions, but his reluctance to bend and negotiate trade agreements led to food shortages and worker unrest while profiteers grew rich on the misery of others. There were a small number of high-profile 'incidents'. Just after Lenin had passed through Stockholm in April 1917 on his way to St Petersburg and revolution (pausing only to meet some fellow socialists and to buy the coat he subsequently wore to address the Russian crowds), Sweden teetered on the brink of serious unrest caused by heavy-handed policing of hunger marches.[1] The hard lessons learned from this painful experience were to be applied in the Second World War.

FIGURE 3 Stockholm women's hunger march, 1918 – one result of the Government's inflexible approach to upholding Swedish 'rights' in international law during the First World War.
(PA Photos)

The crisis was defused by the dismissal of Prime Minister Hammarskjöld (now nicknamed '*Hungerskjöld*') and a general election which led to the formation of the first Liberal-Social Democrat Coalition Government. The subsequent Swedish constitutional reforms of 1917–18 took place in the shadow of more dramatic revolutionary 'reforms' a few hundred miles to the east in St Petersburg. While Russia was adopting a Bolshevik agenda, Sweden was taking the first steps on a Social Democratic programme of universal suffrage, workers' rights and better living conditions for all. These ambitions would not be realised fully for many decades but parliamentary democracy was firmly established after the overdue reduction of royal authority in government.

SOCIAL DEMOCRATIC PROGRESS, DEFENCE AND FOREIGN POLICY, 1920–1939

Sweden entered the uncertainties of the 1920s with parliamentarianism supreme and the rise of the left having altered and fragmented the party political landscape. No party could now command a majority in the *Riksdag* (Parliament) and so for thirteen years until 1933, Sweden was ruled by a succession of eight minority governments. Politicians struggled to find solutions to intractable economic dislocation caused by war and its aftermath as in the rest of Europe in the 1920s and 1930s. Sweden was not immune from widespread unemployment arising from collapsed markets and industrial overcapacity. Against a background of financial crisis and joblessness, the two questions of social welfare and defence-spending still dominated political debate.

In March 1920, the Social Democrats formed their first-ever Government led by Hjalmar Branting in which former firebrand Per Albin Hansson was appointed Minister of War. He was to hold this post again in two later Social Democrat Governments (1921–3 and 1924–6). These periods in office gave him the authority and insight required to carry out swingeing reductions in defence expenditure in 1925 by a third or one million kroner. Seventeen regiments were disbanded and the navy was greatly reduced. Per Albin was vilified by the right, and even the liberal press such as Torgny Segerstedt's *Göteborgs Handels-och Sjöfartstidning* (G.H.T.) expressed opposition to the measures. The cuts weakened Swedish defence materially and psychologically for the next decade but Per Albin was unrepentant. It was no part of the future vision of the Social Democrats to satisfy a reactionary monarchy and military establishment.

As early as September 1921, Per Albin had given a speech in which he first formulated the Social Democrat welfare state vision of 'making Sweden a good home for all Swedes . . .'[2] This would later be termed '*Folkhemmet*' and its association of community, safety, welfare and family attracted a broad spectrum of support, both in the cities and in the countryside. This visionary concept was the cornerstone of Per Albin's political philosophy and he became its visible symbol. Its achievement depended heavily on future political consensus and economic prosperity. After the instability of the Twenties, the Thirties witnessed the beginning of an era of Social Democratic hegemony. After deft negotiations with the Agrarian Party in September 1936, Per Albin brought them into a Social Democratic-led, two-party Coalition Government and simultaneously deprived the Conservatives of any hope of forming a government. This 1936 Coalition Government had Social Democrats Per Albin as Prime Minister, Rickard Sandler as Foreign Minister, Gustav Möller as Social Minister and Ernst Wigforss as Finance Minister.

What were Sweden's strategic interests between the wars, and how would its policy-makers deal with the changing situation? To the east Russia was now almost totally bottled up in the Gulf of Finland. Vital sea access to Leningrad was potentially threatened from the north by Finland which had declared its independence in 1917, and from the south by the new state of Estonia. Further to the south, Latvia and Lithuania occupied the remainder of the former Russian Baltic coastline. There had been minor border wrangles among the Baltic States and between Lithuania and Poland but the biggest Baltic question was the viability of Estonia, Latvia and Lithuania as independent entities overshadowed by their recent former ruler, Russia. In order to maintain stability on its Baltic doorstep, it was in Sweden's strategic interest to support these new states in their quest for political and economic progress. They could act as a buffer to Russia and perhaps avoid a repetition of their occupation by Germany in the latter years of the First World War.

Another consequence of Finnish independence from Russia was the issue of the Finnish Åland Islands. Lying only twenty miles from the Swedish coast and fifty miles north of Stockholm, they command the entrance to the Gulf of Bothnia (containing about 1,000 kilometres of Swedish coastline and the iron ore exporting ports of Luleå and Gävle) and were populated almost entirely by 10,000 Swedish speakers. The islands had been part of the Russian Duchy of Finland but were demilitarised in 1856 to contain Tsarist influence in the Baltic as part of the Crimean War settlement. In 1918 a Swedish attempt to satisfy the islanders' appeal for reunification with Sweden resulted in a stand-off with the new Finnish army. The Ålands would remain as a *leitmotiv* of Swedish policy for the coming decades. Also, Finland now formed the northern barrier between Russia and Sweden. This bulwark began territorially in the west of Finland and at the Åland Islands yet for Swedish strategists, the Finnish eastern borderlands of Karelia were traditionally regarded as the first Swedish line of defence against Russia.

To the west, meanwhile, the neighbouring countries of Norway and Denmark bordered the shores of the North Sea and Atlantic where the British Navy dominated the seas up to the Skagerrak and implicitly protected them from sea-invasion. During the First World War, these countries had also been neutral but like Sweden had been subject to Allied blockade to the detriment of their economies and sustenance. To the south lay the vengeful German neighbour bent on overthrowing the Versailles settlement and creating *lebensraum* to the east. Despite the intrusion of Danzig and the Polish Corridor,

Germany's Baltic coast remained broadly similar to its pre-1914 position and Sweden continued to lie within the German sphere of influence. During the First World War, the main role for Sweden had been its shipments of iron ore to the blast furnaces of the Second Reich. Its Third Reich successor would expect no less – whether Sweden was neutral or not.

The question of defence expenditure reared its head again in the autumn of 1930 when a *Riksdag* all-party Commission evaluated two radical alternatives: disarmament or re-armament. Disarmament was quickly rejected and pressure for substantial re-armament against a deteriorating international situation influenced the Commission when it reported in 1935. The Anglo-German Naval agreement of 1935 represented a setback for Swedish interests in that the British Navy in effect deserted the Baltic. The Italian invasion and conquest of Abyssinia demonstrated the inability of the League of Nations to protect small nations and so despite dissension within the Social Democrat party, a new defence budget based on a ten-year programme of rearmament, was adopted in 1936.

The new budget allowed the army to aim to develop a new deployment by the beginning of 1940: six divisions and a partly-mechanised cavalry brigade. The navy's disappointment at failing to secure funding to replace its three, twenty-year-old battleships was mollified by ordering two destroyers and six submarines while defensive coastal artillery was strengthened. It was in air strength, soon to be crucial, that the planners miscalculated. As early as the 1925 cuts, Per Albin had intended a strengthening of the air force but rising costs and technical development had kept this out of reach. There were only 150 mainly obsolete planes against a planned complement by 1935 of 250 machines. Critically, the emphasis also switched from fighters to bombers with the intention to destroy enemy aircraft on the ground rather than in the air. This strategic error would soon leave Sweden's territory and her cities in particular, vulnerable to threats of air-raid attack.

Throughout the Twenties and Thirties Sweden was on the sidelines in European events and the fall in the barometer of international relations from 1935 onwards was of great concern to the Swedish Foreign Ministry (*Utrikesdepartementet* or *UD*) if not to Per Albin himself. There was, however, little prospect of meaningful Nordic cooperation. The weakening of the League of Nations also forced Sweden in 1936 to re-adopt a decisive policy of neutrality as a main safeguard of the country's security. As a leading historian commented: 'not even the Scandinavian countries could now simply count on

FIGURE 4 Gloster Gladiator fighter aircraft, 1939. The British Gloster Gladiator was the backbone of Swedish fighter defence in 1939 but its maximum speed was slower than Russian and German bombers. There were only 33 operational aircraft in one squadron. In September 1939, the *Luftwaffe* had 1,179 fighters and 1,180 bombers.
(PA Photos)

Swedish assistance when in danger of war.'[3] Inter-Scandinavian discussions continued in June 1937 when Sandler sounded out his Danish and Norwegian counterparts, Peter Munch and Halvdan Koht, regarding closer cooperation with Estonia, Latvia and Lithuania. Their response was lukewarm as they wanted closer ties with Sweden itself and rejected commitments to states which might bring them into conflict with Russia. Sandler persisted but failed to link the buffer states on Sweden's western frontiers, Norway and Denmark, to those of Finland, Estonia, Latvia, and Lithuania to the east. All of the Scandinavian countries anticipated that their declarations of neutrality would again enable them to remain outside a great powers' conflict. It was not in their interests to tie themselves too closely with any other state in the worsening situation.

For Sweden, the unease created by the Munich crisis was not so much a fear of a rapacious Germany but the prospect of a conflict between Germany and Russia which could bring the warring parties close to the Swedish border, as during 1914–1918. It was against this background that the Foreign Minister, Rickard Sandler, launched a major initiative to settle the question of the Åland Islands. The attempts by the islanders between 1918 and 1921 to break away from newly independent Finland to re-unite with Sweden had been thwarted by a 1921 League of Nations ruling. The signatories to this Åland Islands Convention were by 1938 unable to oppose a determined Soviet refusal to be bound by it. Sweden felt, together with Finland, that it was vital to control the Ålands in case of war. The creation of the Stockholm Plan with Finland in 1939 set out measures which both countries would jointly take to defend the Ålands. Russia's refusal to agree in early 1939 forced Sweden to withdraw the Plan and represented a loss of prestige for both Sweden and, even more so, for Sandler. 'We ought never to have embarked on this', sighed Per Albin.[4] The Russians were concerned that a German-leaning Finnish military could allow Germany to benefit at the expense of Russia. In addition, they were unwilling to see this cooperation pulling Finland towards Scandinavia. It was not in Moscow's interest to strengthen Nordic solidarity and neutrality.

One feature of the Government's public pronouncements on foreign policy issues was their blandness, at times amounting to vagueness. This circumlocution is noticeable in many of Per Albin's speeches ('tepid' according to *UD* diplomat Sven Grafström) which strained to avoid identifying the great powers and linking them in any way to problems or advantages affecting Sweden.[5] There were good reasons for this. The great powers carefully monitored all official and semi-official utterances from the neutrals to assess whether there was any change which might be advantageous or detrimental to their own positions. So, without mentioning Hitler and the Nazis, Per Albin's wartime position was presaged by a speech that he gave in Oslo in May 1938 as Europe slid towards the Munich crisis. He declared that in principle:

> The Swedish (Social Democrat) Party is not prepared for absolute neutrality. We say instead 'we shall keep ourselves out of war.' But can we also achieve that? If a situation arises where we cannot keep ourselves out, then we must ensure that we come in on the right side. Even as a neutral, we must have our thinking directed to where our natural position is. We must look further than neutrality.[6]

He had managed to signal that he considered 'purist' neutrality to be an insufficient national policy while making it clear that for democratic Sweden there was a 'wrong' side which would shortly make its wishes felt.

The failures of Sweden's 1914–18 neutrality were also implicitly recognised in a perceptive and prescient guidance note for Swedish Heads of Mission drafted in 1939 by Erik Boheman, the UD's Secretary-General and its most senior civil servant. It contained five key forecasts. First, although neutrality would be the foundation of Swedish policy, neutrality's strict legal position would again be disregarded by the belligerents. As Roger Ogley has pointed out, the Hague Conventions can only operate if all belligerents respect a country's neutrality, and respect became increasingly threadbare in twentieth-century total warfare.[7] Secondly, no belligerent would have any motive to involve Sweden in war. Thirdly, iron ore would be the key trading issue. Fourthly, this trade would place Swedish neutrality under extreme pressure. Finally, Boheman concluded that:

> To a certain extent, neutrality must in its application be 'negotiated', above all in the commercial sphere. But the political and strategic prerequisites for its maintenance by no means appear ruled out.[8]

Boheman's note advocated the policy of *negotiated* rather than strictly *legal* neutrality, a policy which the Coalition Government was to follow.

The British declaration of support for Poland in April 1939 was intended to set a boundary to Germany's eastern ambitions. That tactic was fatally weakened by the failure of the Western Allies in August to strike a deal with Soviet Russia and led to the subsequent Russian pact with Nazi Germany. The core demand which the Soviet negotiators made unsuccessfully to the western representatives was the right to intervene in the neighbouring Baltic countries of Poland, Lithuania, Latvia, Estonia and Finland in order to protect Russia against invasion. This right was concealed in a secret protocol to the Molotov-Ribbentrop Pact in August 1939 when the two ideological enemies temporarily put national ambitions first.[9] The delayed Finnish time-bomb would explode under Swedish foreign policy after the Russo-German occupation of Poland.

A CHANGING SOCIETY, 1918–1939

Sweden had altered substantially in character during the economically challenging years between 1918 and 1939. Urbanisation continued its pre-war trend increasing pressure on housing. In 1920, 45 per cent of the 5.9 million population lived in towns compared with 30 per cent in 1900, a huge increase of over a million. The resulting accommodation crisis encouraged innovative, socially aware, simpler architectural design with a functional emphasis.[10] The Stockholm Exhibition in 1930 celebrated this style breakthrough as well as providing a showcase for a new, confident, Swedish economy. For many, the exhibition marked the beginning of modern, urbanised Sweden with hygienic housing replacing the rural squalor and urban slums that characterised living conditions for the working class in the nineteenth and early twentieth centuries. These were breeding grounds for disease, particularly tuberculosis, and created social tensions. Such conditions were targets for the Social Democratic social-economists, Gunnar and Alva Myrdal, who co-authored a 1932 book entitled *Crisis in the Population Question* (Kris i befolknings-frågan). It offered the basic premise that social reforms were needed to enhance individual liberty, such as crèches for working women, while also promoting child-bearing. Controversially, it also advocated forced sterilisation of the mentally deficient to limit the spread of genetic mental incapacity and prevent children being raised by incapable parents. From 1921, along with the vote, women were now increasingly able to gain access to contraception. The family planning organisation, *RFSU*, was founded in 1933 and in 1938 legalised abortion was introduced after a campaign to end an estimated 10,000 illegal abortions annually. The growth in women's rights was mirroring wider social changes in dress, fashion and employment. Yet women in the civil service had to leave after marriage and domestic service remained as a major occupation.

For many men, the economic circumstances of the nineteen-twenties and early thirties meant shrinking job opportunities, long periods of unemployment, wage reductions, strikes and lockouts, occasionally with violence. In the Norrland timber town of Ådalen in 1932, the army opened fire on demonstrating unarmed strikers, killing five and wounding five more. From the mid-1930s, the economy began to improve, leaving behind a low point in 1932 when an estimated 11,000 children were approaching starvation. The Social Democratic Government had introduced community work projects for the unemployed from 1932 but the introduction of workers' rights such as paid holidays in 1938 indicated the extent of economic improvement. The economic turmoil of the period had left its mark politically on Sweden, as in other western democracies, with a rising interest in both Communism and Fascism.

In 1924 the group of Social Democrats who had left in 1917 to form the Communist Party fragmented again. A liberal group led by Per Albin's old adversary Zeth Höglund split from the purist, Moscow-leaning faction under Karl Kilbom and eventually returned to the Social Democrat mainstream in 1926. The left's chronic instability continued through the 1930s with further splits leading to electoral failure for all radical left parties except the Communists. The far right was no less fragmented and no more successful. Two main groups evolved, the Swedish National Socialist Party under Birger Furugård and the breakaway National Socialist Workers Party led by Sven-Olof Lindholm. While these failed even to achieve the one per cent of the vote required for *Riksdag* representation, they were more successful in local elections. Other organisations such as the secretive and extreme 'Brown Guard' (who regarded Lindholm as a traitor to Hitler and Germany) were more interested in extra-democratic activities. One estimate of overall membership of Nazi organisations puts it around 30,000 in the mid-1930s.[11]

Although these extremist failures meant that Swedish politics would remain democratic, the inability of European democratic institutions to address economic problems and the chronic instability of governments in the twenties led many outwith the far right to look to Italy and particularly Germany as examples of decisive leadership and vitalising politics. Traditional Germanic cultural ties coupled with fear of the Soviets and the apparent success of the new, modernising Nazi brooms in sweeping out unemployment, acted as powerful magnets for those who were not convinced by the faltering Social Democrat steps towards a new Sweden.

A steady stream of Swedish visitors marvelled at the new Germany, its leadership and institutions. A high-level military delegation presented Hitler with a statuette of Karl XII, Russia's scourge and hero of Narva, on the Führer's birthday in April 1939. Hermann Göring, whose first wife was Swedish, had been decorated by King Gustav a few months earlier. However, although some sportsmen, writers and journalists were dazzled by the Berlin regime, its racist, anti-democratic policies were becoming more evident and some of the results were beginning to affect Sweden itself in the form of Jewish refugees.

Anti-semitism was neither a specifically German or Nazi phenomenon but was Europe-wide with its roots in the Middle Ages. In Sweden, Jews were not permitted to live where they pleased until the 1850s while anti-semitic sentiments could even be found in the works of the late nineteenth-century progressive author, August

Strindberg.[12] The eastern European pogroms during that period also created Jewish immigration into Sweden causing concern among small businessmen about Russian and Polish-Jewish 'parasites' and 'downright riff-raff'. After 1918 there was a gradual growth in anti-semitic groups and many of their members joined the fledgling Swedish Nazi parties in the 1930s.[13] Göteborg, with its high urban unemployment, was particularly fertile ground for both. Nevertheless, in its anti-semitic characteristics Sweden was by the 1930s in step with most other main-stream, democratic European societies, Britain and France included.

In Sweden, Jews – along with Catholics – had traditionally been discriminated against on religious grounds but when nineteenth-century scientific racial studies developed into full-blown eugenics in the twentieth century, this distinction shifted to racial characteristics. To underline the contemporary respectability of such work, the State Racebiology Institute opened in 1922 with all-party agreement. Their well-meaning focus on the categorisation of people in order to cultivate and safeguard the Swedish 'race' leading to improved lives for all, nevertheless increased the separateness of the Jewish community and of course boosted Swedish interest in Nazi racial theories.

The defensive political mindset that supported the protection of race also led to the discussion of forced sterilisation for the 'mentally deficient' as early as 1922. This practice began in Sweden in 1935 following its earlier introduction in thirty-three American States, as well as Denmark, Norway and Finland. Forced sterilisation in Sweden persisted until 1975, claiming over 60,000 victims and its widespread acceptance can be gauged by only one politician opposing it at the time of introduction. Racial theory had also entered mainstream Swedish opinion facilitating open discussion of 'the Jewish question' but would provide a later unwelcome cultural association with the genocidal policies in Berlin. While Swedish emphasis was on the elimination of genetic defects, the Nazi emphasis was on the elimination of racial groups.

The new regime in Germany was active in its persecution of German Jewry and from 1933 to 1938, 150,000 fled. About 3,000 refugees entered Sweden up to 1939 despite restrictive policies similar to those applied by most western states at that time. Sweden introduced openly protective immigration controls for the first time in 1927 reflecting the country's growing xenophobia.[14] These were reviewed in 1936 and further tightened in 1938 against Jewish refugees yet influential voices were raised in anger at the treatment of Jews in Germany and Sweden. Foremost among the newspapers was the *GHT* under Segerstedt which published atrocity reports from Germany with headlines such as: 'Jews whipped to death in concentration camp.'[15] On Swedish radio, the humanitarian activist Nathanael Beskow roundly criticised Swedes for their 'national selfishness' in ignoring the plight of refugees.[16] The corresponding political debates were now openly tinged with racism – frequently disguised as unemployment concerns – and immigration restrictions would not be eased until the Holocaust reached the borders of Sweden.

Mass media in the form of press and radio were growing and the inter-war period was also particularly productive in arts, literature and the youthful medium of cinema. Alongside the established national newspapers such as Dagens *Nyheter (DN)* and *Svenska Dagbladet (SvD)* was an active regional press including *Norrbottens Kuriren* and *Sydsvenska Dagbladet*. The newspaper press covered the political spectrum from the far-left communist *Ny Dag* to the pro-Nazi *Aftonbladet* and most papers had some direct or indirect connection to a political party. The Swedish press began to be closely watched by Germany for signs of support or criticism following Hitler's takeover in 1933. *GHT* was described as being dominated by 'Jewish capital' and *SvD*'s Gustaf Stridsberg as 'England-friendly' by a diplomat reporting back from the German Legation in Stockholm.[17]

Radio had been established in 1923 with an organisation, *Radiotjänst AB*, based on the British model of John Reith's independent BBC. Education and information were the public service broadcaster's aims and the new monopoly was jointly owned by the state and the press, who were given this element of control as reassurance that newspapers would not be eliminated as a result of the new medium. *Radiotjänst* surged forward with its content of popular educational programming for licence payers that included lectures and talks but it was not until over a decade later that a news and comment programme, *Dagens Eko,* was introduced in 1937. Notably, *Radiotjänst*'s social reportage was distinctly progressive.

Swedish cinema was also progressive, particularly the director Victor Sjöström who enjoyed a successful creative partnership with the novelist Selma Lagerlöf. The young film actress, Greta Garbo, developed her craft in Sweden before her Hollywood years. Not all Swedish films were of the quality of Garbo's classic, *Gösta Berlings Saga*. A particularly popular genre, *pilsnerfilmen*, portrayed crude stereotypes of upright characters overcoming their adversaries including, for example, usurious Jews.

Literature was particularly energetic with the emergence of the 'proletarian' authors in the early 1930s. The work of writers like Harry Martinson and Ivar Lo-Johansson, while creating literature of superb quality, equally disclosed unpleasant aspects of Swedish society that the middle classes had previously ignored. Musically, artistes like Evert Taube introduced the more exotic rhythms of South America into Swedish repertoires. Taube, like Martinson, had been a merchant seaman in Sweden's global fleet and both used their exotic experiences to enhance their art.

In the twenty years since the end of the First World War, Sweden had become a more progressive, modern, and urbanised country with the stirrings of major social change amplified by an almost continuous Social Democratic presence in government from 1932. In the 1930s Sweden was in the forefront of rational, research-based social policy but although forced sterilisation appears dissonant alongside new pension arrangements, the policy objective was consistent: to improve the economic and social welfare of the Swedish population based on political consensus. As a society, it remained stratified by class, hobbled by deference, rigid with formality and xenophobic, particularly towards Jews. Although in its anti-Semitism, Sweden was firmly in the mainstream European tradition, Swedes largely rejected extremist Nazi policies and brutality. Yet, the combination of interest in racial categorisation and narrow nationalism coupled with a tradition of national self-preoccupation meant that most failed to appreciate the urgency of the pre-war plight of Jewish refugees. Many Swedes were only one generation away from grinding poverty, disease and malnutrition, both urban and rural. Not surprisingly, their first concern was for their own economic welfare. The nation was changing slowly from a rural-based society to an urban one but cultural and social change was lagging behind a steady shift in employment and residential statistics.

Sweden's modernisation, like its politics, was a gradual process. In 1939, the committed neutral remained as vulnerable to great power pressure as in 1914–18 but had survived and learned from that earlier bruising experience. Its neutrality policy was now based on self-interest and flexibility rather than purist and brittle legal interpretations of neutrality. The investment in defending neutrality was too little and too late but Per Albin, having cut expenditure on arms, was now faced with the consequences. He would become the personification of the policy of remaining out of war for the benefit of Sweden's people and would not deviate from that aim for the next five challenging years. While living in London in October 1915 where he was working as a foreign correspondent, Per Albin had been invited to join the British army in its war against Germany.[18] Almost thirty years later in 1942, Winston Churchill also hoped Per Albin and his Government would join Britain against Germany.[19] On neither occasion were these hopes realised.

Notes

1. Lindqvist, Drömmar och verklighet, p. 182.
2. Ibid. p. 292.
3. Carlgren, Sverige och Baltikum, p. 34.
4. Isaksson, Per Albin, p. 377.
5. Grafström, Anteckningar, 1 May 1940.
6. Isaksson, Per Albin, pp. 365–6.
7. Ogley, The theory and practice of neutrality, p. 8, and Best Humanity in warfare, pp. 244–62.
8. Carlgren, Svensk utrikespolitik, pp. 13–14.
9. Article I. In the event of a territorial and political rearrangement in the areas belonging to the Baltic States (Finland, Estonia, Latvia, Lithuania), the northern boundary of Lithuania shall represent the boundary of the spheres of influence of Germany and USSR.
10. Dahlberg, Hundra år i Sverige, pp. 94–151.
11. Heléne Lööw, quoted in Svanberg & Tydén, Sverige och Förintelsen, p. 60.
12. Strindberg, Det nya riket.
13. Svanberg & Tydén, Sverige och Förintelsen, pp. 58–60.
14. Utlänningslag (1927:333) Aliens Act of 1927 (1927:333).
15. Svanberg & Tydén, Sverige och Förintelsen, pp. 99–100.
16. Ibid. pp. 108–9.
17. Thulstrup, Med lock och pock, p. 27.
18. Arbetarrörelsens arkiv, Stockholm, Per Albins Brev, Letter from Capt. Thomas P. Mills asking Per Albin to join up 'as one of the unmarried men of military age living in St Pancras . . .' 18 October 1915.
19. 'I feel it most important that Sweden should be in with us all before the end . . .' National Archives, London, WSC to Roosevelt 25/10/42 PREM 3/417/1.

2

Wartime Power and Personalities

During the 1930s, the Swedish political landscape became increasingly dominated by the Social Democrats, who had governed since 1936 in coalition with the Agrarian Party. This Government collapsed in December 1939 due to disagreements over foreign policy and Finland. There were 'activists' within the Cabinet and the wider political community who wanted a more vigorous stance in supporting Finland. The Finns were resisting Soviet pressure to concede territory to improve Russian defence, a position which quickly developed into the Russo-Finnish Winter War. The most prominent of those activists was Foreign Minister Rickard Sandler whose Finnish policy was strongly opposed within the Cabinet, leading to his resignation. Among his strident critics was party colleague and Finance Minister Ernst Wigforss. Wigforss feared that further commitment to Finland would lead to Swedish hostilities with Russia, the geopolitical enemy that the military establishment longed to attack and the ideological enemy that the right-wing politicians yearned to eliminate. Two weeks of tough negotiations by Per Albin took place to bring the other parties into a broad-based Coalition Government. This was not a simple coming-together of political rivals under the banner of national unity to deal with the problem of the Winter War and the wider Allied-German conflict. Rather, it was the result of some prolonged bargaining, particularly with the Conservatives. The resulting wartime Coalition Government was to last until the end of July 1945, its durability tested by many external and internal stresses and strains. How did Swedish institutions and politicians operate to form a working democracy?

THE PARTIES, THE KING AND THE CABINET

The Conservatives (*Högern*) led by economics professor Gösta Bagge had their roots in conservative and patriotic segments of the country and had gradually adopted economic liberalism in place of their early protectionist policies. The party was fiercely antagonistic to the Communists and many even suspected Per Albin to be a fellow-traveller. Some commentators felt that Bagge avoided making clear to his party that the Germany they had earlier valued as a bulwark against communism was not now the same Germany following the Nazi takeover.[1] Opposition to Bagge's commitment to an activist, interventionist policy towards Finland and enmity to the Soviet Union posed the greatest threat to Per Albin's Cabinet unity. Bagge also believed that a positive relationship with Germany could facilitate his ambitions for an activist Finnish policy.

The People's Party (*Folkpartiet*) was the successor to the Liberals who had attained free trade and universal suffrage in conjunction with the Social Democrats by 1921. Thereafter, their star had waned with the rise of their former partners but under their 'Norrland free-liberal' leader, Gustaf Andersson, they regained some of their former strength, particularly with the ideological commitment to new socio-liberal economic thinking represented by professor Bertil Ohlin as a counterweight to the Social Democrats' state planning. Their liberalism gave them a particular detestation of extreme left and right in Swedish politics. Andersson also opposed Finnish activism and advocated a cautious, isolationist policy.

The Agrarian Party (*Bondeförbundet*) had evolved from its pre-1914 origins as a political movement to safeguard country and farming interests into a more broadly based national movement. In 1933 a younger cohort led by Axel Pehrsson-Bramstorp struck a deal with Per Albin and the Social Democratic government to support their economic recovery programme in return for safeguards for the farming community – the so-called 'cow-trade'. This in turn led to Pehrsson-Bramstorp becoming leader and Prime Minister in a short-lived government in 1936 which gave way to the Agrarian two-party coalition with the Social Democrats. Janne Nilsson became Defence Minister in charge of re-armament, with veteran politician Karl-Gustav Westman as Justice Minister and Pehrsson-Bramstorp as Agriculture Minister. The choice of Nilsson meant that Per Albin could distance the fractious Social Democrats from the politically divisive policy of re-armament and reward the Agrarians for their participation, but on Nilsson's sudden death in 1938, he was replaced without delay as Defence Minister by Social Democrat Per-Edvin Sköld. Pehrsson-Bramstorp shared Andersson's caution and Per Albin's desire for consensus. He proved to be a stabilising influence in the Cabinet and focused on domestic rather than foreign policy.

The Social Democrats had at last gained a stable majority in 1936 through their coalition with the Agrarians when they had simultaneously consigned the other parties to permanent parliamentary opposition. The 'cow-trade' which allied the Agrarians with the Social Democrats to address the economic crisis of the 1930s had led to new economic thinking from Wigforss and the economist Gunnar Myrdal. The pragmatic Per Albin saw to it that Marx was superseded by Keynes in the core economic thinking of the Social Democrats. To buttress the new economic direction, the two powerful bodies in the economy, the employers' federation *SAF* and the trades unions' association *LO*, concluded an historic agreement at Saltsjöbaden in 1938 to minimise workplace conflict by regulating collective bargaining and strike action. The Saltsjöbaden agreement ensured that despite wartime economic strains, industry kept producing. Labour disputes, a potential source of national disunity and so much a feature of the preceding decades, had also been temporarily tamed. From this broad political base, progressive social policies were introduced which limited the lure of communism while providing the Swedish population with tangible benefits to reduce the attraction of a Nazi alternative to Swedish democracy. Per Albin had gradually moved to command the centre ground of Swedish politics which eased the acceptance of his national leadership by the opposition parties in December 1939.

King Gustav V, who reigned from 1907 to 1950, was not merely a national symbol and constitutional necessity but also a significant participant in policy discussions throughout the Second World War – as he had been during 1914–18. The Advisory Council for Foreign Affairs, *Utrikesnämnden*, was chaired by him on fifty-three of the sixty-five wartime meetings during 1939–45, when his personal engagement and independence of outlook was evident. He preferred pronouncement to discussion and remained a force that the politicians had to reckon with. Although in his eighties by 1939, he was sharp, incisive and committed. His relationship with his former constitutional adversary, Per Albin (in his earlier radical phase), has been described as formal and professional but Wigforss found him genial and friendly with his Ministers.[2] Yet he cut over Per Albin on one occasion in Council to declare 'That is my view and I have chosen to express it.'[3] As a veteran of domestic and international conflicts, he believed that his role was to support Coalition Government policy publicly while privately adding his advice and experience to their deliberations in the *Utrikesnämnd* and in the weekly Council (when decisions were formally ratified), as well as occasionally at informal meetings. At times, he was to take advantage of some unclear constitutional areas governing his conduct as head of state in order to undertake some personal initiatives to further Sweden's best interests – in his view. He explained his approach to Nils Quensel in 1940.

> Under normal circumstances, a constitutional monarch can and ought to restrain himself from becoming involved in the business of government but now . . . I do not look so much to the Constitution but consider that each and everyone must aim to serve the nation as best he can.[4]

When Per Albin began to form the wartime Coalition Government in December 1939, the Conservatives under their leader Gösta Bagge had decided that the international threat justified their conditional participation. With support from the King, they first tried to emulate the 1914 solution of bringing in non-political Ministers to form a 'government of talents' but those proposals were dismissed by Per Albin. Bagge and the Conservatives were also concerned to safeguard Sweden's options to support Finland, short of Swedish army intervention. Their supporters in the country were not entirely behind this and preferred to align with the Social Democrats and the People's Party in a more cautious approach. Bagge's negotiations with Per Albin barely succeeded in establishing that Conservative participation would bind them to non-intervention in Finland only if there were no major changes in the situation. Per Albin also gave a verbal assurance that equipment supplies to eager Swedish volunteers could be made from Swedish reserves. In the new Coalition the Social Democrats retained the key posts of Prime Minister (Per Albin Hansson), Finance Minister (Ernst Wigforss), Defence (Per Edvin Sköld) Social (Gustav Möller), and Supply (Hermann Eriksson). The previous Agrarian Party coalition partners Axel-Pehrsson Bramstorp (Agriculture) and Karl-Gustav Westman (Justice) also retained their posts. Westman had been a junior member of Hammarskjöld's ill-fated 1914–17 Cabinet and so had experienced at first hand the disastrous outcome of Hammarskjöld's principled stand against a superior power which held all the advantages.

Five earlier Ministers, including Gunnar Hägglöf, the young Per Albin protégé and later trade negotiator, and Sandler left to make way for the incoming Ministers. These included the Conservatives' Gösta Bagge (Ecclesiastical) and Fritiof Dömö (Trade), the People's Party's Gustav Andersson (Transport & Communications) and Torvald Bergqvist (without portfolio). Per Albin also selected his own 'talents' from outwith the *Riksdag* . They were Hermann Eriksson, Chairman of the Cooperative Association (Supply) and Christian Günther, a career diplomat most recently Minister in Oslo (Foreign).

FIGURE 5 The wartime Coalition Government, 1939. All parties except the Communists – the wartime Swedish Coalition Government Cabinet at the Palace for their first formal Council meeting with King Gustav V on 13 December 1939, pose inexpertly for a group photo. Left to right: Gösta Bagge, Church Minister; Gustav Andersson, Communications Minister; Thorwald Bergquist, Minister without portfolio; (hidden behind Bergquist) Gustav Möller, Social Affairs Minister; Karl Gustav Westman, Justice Minister; Nils Quensel, Minister without portfolio; Christian Günther, Foreign Minister; Fritiof Dömö, Trade Minister; Per Albin Hansson, Prime Minister; Ernst Wigforss, Finance Minister; (hidden behind Wigforss) Per-Edvin Sköld, Defence Minister; Axel Pehrsson Bramstorp, Agriculture Minister; Hermann Eriksson, Supply Minister.
(SVT Imagebank)

This group would remain largely unaltered throughout the war and were later joined by a changing handful of Ministers without Portfolio including Nils Quensel, Knut G. Ewerlöf and Per Albin's 1946 successor, Tage Erlander. This all-party Coalition was unique in Swedish Parliamentary history but it notably excluded the Communists who had only five members in the Second Chamber. Following the formation of the Coalition, Per Albin created an inner war-cabinet of Sköld, Eriksson, Wigforss and Günther, joined in 1941 by Supply Minister Axel Gjöres. The composition of this group (excepting Günther) reflected both a political affiliation to Social Democracy and the importance of trade and supply issues for policy decisions.

During the two-month Cabinet crisis in October and November 1939 dominated by disputes over Finland between Sandler and Wigforss, Per Albin had demonstrated several characteristics which were to typify his leadership style in Cabinet and that his detractors were to criticise in their diaries, sometimes to their close colleagues – but not to his face. His belief that most problems sorted themselves out over time militated against active decision-taking – which frustrated his more proactive Cabinet colleagues. In late 1939, he told Gunnar Hägglöf that in politics, one should never be hasty.

> Besides, if I hesitate, it means that I, like most of my colleagues in the group, am very cautious. You say that you found them sitting on the fence. It's hardly surprising when we're faced with such new and damned complicated problems.[5]

Not everyone appreciated those qualities. Bagge expressed his frustration, while a member of the Coalition Government, at being unable to attack Per Albin's 'unsuitability'.[6] Trade Minister Hermann Eriksson added in March 1944: 'P.A. is the most cowardly idiot imaginable and it is only the phenomenal luck that he and Günther enjoy, that has made it go as well as it has.'[7] Per Albin had indeed wavered in 1939 at the height of the Sandler–Wigforss conflict when he both doubted his own abilities as a wartime leader and expressed interest in resigning.[8] But he was no coward. He valued consensus above debate. This meant that in his preferred role as moderator, he frequently deflected discussion or sought ways whereby contentious issues could be sidelined or postponed. He would also use body language to signal his disinterest or displeasure at the course of a discussion.[9] Dangerously, he felt that he was closer to public opinion than his colleagues when it came to orienting policy and concessions towards the Allies and away from Germany. He believed that he was more in tune with the man in the street than his right-wing colleagues with their narrow contacts and limited social circles. Yet, as his biographer emphasised, his conscious alignment with the attitudes of the average Swede gave him a public aura of common-sense and tolerance for the views of others in marked contrast to the ideologues at home and abroad.[10] Conversely, in Cabinet, he sometimes closed down discussion on valid policy options to avoid the type of open dispute exemplified by Sandler and Wigforss that had been so damaging to Cabinet unity and to his authority.[11] Per Albin knew that he had to find a way of controlling the combative Wigforss whose inclusion in the Cabinet was essential for full Social Democrat Party support. Wigforss could take issue with Cabinet colleagues on any aspect from foreign policy to butter supply. Bramstorp said: 'Wigforss is not so bad when you get him in private. He winds up and runs to and fro on the floor for a bit – then he settles down.'[12] The problem was that he could create friction and dissent while Per Albin sought calm and unity. Erik Boheman left an insightful pen portrait of the wartime Cabinet in session.

> Per Albin sunk in the Chairman's seat with Günther on his right, cool and collected behind the pince-nez, Wigforss with his mercurial gestures, Sköld somewhat sullen and rather superior, Möller's thoughtful hawkish features, K. G. Westman's sarcastic smirk, Rasjön (Andersson) with his aesthetic profile, Bramstorp confident, certain and rather confused in his thinking, Bagge nervous and worried, followed by an always sensible and discerning Ewerlöf, Hermann Eriksson, Gjöres, Quensel and the others.[13]

Swedish wartime foreign policy decisions were reactive rather proactive, driven by the demands of the belligerents and the war situation. As well as foreign policy, supply and economic issues were a staple of the wartime Cabinet as Westman's diaries reveal but there were three factors which coloured their deliberations. Firstly, the Social Democrats, although dominant as the largest party, nevertheless attempted to ensure that collective political responsibility was taken for all decisions, particularly the unpopular ones, in order to avoid electoral punishment by disaffected voters. Secondly, foreign policy discussions were dampened in the *Riksdag*. Members were expected to trust the judgement of their party leaders in the Cabinet, not to be told too much for security reasons, even in secret sessions, and to avoid damaging dissension that might indicate exploitable disunity to the circling great powers. This *Riksdag* passivity was described as 'totalitarian parliamentarianism' by Government critics and allowed Ministers to act increasingly without full parliamentary scrutiny, notwithstanding attempts in the *Riksdag* to hold them to account. Thirdly, the media were self-restrained in their discussion of Sweden's foreign policy and administratively restrained from reporting on certain topics, in particular German aggression and human-rights crimes, especially up to 1943. These factors initially permitted the Coalition Cabinet a large measure of freedom of action in foreign policy but the absence of wider support among the political and press community would later lead to increasing criticism of the Coalition when the pressure was off and the facts emerged.

The Cabinet became disproportionately important in decision-making. *Riksdag* scrutiny was at times sidelined despite attempts by some *Riksdag* Committees to interject but the *Riksdag* never became an 'empty formality', particularly when important decisions were taken.[14] However, the views and inclinations of individual Cabinet members became overly significant. Per Albin strained to achieve Cabinet consensus which was largely maintained for domestic policy but was subjected to severe strains at crucial decision points in foreign policy. Significantly, the new Coalition Cabinet represented a major change to the fractious party arguments during the Twenties and Thirties on issues like disarmament and economic recession. Yet, the party rivalries were merely postponed and personality clashes were sublimated rather than eliminated.

Between 1939 and 1945 all the main Swedish political parties were agreed on the objective of keeping Sweden out of the war, though it was perhaps the 'lowest common denominator' of agreement in a nation of disparate opinions.[15] Debates over foreign policy arose out of differences over the extent and nature of the changes needed to achieve this aim while safeguarding neutrality status. Sweden also had to reconcile non-belligerency with maintaining neighbourly Scandinavian relationships, upholding democratic institutions and culture, preserving independence, sustaining a modern economy and providing essential food and fuel for its people. These adaptations had to take place while under pressure now from Germany, now from the Allies and with an eye to possible Russian reactions. The key policy debates concerned the degree to which Sweden should be involved in the struggles of Finland and Norway, the scope of concessions which should be made to the Germans under duress, the speed at which these concessions – coupled with trade reduction – should be withdrawn, and the extent of freedom of expression for press and political comment.

THE DIPLOMATS

Per Albin was neither experienced nor comfortable with foreign policy issues. His indifference to ideology or crusades was matched by his disinterest in diplomatic minutiae. His long political career had been grounded in domestic politics and as Prime Minister he had been initially in some ways a hostage to Sandler's long experience and knowledge of international diplomacy. This meant that one other significant outcome from the Sandler *débacle* was Per Albin's determination, when forming the wartime Coalition Government in December 1939, to prevent party and ideological disputes intruding into the Foreign Minister's important task of pursuing the policy of remaining out of the war. He also wanted someone who he could trust to stick to this policy and he selected Christian Günther, a career diplomat. Until then, Günther had been remarkable only for his somewhat unconventional past as a literary dilettante until his thirties when he entered the Civil Service, but his personal qualities were to contribute to Sweden's success in delivering the prime policy objective. His dismissive view of Per Albin was that 'he lacked the ability to understand foreign policy problems but that he did not comprehend his failing.'[16] However, the same could also be said of Günther and party politics.

Günther personified *realpolitik* with his austere, dry manner and a first-class instinct for protecting Sweden's position while successfully maintaining a front which obscured his real opinions. He also possessed the ability to assess a complex diplomatic situation from many angles. While Günther was assiduous in briefing politicians and journalists on the Government position, he did so at length but with clarity in contrast to the reserved obscurantism of Sandler ('the best way to preserve independence was through independence').[17] However, Günther's style so verged on the tedious that UD diplomat Sven Grafström complained: 'more numbing than usual. I simply do not understand how one can turn so intrinsically interesting a subject so creakily dry.' Günther also succeeded frequently in numbing the press, perhaps his intention.[18] Without any party membership, he was dependent on senior politicians for support and security in his post. In the early years of the war with Germany in the ascendant, he leaned somewhat towards Bagge's activist perspective but after 1942 towards Per Albin's cautious approach when changing course. 'You cannot turn an old ship of state on a coin.'[19] Above all, Günther retained his *sang-froid* in the face of some intense political and diplomatic pressure.

Günther's *realpolitik* was often seen, and still is by his detractors, as a predisposition to Germanophilia or even for covert Nazi sympathies – an astonishing claim for a man with a cherished Jewish daughter-in-law, although, in 1940, he expressed the naïve belief that Jewish antecedents might affect an individual's judgement.[20] His apolitical position meant that he would never be able to satisfy those politicians and journalists who believed that Sweden's foreign policy should be driven actively by nobler ambitions and moral precepts in the face of totalitarian aggression. Günther's appetite for ideological causes and honourable acts was constrained by the necessity of focusing on detail in order to minimise damage to Sweden's position while trying to leave nothing to chance. He was notably thick skinned and when press attacks on his policies increased in 1944, he seems to have been almost indifferent at a time when Grafström believed that he 'would barely pass the judgment of history.'[21] His defining characteristic throughout was to try to keep the diplomatic temperature as low as possible and avoid prestige issues with the belligerents which inflamed situations. He preferred to take the pragmatic approach of recognising superiority and accommodating it. He stressed to each great power that to maintain a strongly independent Sweden was in *their* best interests because Sweden could and would assist those interests – when they did not directly conflict with Sweden's own. He attempted to steer clear of taking sides for fear of being fastened to a damaging position, and to evade formal commitments in the fluid situation of a global war. He made few notes of meetings and Boheman once joked that if Sweden had not cracked the coded German despatches to Berlin, Günther's colleagues would not have known what he had said in key discussions.[22]

Günther was ably supported in the Swedish Foreign Ministry by a raft of outstanding diplomats: for example Erik Boheman, Gunnar Hägglöf and Staffan Söderblom. They and others were also described by Grafström as 'the *UD*'s self-regarding and plotting 'brains trust' (sic).[23] The best people had been retained in Stockholm to provide the necessary support to Günther while the Ministers in the key locations, Vilhelm Assarsson in Moscow, Arvid Richert in Berlin, Björn Prytz in London and Wollmar Boström in Washington tended to be of a lesser diplomatic calibre. Prytz was even superseded by Boheman in important discussions after a number of errors (*en rad dumheter*).[24] This did not mean that they were ignored, but rather that the careful diplomatic assessment of options and formulation of responses to the many pressures and demands on Sweden were carried out by a relatively small, high-level team in the UD. For officials like Erik Boheman, the war meant anxiety, pressure and intense activity.[25] A sympathetic colleague also noted 'in these times (1941), living under the weight of his Jewish blood and feeling unease and doubt about the future.'[26] This pressure took its toll and at least one suffered a breakdown after the war. Chain smoking – another sign of stress – also seems to have been widespread, judging by contemporary photographs.

THE PARLIAMENTARY SYSTEM

Swedish democracy in 1939 was, like its European counterparts, the result of centuries of change, struggle and compromise. The institutions which characterised Parliamentary democracy in 1939 had changed somewhat since 1914. The *Riksdag* consisted of two Chambers, each with a speaker. The Upper Chamber was elected indirectly and was considered to represent 'education and wealth'. Elections for the Lower Chamber were open only to men until 1921 when a universal and equal franchise was introduced for men and women alike and the *Riksdag* finally achieved a system of democratic representation. The growth of the modern political parties from the second half of the nineteenth century was a stimulus to increased representation. As outlined earlier, the emergence of the Social Democrats and Liberals had forced the King to relinquish his power to select Governments and set policy. 'Parliamentarianism', the term for this power-shift, was eventually accepted in 1917 by Gustav following the Liberal and Social Democrat electoral success. Even so, he retained a significant but somewhat loosely defined role, aspects of which influenced events during the Second World War. Parliamentary government, as in Britain, remained a matter of flexible custom and tradition rather than rigid constitutional laws.

The power in the *Riksdag* became increasingly concentrated in the directly elected Lower Chamber and Governments were formed on the basis of achieving a working majority (frequently a minority between 1920 and 1936) from a coalition of parties in the *Riksdag*. Government was based on the 1809 constitutional 'Instrument of

Government', which was largely influenced by the principle of a separation of powers. An important factor was the distinction between legislative, judicial and executive power. The independence of the courts and the press was a further characteristic of Swedish constitutional democracy which was to prove significant during 1939-45. Executive power in 1939 rested in the Cabinet, composed of ten departmentally responsible Ministers with collective responsibility, headed by the Prime Minister. The Ministerial portfolios, for example foreign policy, were matched by *Riksdag* Committees *(Utskott)*, each with a Chairman, whose fifteen-man composition reflected the party representation in the *Riksdag*. Specifically for foreign policy, the Swedish Constitution also provided for an Advisory Council for Foreign Affairs *(Utrikesnämnden)* which was normally chaired by the King, placing him at the centre of decision-making. It consisted of nine members of the *Riksdag*, usually all the party leaders and confusingly also some of the members of the *Riksdag*'s Foreign Affairs Committee *(Utrikesutskottet)*. The *Utrikesnämnd* was where key foreign policy discussions took place in the utmost confidence while the chairmanship and opinions of the King added a particular authority. The *Utrikesutskott* was less important and acted more as a *Riksdag* sounding board for Government thinking and political opinion. For particularly important and confidential issues, the *Riksdag* often went into secret session but as the pressure of wartime decision-making grew on the Coalition Cabinet, Ministers' powers of independent action also increased.

Within this democratic framework, the electorate voted alternately every two years. Municipal *(Kommunal)* quadrennial elections voted for the local politicians who selected the Upper Chamber members. *Riksdag* quadrennial elections voted directly for the *Riksdag* members of the Lower Chamber. Municipal elections took place in 1942 and 1946 while *Riksdag* elections took place in 1940 and 1944. These enabled the politicians to promote their parties and assess the mood of the country as well as to provide useful indicators of Swedish opinion during these wartime years. The number of those voting rose steadily from 1.7m in 1921 to 3.1m (71.9 per cent) in 1944. Particularly notable during the inter-war years was a growing centralisation and representation of specific interest groups such as employers, within national organisations which increasingly functioned alongside government, and whose leaders also became significant in consultation and influence with the government.

Sweden had developed and reinforced its liberal, democratic institutions since the beginning of the century. This enabled the country's politicians to see off the fractious extremists during the Twenties and Thirties by offering realistic alternatives to Nazi and Bolshevik visions of society that were achievable only by abuse and violence. Party conflict took place within a parliamentary setting and not on the streets. Sweden was indeed a working democracy in 1939 though its institutions would be soon tested by the demands and expectations of both the totalitarian and democratic belligerents.

Notes

1. Grafström, *Anteckningar*, 17 April 1942.
2. Carlsson, *Gustaf V och andra världskriget*, pp. 336–8.
3. Westman, *Politiska anteckningar*, 12.9.1941.
4. Quensel, *Minnesbilder*, pp. 234–5.
5. Hägglöf, *Möte med Europa*, p. 219.
6. Westman, *Politiska anteckningar*, 14.6.1940.
7. cited in Johansson, *Per Albin och kriget*, p. 417.
8. Isaksson, *Per Albin*, p. 362.
9. Boheman, *På vakt*, p. 37.
10. Isaksson, *Per Albin*, p. 417.
11. Wigforss shouted at Sandler in Cabinet: 'You must not be so bloody cowardly. You are sure to face the consequences!' Hägglöf, *Möte med Europa*, p. 206.
12. Westman, *Politiska anteckningar*, 31.10.1939.
13. Boheman, *På vakt*, p. 43.
14. Westman, *Politiska anteckningar*, 21.6.1940.
15. See for example Estwall, *Ett folk, ett rike, en åsikt?* in Andersson & Tydén (eds), *Sverige och Nazityskland*.
16. Westman, *Politiska anteckningar*, 21.6.1940.
17. quoted by K. G. Westman 13.6.1940 in Wahlbäck, *Regeringen och kriget*, p. 99.
18. Ibid. 25.11.1943.
19. Wahlbäck & Boberg (eds), *Sveriges sak är vår*, p. 159.
20. Westman, *Politiska anteckningar*, 13.6.1940.
21. Grafström, *Anteckningar*, 25 August 1944.
22. Ibid. 25 August 1944.
23. Ibid. 14 October 1939.
24. Westman, *Politiska anteckningar*, 15.9.1939.
25. Boheman, *På vakt*, p. 308.
26. Grafström, *Anteckningar*, 4 August 1941.

3

Isolation, 1939–1941

In early September 1939, Sweden responded diplomatically, economically and militarily to the conflict that would become the Second World War. Between 1 and 3 September the country's neutrality was again declared, shipping lanes and harbours were closed to foreign warships, unnecessary journeys prohibited to save petrol and 70,000 reservists were called up. The Government made it clear that it wished to maintain trade as far as possible with countries which respected Sweden's neutrality and integrity.[1] Within the two-party Coalition Government, in power since 1936, an air of cynicism and resigned acceptance of the situation permeated the politicians. Westman, the Justice Minister wrote: 'A world war every twenty-five years – it's an unpleasant and expensive educational method.'[2] Per Albin was even more bitter, complaining that everything he had tried to accomplish, his *Folkhem* vision, would soon be wasted on 'military operations, artillery, cruisers and planes.'[3] Two major issues were now on the Government's agenda: regularising the trade position with the belligerents and safeguarding the Ålands.

TRADE AGREEMENTS, DECEMBER 1939–JANUARY 1940

The priority for trade was to conclude an agreement with Britain as a precursor to negotiating with Germany whose aims were expected to include maintenance of iron ore shipments. A British *aide-memoire* to Sweden on 7 September, clearly well-prepared in advance, envisaged an agreement based on a restriction of re-exports of western goods to

Germany and a limitation on trade with Germany, particularly iron ore, to pre-war levels.

Negotiations with the British started in late September and the agreement was signed on 7 December 1939. Both British and Swedish objectives were largely met. Pre-war levels and re-exporting limitations were accepted by the Swedish negotiators while a minimum of controls and bureaucracy for Sweden was accepted by the British. The 1939 Anglo-Swedish War Trade Agreement (WTA) represented a favourable outcome for Sweden which was in the weaker position due to the British continental blockade. The long-term consequences were that Sweden would become more dependent on Germany for coal, coke, steel, chemicals, machinery and instruments.

With the WTA signed, the Swedish negotiators could now approach the Germans whose short-term concern was the continuity of iron ore supplies. The Swedish negotiators opened with offers of seven million tonnes for 1940 and the normalisation of export levels to the average for 1933–8: that is, the British proposal. These were rejected by the Germans who adjourned talks and mined the southern Swedish coast in late November to maintain pressure. A revised offer of ten million tonnes and 1938 levels of exports was now tabled (structured in such a way as to enable Sweden to argue that it had kept its verbal commitment to Britain) together with a pricing mechanism favourable to Sweden. This formed the basis for the agreement concluded with Germany in January 1940. In spite of the British blockade and with few concessions, Sweden had succeeded in achieving the maintenance of its trade with both warring parties. The Coalition Government had accomplished in a few short months what Hammarskjöld's First World War Government had failed to achieve over several years.

THE ÅLANDS, FINLAND AND THE WINTER WAR, OCTOBER 1939–FEBRUARY 1940

A more intractable problem with a significantly higher political profile was the Åland Islands and Finnish security. The initial relief in Stockholm created by the Molotov–Ribbentrop Pact apparently reducing tension between the two great powers in the Baltic gave way to new misgivings when, at the end of September, the Estonians were forced to concede naval and air bases to the Russians. It now appeared to the region's politicians that the Russian agreement with the Germans would allow Stalin to recoup some of Russia's earlier territorial losses from 1917 and thereby threaten Sweden and Finland as well as the fledgling Baltic states. In October 1939 Foreign Minister Sandler, who had unsuccessfully tried to promote the Stockholm Plan once more urged an 'activist' policy of military cooperation with the Finns including mining the seas around the Åland Islands, and so to deny access to the Russians *in case* they attacked. The anti-Russian Commander-in-Chief, General Thörnell, even wanted troops to be dispatched immediately to the Ålands. More cautious voices in the Government, particularly Ernst Wigforss, the Finance Minister, stridently rejected such activism due to its potential for drawing Sweden into war with Russia.

At the beginning of October the Finns had been invited to Moscow for 'discussions' which turned out to be a three-point demand for a Soviet naval base, a redrawing of the border and a defence treaty. The Finnish Prime Minister, Social Democrat Väinö Tanner, looked to Sweden for support. The political pressure on the Swedish Government was enormous with widespread national sympathy for the Finns manifesting itself in a huge public demonstration of support in Stockholm for their threatened neighbour. It took place on the occasion of a Scandinavian Heads of State meeting in the capital on 18 and 19 October promoted by Sandler. Despite this and Sandler's urgings, Per Albin and the Cabinet rejected any further military ties, fearing a slide towards war, not just with Russia but also with its Pact partner, Germany. While Per Albin stood firmly by the decision not to send troops to the Ålands, he had remained indecisive about Sandler's proposal to mine the Åland Sea, which was supported by Sköld. Sköld saw it as a military preventative measure to keep the great powers out of the northern Baltic while Wigforss saw it as leading to war with Russia. It was an issue over which he had threatened to resign and then go into public opposition. The Cabinet discussions between Wigforss and Sandler in those days were strained and impatient, with Wigforss openly expressing his distrust of Sandler with regard to Finland and Per Albin unable to exert authority over his fractious party colleagues. The refusal to send troops to Finland outraged the activists in the military as well as Sandler.

On 30 November the Russians attacked Finland to open what became known as the Winter War following the rejection of their demands. Instead of collapsing within weeks like Poland, the beleaguered Finns were to hold off the Red Army for the next two months. On 1 December the Finnish Government requested that Sweden send troops to Åland to allow the Finns to withdraw their forces there to fight the Russians. Wigforss argued that this issue had previously been decided, but it went for wider discussion on 2 December to the *Utrikesnämnd* where in contrast to the Cabinet, the unity of the parties centred on maintaining a non-belligerent position regarding Finland – that is no troops – while providing the greatest possible material assistance in the shape of supplies and loans. Correctly realising that his position was untenable in the face of such a determined rejection of his policy, Sandler resigned that day. Per Albin acted decisively and with considerable energy to regain his authority. The Coalition Government was reshuffled, both to exclude Sandler with his principled but dangerous 'activist' policies, and to broaden party representation. Westman put himself forward as Sandler's successor but Per Albin did not bite.[4] Per Albin's shrewd move was to replace Sandler with the apolitical diplomat, Christian Günther, whose skill at racetrack betting would be matched by his handling of the great powers. Activism had been replaced by adaptability.

Per Albin was able to rise above the party conflicts of the 1920s and 1930s to form the wartime Coalition, which he did without reference to his party colleagues and party committees. This administered a timely warning shot to Wigforss, who resented and feared being excluded from the discussions, and Sköld, who having partly supported the Sandler line was relieved to have retained his post, unlike the unfortunates Forslund and Engberg who were consigned to political oblivion. He had also seen off a challenge from the right, supported by King Gustav, that aimed at replacing him and his depleted authority with an apolitical 'strong-man', Torsten Nothin, at the head of a 'true coalition government' by refusing to join it.[5] Additionally, Bagge's attempt to exclude the Social Democrat's veteran left-wing bogey-man, Gustav Möller, was unsuccessful. Even right-winger Westman appreciated Möller's anti-communist credentials.[6]

In dismissing Sandler and including Bagge, Per Albin, in his role as Social Democrat leader, had removed an activist from his own party and replaced him with another from the Conservatives. Bagge and Wigforss would balance one another while Per Albin in his role as Prime Minister could distance himself from their conflicts. For example, Westman recorded the following 1941 Cabinet incident over a proposal by Bagge.

> Wigforss persisted in his obstinate opposition despite Bagge's attempts to persuade. Per Albin interrupted the meeting with some

conciliatory words and postponed the decision. Bagge became angry, took his papers and flung them on the table, said angrily that he should resign etc., which caused a stir.[7]

Bagge sought to maintain his influence by seeking support from Günther for a more activist policy towards Finland. Bagge's relationship with Per Albin was strained from the outset, partly due to Bagge's enthusiasm for Finland and hostility to Russia but also due to differences in perspective. Bagge regarded Sweden as having an historical mission in the east whereas Per Albin stuck to the basics of protecting the Swedish people from military and political adventurism. Bagge chafed at Per Albin's style and continually complained that he 'opposed him (Bagge) as usual and will not do anything.' Per Albin complained that Bagge 'still customarily pushed his views as if he was in opposition.'[8] Although he still had to tolerate fractious colleagues, Per Albin had now assumed the role of 'Father of the Nation' (*Landsfader*), a part into which he grew as the war progressed and his political stature increased.

Sweden's position had now become more precarious for three reasons. Firstly, public and military agitation for support to Finland against Soviet aggression threatened to destabilise Sweden's policy of neutrality and remaining outside the wider conflict. Secondly the Allies spotted an opportunity in northern Sweden to seize control of the Narvik-Luleå railway and with it Sweden's iron ore by claiming to require troop transit there through Norway and Sweden to help Finland. But Boheman noted later that the Germans made it clear that if Allied troops set foot in Sweden, counter-measures would arrive 'like a letter in the post'.[9] Thirdly, if the Red Army succeeded in overcoming Finland, Russia would again border Sweden. Additionally, Sweden feared that any cooperation with the Allies risked the dreadful prospect of drawing Russia in alongside Germany and turning Scandinavia into a battlefield.[10] Everything pointed towards Sweden seeking to broker an early end to Finnish-Russian hostilities.

The Government had modified its stance in the conflict from neutral to that of 'non-belligerent' in order to placate Bagge, the Conservatives and popular sentiment that was still pressing for substantive support to Finland. This status enabled material support to be given to hard-pressed Finland in addition to the humanitarian support afforded to refugees, particularly children, affected by the hostilities. Material support was given a low profile to avoid unnecessarily irritating the Russians. Sweden supplied 84,000 rifles, 575 machine-guns, 85 anti-tank guns, 104 anti-aircraft guns, 112 howitzers and field-guns, 25 aeroplanes, 30,000 shells and 50,000,000 cartridges, partly from its own meagre supplies and partly by diverting export orders from Germany to Finland.[11] Britain and France also supplied arms but only in irregular deliveries of sometimes obsolete equipment. By comparison, most of Sweden's deliveries were modern and free-of-charge. In addition to the material, a 'Finland Committee' was formed with the goal of providing 7,500 volunteers to defend Lapland and the northern rail links there with a longer-term option of greater Swedish intervention. They were successful in signing up a corps of 8,260 Swedes and 727 Norwegians, armed from Swedish military sources, whose eventual and honourable engagement in the Finnish cause came too late to affect the outcome. Humanitarian aid was organised in Sweden by two groups: the National Association for Finland, and Central Finland Aid. The former collected money while the latter collected clothing and organised the reception of the 'war children' from Finland. About 9,000 under ten years old were sent to safety in Sweden by boat, train and air during the Winter War. More would follow in later years.

In this way, the political energy generated by the protests against the Government's passivity was redirected into displacement activities of aid and support, while Swedish efforts to end hostilities continued. The Finns had succeeded initially, against all predictions, in holding the Red Army but in early December Finnish approaches through the Swedes to re-open negotiations with the Russians were rejected. In late January the Russians, through their colourful but non-doctrinaire Stockholm Minister, Mme Kollontay, dropped their insistence on dealing only through their Finnish puppet Communists and indicated a willingness to negotiate directly.[12] Stalin valued security for Leningrad over the prospect of attempting to impose Finnish Communist Otto Kuusinen on Finland, and a potential slide into the wider European conflict.[13] As Wilhelm Carlgren wrote: 'Finland was now fighting for her frontiers, but no longer for her survival.'[14] To the relief of the Swedes, these borders did not adjoin Sweden. Significantly, the King publicly supported Per Albin in his refusal to increase Swedish involvement, deflating Per Albin's activist opponents and further increasing his authority. Continued Swedish refusals to escalate their support from aid to entering the war, coupled with military reverses and Per Albin's emphasis on beginning negotiations, obliged the Finns to talk to the Russians who had predictably raised their demands.

On 13 March the Finnish negotiators led by Prime Minister Ryti signed the peace treaty which ended the conflict. Finland ceded

22,000 square miles of territory in Karelia, Viipuri, Sordavala, Petsamo and the whole of Ladoga-Karelia, home to 12 per cent of the Finnish population.[15] Hanko was handed over as a naval base for an annual rent but the war cost Russia dearly. Molotov had lied to the Supreme Soviet when he stated Soviet losses as 48,747 dead and 158,000 wounded. According to 1992 estimates based on the Soviet archives, losses were 131,000 dead and 325,000 wounded.[16] Khrushchev allegedly put their losses even higher at one million dead.[17] Despite Russia having achieved its war aims, the loss in prestige was damaging while the Red Army's leadership weaknesses and inept performance following Stalin's purges was noted throughout Europe, and particularly in Berlin.

IRON ORE AND BELLIGERENT PRESSURE, NOVEMBER 1939–APRIL 1940

The ambiguous Swedish role of aiding Finland while brokering the peace had also been carefully observed, especially in Moscow. Persistent Swedish fears of instability in Scandinavia resulting from the Winter War leading to a threat to the country's security were fully justified. The armies of Britain and France sat idle on the French borders throughout the autumn and freezing winter of 1939. Apart from leaflet drops and minor naval actions, the war justified its 'phoney' label. The Allied strategy was to advance into Belgium to counter the anticipated German attack there. This passive, defensive mentality was symbolised by the Maginot Line and dominated by the French politicians' desire to avoid heavy losses on home territory during a necessary period of rearmament to catch up with Germany. Pressure mounted for action and the Winter War offered the opportunity to engage the German-Russian alliance well away from French territory.

The strategic importance of supplies of Swedish iron ore to Germany had, in the absence of more aggressive thinking in Paris and London, begun to divert the attention of politicians there. One in particular was the newly appointed First Lord of the Admiralty, Winston Churchill. Interrupting those supplies became a war aim of the Allies in late 1939 and whereas the WTA allowed Sweden to maintain ore exports at earlier levels, the Allied intention was to disrupt these militarily. In late November, Churchill advocated the mining of Norwegian coastal waters after, in September, unsuccessfully proposing a naval expedition to reclaim the Baltic from the German navy. The Allies had previously assumed that, during winter when the Gulf of Bothnia was frozen and the Swedish ore port of Luleå closed, ore-carriers departing from the Norwegian ore port of Narvik would be exposed to British naval interception. These ore ships could however proceed within neutral Norwegian territorial waters which meant that in attacking, the Allies would have to infringe Norwegian neutrality. This consideration again caused Churchill's scheme to fail but his persistence resulted in a further proposal for the British navy to be allowed to operate in Norwegian waters. This request was communicated in January 1940 to Stockholm and Oslo, receiving an outraged reception in both. The predictably adverse reaction caused Prime Minister Chamberlain and Foreign Minister Halifax to shelve the idea for the time being.

Of course, control of the railway connections between the Swedish ore mines to both Narvik and Luleå would also mean control of ore exports but seizure would require a violation of Norwegian and Swedish neutrality. The Winter War appeared to offer a possible excuse for the Allies to avoid that violation and still take control of the ore mines. During December 1939, the British began to consider the possibility of Sweden and Norway becoming so alarmed by the resurgent Russian threat that they would seek protection from the Allies – the price being the cessation of iron ore exports to Germany. Even if they did not seek protection, the Allies could intervene to help Finland under the guise of a League of Nations appeal. This intervention plan would take the form of landing troops in Narvik, supposedly *en route* to Finland but in reality to secure the ore mines. This complicated and unrealistic proposal could only succeed with the cooperation of both Norway and Sweden and would require the Swedish Government to increase its previously circumscribed support to Finland. Nevertheless, the existence of the intervention plan was sufficient for Halifax and Chamberlain to block Churchill's mining proposal on 12 January 1940 but still left them with the requirement to press on with some kind of intervention operation.

Churchill deliberately raised the temperature in a broadcast on 20 January 1940 when, in order to prepare opinion in Scandinavia for the intervention plan, he forecast that the war would eventually engulf the region. The French, under pressure for their inactivity, now began to show interest in the intervention plan, sharing the same wishful thinking as the British about likely Norwegian and Swedish reception. On 16 February Churchill ordered a violation of Norwegian territorial waters in order to rescue 300 British seamen imprisoned on board the *Altmark* in Jøssingfjord. This successful operation sealed Norway's fate because as a result, Hitler and his admirals noted that neither did the British respect Norwegian neutrality nor the Norwegians assert it.

The Finns, desperate in the face of the new Russian offensive, again sought Allied men and equipment and the Allies requested transit across Norway and Sweden for these on 2 March 1940. This spurred the mediation effort by Sweden between Russia and Finland so that by the time of the British Cabinet decision on 12 March to send an intervention force, the Finns had agreed terms with the Russians, thereby removing the Allied pretext. This left only Churchill's original proposal to mine Norwegian waters, but now with the added intention to land Allied troops to secure certain important Norwegian ports. Churchill secured French approval for this on 5 April and was triumphant that his initiative to block iron ore exports and defend Norway against Germany had been adopted. On 9 April 1940 after the mining had taken place but before Allied forces had landed, the Germans struck with a better and more realistic military operation which paid no heed to Scandinavian neutral sensibilities. Denmark and Norway were invaded by land, sea and air.

OPERATION WESERÜBUNG, 9 APRIL 1940

Although the Scandinavian governments were not taken completely unaware by the invasion, code-named 'Weserübung' by the Germans, because intelligence on the preparations had been available since March 1940, Günther had been confident that Weserübung was aimed at Norway and Denmark, not Sweden. On 9 April as the German troops landed, Prince Viktor zu Wied, German Minister in Stockholm, briefed Günther on the invasion at 5 a.m., and at 7 a.m. gave him a four-point note. Germany required Sweden to maintain neutrality, restrict its naval activity to coastal territorial waters, maintain telecommunications between Norway and Germany and continue iron ore exports.

These requirements foreshadowed much more onerous demands which the German Commander, Keitel, pressed the German Foreign Ministry to put forward in early April.[18] Fearing British naval attacks on troopships between Norway and Germany as well as needing shipping to support the forthcoming western offensive, Keitel insisted that Sweden be asked to allow German troops to cross Sweden by rail to Norway. German diplomatic pressure began to be applied to Sweden to secure transit, initially, in April as a priority to supply the campaign against the Norwegian and Allied troops, and later to maintain the garrison after the fighting had ceased in June.

Most pressing for Sweden in the aftermath of *Weserübung* was how to respond to the new geopolitical situation. Before *Weserübung*, Sweden had begun to demobilise following the tensions of the Winter War, leaving only about 85,000 men under arms. The absence of Swedish military vigilance in the face of incoming intelligence about German preparations pointed to miscalculations by the Swedish leadership, despite various explanations later.[19] Sweden was unprepared to take on the German war machine on April 9. As concern about a German invasion of Sweden changed into fears of complications arising from continued fighting in Norway, Swedish policy makers were forced into hard choices.

Taking Sweden's aim of remaining outside the conflict as the starting point, Sweden responded to Norway's request to allow refuge for King Haakon and Crown Prince Olav by stating that Sweden could not guarantee immunity from internment. A tough neutral line would be followed. Per Albin broadcast a speech on 12 April in which he decisively repeated that position, despite indicating sympathy for Sweden's neighbours. Strict neutrality meant no help to the Germans but neither to the Norwegians nor to their new British and French allies. In sharp contrast to Sweden's military aid to Finland, none would be forthcoming for the Norwegians. The threat was now on Sweden's border instead of distant Karelia and suggestions of support from Nordic activists now fell on the stony ground of potential German retaliation. Even the British Legation in Stockholm destroyed its secret records and prepared for evacuation.[20] Yet, while some Swedes attempted surreptitiously to provide helpful campaign advice, the British obsession with seizing the iron ore mines partially blinded them to the strategic realities of the Norwegian campaign.[21] Meanwhile in the Foreign Office, Halifax and his officials longed for a German–Swedish conflict. 'I would do anything to bring it about', wrote Alexander Cadogan in May while Halifax fretted about a joint German–Swedish attack.[22] British duplicity and ineptitude was manifest and damaged Swedish confidence in Britain.[23]

The Norwegian army continued to fight the *Wehrmacht* until 10 June but with the German May offensive in the Low Countries,

British and French forces began to be evacuated from Norway, ending with the Norwegian King and Government's departure to England on 9 June. But back in April, the threat of the British and French had stimulated Keitel to raise again with the Nazi hierarchy the issue of secure transit across Sweden for his troops. An extraordinary two-month episode in Swedish–German relations had begun, opening with Sweden's firm rejection of German transit and ending with a resigned concession. These two months were characterised by German threats and Swedish resolve to maintain national freedom of action and safeguard the population. Sweden would never again receive greater attention from the Nazi leadership. The concession was made only when all alternatives other than to face down the unbridled Germans were exhausted.

THE 'LEAVE TRAFFIC' CONCESSION TO GERMANY, APRIL 1940–JUNE 1940

This episode of the transit concession sheds light on the complexity of diplomatic and economic issues with which Swedish policy-makers had to deal and which were not fully appreciated by any of the other parties. It also signifies the first major Swedish concession to Germany and a decisive break with strict Swedish neutrality causing an adverse effect on Sweden's relations with Norway and the Allies.

First, German demands were supported by a triumphant, technologically and numerically superior military, reinforced economically by blockade to the west and diplomatically by the Molotov-Ribbentrop Pact with the Soviet Union. It was not clear to the Swedish Government in April 1940 that Germany would stop at occupying Norway and Denmark and so invasion across the border as well as *Luftwaffe* bombing raids from north Germany and occupied Denmark were a real possibility. The fog of war was enveloping Swedish decision-making. Secondly, the Western Allies were retreating militarily and diplomatically, not only from Norway but also from mainland Europe in the wake of German success. Allied failure to protect Denmark and Norway from invasion served to underline Swedish isolation in the face of German threats. Thirdly, while Norwegian military failure could be (and was) ascribed by some Swedes to Norwegian Government incompetence, the spectacle of fellow democratic Scandinavians being subjected to the violence of a military occupation was disturbing for the Social Democratic movement and Swedish opinion leaders.[24] They looked to the Swedish Coalition Government to do whatever was possible to help the Norwegians and those aspirations had an influence on domestic politics. The policy of remaining outside the war and refusing military transit to the Germans while hostilities continued in Norway began to splinter Swedish thinking. As the shock of April gave way to the realisation of May, Swedish diplomacy struggled to keep abreast of the changing kaleidoscope of possible outcomes.

How did the Germans secure the concession? Since Keitel's initial request for the German Foreign Ministry to obtain it diplomatically prior to the invasion, the situation in Narvik had deteriorated for the *Wehrmacht* and a febrile Hitler began to panic about a possible defeat there. This elevated the transit issue to one concerning the prestige of the Third Reich and its *Führer*. Shortly after the April 1940 invasion, arising from Keitel's pressure, the Swedish Minister in Berlin, Richert, had been asked to request that a delegation of Swedish representatives travel to meet Hermann Göring to give assurances that Sweden would not attempt to join in any Allied action against the German invasion of Norway. Göring was then responsible for Swedish relations ('*Schwedenreferent*') due to his ability to speak Swedish and presented himself to the Swedes as 'Sweden's friend' within the Nazi cabal. A Swedish delegation met Göring on 15 April and was harangued for an hour about the suspicions harboured in the Nazi hierarchy concerning Swedish intentions regarding iron ore and the Western Allies. Admiral Tamm reassured Göring that Sweden would defend its borders against any enemy and when discussions resumed the following day, Göring moved to the possibility of non-military 'supplies' such as clothing, being transported through Sweden. Hägglöf, the diplomat on the delegation, recalled in his memoirs that he stressed the impossibility of conceding military transit while Norway was still fighting and that Göring responded with an attack on Swedish press criticism of Germany and the Nazis. Next day Tamm personally had to reassure Hitler by repeating his reassurances that Sweden would stand firm against any aggressor. This satisfied Hitler, particularly when reinforced with a letter in the same vein from King Gustav. The effect of the assurances lasted only a few weeks despite being sweetened by a further Swedish concession on 25 (or 19) April to allow transit of 'civilian supplies' including fuel oil to the German forces.[25] But Sweden still held out and refused German demands for the transit of military supplies and rejected Göring's suggestion of a like-for-like artillery piece exchange to reinforce the beleaguered German force in Narvik.

As the military situation deteriorated for the Germans in Narvik, a smaller delegation was again summoned to meet Göring at his field headquarters on 11 May 1940 during the invasion of two of Sweden's diminishing number of fellow-neutrals, Belgium and Netherlands. Göring had earlier suggested to a delegation member, businessman Birger Dahlerus, that Sweden could permit the transit of some military supplies under a Red-Cross disguise. Now, a jubilant Göring quickly moved on to the transit question, making it clear that Swedish concerns about neutrality took second place to Germany's prestige and that of the *Führer*, particularly since Sweden had allowed the transit of supplies to Finland during the Winter War. He emphasised that Germany could easily bomb urban areas to secure concessions but did not wish to do so. Various helpful contacts in the German authorities also warned Hägglöf about Hitler's potential to strike at Swedish cities. The war of nerves had escalated sharply.

With no further progress, the delegation returned to Stockholm and after reporting, one member made it clear to the Cabinet that he thought Germany would win the war, based on what he had seen and heard. Per Albin told Hägglöf that Sweden would still not change its decision. Göring's failure to extract any concession led to the responsibility for Swedish contact returning to Foreign Minister Ribbentrop. Nevertheless, the Germans had cajoled and threatened Sweden in equal measure first to allow humanitarian transits consisting of food and medical supplies (19 April), then repatriation of wounded soldiers from Narvik (20 April) and unarmed seamen (15 May) over the Swedish rail network that springtime. For Hitler and Germany, this indicated a Swedish predisposition to assist. Richert was now called in by Ribbentrop on 16 May to receive an official request for transit of 100 carriages of equipment. Richert arrived in Stockholm on 17 May to brief the Cabinet personally on Ribbentrop's and Göring's latest thinly veiled demands and threats including: 'If you want a quarrel with us, you will get it'.[26] When the *Utrikesnämnd* met on 18 May Östen Undén and Sandler were against weapon transit but an overwhelming number of members were in favour. Commander-in-Chief Thörnell also warned the *Utrikesnämnd* that this would be a bad time to resist Germany due to Swedish military weakness and reliance on Germany for future military supplies. The military had no appetite to support a rejection by the politicians. Nevertheless, the demand was again refused. The Government realised the risk it was taking but considered that to concede now would amount to entering the war on the side of Germany and perhaps having to suffer Allied retaliation as a consequence.[27] Meanwhile successful German advances in the Low Countries and Allied failures in Norway, coupled with military and diplomatic vulnerability, had increased the feeling of despair in Stockholm. Richert's frequent reports of further German attempts, now by Göring, now by Ribbentrop, to coerce Sweden into transit of war materials contributed to the atmosphere of isolation and hopelessness. The Government genuinely expected that their continued refusal would result in German action but the deteriorating position in France was making an Allied counter action appear increasingly unlikely.[28] On 18 May the army was on full alert for a German attack but on 20 May when German panzer columns had reached the English Channel, the *Riksdag* party groups gave their support to the Government policy of refusal.

Unfortunately, the primary Swedish tactic of refusing transit, on the grounds that the ongoing hostilities between Norwegian and German troops made it unthinkable to support action against fellow-Scandinavians, had painted Sweden into a tactical corner. Sweden had relegated its neutrality status argument to a secondary position and the cessation of hostilities in Norway would inevitably bring about a German ultimatum on transit. This was not long in coming. Before that, there was a final diplomatic diversion away from the core issue of transit by a half-baked idea, suggested by the self-appointed go-between, Birger Dahlerus, for Sweden to guarantee a neutral zone around the disputed Narvik area and to designate northern Norway as a neutral de-militarised zone under Swedish control. This was taken up in desperation and promoted by Sweden to both the Allies and Germany without any enthusiasm from Norway. The advantages to Sweden were that this so-called 'Narvik Plan' would remove the contentious requirement for transit to support the German troops in Narvik and also safeguard the ore mines in Sweden from action by both sides. The advantages to the belligerents were less clear and varied according to who had the upper hand in the area. By 28 May the Wehrmacht had been driven out of Narvik towards the Swedish frontier but at the same time, Allied forces were being evacuated from Dunkirk. This caused the British and Norwegians to re-think their opposition to the 'Narvik Plan' but of course dissipated any German interest when they confidently anticipated

British military withdrawal to defend Britain. Wigforss and Sköld expressed resistance at a Cabinet meeting on 30 May in a discussion about the anticipated German demands for transit. Westman regarded this as willingness to go to war on an issue that did not threaten any vital Swedish interest and retorted: 'If the Norwegian government surrenders, then we will be placed there with *our war*!'[29]

However, the departure of the Western Allies from Norway on 7 June (which Günther and the Cabinet had learned about on 3 June) and the Norwegian surrender on 11 June now allowed Ribbentrop to point out to Richert in Berlin on 16 June that the previous reason for refusal had now disappeared. Sweden was now free, in the opinion of the German leadership, to redeem its earlier refusal. For them, neutrality was no longer the issue. In fact, a further German request for transit of vehicles, boats and non-military material had been agreed on 15 June with Wigforss and Bramstorp stipulating 'provided that the content is of a peaceful character.' Ribbentrop knew that with the Allied departure from Norway, there was no longer any risk of Sweden joining the Allies. He further stated that: 'refusal would be seen as an unfriendly act' – tantamount to an ultimatum. Richert again travelled to Stockholm to present these latest demands to the Cabinet which met on 18 June four days after the fall of Paris, three days after the fall of Verdun, two days after the invasion of Lithuania by the Soviet Union and one day after the invasion of Latvia and Estonia by the Russians. The totalitarian tide was rushing towards the shores of Sweden while democracy was ebbing away elsewhere. Westman described this as feeling like 'living in front of the muzzle of a loaded cannon.'[30]

The Swedish Cabinet discussed the demands with Richert present. Historian Wilhelm Carlgren described the meeting as one of form – how to concede – rather than of substance – whether to concede or not.[31] That view was certainly shared by Grafström who believed that the decision had already been taken on 17 June.[32] No one present at the meeting opposed a compliant response to Berlin. The meeting started at 9 a.m. with Richert's report on Ribbentrop's demands that stressed that it was essential to answer 'yes' to avoid an attack. Per Albin introduced the discussion by restating the position and emphasising that the German demand was contrary to what he had earlier stated was Sweden's neutral position. He reviewed all the arguments and stressed that if the decision was taken to overturn the content of Swedish neutrality, the Swedish people would have to be told that the reason was the German threat in the current situation. He gave the impression that such a policy reversal was unthinkable but typically did not indicate his own position.

Günther supported Per Albin by covering all the options and outcomes which could ameliorate the decision but believed that a war with Germany at this point would be hopeless. He had previously told Westman in May that he was against going to war to support an unrealistic Norwegian position.[33] Sköld agreed with Günther but warned of possible British reprisal raids for example, on Göteborg's railway yards. The military and economic reasons for concession were obvious and pressing. Sköld was then interrupted dramatically by Günther announcing a telegram from the Swedish ambassador in London, Björn Prytz who had met Under-Secretary R.A. Butler of the Foreign Office on 17 June. The telegram reporting this discussion was read out to the already dejected cabinet and summarised by Günther to the *Riksdag*'s *Utrikesutskott* later that day.

> In discussion today with Butler Foreign Office he confirmed that the French unconditional surrender concerned fleet or colonies. Everything had been tried yesterday to support Reynaud but in vain. Britain's official attitude is for the time being that war must continue but he asked me to rest assured that no opportunity would be missed to reach a compromise peace if the prospect offered reasonable terms, when no '*diehards*' would be allowed to stand in the way. He considered that Britain had greater negotiating opportunities than could be got later on and that Russia would play a greater role than the USA if discussions got started. During the discussion, Butler was called into Halifax who sent word that '*Commonsense not bravado would dictate the British Government's policy*', on which Halifax said he understood that such a message would be welcomed by the Swedish Minister but that it should not be interpreted as '*peace at any price*'. In discussions other members of Parliament showed clear expectation if and when prospect of negotiations arose, possibly after 28 June Halifax may succeed Churchill.[34]

[Italics quote the original English text in the telegram – author's translation.]

The telegram supported the Swedish Cabinet's suspicions that no help would come from the British who were also apparently about to sideline 'diehard' Churchill and seek terms from Hitler. There was also relief that Allied retaliation would be unlikely if transit was conceded. The unanimous Cabinet decision was to open negotiations with the Germans. Next, the *Riksdag's Utrikesutskott* was convened at 12.00 to discuss the Cabinet view and after summarising the situation, Günther recommended a compliant answer. With the exception of Undén and Sandler, there were no objections to the Government position. Following these two decisive meetings, Günther advised zu Wied that Richert would reply positively the following day to the German demand. It is significant that Per Albin and the Coalition Government, envisaging widespread disquiet, took great pains to ensure that the unpopular decision received as wide a political consensus as possible in the circumstances. This was to avoid it being portrayed as being taken by a small, unrepresentative group.

Germany's Russian ally had already pacified Finland and now occupied Estonia, Latvia and Lithuania between 15 and 18 June to complete Sweden's isolation. Negotiations with the Germans on the mechanics of transit were opened on 19 June and completed on 8 July. The Allies had lost militarily in Europe and thanks to Butler, they had relinquished the moral high ground with Sweden. This made subsequent British protests regarding the concession ring hollow in Stockholm. The Western Allies had in fact surrendered almost all influence on the Scandinavian situation when they withdrew from Norway and later from France. This removal of the possibility of Allied reprisals was one of the factors which led the Government to concede. Britain and France, who only a few months previously had been strong-arming Sweden into conceding transit for their troops to Finland were now reduced to diplomatic hand-wringing that Sweden was on the slippery slope to becoming a German satellite. British Minister Victor Mallet was instructed on 18 July to give 'a determined recital of all our grievances' and attempt to 'check them in their downward career towards complete subservience to Germany.'[35] Per Albin openly admitted to his colleagues that Sweden was no longer neutral due to the concession. The UD denied to Britain that Sweden's concessions broke her neutrality in view of the current military and political circumstances – a position recognised privately by Mallet but not shared by him with his Swedish counterparts. The Russians by contrast were keen to support Sweden as a neutral and following the concession Sweden was seen by the Soviet Union as a buffer zone against Germany. Russian support could not fully replace the counterbalance to Germany which the Western Allies had represented – but for beleaguered Sweden, it was nevertheless welcome.

What did the concession really amount to? The Swedish Government recognised that there would be no benefit – and a number of disadvantages for Sweden – if a military transit agreement continued to be refused by Sweden after British troops left Norway. When the Norwegians established their collaborative Government with the Germans, the effectiveness and tyranny of the occupation was not heightened by the occupying forces having a safer means of reinforcement. While it may have deprived the Allied forces of a limited opportunity to sink German troops, the reality is that transit did not damage the Allied war effort in any material way. The records indicate that there was at that time no intention by Germany to invade or bomb Sweden but of course this was not known to the Swedish leadership. Given the brutal disregard by the Nazi leadership for the sovereignty of Europe's neutrals and its aggression to opposition of any kind, it is difficult to criticise the Swedish Government's assessment that a refusal of transit would most probably have led to military action against Sweden. The criticism that refusal would have been the correct course in a moral sense, implies a full appreciation of the genocidal horrors yet to come. In strategic terms criticism also suggests that refusal would in some way have benefited the Swedish state. Sweden's inevitable defeat in an armed struggle may have led to a post-war European settlement by a victorious Germany and its Soviet ally. A 'Reichskommissariat Nordenland' comprising Sweden, Norway and Denmark with Finland re-integrated into Russia as a Soviet Republic is not too far-fetched an alternative scenario.

The real significance of the concession was political. It demonstrated that a democratic country could be forced by a dictatorship to abandon strict neutrality in order to uphold its democracy and independence. Per Albin resignedly noted in his diary over the next few days:

> So now we have broken our precious and strict neutrality from the knowledge that it is unreasonable in the current situation to take the risk of a war.

> Day-after feeling. It pains me that we should be compelled to give way to superior force but I cannot see the possibility of going any other way. [36]

The decision exemplifies a functioning Swedish democracy at a time of extreme national danger. Conceding transit to German demands was not, as some would characterise it, an undemocratic decision taken by an unrepresentative group of compliant moral cowards. As early as 27 May Günther had put the point to the *Utrikesnämnd* and Per Albin recorded a general reluctance to take the risk or face the decision.[37] The fact that Russia had indicated a restraining interest on German ambitions towards Sweden coupled with Sweden's ability to put the iron ore mines out of action and deny Germany those strategically important supplies provided some limited means of moderating German demands.

Having secured the principle, the Germans now demonstrated their superior position with extensive demands for significant use of the Swedish rail network during the two weeks of negotiation in June on the operation of transit. Troop transit became known as 'Leave Traffic' to reflect the carriage of German soldiery on leave ('*Permission*'). Günther personally took part in the discussions, which indicates the significance which Sweden placed on the detail of the concession. On the German side was Hitler's special envoy Karl Schnurre whose arrogant negotiating style was particularly loathed in Stockholm. Boheman later wrote: 'Thank God I gradually extricated myself from having anything to do with him'.[38] Schnurre may also have been foremost in Günther's mind when he wrote:

> During the years 1940–42 the *UD*'s relationship towards the pushy, and also to us, arrogant Germans was characteristic of an interminable wrangle about everything. I cannot recall a single subject or a single question where we had the same understanding and that any consensus could be established.[39]

Of particular interest was the whittling down of the German opening position for the unfettered use of the Swedish rail network. There were three particular routes which the Germans wanted to use. First, their focus was on the southern route which allowed for the troops on leave from south Norway (Kornsjø) to transit to the Swedish Baltic port of Trelleborg which connected by ferry to Germany. The north-south route from Narvik to Trelleborg was second and finally there was the interchange of troops between the Norwegian cities of Trondheim and Narvik through Sweden by a 'horse-shoe' route to avoid the exposed sea passage. Perhaps bearing in mind the failure to control British transit traffic through Sweden to Russia during the First World War, Günther and his team succeeded in imposing important restrictions on the Germans: troops had to travel unarmed, limited to 500 troops per train, only one train per week (Narvik) or per day (Kornsjø) and all incoming numbers to be matched by outgoing numbers. In this way, Sweden tried to ensure that transit was not used to strengthen the German garrison in Norway and that a sizeable German force would not be able to carry out an act of war on Swedish territory during their passage. Sweden was not only concerned about Allied reactions but also did not want to encourage fears in the Kremlin about Sweden moving closer to Germany which might attract another pre-emptive move against Finland. In London, the mood was hardening against Sweden due to similar fears about closer ties with Germany. British Minister Mallet defended his view against a sceptical Churchill that a neutral Sweden was worth supporting. Mallet's arguments rested on access to intelligence, Swedish rearmament, limits on exports to Germany and contacts with resistance groups in occupied lands and he prevailed.[40]

Sweden now began to live with the realities of encirclement, transit, German hegemony, Allied criticism and Russian concerns about future Swedish neutrality. Mid-1940 was not a time for faint hearts in the Swedish leadership. Alfred Rosenberg, the Nazi chief ideologue's briefing to foreign journalists in early July on the 'New Order' in Europe – in which the Scandinavian countries would share a common political and economic front under German leadership – was taken in Stockholm as the precursor of future German foreign policy while the concept was comprehensively rejected in the Swedish press. For the next twelve months until the German invasion of the Soviet Union, Sweden had to deal with four main issues. Firstly, concerns continued about the likelihood of Finland being subject to further Russian aggression while Germany's attention was diverted by the war in the west. Secondly, following their success over transit and the 'New Order' speech, the Germans continued to press for further concessions from Sweden and tighter economic and political relations. Thirdly, the consequences of the blockade for the Swedish economy and the welfare of its people gained greater prominence. Finally, the domestic political situation was tense, both from opponents of the policy of accommodation with Germany and those who were tentatively trying to seek a *modus vivendi*.

CLOSER TIES WITH FINLAND? APRIL 1940–DECEMBER 1940

Due to understandable Swedish concerns about a possible attack following *Weserübung* in April 1940, the Ålands again appeared on the agenda of Swedish-Finnish relations. On 25 April Günther told the Finns that Sweden had now decided to participate in the defence of the islands. The Finnish leadership had other ideas because they were now considering seeking closer ties with Germany to counter Russian aggression and did not want any complications over the Ålands. This delayed any meaningful response. The Soviet Union was also attempting to obtain a better defensive position in the Ålands when on 27 June they presented a demand that either Finland withdrew her troops from the Islands or enter into a joint defence agreement.[41] In July 1940, Swedish feelers in Moscow revealed that the Russians would be satisfied with a return to demilitarisation but the Russians continued to increase pressure on Finland with new demands for Soviet troop transit. With relations apparently worsening, Günther proposed that to discourage the Russians, Sweden should advise them that an attack on Finland would be regarded as an attack on Sweden. Not surprisingly, following the rejection of Sandler's 'activist' policy barely six months earlier, the Government also dismissed Günther's proposal. Finnish hopes of active intervention on their behalf by Germany seemed to be still-born despite Finland concluding a transit agreement, in return for German arms, with Germany in August. This would not only help to garrison Norway but also establish German depots for their later attack on Russia. Hitler was careful not to arouse Russian suspicions and so declined to become involved in the Russian–Finnish disputes.[42]

Sweden was now anxious to deflect Finland from its course of closer relationships with Germany but was reluctant to offer compensating assurances of closer Swedish commitment in the event of Russian aggression. Instead, Sweden attempted in Moscow and Berlin to promote the idea that a Swedish-Finnish agreement to maintain the status quo, that is neutrality and demilitarised Ålands, would address the concerns of both Russia and Germany. Responding to feelers from Finland in September Sweden went so far as to consider a re-union between the two countries with foreign policy and defence policy firmly under Swedish direction. Notwithstanding Swedish assurances, this proposal was seen by Moscow and Berlin as a complicating Swedish interference, and provoked a strong and negative response in early November. Sweden and Finland now had to drop the idea. Their suspicions of Russia were justified in mid-November when Molotov attempted unsuccessfully to persuade Hitler to give the Soviet Union a free hand in Finland. A repeated attempt by Günther in December 1940 to secure Russian and German interest in a Swedish–Finnish neutrality agreement was also rebuffed. Neither wanted Swedish interference in Finnish policy because they both had other plans for the future of Finland. Russia still regarded Finland as a vassal state and an Achilles heel in its defences against Germany. Germany was now in the initial stages of preparing for the invasion of the Soviet Union that would involve Finland. Swedish security concerns were a secondary issue in relation to the ambitions of Sweden's mighty neighbours to the east and south.

Closer Ties with Germany? June 1940–August 1940

Sweden increasingly found herself on the receiving end of unwelcome attentions from Germany with regard to further concessions and closer relations. The main concessions which Germany now pursued concerned press freedom and further military transit through Sweden. Germany complained about Swedish press and radio on no fewer than twenty-five occasions in July and August 1940, a sharp increase from the forty during the previous ten months since September 1939.[43] The extraordinary sensitivity of the German leadership was due to criticism from a country within Germany's sphere of influence being regarded as *lèse-majesté* of the *Reichsführer*, resulting in a high diplomatic profile for the Swedish media's attitude. The various representations by the German Legation and Göring amounted to pressure to rein in the Swedish press and this was done both discreetly and openly by the Coalition Government, King Gustav, and Günther. They worried that the raising of diplomatic temperatures could lead to problems elsewhere in the Swedish-German relationship at a time when stability there was valued more than untrammelled free speech.[44] The media were cowed by concerted Government efforts to appeal to their sense of responsibility while for the extreme cases like Torgny Segersted's newspaper, *GHT*, critical editions were confiscated. This was partly the politics of gesture and when the Coalition Government demonstrated action to meet the criticisms, the number of German protests reduced. These restrictions of press freedom indicated the willingness of the Coalition Government to accommodate German sensitivities when Swedish security was believed to be threatened.

Germany also expressed interest in the positioning of Sweden within the new German-centric European constellation. Various German officials declared themselves disappointed that Sweden was failing to adjust to the new situation, as evidenced by the Coalition Government's unwillingness to yield to every German demand. In fact, there had been an interest in policy adaptation, a 'new course', within the Social Democratic party initiated by Allan Vougt, a close associate of Per Albin. This was based on Vougt's discussions with fellow Social Democrats in Denmark who somewhat optimistically wanted to accommodate the Germans in such a way so as to preserve the leading Social Democratic position within Scandinavian politics even after the widely expected German victory in Europe. Vougt's initiative petered out in the face of Per Albin's lukewarm response.[45] A Scandinavian Social Democrat 'New orientation' conference in Stockholm in mid-August 1940 attended by Danish Prime Minister Stauning and Per Albin came to nothing. Significantly, not only were there no minutes, but also no common Danish-Swedish policy emerged on 'positive' adjustment to the Germans.[46]

Göring suggested that Sweden could find a position similar to Bavaria in a 'Greater Germany' while a diplomat patronisingly likened Sweden to Yugoslavia or Hungary. The overall theme was that Sweden should take a stronger initiative to align herself with Greater Germany – before she lost the opportunity to do so. This uncannily foreshadowed Churchill's later pronouncements that Sweden should join the Allies 'before the end.'[47] Sweden prudently fended off both sets of blandishments. However, as the German juggernaut rolled towards the invasion of Russia, Sweden would encounter more urgent and serious demands for further concessions.

TRADE, SUPPLY AND THE BLOCKADE, APRIL 1940–FEBRUARY 1941

The consequences of encirclement by Germany for the Swedish economy and the welfare of its people after April 1940 were dramatic and severe. The Germans immediately re-negotiated their 1939 trade agreement which in effect abandoned the earlier principle to maintain so-called 'normal' pre-war trade levels, while Britain quickly restated its adherence to the WTA. The principle of 'normal' had been particularly important in 1939 in securing British agreement and Britain attempted in vain to get Sweden to comply with the WTA tonnages to put a limit on exports to Germany.[48] Also, in response to the situation that a significant amount of Swedish shipping (about 1 million tonnes) was left outside the double British and German blockades, Britain undertook in September 1940 to charter 60 per cent for Allied use and allow bunkering in British ports. However, since 9 April Britain had refused to allow Sweden to trade through the blockade, one of the few remaining British means to exert pressure. Swedish representations argued that continuing refusal would weaken Sweden's ability to resist German pressure and furthermore would lead to Sweden being subsumed entirely into the German economic structure. Britain relented and allowed four ships into and four ships out of Göteborg per month, subject to British naval controls. German agreement was also necessary to allow shipping through their Skagerrak blockade but that took a further three months until February 1941 to achieve. Both Britain and Germany would continue to use this trade with the west, the so-called 'Safe-Conduct Traffic', to pressurise Sweden throughout the war.

In essence, between March 1940 and May 1945, Germany had total control over supplies of coal and coke while the Allies had partial control over supplies of fuel oil using the 'Safe-Conduct Traffic' which the Germans also jointly controlled. Manufacturing industry, process industry, and power generation depended to a large extent on coal and coke. Modern warfare depended on fuel oil and the Swedish requirement for that grew as rearmament increased the amount of military equipment during the war. This dependency gave the belligerents a stranglehold over the Coalition Government that influenced some of the foreign policy decisions taken later.

Domestic Political Pressure and the Election, June 1940–September 1940

As historian Alf Johansson has written: 'The weeks following the transit concession were a hard time for Per Albin.' He attempted to minimise its significance but it was clear to the Swedish public as well as to Per Albin's opponents that neutrality had been severely compromised. Press opinion covering the transit concession, which had leaked out in advance of any official announcement, downplayed any effect on Norway and the war in general. While Per Albin's initial public pronouncements trivialised the concession, he admitted to the Riksdag in secret session on 21 June that it marked a change in neutrality policy.[49]

The press reaction took three positions. At one extreme were those who followed the initial Government line and dismissed the concession as almost a mere logistical issue. At the other were those who saw the concession as a step towards entering the war on Germany's side. Between those two positions were those who urged their readership to trust the Government's judgement while warning against trivialising the issue. There was initial disquiet over the rumour that Swedish army escorts were under orders to treat the German transit troops respectfully, but the Social Democratic party reaction seems to have been to press Per Albin to speak reassuringly to the nation. He did so on 28 July 1940 when he re-stated that the concession did not mean abandoning either Swedish neutrality or the right of self-determination and that the Government's position was not determined by any political ideology.

The September 1940 election campaign was understandably restrained in the circumstances but Per Albin and the Social Democrats benefited from the prevailing mood. His reputation for sound judgement had been boosted by the collapse of the Western Allies which showed that his opposition to an active intervention in the Winter War – an intervention which would also have required Western Allied support – was correct. Intervention would also have sucked Sweden into an unsuccessful war against Russia. Following a campaign based on Per Albin's reputation as a leader for troubled times, the Social Democrats on 15 September gained absolute majorities in both Chambers of the *Riksdag*. This also gave them the unwelcome burden of greater responsibility for the decisions taken by the Coalition Government whose representative Cabinet membership remained unchanged. Following the election result, Per Albin received a one-word telegram from a political opponent: 'Condolences!' His responsibility as Prime Minister was about to get heavier in the summer of 1941 as Hitler squared up to Stalin.

Neighbouring Occupation, Oppression and Resistance, April 1940–December 1942

The invasions and occupations of Norway and Denmark had a traumatic effect on Swedish political and emotional attitudes as well as on the country's geo-political position. Although Scandinavianism had failed to produce common defence and foreign policies against the totalitarians, the reality of the German action saw Sweden's previously close relationships with its neighbours brutally disrupted. The three nations' peoples and politicians could communicate with each other in their own languages, shared common historical and regal connections back over 1,000 years, had intermarried, traded, and developed political parties, policies and institutions that had more in common than different. This created bonds which would not break during the war but would be severely tested by the strains arising from Sweden's policy choices. Germany had transformed Sweden's neutral neighbours, first into unwilling combatants then into involuntary members of the Third Reich, something which the Swedish leadership had determined would not happen to Sweden.

Norwegian Defiance

Once hostilities had ceased in Norway in 1940, the Norwegians had two governments, a government-in-exile in London tied to British policy and a German-led administration in Oslo under *Reichskommissar* Terboven which contained members of Vidkun Quisling's fascist *Nasjonalsamling* Party. Swedish policy towards both until 1942 was primarily determined by cautious assessment of the extent to which relations with either could cause problems with Germany.

As early as 10 April the President of the Norwegian *Storting* (Parliament), C. J. Hambro, arrived uninvited in Stockholm following the invasion with the intention of broadcasting a message to the Norwegian nation on Swedish radio (*Radiotjänst*). The Germans warned that this would be regarded as an unfriendly act and a breach of neutrality which forced the Coalition Government to interfere with *Radiotjänst* independence and prohibit Hambro's speech.[50] The transit concession was added to Swedish refusal of temporary refuge in Sweden for the fleeing Norwegian King and later, non-recognition of the Norwegian government-in-exile's representative in Stockholm. The Norwegians meanwhile were maintaining an effective diplomatic offensive, critical of Swedish transit concessions in London which together with British dissatisfaction damaged Sweden's standing in Washington.

Civil liberty in Norway gradually deteriorated for its citizens and created a growing resistance movement against the Government. From 1940 to 1942, the *Nasjonalsamling* Government's attempts to create National Socialism in the country met an entrenched Norwegian democratic culture which was integral to Norway's national identity. These attempts provoked defensive resistance. For example in late 1940, when the Government tried to take control of the National Athletic Association, athletes refused to compete – a boycott which lasted until 1945. Further opposition occurred with the replacement of judges, the arrest of trade unionists and later in 1942, 1,200 teachers who had refused to implement a new Nazi curriculum in the schools. This also led to a complete break between the Church and the regime. Yet, *Nasjonalsamling* membership increased by 65 per cent from 26,000 in 1940 to just under 43,000 in early 1942 indicating perhaps more than nominal levels of collaboration.[51] The *Nasjonalsamling* paramilitaries, the *Hird* (the equivalent of the German *SA*), were active in beating up protesters and resisters which only increased opposition to Quisling and the *Nasjonalsamling*. The Germans were ruthless when attacked, for example taking hostages, sending civilians to concentration camps and destroying property, but for most Norwegians, life went on as before. For some groups such as farmers and fishermen, living standards actually improved under the occupation.[52] Initial Swedish guilt for the suffering of their neighbours found popular expression in collections and humanitarian efforts and political expression in the pages of *Trots Allt!* and *G.H.T.* Towards the end of 1940, the Swedish Red Cross sent humanitarian aid and 624 pre-fabricated houses over the border to the war-damaged areas but as the oppression increased, so did Swedish anger. From the beginning of August 1941, a state of emergency had been in force which was followed by strikes in September. The Germans decided to make an example by executing two leading trades' unionists but instead created martyrs around whose fate the labour movement in Sweden began to stir. The Trades Union (*LO*) Conference denounced the atrocity in a text, later broadcast on the BBC, which a sympathetic Per Albin nevertheless felt could have been phrased more diplomatically. The *LO* had defiantly asserted that the German working class would not support such executions. Günther typically urged restraint on Swedish press comment.[53] Swedish public opinion was nevertheless outraged and that disquiet put pressure on Coalition Government policy.

In Cabinet also, Norway was on the agenda in 1941. The refusal to recognise the Norwegian government-in-exile as the sole Norwegian authority, the continuing non-recognition of their representative in Stockholm, and the legal process over the ownership of Norwegian merchant ships stranded in Göteborg on 9 April 1940, sustained Norwegian antagonism in London. Furthermore, some of the 3,000 Norwegian refugees in the country were considered to be a security risk, closely monitored by the Swedish secret police and a few even administratively detained. Per Albin refused to pressurise the Germans on behalf of the Norwegians, believing correctly that it could limit Swedish influence in other areas and more importantly, prove completely ineffective against the internal policies of a ruthless occupier. Initially, Per Albin's unpopular refusal to act despite the widespread condemnation of German atrocities was more dictated by German strength but as the German military position weakened after November 1942, the bolder Sweden became.

Before this occurred, more stories arrived in Sweden of German atrocities arising from the treatment of the 10,000 Norwegian prisoners in Norway and Germany but reports of these abuses were officially suppressed in the media, most notoriously in March 1942. Seventeen newspapers were simultaneously confiscated when they printed a syndicated report of German torture of Norwegian resistance members. The clamour over this suppression policy combined with rising public opposition to German transits led to an overall hardening of opinion against the Coalition Government's 'caution first' policy towards the Germans. This caution significantly did not preclude the reception in Sweden of several hundred Norwegian Jews who were able to escape a round-up for deportation in autumn 1942. They fled, sometimes with Swedish assistance, to safety over the border, an event which the German legation noted cynically, having apparently swallowed the Swedish case that these refugees' activities would be heavily restricted.[54] Of those who had not fled, 532 were deported by sea, not through Sweden, to their deaths in Auschwitz in December 1942. This brutal incident caused a significant transformation both to Swedish attitudes regarding the Germans and to Sweden's refugee policy, shifting 'from indifference to activism', as one analyst puts it.[55]

Danish Cohabitation

In contrast to Norway, there was no significant armed resistance when the Germans invaded Denmark. An invasion that began around 4 a.m. led to the Danish decision by 6 a.m. not to resist and the small-arms skirmishes ended shortly thereafter. Danish military losses were 16 dead and 23 injured.[56] The Germans succeeded in securing the cooperation ('*forhandlingspolitik*'), from the sitting Government regardless of the absence of any formal agreement for their 'protective' occupation. Germany might have also succeeded in achieving similar cooperation in Norway if Quisling had not forced himself onto the German agenda and rendered any deal constitutionally impossible.[57] Furthermore, Denmark had signalled its likely cooperation with Germany by signing one of Hitler's renowned 'non-aggression' pacts in May 1939.[58]

During the early occupation, life went on much as before because the sitting Government continued until August 1943 and many Danes did not feel much difference in their daily lives. There was generally little attempt to change public administration while the small army and navy remained intact. There was no government-in-exile to create split loyalties as in Norway and the compliant Danish Government were treated by Germany at arms' length as a foreign administration through the Foreign Ministry. Initially for Sweden, the Danish occupation was much less problematical than that of Norway. For a start, Sweden did not share a land border and Germany enjoyed easy land access to Denmark. Without hostilities, there were no German demands to succour the invading force and no refugees from the fighting to be accommodated. There were no competing governments and the Western Allies had no excuse to become involved in Danish affairs. What was complicating for the Swedish Social Democrats was that their party comrades in Copenhagen had reached the sort of accommodation with the Nazis that some in the Swedish party were beginning to contemplate in mid-1940, albeit in order to lubricate the release of Norway and Denmark from the German yoke on the latter's anticipated victory.[59]

Nevertheless, the Danish example of Social Democratic cohabitation with the occupiers offered a Scandinavian working model for Sweden to observe, while the Swedish leadership contemplated consequences arising from the probable German domination of Europe. This model apparently safeguarded their democratic institutions and protected their citizens, including the Jews, from civil rights abuses in return for passive acceptance of German hegemony and continued trade. With this example, it is hardly surprising that the Swedish leadership kept its options open. They refrained from taking steps that could hamper a frictionless accommodation with Germany should that become necessary in order to retain some of Sweden's democratic freedoms within a totalitarian federation.

It took some time to get going but the first signs of a Danish resistance movement began in late 1941, gathered tempo into 1942 and broke the surface in the summer of 1942 with demonstrations, illegal newspapers and the first really organised sabotage as opposed to individual or amateur initiatives. It is significant that the initial resistance was against the Danish Government due to their cohabitation policy. This had created a backlash of resentment among Danish Communists who were free to oppose it following the invasion of Russia in July 1941 when the Danish authorities began to intern party members at the behest of the Germans.[60] By January 1942, the Danish Communist Party, *DKP*, was in the vanguard of organising groups of saboteurs.[61] *Frit Danmark* was one of the highest profiled resistance newspapers and a conservative politician and former minister, John Christmas Møller, was one of its founding contributors. Møller later escaped to London via Sweden with his family in April 1942 to become Chairman of the Danish Freedom Council, formed by Danish nationals who had fled to London.

Quisling's equivalent in Denmark was Fritz Clausen, a small town doctor who also led the electorally insignificant *DNSAP* (*Danmarks National Socialistiske Arbejderparti*) with about two per cent of the vote in 1939 and 1943 elections.[62] The Germans used him after 1940 as the extremist threat to force Prime Minister Stauning's Government to toe the German line but the *DNSAP*'s political failure led to Clausen's demise after the 1943 election. The man whom Hitler had once suggested could take over Denmark, to the horror of the German Foreign Ministry, then joined the SS and his party crumbled. For Swedes, travel in Denmark was unrestricted and normal trade took place between the countries but Swedish visitors began find that the resistance was gathering momentum under continual British encouragement. Much of that was organised by the British Special Operations Executive (SOE) from their offices in the British Legation in Stockholm.

SWEDEN AND BARBAROSSA, DECEMBER 1940–JUNE 1941

Hitler's decision in December 1940 to invade the Soviet Union in June 1941 was to place a strain on Sweden's policy of remaining out of the war – a strain which almost broke the Coalition Government. The attack was code-named *Operation Barbarossa*.

Sweden entered 1941 with apparently reasonable relations with the Germans. Although persistent, muted criticism in the Swedish press about German actions in occupied Norway and Denmark resulted in the familiar round of irritated protests, Germany had nevertheless consented in February to allowing 'Safe-Conduct Traffic' through the German blockade. However, the careful monitoring which Günther's negotiations had imposed on the rail transit began to show a build-up of German troops in Norway in contravention of the agreement. The Germans attempted to explain this away to a sceptical UD using convoluted statistics and circumstantial reasons – for instance, a reduction in soldiers' leave due to ice. The Swedish Government, unaware of the troop build-up for *Barbarossa*, feared that the raid in March 1941 by British commandos on the Norwegian island of Svolvær, less than sixty miles from the sensitive port of Narvik, had perhaps moved the Germans to decide on a pre-emptive strike and occupy Sweden. That would remove any risk of an Allied landing joining up with the Swedish army to invade Europe via the north-western flank. The German Legation now advised Sweden that a further 76,000 troops were to be transited through Sweden. This led to the so-called 'March Crisis' when the Government decided to respond to fears of German invasion by mobilising a further 80,000 reservists. The following day, the German figure of 76,000 was 'corrected' to 16,000 to which Günther agreed, provided that the transit took place by 23 March. Further concessions were made regarding the passage of guns and supplies but Günther maintained overall limitations despite some elasticity. Germany now relaxed its pressure and April passed without any significant demands.

Finland was however being increasingly pressurised by Russia. The Russians wanted control of the northern port of Petsamo (Pechanga) on the Barents Sea and its adjacent nickel mines which were strategically important. In contrast to their reluctance the previous summer to become involved in Finnish-Russian disputes, Germany now supported Finland against Moscow. Russia backed off and Finland moved closer to Germany. The Swedish attaché in Helsinki reported in mid-April that Finnish-German staff discussions were at an advanced stage and he was further told by his German counterpart that the attack on Russia would take place in early or mid-June. Günther's forecast of war between Germany and the Soviet Union was becoming reality and despite Finnish assurances of neutrality, made during his visit there on 6–7 May, it seemed clear that Finland would be involved.

With hostilities approaching, General Olof Thörnell, the anti-Russian Swedish Commander-in-Chief who was on good terms with the *Wehrmacht*, on 21 April requested formal instructions from the Government in the event of a German-Russian conflict.[63] In addition, he reviewed Sweden's weak military position relative to Germany, said that a war with Germany to prevent German support to Finland was 'absurd', and proposed a list of active measures, including occupation of the Ålands. This request polarised thinking among the politicians – causing an extended debate between the activists who included Günther, and the isolationists who included Wigforss – but resulted in Thörnell simply being told in early May to defend the country's neutrality in all circumstances, even against Germany.[64]

Germany was preparing Sweden for more concessions to help

Barbarossa. Pressure was put on Swedish trade when at the end of March Germany withdrew the 'Safe-Conduct Traffic' consent and reduced exports to Sweden, particularly vital metals and fuel. Berlin resumed its litany of complaints about Swedish press comments and Swedish limitations on the transit agreement. German envoy Karl Schnurre, now appointed as transit negotiator, again appeared in Stockholm on 24 May. He was returning from a mission to Helsinki to agree military coordination during *Barbarossa* – less than four weeks away. In Stockholm, he indicated the German leadership's dissatisfaction with Sweden, advised that there were no concrete requests from Germany at present and hoped that a more cooperative future could be anticipated, to which Per Albin responded in his usual ambiguous way stating that Sweden 'had always been and still was prepared for international cooperation on a voluntary and independent basis.'[65] Günther had gone somewhat further and reassured Schnurre that 'we understand and appreciate Germany's protecting hand over Finland and in no way wish . . . to disturb the relationship between Finland and Germany.'[66] Schnurre reported favourably to the Nazi leadership at which Hitler reversed his earlier view that Sweden would not grant further transit.

Per Albin had given an accommodating answer to Schnurre in order to address the deterioration which had taken place in German-Swedish relations following the March crisis. Schnurre had hinted that a concession on transit would ease the German 'Safe-Conduct Traffic' suspension. Sweden feared that such a concession would cause the British to suspend it. Overwhelmingly, the balance of power in June forced Per Albin and Günther to recognise reality and prepare for a concession which would not drag them onto the German side. Günther however aligned himself more closely to Bagge's activist view that involvement in the forthcoming conflict could offer Sweden an opportunity to end the Russian threat to Finland and by extension to Sweden. The restraining interest of Russia was now nullified and the activists were again encouraged.

At the beginning of June Finland took on the character of a German forward deployment area. Large troop concentrations together with troopship embarkations were reported from Germany and Finland. In the first week of June the Finns at last informed Sweden of the presence of German troops while stressing insincerely that war was not inevitable. Sweden took preventative measures by cancelling leave for troops stationed in Norrbotten and heightening the alert on the Baltic island of Gotland. The picture facing Swedish decision-makers was nevertheless a confused one with no firm indication of war among the overwhelming intelligence about preparations and troop movements. Even the usually well-informed Richert was unsure of whether the Germans intended blackmail or hostilities with the Soviet Union.[67] On 7 June Boheman disclosed to the visiting Stafford Cripps (accompanied by Mallet) that Swedish intelligence from Germany confirmed that the attack would take place on 21 June.[68] Germany had reduced its pressure on Sweden, helped by the increased vigilance by Swedish authorities over press coverage, but the first indications of German demands were appearing. On 19 June the German military attaché in Stockholm floated hypothetical questions in the event of a German-Russian war. Midsummer and the next concession demand were not far off.

ANOTHER CONCESSION, JUNE 1941

On 22 June, the day of the invasion of Russia, Schnurre met Günther at 7 a.m. with a list of demands from German High Command, OKW, at the top of which was a 'one-off' request for transit over Swedish railways of a single Division of troops under General Engelbrecht from Norway to Finland. Günther countered with the previously successful suggestion that sea transport could be used. Schnurre not only ruled that out but added that a refusal by Sweden would be seen as 'an unfriendly act'. Sweden would not be exposed to the threat of war but should interpret her neutrality to the advantage of Germany.[69] Concession would clearly represent a further break with the legal basis of neutrality. Schnurre sought to make the concession appear as acceptable as possible: crucially it would be one-off, the Engelbrecht Division would not remain on Swedish territory and Sweden would not be asked to join the joint Finno-German invasion. Günther seems to have decided to agree, having feared worse demands such as the occupation of Gotland, and believed that a further concession would not significantly worsen relations with Britain. He agreed to other requests on mining and significantly a provisional, non-binding transit-planning exercise with German military representatives, and told Schnurre to expect an answer on the Engelbrecht Division in four days time. Given these minor agreements, Schnurre must have been fairly confident of success for a major transit concession.[70] In contrast to May 1940, no actual military threat was made by the Germans but Boheman's belief that a refusal would have created a deterioration leading to conflict must have been widely shared in Stockholm.[71]

The demand triggered a furious debate in the Cabinet, in the *Utrikesutskott* (*Riksdag* Foreign Affairs Committee) and in the *Riksdag* itself where 'one-off' made little difference to the principled opponents to the concession. The German request for transit was regarded as a severe test of the Coalition Government's resolve to maintain the appearance of neutrality and the reality of independent decision-taking. Once more the Coalition Government was plunged into a decision of strategic importance, this time fundamentally entangled with Sweden's aspirations and fears regarding the old Russian enemy to the east and the new German enemy to the south. The characteristics of this concession decision were different from the 1940 case due to two new factors: firstly the role of the monarchy and secondly, a more widespread *realpolitik* view within the Government and the *UD* that Germany would now win the war and that Sweden would have to adjust to that outcome. Also, when Per Albin and Günther had briefed King Gustav V on the demands, the King strongly supported the concession on the grounds that he was unwilling to take responsibility ('*kunde inte ta ansvaret*') for the country going to war over a contribution to the Finnish-German cause against Russia. Per Albin chose to interpret his remarks as a threat to abdicate – an interpretation which he would put to good use.[72] 'It was bloody good that the old chap said that, which I will use in my party group.'[73] Per Albin's other trump card was the 'one-off' proviso.

On 23 June Günther presented the case for acceptance to the Cabinet citing *inter alia* Boheman's view that a refusal could result in Sweden and Finland disastrously ending up on opposite sides in the war and stressing that allowing it should be viewed as support for Finland rather than as a concession to Germany. Günther advised acceptance but did not reveal that he had authorised *non-binding* working discussions between the *UD* negotiators and the Germans for the arrangements. The Cabinet was also told of King Gustav's 'threat' but similar to June 1940, Per Albin did not reveal his own position although Bagge detected a predisposition to accept. The political essence of the task for Per Albin was to get all parties, most of all his own, to subscribe freely to an unpalatable decision. Failure to do so might lead to a decisive crisis with the Germans, which could bring down the Government and allow more pro-German politicians to take over. Per Albin acknowledged the non-neutral nature of the transit and the negative effect on the Swedish people. He stressed that the *Riksdag* must be fully consulted. The three Cabinet opponents argued that conceding transit would mean entering the war on Germany's side, four agreed with Günther and two expressed no view – of whom one later claimed his opposition.[74] The *Utrikesnämnd* chaired by the King was also divided. The Conservatives and Agrarians moved to back Günther on the basis of defending Finland. The People's Party and more importantly the Social Democrats were also divided. Undén and Sandler were against but Per Albin kept the discussion open and both the King and Crown Prince supported Günther's line.

The *Riksdag* members met as party groups the following day and took on the same divided characteristics of the *Utrikesnämnd*. Pro-Finnish, anti-Soviet sentiments and an element of Germanophilia contributed to the Agrarian and Conservative *Riksdag* groups concurring with concession when they met on 24 June. Bagge had also reminded the Conservatives of the importance of internal unity in the face of the external threat. The People's Party group met and although its leader, Andersson, repeated Bagge's message, nine out of thirty-six voted for rejection. The right-wing parties had agreed to make the concession with the King's threat in prospect. In preparation for the Social Democrat group meeting where a damaging and irreparable split could most be anticipated, Per Albin met the party members of both the *Utrikesutskott* and the Cabinet to go over the issue. Instead of mentioning the King's threat, he suggested that the Government might be replaced, with a loss of power for the party, if the request was rejected and followed this up with a warning of the potential hostile reaction from Germany. Wigforss led the opposition and called for a vote after a majority of speakers had urged rejection. The result was an emphatic 159 to two against, perhaps reflecting an element of grand-standing rather than responsibility. Per Albin deftly called for a second vote, reminding the group of the possible consequences, including splitting the Government. This divided seventy-two to fifty-nine in favour with thirty abstentions. The first vote reflected conscience and the second reality.

When the Cabinet reconvened, Per Albin stated that the Social Democratic group opposed the concession provided the other parties supported that decision. He then turned on Günther and said that a commitment from him not to recommend further concessions would help to ease the Social Democrat fears. The Cabinet were confused, not knowing if the Social Democrats had said no. Per Albin then offered the solution. He personally was opposed but if the concession could be limited to a one-off he would agree for practical purposes. Bagge seized on the opportunity to avoid a Government melt-down and reinforced the one-off agreement. Per Albin then offered the other parties the opportunity to re-consult their groups. No other

Cabinet members took up his offer and with the Social Democrat members also remaining silent, the decision to agree was taken. The party leaders all announced their agreement to go along with the Social Democrats' line and none of the Cabinet were prepared to split the Government and cause it to fall over the issue.[75]

The *Riksdag* was next to be consulted in secret sessions on 25 June with the Communists excluded. Günther led the discussion in the Lower Chamber where the debate passed without incident. Per Albin spoke to the Upper Chamber where about thirty Social Democrats and a handful of People's Party members expressed their disquiet but were countered by an equal number from their own parties agreeing with the decision. The Cabinet again met later that day formally to ratify the decision and while Social Democrat members Wigforss, Gjöres, Sköld and Möller all noted their opposition, there was no repeat of the resignation threats which had characterised the break-up of the Coalition Government in 1939. Per Albin had achieved the nigh-impossible task of consolidating Social Democrat unity around a detested concession while shackling Bagge, Günther and the activists with its 'one-off' nature and so preventing later agitation for further significant concessions to the Germans. The crisis had in fact stabilised the Coalition Government by excluding future activist tensions and locking all parties in to the Government's foreign policy. Later on that day, the decision to concede transit was formally taken in Council and thanks to Günther's advance negotiations, the Engelbrecht Division began to entrain for their 'crusade against bolshevism'. The first troops rolled through Sweden that very night under the midnight sun on their way to engage the Red Army on the Finnish frontier. It was emphasised to the Germans that this was a 'one-off' concession but Schnurre and his superiors were to aspire to much more in the coming months.

In this democratic decision, Per Albin and Günther had a vested interest in securing Government unity for concession, having chosen to hint at a favourable response to the Germans in advance of the Government meeting, based on their *realpolitik* view of the requirements of the situation. This brinksmanship could have backfired badly if the opponents had been in a majority and perhaps have led to the collapse of the Government and its replacement by less resistance-minded politicians. It is however clear from the voting patterns that a majority of the *Riksdag* politicians were ultimately in favour of concession and needed only some coaxing from Günther and Per Albin, buttressed by the spectre of national disunity, to take the broader view. Whatever might be said later – and there were to be many versions of this event, exceeded only by the number of interpretations – Per Albin with the support of Günther had led his country and his Cabinet into taking an unpalatable decision in a democratic manner. The one-off nature of this concession conferred on it a shred of honour and helped salvage Swedish self-respect. It also set a limit on German ambitions and despite repeated German attempts, it remained a one-off.

REELING BUT RESISTANT

Sweden had experienced a spiral of set-backs since September 1939 which had struck the country militarily, economically and politically. Scandinavia had briefly been turned into a battleground due to Hitler and Stalin's aggression and a totalitarian takeover of Sweden could not be ruled out. Swedish defence capability on the ground was poor and in the air was effectively non-existent leaving the country open to *Luftwaffe* attack, the implied threat which the Germans used to secure the Norwegian transit concession and later the Engelbrecht transit. The occupation of Denmark and Norway cut Sweden off from almost all western trade forcing the country unexpectedly to rely on Germany for crucial supplies of coal and fertilisers without which the Government feared that industry could collapse, rearmament would falter and people could starve. The main German *quid-pro-quo* was continued supplies of iron ore coupled with Swedish political passivity and neutrality. The all-party unity in Swedish politics was symbolised by the Coalition Government Cabinet with the Social Democrats uncomfortably in the driving seat and although there were limitations on open political and media debate, democratic institutions were maintained. The Swedish leadership was acutely conscious of the dangers of the situation, now from Russia, now from Germany, but was able to construct, negotiate and maintain positions within a neutral status which could accommodate unpredictable changes in the fortunes of war. Fortunately for Sweden, none of the belligerents was prepared to challenge Swedish neutrality militarily, no matter how much that status was flexed, because each could derive or anticipate benefits for itself when the power balance altered in its favour.

Like Charles Dickens' ill-fated character Mr Micawber, Sweden hoped that 'something would turn up.' And Westman's diary note of a September 1941 Cabinet meeting even admitted the possibility of a Russian victory.[76]

Notes

1. Hägglöf, Svensk krigshandelspolitik, p. 39.
2. Wahlbäck, Regeringen och kriget, p. 20.
3. Hägglöf, Möte med Europa, p. 197.
4. Westman, Politiska anteckningar, 8.12.1939.
5. Ibid. 14.12.1939.
6. Ibid. 8.12.1939.
7. Ibid. 27.2.1941.
8. Isaksson, Per Albin, pp. 398–9.
9. Boheman, På vakt, p. 97.
10. Ibid. p. 104.
11. Meinander, Finlands historia, p. 201.
12. Mallet, Memoirs, pp. 106–10.
13. Boheman, På vakt, p. 108.
14. Carlgren, Svensk utrikespolitik, p. 36.
15. Engle & Paananen, The Winter War, p. 143.
16. Meinander, Finlands historia, p. 212.
17. Quoted in Engle & Paananen, The Winter War, p. vii.
18. Wilhelmus, 'Det tyska anfallet mot Skandinavien', pp. 70–1.
19. See for example, Hugemark, 'Överraskning i teori och praktik', pp. 106–7.
20. Mallet, Memoirs, p. 84.
21. Boheman, På vakt, p. 115 & Mallet, Memoirs, p. 77.
22. National Archives, London, FO 371/24832, 11 May 1940 (annotations).
23. Mallet, Memoirs, p. 91.
24. Westman, Politiska anteckningar, 15.4.1940 and Boheman, På vakt, p. 111.
25. Carlgren, Svensk utrikespolitik, p. 166 (but Grafström dates the first transit to 19 April).
26. Westman, Politiska anteckningar, 16.5.1940.
27. Johansson, Per Albin och kriget, p. 164.
28. Carlgren, Svensk utrikespolitik, p. 171.
29. Westman, Politiska anteckningar, 30.5.1940.
30. Ibid. 30.5.1940.
31. Carlgren, Svensk utrikespolitik, p. 184.
32. Grafström, Anteckningar, 31 October 1944.
33. Westman, Politiska anteckningar, 31.5.1940.
34. RA. HP39A UD723 17.6 (18.6), cited in Carlgren, Svensk utrikespolitik, p. 194, n. 2.
35. FO 371/24859 18.7.40 cited in Carlgren, Svensk utrikespolitik, p. 188, n. 155.
36. Wahlbäck & Boberg (eds), Sveriges sak är vår, p. 114.
37. Per Albin Hansson 27 May 1940 in Wahlbäck, Regeringen och kriget, p. 95.
38. Boheman, På vakt, p. 46.
39. RA. UD Handbrev Series 3 Christian Günther's Private Archive 1939–1945, 5 February 1945. Letter to Ivar Harrie of Expressen.
40. Mallet, Memoirs, pp. 98–9.
41. Carlgren, Svensk utrikespolitik, p. 200.
42. Ibid. p. 220, n. 123.
43. Ibid. p. 216.
44. Ibid. pp. 216–18.
45. Johansson, Per Albin och kriget, pp. 184–91.
46. Ibid. p. 190.
47. Leifland, 'They must get in before the end'.

48. Mallet, *Memoirs*, p. 88.
49. Johansson, *Per Albin och kriget*, p. 176.
50. Lindal, *Självcensur i stövelns skugga*, pp. 72–7.
51. Andenæs, Riste & Skodvin, *Norway and the Second World War*, p. 69.
52. Grimnes, *Norge under okkupasjonen*, pp. 41–2.
53. Johansson, *Per Albin och kriget*, pp. 285–7.
54. NA GFM EO35765 4.12.42 Juden im Schweden.
55. Levine, *From indifference to activism*.
56. Hæstrup, *Besættelsens Hvem-Hvad-Hvor*, p. 19.
57. Grimnes, *Norge under okkupasjonen*, p. 12.
58. Christensen, Lund, Olesen & Sørensen, *Danmark besat*, p. 55.
59. Johansson, *Per Albin och kriget*, pp. 186–7.
60. Hæstrup, *Besættelsens Hvem-Hvad-Hvor*, p. 168.
61. Christensen, Lund, Olesen & Sørensen, *Danmark besat*, pp. 311–13.
62. Hæstrup, *Besættelsens Hvem-Hvad-Hvor*, p. 112.
63. See Cronenberg, 'Och får jag tag i den fan-', p. 278.
64. Carlgren, *Svensk utrikespolitik*, pp. 270–1.
65. Ibid. p. 280.
66. Cited in Isaksson, *Per Albin*, p. 404.
67. Carlgren, *Svensk utrikespolitik*, pp. 290–1.
68. Mallet, *Memoirs*, p. 111.
69. Carlgren, *Svensk utrikespolitik*, p. 300.
70. Ibid. p. 302.
71. Boheman, *På vakt*, p. 178.
72. '. . . jag måste tolka så att han hällre avstode från tronen . . .' Per Albin Hansson 22 June 1941, in Wahlbäck, *Regeringen och kriget*, p. 168.
73. Isaksson, *Per Albin*, p. 474.
74. Carlgren, *Svensk utrikespolitik*, p. 304.
75. Ibid. p. 306.
76. 'Om Ryssl. segrar . . .', Westman, *Politiska anteckningar*, 10.9.1941.

4

Towards the Turning Point, July 1941–July 1943

The period between July 1941 and January 1943 initially saw Sweden trying desperately to protect itself from the consequences of a rising tide of German success in the east. Then, as the German zenith passed, Sweden began to prepare for the adjustments required to accommodate the growing power of the Western Allies, who after December 1941 significantly included the formerly neutral United States. Sweden also kept an eye on the advancing Red Army and the prospects for Germany's co-combatant, Finland, in the event of Soviet success. It took until 1942 for Sweden to realise that the seeds of Germany's downfall had been planted by Hitler's catastrophic decision to wage war on two fronts. However, Sweden was sandwiched between these two fronts and increasingly had to satisfy both sides as opposed to accommodating the Germans. The nadir of concessions to Germany took place between the Engelbrecht concession in July 1941 and the release to the Allies of the previously embargoed Norwegian ships the following year, March 1942. By then, it was clear that the Soviet army had put a brake on the *Wehrmacht*'s campaign in Russia. German setbacks, however, did not mean an easing of the difficulties for Sweden. Indeed, Sweden had to work harder on the diplomatic and trade fronts in order to maintain its position as an independent, self-determining state.

GERMAN FLIRTATION AND ALLIED WEAKNESS; AFTER ENGELBRECHT, JULY 1941–FEBRUARY 1942

The two powers most disadvantaged by the Engelbrecht concession in June 1941, Britain and Russia, protested without any real enthusiasm. Britain did not even formally present a protest note while the Russian Minister, Mme Kollontay, was at pains to indicate that they were only protesting because Britain had done so. Both countries impotently accepted that there was little else that they could do and more significantly, little else that Sweden could do in the circumstances. For Russia, the limited transit concession was infinitely preferable to more tangible Swedish participation along with Finland in the invasion.[1] Together with the USA, they were more concerned with Sweden's continuing position as an independent country rather than damage to its status as a strictly neutral power.

Against the background of early military success against the Soviet Union, Germany now attempted to press home its perceived advantage with a wider agenda of military and diplomatic initiatives. The German navy attempted to extract Swedish cooperation with a proposal to seize any Soviet warships forced out of their home harbours by the advancing German forces and taking refuge in Swedish ports. Within two days, the Germans were told that this was not possible. The Germans did succeed in persuading the Swedish navy to lay mines in the Baltic Sea off Öland which completed a German barrier across the southern Baltic. The Swedish minefield protected any vessels in Swedish territorial waters but the barrier was a clear defence for the German navy against the Russian fleet. Schnurre's original list of demands, headed by the Engelbrecht transit, was largely met in subsequent negotiations carried out separately by the *UD*'s Erik Boheman. These included permission for German and Finnish planes to over-fly Sweden in an emergency without risk of being shot down, three Swedish airfields being designated for emergency landing, and regular overflights by 'courier planes' between Norway, Germany and Finland. The *UD* generally avoided formal, written agreements on concessions wherever possible. To do so would tie their hands for the future. However, in the case of the Engelbrecht transit, while a Swedish note gave consent, it also confirmed the one-off nature of this concession.

On the diplomatic front at the beginning of July 1941, Schnurre attempted to engage Günther informally in discussions regarding Swedish volunteers for the *Wehrmacht*. He also sounded out interest in signing up to a 'Scandinavian Pact' under German leadership which respected Sweden's wish to remain out of the war but also her position as the leading Scandinavian power. Günther again rebuffed this on the grounds that it would signify Scandinavian adherence to the Axis. In response, Schnurre warned that Sweden would be regarded negatively in Berlin. The next significant demand from Schnurre, for the transit of a further division barely a month after the Engelbrecht concession, was made on 31 July. Günther immediately refused, partly on the grounds that the Engelbrecht transit had been 'one-off' and partly because German troops had successfully been transported by sea to Finland, escorted by Swedish warships while in Swedish waters. Schnurre and Berlin accepted the Swedish refusal with little protest which perhaps indicated a strengthening of Sweden's position. The trend of escalating German demands worried Günther who considered them as preliminary to future German pressure to conclude a treaty binding Sweden to Germany. How long would the Nazis tolerate uncooperative behaviour from a country surrounded by their forces and whose economy they could control through restrictions and sanctions? Although the UD did not exclude a medium-term scenario of a weaker Germany with increasing military difficulties, problems for Sweden could still arise from increasingly desperate German attempts to improve German defences.[2]

One measure which the Government considered in late 1941 demonstrated Per Albin's authority in the Cabinet and exemplified his procrastinating approach to difficult or sensitive policy issues. Bagge, having failed to commit Sweden in the east, now turned to banning the Communist Party in Sweden. Günther welcomed this as an easy way of gaining German goodwill but Per Albin cunningly countered by adding the proscription of extreme right-wing groups to the proposal. This 'double-sided' tactic prolonged discussion as to which groups should be banned. Tensions surfaced in Cabinet again between Bagge and Wigforss. Per Albin recorded his relief at 'a resignation threat from either side' which tested the Cabinet balance. In January 1942, when the Germans expressed displeasure over the 'double-sided' proposal, Per Albin was able to drop it and avoid a damaging concession to German interests.

German disappointment at Sweden's indifference to joining their 'crusade against bolshevism' surfaced in September 1941 when Sweden was again warned about critical press coverage which indicated a 'hostile attitude to Germany'.[3] But the real pressure arose from the presence of Norwegian merchant ships which had been stranded in Swedish ports when Norway was invaded in 1940. Beginning in late 1940, Stockholm-based George Binney of the British Ministry of Economic Warfare (MEW) planned a break-out, *Operation Rubble*, from Brofjord near Göteborg. In late January 1941, five of these ships broke through the German blockade successfully. The Norwegian government-in-exile had requisitioned the ships and they were loaded with goods vital to the British war effort including ball-bearings. The Germans now claimed that the remaining twelve ships belonged to the occupied Norwegian state and disputed the right of the government-in-exile to dispose of them. The Swedish response to the dispute was to submerge it in the legal quagmire of an embargo process allegedly on behalf of the Norwegian owners but really for the occupying Germans. The case would take months to grind through the Swedish courts and Sweden was able to postpone having to take a decision. Boheman made it clear to Mallet that Swedish interests meant recognising the reality of German power: British support to Sweden would not extend beyond friendly advice in the event of a dispute with Germany. Sweden was placed in the unwelcome role of arbiter between the two belligerents in a dispute which was as much about prestige as military advantage. An added complication was that the case involved the property of Sweden's occupied neighbour and their citizens who crewed the vessels.

Sweden was approaching 1942 in a delicate relationship with a victorious Germany. In late October 1941, Günther declared to a secret session of the *Riksdag* that due to the changes in Europe, Sweden must now recognise reality in the shape of demands made and criticism directed at Sweden by the belligerents. He reaffirmed the desire and intention to remain out of the war and to resist if either side attempted to involve Sweden against the other. This declaration was endorsed by the parties in the *Riksdag* and welcomed in Berlin which nonetheless remained critical of the Swedish Government. To address German criticisms, a somewhat submissive document was prepared by the *UD* in which the totality of Sweden's 'considerable services' to Germany between July 1940 and October 1941 was laid out. These included 670,000 soldiers transited to and from Norway, 5,000 supply-laden rail wagons to the *Wehrmacht* in Finland, seventy German supply vessels escorted through Swedish waters, sixty overflying courier flights a week, the establishment of a transit supply depot at Luleå and lastly the maintenance of exports of 45,000 tonnes of iron ore per day from the port at Luleå following the reduction in exports from Narvik due to damage to facilities there caused by the fighting in 1940.[4] The previous month, a message to Hitler from the King, had expressed 'warm thanks for his decision to crush bolshevism, a danger not only for Scandinavia but for the whole of Europe and extended his best wishes for the great success which had been so far achieved.' These two documents mark a particular low point in Sweden's subservience to the Germans. Per Albin had advised against the King's letter but it is not clear if Günther knew or approved of it.[5]

Despite the apparently cordial exchanges between Stockholm and Berlin, there was an undercurrent of nervousness due to the German setbacks on the eastern front. The Swedes had learned to what lengths Hitler would go to pressurise and threaten Sweden for concessions when his troops were cornered at Narvik so how might Sweden be affected by German reverses in December 1941? One possibility was a German pre-emptive move against Sweden to block any Western Allied plan to invade Norway and join up with the Swedish army. In Berlin, Richert certainly gave weight to the rumours of such a move which circulated there.[6] These caused the government to increase military alertness on 18 February 1942 which was explained to the Germans as a seasonal exercise that showed also that Sweden was on standby in case of any move by the Western Allies. A further reassuring message was sent from the King, on his own initiative, to Hitler

> giving his royal word that Sweden would never permit [an allied action in north Scandinavia] across Swedish territory and was firmly resolved to resist such a move which the Swedish forces were capable of doing. [7]

Hitler had in fact feared a Western Allied landing in January 1941 and also the unlikely scenario that the Swedish army would join in to gain Petsamo and Narvik.[8] Every Murmansk convoy was feared to be an invasion fleet. While Hitler may have considered a move against Sweden, the *Wehrmacht* strength simply was not adequate for a knock-out blow, given the commitments on the eastern front. With his close shave at Narvik during May–June 1940 in mind, Hitler did not want to begin a drawn-out action which would allow the Western Allies time to mobilise forces to assist Sweden. His concerns regarding the trustworthiness of Sweden in the event of an Allied action remained. Despite the official reassurances, Hitler believed that public opinion could force a change of government to one that would side with the Western Allies and expose the northern flank of the Third Reich. Sweden now achieved some security from her armed readiness which together with the assurances meant that Swedish-German relations improved again – this time without any concessions.

OPERATION PERFORMANCE, MARCH 1942

The spring of 1942 saw the issue of the Norwegian ships reappear on the diplomatic agenda. The Swedish Supreme Court ruled on 17 March in favour of Britain in terms of their ownership and they were free to leave Göteborg with their valuable cargoes of bearings and metals. Ahead of them lay the German navy blockade across the Skagerrak. Britain had been intransigent in the exchanges with Sweden regarding the ships: nothing less than unconditional release of these vessels would satisfy the British negotiators. This hard line arose partly as a result of the German reverses in Russia and partly from rediscovered British confidence generated by the Russian and American entry into the war which signified the end of Britain's isolated stand against Nazi Germany.

In *Operation Performance* the ten ships put to sea on the evening of 31 March but the German navy sank three, another three were scuppered by their own crew and a further two, *Lionel* and *Dicto*, fled back into Göteborg. Only two eventually made it to England. The whole episode had been planned in meticulous detail by the British SOE and was again led by the swashbuckling George Binney (later knighted) who had arranged for weapons to be smuggled, first into Sweden and then aboard the ships to defend them against German attack. The German reaction was somewhat muted compared to the bombast of the previous autumn. Their protests centred on the fact that Sweden had not acted neutrally in the matter, for example in allowing the two surviving vessels to return to Göteborg. Initially, the Germans were unaware of the arms smuggling but after news of a formal Swedish protest to Britain, their complaints encouraged Günther unusually to commit in writing that the two surviving vessels would 'not again leave the harbour'.[9] This commitment would weigh heavily around the Government's neck in the months to come. The Germans satisfied themselves that the breakout had amounted to a pyrrhic victory for the British but the achievement was prestigious for hard-pressed Britain at a point in 1942 when the war elsewhere was going badly. The illegal arming of the ships also led to Binney's expulsion. The positive aspect for Sweden was that the vital 'Safe-Conduct Traffic' was not interrupted by Germany as a result of the break-out but negatively, the presence of the two remaining ships *Lionel* and *Dicto* in Göteborg harbour meant that Sweden risked being reluctantly drawn into another prestige conflict between the Western Allies and Germany.

British assertiveness in its relations with Sweden now manifested itself in the outright refusal to recall, as Sweden demanded, two diplomats who had been involved in arms smuggling with Binney. Britain threatened to stop oil supplies by the 'Safe-Conduct Traffic' if Sweden insisted on recall – which it dropped. Additionally and more threateningly for Sweden, the British Government now wanted to link Swedish import quotas with a reduction and limitation of the concessions which the Germans presently enjoyed. A new note of firmness and intimidation now entered the diplomatic dialogue between the Western Allies and Sweden. This was more pronounced in the exchanges with Washington than with London but this harsher tone represented another shift in the relations between Sweden and the Western Allies which mirrored the fortunes of war. Allied policy was now to reverse the tide of concessions made to Germany and to begin to secure some concessions in their favour.

ALLIED PRESSURE TO END CONCESSIONS, APRIL 1942–DECEMBER 1942

In April 1942, Sweden requested an increase of 30,000 tonnes of imported oil per quarter to the existing quota and cited Swedish defence requirements against German invasion as the reason. While the defence case was dismissed in London and Washington, the Western Allies made a counterproposal in mid-June based on imposing reductions on the Swedish concessions to Germany. For example, transit of troops and materials to Norway should be limited to 75,000 men each way and a maximum of 2,500 tonnes respectively, no oil to be transited, and statistics to be provided to the Allies.[10] Günther now set about the awkward task of persuading the Germans to reduce their loading on the overstretched Swedish rail system – as the case was presented to the German transport officer in Stockholm.[11] This technical rail discussion which the Swedes tried to promote in July was replaced by a political discussion which saw the return of the objectionable Schnurre to Stockholm in early August 1942, an event which Günther had hoped to avoid. Schnurre refused to accept the Swedish case for reduction and indeed asserted the German requirement for unlimited use to meet *Wehrmacht* needs. He nevertheless agreed that if Sweden abandoned the attempt to limit the volumes, Germany would attempt to reduce its traffic. When these reductions failed to materialise, Sweden imposed more limited reductions in September than had been proposed in July and further reductions by the German side were noted in November by the

Swedes. The ground had begun to shift from under the confident German position after the summer of 1942 and the Swedes carefully followed the changes. Despite the usual crop of complaints about unfavourable Swedish press treatment of the German campaign – military deadlock or even defeat were now options being discussed openly – Swedish concerns about German invasion returned and Günther once more urged the press to rein in their comments, which in his view only complicated a tense situation. Swedish opinion became even more hostile following a round of executions in Trondheim on 6 October and the deportation of 532 Norwegian Jews to Germany on 25 November as part of the Nazi 'Final Solution'.[12] The Holocaust had reached Sweden's borders but the British army victory at El Alamein in early November and the landing a few days later of the Anglo-American forces in north Africa focused Swedish attention on a future Allied victory. The Swedish military took several steps in December to put the army on alert in response to the threat of a German attack that reflected the Government's belief that an attack was still possible in the unlikely event of an Allied landing in Norway. German demands now eased off but several requests in November for additional transit were rejected. On the German trade front, Swedish negotiator Hägglöf was also pressing for more favourable terms during the discussions for the 1943 Agreement. The Germans, seeking to maintain their important trading relationship with Sweden, undertook to continue their high 1942 levels of supplies of coal, coke and chemicals. The Germans tentatively tried to tie their proposals, for restrictions on Swedish exports by air to the Western Allies, to the continuity of the 'Safe-Conduct Traffic', but this was rejected by Günther on the basis that Swedish policy had to be even-handed.[13]

The Allies had meanwhile shown little interest in pursuing their attempts to persuade Sweden to limit the German concessions. The Swedish response had elicited little reaction from the Allies which seems to have been the result of the shift in the Allied power from London to Washington. The British reluctantly accepted that key decisions would now be taken there. Washington decision-taking itself was somewhat fragmented as the State Department wrestled with the Pentagon for primacy in war policy. To add to the complexities for Sweden, the prevailing climate in Washington was hostile. Since Hägglöf's visit in 1940 and the United States' entry into the war, new people had taken a critical view of Sweden's application of neutrality. Nevertheless, as a precursor to negotiations on oil, Britain persuaded the Americans that an independent Sweden was a useful resource for the Allied war effort *inter alia* because of the supplies of materials like ball-bearings and intelligence advantages, not least in relation to operations in neighbouring occupied countries.[14] The basis for new negotiations was an Anglo-American memorandum submitted to Sweden on 18 September 1942. Erik Boheman, *UD* Secretary, was to play a key role in the discussions which would symbolise the end of the primacy of German considerations in Swedish policy while the subsequent intensification of Allied pressure on Sweden would be led by the unsympathetic Americans. The Anglo-American memorandum now proposed even further limitations on transit concessions than had been suggested in mid-June together with a demand that Swedish escorts of German vessels should cease. To reinforce the point, Washington also detained the cargoes due to be loaded on to the 'Safe-Conduct Traffic' from the United States.

Boheman set off at some personal risk on the civil air service between Sweden and St Andrews in Scotland. The Germans were to attack the service the following year with loss of life. Arriving in London, in October 1942, he was cordially received at the British Foreign Office and the powerful MEW. Boheman put the Swedish case to officials, military, and politicians including Churchill who, while they were sympathetic to the position in which Sweden found itself and in agreement that Allied support should be given to help Sweden defend itself, were equally firm that the concessions made to Germany must be withdrawn. Churchill also told Boheman (who had described Churchill in 1940 as 'old and scared') that he thought that Sweden had so far followed a wise policy, admitted that Britain had exaggerated the importance of iron ore exports at the beginning of the war, and said that Stalin did not intend to take over Finland unless absolutely forced.[15] Britain had no interest in seeing Sweden at war with Germany.[16] 'Under no circumstances do we want another victim. We want your country preserved.' The policy question for Sweden at this point was how far and how fast concessions to Germany should be withdrawn. Withdrawal had to be at a level and pace which would not provoke the Germans into military or trade retaliation, including the suspension of the 'Safe-Conduct Traffic', while procuring Allied supplies and ensuring their import by the 'Safe-Conduct Traffic'. This naturally caused some animated discussion within the Coalition Government.

In London, Boheman largely met the Allied demands, for example the requirement that the additional oil quota should be used exclusively for defensive military purposes, while stipulating a few reservations on Sweden's ability to meet them all. He emphasised that Sweden had absolutely kept to the WTA but after Denmark and Norway had been invaded in 1940, isolated Sweden was forced to replace its western imports with those from Germany which required increased exports to the Allies' enemy. Despite Boheman's concessions, the American negotiators in London lacked authority to agree to the increases in oil quotas from the United States which meant that Boheman would next have to travel there to meet the hawks in the Roosevelt administration. Churchill personally dictated an introduction to Roosevelt for Boheman in order to smooth the way for what promised to be a more difficult reception.

Sweden did not enjoy the same extensive relationship with the United States as with Britain. There was no WTA, shipping agreements and little background understanding between officials. Moreover, some hawks in Washington were arguing that a complete blockade of Sweden might better serve Allied interests. This would limit Sweden's ability to supply Germany and so shorten the war while an invasion of Sweden by Germany was now unlikely. There was also doubt that Sweden was really independent of Germany. How much of this critical attitude can be ascribed to active Norwegian diplomacy since 1940 is difficult to tell but Trygve Lie, the Norwegian Government-in-exile's Foreign Minister (who had built up strong relationships in Washington due to his advocacy of a post war NATO) was worried that Sweden would secure the benefits of neutrality and victory and so continue to dominate Scandinavia at the expense of its neighbours. Even the British Foreign Office agreed that Sweden should not benefit from the war.[17] Against this background, Boheman had his work cut out to achieve the oil quota increase Sweden wanted, particularly as the Americans again moved the goalposts by adding two further requirements: the freedom for the two remaining Norwegian ships, *Lionel* and *Dicto*, to sail from Göteborg and permission for the Allies to charter even more of the Swedish merchant fleet.

Boheman now considered it important to yield to the Allied demands due to continued Allied military success against Germany. Back in Stockholm, his views caused tensions because Per Albin and Günther simply did not want to defer to the Allied demands too quickly. Boheman's patient discussions altered views in Washington to the extent that he was able to agree on 1 December 1942, that two Swedish oil tankers would be allowed to sail and that the Norwegian ships issue would be held in abeyance until an Allied delegation arrived in Stockholm. A plethora of other issues were, however, not resolved but the main gain for Sweden from Boheman's visit was that a channel had been opened up and that the 'Safe-Conduct Traffic' had been maintained.

THE POLICY SHIFT AND *LIONEL* AND *DICTO*, DECEMBER 1942–JANUARY 1943

Unfortunately for Boheman and Sweden, the fragile agreement on the oil tankers did not survive for long. The Allies chose to turn the release of the Norwegian ships into a symbolic concession in return for continued Swedish trade and supply from the west. The Allied delegation from the British MEW arrived in Stockholm in mid December and demanded the ships' unconditional release. Minister Mallet joined them a few days later and threatened to cut off the 'Safe-Conduct Traffic' imports. The Americans joined in the pressure and Günther was thus faced with the dilemma of conceding to the Allies that which he had told the Germans would never happen. His written assurances came back to haunt him when, as Allied military success and the German difficulties in Russia grew, the Allies decided to make the release of the ships both into the type of prestige issue that Günther feared and a bargaining counter for supply of oil to the hard-pressed country.

The Coalition Government was now forced to contemplate the enormity of the policy shift required. On 21 December Günther told his Cabinet colleagues of Mallet's representation and his own subsequent refusal, which was unenthusiastically approved by the Cabinet. Bagge and Per Albin both indicated that they thought that it was unwise to change the policy at this juncture on the basis that this would risk German suspension of the 'Safe-Conduct Traffic'. But only one week later, the support for Günther and his position had ebbed. Orders given to the Navy to prevent the ships' departure – with force if necessary – had caused concern in Social Democrat circles meaning, as it did, firing on unarmed British ships to accommodate German expectations. Furthermore, Boheman had now returned from Washington and on 29 December recommended acceptance of the Allied request to the Cabinet. This caused Bagge mischievously to point out that Günther and Boheman seemed to be at variance.

Günther still had not encountered any real opposition: the *Riksdag*'s Foreign Affairs Committee *(Utrikesutskottet)* meeting on 30 December (which Boheman also briefed) agreed with his view that while the cargoes could be released, the ships could not. Meanwhile,

Utrikesutskottet Chairman Östen Undén had changed his view following consideration of Boheman's briefing to the Committee. Per Albin also began to waver, partly due to Boheman's influence and partly due to the tide of public opinion running strongly in favour of the Allies. Swedish diplomacy now switched to attempting to get an assurance from the Germans not to suspend the 'Safe-Conduct Traffic' if the ships were allowed to leave and to limit any retaliatory action. While this was happening, Günther had determined to release the ships, whether or not the Germans agreed. In this decision, he probably gave more weight to the drama unfolding at Stalingrad and the future power balance than to inevitable German objections. In Berlin, Richert was able to secure assurances that no retaliatory action would occur as a result of the ships' release. Boheman told Mallet on 11 January that the ships would be released subject to assurances that the 'Safe-Conduct Traffic' ships would remain at Sweden's disposal, should the 'Safe-Conduct Traffic' be interrupted. Günther now took the risk and confirmed the release at which point the Germans, contrary to previous assurances, stopped the 'Safe-Conduct Traffic' on the 15 January.

The two ships never broke out of the blockade despite an attempt on 17 January 1943. After October their valuable cargoes of ball-bearings and special steels were subdivided, transhipped in great secrecy onto five specially converted unarmed British motor torpedo boats (MTBs) in Lysekil and taken to Hull in nine trips. The MTBs superior speed put them out of reach of the German blockade force and none were lost despite having to navigate the North Sea under cover of darkness in appalling winter conditions. The Swedish navy was instructed to ensure that there was no German intervention in Swedish territorial waters.[18]

The Allies had succeeded in forcing a prestige-laden decision in their favour. This was the first significant concession to the Allies in the new war situation and one to which Günther and Per Albin had difficulty in adapting. After two and a half years of constant threats and menace, their now ingrained reluctance to risk antagonising the Germans had led them to lose some authority in the Cabinet through a hasty reversal of policy. Their defensive stance would be further tested and they would again have to concede ground in the face of stiffening Allied demands. Significantly, the final decision does not seem to have been endorsed by the Cabinet, *Utrikesutskottet*, or *Utrikesnämnden* unlike previous decisions of this importance. Possible reasons for this include an understandable reluctance by Günther publicly to expose his policy setback. Another explanation is that neither Per Albin nor Günther wanted at this stage to stimulate further debate amongst those politicians who were now advocating a harder line towards Germany for a speedier withdrawal of concessions in order to influence Allied attitudes to Sweden. Both Per Albin and Günther wanted to pace the withdrawal of concessions with the changing war situation but above all to minimise both the risk of retaliatory German military action and difficulties with the Germans over the all-important 'Safe-Conduct Traffic'.

So for Sweden, the efforts to increase oil quotas and maintain the 'Safe-Conduct Traffic' without significant disruption to their relationship with Germany had failed. The larger picture of the struggle between democracy and Nazism was secondary to the desperate Swedish attempts to secure and maintain their own precarious supplies. The Swedish Cabinet was focused entirely on the consequences to Sweden of being seen to give way to the Allies and possible German retaliation against the 'Safe-Conduct Traffic'. The moral debate was secondary to the fact that the Western Allies had successfully secured Swedish compliance by unsubtle pressure against a backdrop of German military setbacks. This overt demonstration of Allied strength struck a chord with the Swedish public who were tired of concessions to Germany and longed for a change of policy. What they perhaps did not appreciate fully was the risk which such an about-turn could carry when their country was still surrounded by German occupied territory.

GERMAN REVERSALS AND THE END OF SWEDISH TRANSIT, JANUARY 1943–JULY 1943

The beginning of 1943 also saw a change not only in Germany's military success but also in its representation in Stockholm when German Minister Zu Wied was replaced by the more hard-nosed Hans Thomsen. He was faced with the recent reversal in Stockholm that now placed Western Allied requirements ahead of those of Germany. Hitler commented in March 1943, that Sweden now supported the opposition's side domestically and even if they were too clever and careful to show it openly, they 'try to trip me up whenever possible' and they obviously realise 'that I can do nothing to them.' This frustration may have been the basis of the *Wehrmacht*'s operational study in early 1943 for an invasion of Sweden which foundered on the hard reality of insufficient military resources to mount such an attack.[19]

While there was no absolute reversal of direction, the Germans were now firmly reminded that they must respect the rules and agreements with Sweden and that they could no longer expect the same attention and consideration as earlier. The Germans were asked to adhere carefully to their courier flight agreement in February after an emergency landing showed that the aircraft carried military markings and the crew were armed and uniformed in contravention of the agreement. The Swedish Government also reacted sharply to a nervous salvo from an armed German merchant ship against a Swedish submarine in mid-April with a protest note whose firm language was publicised. Transit freight traffic was also reduced in April from seventy to sixty rail wagons per day, the checks for war materials were intensified and discussions were opened to end the German transit depot in Luleå, one of the concessions which Hägglöf had listed in late 1941 in his account to the Germans.

When Grundherr, the head of the Scandinavian section of the German Foreign Office, visited Stockholm in April he was subjected to complaints in firm language about forced labour in Norway and conditions there in general. Thomsen had been called in by Günther a month earlier to be told that anti-German feeling in Sweden was increasing and as a first step, Germany should allow the resumption of the 'Safe-Conduct Traffic' to prevent a worsening of Swedish-German relations. Günther was in a hurry to secure this resumption before the Germans discovered that another round of Allied trade negotiations was due to start in London on 10 May 1943. He feared that the Germans would threaten this resumption as a means of limiting Swedish concessions in London. Eventually, the Germans agreed to resumption on 6 May subject to Sweden assuring them that *Lionel* and *Dicto* would not leave Göteborg that summer.

As early as November 1942, the first explicit request came from the *Riksdag* to end the widely unpopular 'Leave Traffic' from Norway.[20] There had been constant pressure on Sweden from the Western Allies as well as the Norwegians to end it. It had little strategic military value in the war but symbolised at home and abroad, as Boheman pointed out, Swedish dependence on Germany.[21] Norwegian opinion had certainly had an effect on the Government's outlook.[22] There was now open public condemnation of the concessions in sections of the Swedish press while Per Albin's political standing was under pressure.[23] He wanted to continue his careful policy in order to safeguard unity in the Coalition Government and also to maintain the otherwise unobtainable supplies of fuel from Germany which were considered essential for Sweden. The *Riksdag Utrikesutskott* Chairman, Östen Undén, had unsuccessfully tried to pressurise Günther and Per Albin into ending transit by calling them before the *Utrikesutskott* and attacking Günther for continuing the concession. But the *Utrikesutskott* did not hold a hearing and later in the *Utrikesnämnd*, Günther advised continued caution. When Undén opposed this, he was counter-attacked by Per Albin and later humiliated. Despite facing down domestic opposition to the transit, the issue was now linked by the Allies to Hägglöf's forthcoming London negotiations in May and June 1943 for another War Trade Agreement (WTA), this time including the Americans. The objectives of the Allies were for Sweden to reduce its exports to the Axis countries, stop financial credits to Germany and reduce further the 'Leave Traffic' in return for agreement on quotas of goods vital to Sweden. The principle of 'normal' Swedish trade which had underpinned the WTA with Britain had now been abandoned in order to force Sweden to reduce support to Germany and her co-belligerent, Finland.

The Swedish delegation led by Hägglöf was rather exposed. Hägglöf had successfully urged Per Albin prior to the negotiations to allow him to offer transit cancellation to the Allies as a negotiating ploy. However, on arrival in London, he found that the Western Allies had already factored in this offer as a 'given' and instead pressed Hägglöf to further restrict trade with Finland and Germany. The Swedish delegation had been assigned limited scope for manoeuvre by the Cabinet, but as the Allies' demands exceeded what had been envisaged, they had to seek approval from an unresponsive Stockholm or take some decisions themselves without the protection of Cabinet approval in order to make progress. Hägglöf concluded non-binding agreements in London which contained both transit cancellation and trade reduction in return for increased oil quotas. These were greeted with a mixture of dismay and indignation in Stockholm, not least from his UD colleagues, Boheman and Günther.[24] The Swedish delegation provisionally agreed to cancel all German 'Leave Traffic' and most German goods transit by 1 October 1943 and thenceforth to limit all German transit to 120,000 tonnes per annum. If this were not carried out, the Allies could end all exports to Sweden.

Günther had admitted on 6 May that the transit could be ended whenever the Swedish Government decided, because no formal agreement existed.[25] Consequently on 16 June when Hägglöf's agreements were discussed in Cabinet, the discussion was confused, as well it might be when the politicians tried to arrive at a decision which reconciled their desire to find favour with the Western Allies with recognition of the military and economic damage which Germany could still inflict on Sweden. The Coalition Government was faced with the political and diplomatic issues of how to secure the end of the 'Leave Traffic'. Public opinion and media comment were pressing for such a decision, not least because of its perceived advantages to the oppressors of the Norwegian population. Some of this criticism was probably inspired by the British Legation.[26] The Germans had been conditioned to expect reductions or cessation by Günther since April but he wanted to decouple the termination from the recent trade agreement with the Allies.[27] This would take time and with the Allies pressing for agreement, time was in short supply. Significantly, Per Albin was still undecided.

Hägglöf faced hostility from Per Albin and Günther when on 28 June 1943, he urged the Cabinet to accept the poor terms he had negotiated in order to maintain and improve good relations with the Allies with an eye to the future. Per Albin genuinely feared some German military retaliation, having noted in his diary: 'Personally, I believe in a rather strong German reaction, but not necessarily an attack.'[28] Günther dismissed Hägglöf's point about post-war relations as an unknown quantity.[29] Others in the Cabinet argued that the Germans had probably already accepted the possibility of a Swedish cessation and pushed the argument for acceptance. Later, Per Albin came to the view that ending transit was relatively risk-free. He told the Social Democrat *Riksdag* group as much and at the *Utrikesnämnd* on 29 June said that no agreement with the Western Allies would be reached without it while Swedish public opinion expected it. The question was now not so much about *if* transit should be ended but *when*.

Günther believed it was important for relations with the Germans to avoid the impression of surrender to Allied demands and therefore decoupled the ending of transit from the trade negotiations. Although the decision was taken at the Cabinet on 2 July the Allies were to be told simply that it was a decision in principle only, and that it was independent of the trade agreement. Wigforss and Eriksson dissented and wanted the agreement to be included with the trade settlement but Per Albin out-manoeuvred them by replying that if this were the case, it would have to be referred to the *Utrikesnämnd* which would not now meet for some time. What the Cabinet also decided on 2 July was to give notice to the Germans that the 'Leave Traffic' would be ended on 1 August. At the same time, the Swedish army reserves of 300,000 men were called up in case of German military retaliation. The timing of the cessation was favourable however as German attention was diverted away from Sweden towards the fall of Mussolini in Italy and a large Soviet offensive on the eastern front. Hitler had his hands full and the termination was accepted without much trouble. Indeed, the Germans allowed Sweden to present it in a joint communiqué as a Swedish initiative to meet Swedish requirements. The 'Safe-Conduct Traffic' remained uninterrupted.

This decision was a further major shift in Sweden's policy, marking as it did a recognition of Allied success and German failure but it was constrained by the reality of Germany's continuing stranglehold over Swedish trade and the decreasing but ever-present possibility of German military action should the Germans believe that Sweden was abandoning neutrality in favour of an Allied alliance. In fact the ending of transit could be seen as Sweden's return to its pre-June 1940 neutrality. It also marked the return of public opinion as a decisive factor on democratic decision-making in Swedish foreign policy. The unexpectedly restrained response by Germany can be seen as evidence of a failure of judgement by Per Albin and to some extent Günther, who both lost some authority in the Coalition Government as a result of their ultra-cautious line during the discussions on Hägglöf's agreement. Hägglöf had forced the pace for Per Albin and Günther and for the second time in less than six months (the first being the release of the embargoed ships, Lionel and Dicto), their cautious approach to revoking German advantage in favour of Allied benefit was put under pressure from Cabinet colleagues and public opinion. For Sweden, the decision relieved political pressure on the Coalition Government, brought some acclaim in Norway, less so in Britain and the United States, and none at all in the Soviet Union.[30] However, the Allies would soon return for more.

Notes

1. Boheman, På vakt, p. 178.
2. Arnstad, Spelaren Christian Günther, p. 232.
3. '... fientligt inställt land.' Carlgren, Svensk utrikespolitik, p. 328.
4. Ibid. p. 336.
5. Ibid. p. 334, n. 29.
6. Ibid. p. 340, n. 66.
7. Ibid. p. 342.

8. Ibid. p. 346.
9. Ibid. p. 352, n. 123.
10. Ibid. p. 358.
11. Ibid. p. 359, n. 8.
12. Ibid. p. 369.
13. Ibid.
14. Ibid. p. 362, n. 24.
15. Grafström, *Anteckningar*, 11 May 1940.
16. RA HP 1 Ba Boheman to Söderblom 19 October 1942 and Boheman's notes of meeting.
17. Ludlow, 'Britain and Northern Europe'.
18. Lagvall, *Flottans neutralitetsvakt*, pp. 148–9.
19. Carlgren, *Svensk utrikespolitik*, p. 393, n. 177.
20. Molin, in Koblik, p. 287.
21. Boheman, *På vakt*, p. 237.
22. Johansson, *Per Albin och kriget*, p. 307.
23. Ibid. p. 310.
24. Arnstad, *Spelaren Christian Günther*, p. 364
25. Carlgren, *Svensk utrikespolitik*, p. 401.
26. Ibid. p. 399, n. 20.
27. Carlgren, *Svensk utrikespolitik*, pp. 400–2.
28. Isaksson, *Per Albin*, pp. 416–17.
29. Carlgren, *Svensk utrikespolitik*, p. 405.
30. Ibid. pp. 419–20.

5

Eastern Approaches and Western Reproaches: Finland's Continuation War and the Collapse of Germany, June 1941–May 1945

It would be natural to assume that Sweden was entirely focused on its relations with Nazi Germany during the years following the invasion of Scandinavia by the Germans. Certainly, Germany controlled all essential Swedish supplies due to its Skagerrak blockade and represented the most immediate military and political threat to the independent, democratic Swedish state. Yet the Swedish leadership was almost equally preoccupied by relations with the warring countries to the east, that is Finland and Russia, and to a minor extent the Baltic states of Latvia, Lithuania and Estonia. The Winter War had mobilised Sweden to aid its Finnish neighbour against Russian aggression. Sweden had striven to secure a peace in order to protect its borders from Russian encroachment as well as to lower the political temperature in the Baltic region. Domestically, the Government sought to assuage overlapping anti-communist and anti-Russian Swedish opinion. Now that the Finnish army had joined with the German army to recover its lost territory after the German invasion of the Soviet Union, and the Russians had annexed the Baltic states, Sweden was faced with a fresh set of challenges in order to maintain its security to the east.

FINNISH SECURITY AND THE SOVIET UNION, 1940–1941

An obvious question when considering eastern Europe after 1945 is how did Finland escape Soviet control at the end of the Second World War? The answer in short is that, provided Finland conceded

Russia's view of legitimate Soviet security concerns and met them, the possible negative consequences for Russian relations with Britain, United States and Sweden acted as a brake on earlier Russian intentions to annexe Finland during their advance eastwards in 1944.[1] The problem for the Finns in 1941 was that they could not be sure of Soviet objectives regarding Finland. Did they want to acquire more Finnish territory to secure Russia from German attack – as demonstrated by the Winter War settlement – or did they want to completely regain the former Tsarist Duchy as a Soviet Republic? Finnish politicians also referred to the continuing possibility of a Hacha invitation.[2] Such a summons was received by the President of Czechoslovakia from Hitler in 1939 and by the Presidents of Estonia, Latvia and Lithuania from Stalin in 1940 as a preliminary to the loss of their country's independence and the imposition of harsh rule. This meant that Russian demands to take over Petsamo's nickel mine in late 1940 after the Winter War had ended were seen by the Finnish Government as part of the continuous salami-slicing approach by which Stalin would weaken and prepare Finland for annexation. Such concerns not surprisingly drove them to seek security from Germany and Sweden. In August 1940, the Finnish leadership responded to a secret German approach and permitted German troop transit through Finland to Norway in return for weapon supplies.[3] The Finnish troop transit accord was unlimited in both number and duration, starkly contrasting with Sweden's tightly-regulated agreement, emphasising the difference between Finnish willingness and Swedish reluctance.[4] From late 1940, Finnish-German military cooperation grew closer.

This had been noted with nervousness in Stockholm and when the Finns raised the idea of a defensive union with Sweden in September the Swedes saw the opportunity to influence the Finns away from Germany. In order to make such a union palatable to Moscow and to confirm Swedish authority, Günther proposed in October that foreign policy should be controlled by Stockholm and that Finland should not seek revenge against Russia, a significant concession which was accepted in principle by Helsinki. In early November, after the Swedish Cabinet decided to proceed to a further stage, the Russians and the Germans both gave indications that such a union would be unwelcome and in December sent clear messages not to pursue the initiative. Swedish diplomacy had failed to find a way to secure Finland from one totalitarian regime, Russia, without an association with the other, Germany. At this point Finland commenced preparations for the coming operation against the Soviet Union.

FINLAND AND GERMANY, JUNE 1941–DECEMBER 1941

Sweden conceded the Engelbrecht Division transit in June 1941 partly because Finland also requested the concession. This appeal influenced a number of Stockholm politicians but popular opinion in Sweden was by no means as united in support of the Finnish attack – portrayed as a 'defensive move in response to Russian bombing' – which followed soon after the Germans crossed the Soviet border. Finland had tied her fortunes to those of the Nazis and thereby lost left-wing sympathy in Sweden. For Swedish opinion, the Continuation War, as this Finno-Russian conflict became known, was seen variously as a crusade against bolshevism, a recovery of lost territory, a securing of defensible borders and a support to Nazi Germany. There were no more rallies of support as in December 1939 nor did Swedish intelligentsia volunteer for service at the Finnish Front. Indeed, there were less than 1,000 Swedish volunteers in all by August. The question of equipping them in the same way as in the Winter War came up in the Swedish Cabinet and split it. Günther wanted to support them but due to fierce opposition Per Albin delayed the decision indefinitely.[5]

Günther tried in vain to persuade Britain not to declare war on Finland following Finnish disregard of a British warning to halt their advance into Russia at the pre-Winter War 1939 border. Günther feared that such a declaration would only serve to drive Finland closer to Germany. War was declared on 7 December 1941 shortly after the Japanese attack at Pearl Harbor. Hitler foolishly declared war against the United States which also brought them into the European war. As a result, Finnish relations with the United States had also worsened at this point and Sweden struggled to maintain any influence at all with Finland at a time when Finnish armies were in the ascendant against the Russians. Sweden had to take care that any Swedish attempts to help to broker a peace between the Soviet Union and Finland were not seen in Berlin as a move to split the Finnish-German relationship and thereby represent a hostile move against Germany. Stalin, on the back foot after the *Wehrmacht*'s early successes, extended peace feelers to Finland through the Soviet Minister in Stockholm, Mme Kollontay, who raised the subject with Boheman in late December 1941. This approach was rejected in a speech by the Finnish President on 3 February 1942 but the attempt was merely the opening move in an extended and intricate diplomatic effort. This exercise, in which Swedish diplomacy was heavily involved, went on for almost two and a half years until Finland signed an armistice with the Soviet Union on 19 September 1944.

Sweden was naturally concerned to protect national interests which included her relations with Russia, Germany, Britain, the United States, and of course Finland. Finnish interests were fairly low down on the Swedish agenda – provided that any Finnish border settlement with Russia safeguarded Sweden to the greatest possible extent. The prospect of either Russian or German occupation of the Åland Islands unsettled the UD and fuelled their efforts to promote a settlement, but this was Finland's war and the Finnish leadership was keen to slip the reins of overweening Swedish tutelage and take their chances with Germany. Yet, this apparent recklessness did not extend to the Finns fighting Germany's war in Russia or anywhere else. A Finnish regiment which was detached to the *Wehrmacht* was specifically restricted from engaging British forces. Also, Finland was careful to avoid pressing further into Russia than defensive territorial gains would justify or to harm the overall Russian war effort against Germany. For example the Finnish army stopped at Lake Onega and never attempted to cut the vital rail supply route from Murmansk. In particular, Finnish General Mannerheim refused to support any German attack on Leningrad. By this single action, it could be argued that Mannerheim cost Germany the war because the fall of Leningrad may have released sufficient German divisions to take Moscow in 1942 and alter the course of the German campaign in Russia. Mannerheim knew, as a former Tsarist officer, the symbolic nature of Leningrad to Russia and that any Finnish move against the city would have confirmed that Finland's ultimate objective was not the return of her lost territory but the destruction of the Russian state. Such a move would have designated Finland as a strategic enemy of Russia and ensured Finland's ultimate annexation by Russia. Mannerheim understood that Russian national interest came before ideology and that a vengeful Russian government of any political colour would then seek to eliminate Finland permanently. These considerations meant that from December 1941 when the limited Finnish military objectives of regaining the territory lost in 1940 had been achieved, the Finnish-Soviet front was fairly static and quiet – in stark contrast to the bitter battles further to the east between the Red Army, the Russian partisans and the *Wehrmacht* whose outcome would determine the direction of Finnish efforts to secure its future position.[6]

SWEDEN SEEKS A MEDIATION ROLE, MID-1942–MARCH 1944

Sweden waited in the wings to assess how diplomacy could best secure its position with its warring neighbours to the east and south. The key was its relationship with the Soviet Union which, of the three Allies, was initially the least critical of Sweden's relationship with Germany. From mid-1942 as the German success faltered, the Russians emphasised to Sweden that the situation was changing. They now expected a stiffer attitude towards Finland and Germany and a more understanding attitude towards the Soviet Union. The Russians also revived their interest in securing Swedish brokerage for their peace feelers towards the Finns but, in early 1943, Sweden still wanted to avoid any problems with Germany and felt that the outgoing Ryti Government in Finland would not be interested in such approaches. The United States was also warm towards securing a Russo-Finnish settlement with Swedish assistance but the incoming Linkomies Government rejected this American initiative in April 1943. Sweden's special relationship with Finland was clearly valued by both the Soviet Union and the United States but in mid-1943 Germany exercised more influence with the Finnish Government.

Sweden now came under pressure in mid-1943 from USA-British trade negotiations to limit trade with Finland. Additional pressure from Moscow on the Swedish-Finnish relationship provided Sweden with the impetus to adopt a more active role in seeking a separate peace for Finland. The changes in the war situation helped this aspiration in that in September 1943, the Finnish Government asked Sweden, in advance of the Moscow Conference of Allied Foreign Ministers in mid-October, to raise Finland's interest in seeking a settlement that maintained Finland's territorial integrity with Russia. Russia continued its criticism of Swedish concessions to Germany but again agreed to Swedish mediation with Finland in early November through Russian Minister Mme Kollontay in Stockholm. Sweden was relieved to secure this important role which would provide Sweden with some influence in the strategically vital territorial settlement of Finland's borders with Russia.

There now followed an extended series of diplomatic manoeuvres in which Sweden's Erik Boheman was closely involved with both sides (and in great secrecy lest the Germans find out) to reconcile a reluctant and obdurate Finland with an increasingly aggressive and advancing Russia.[7] The Russians made it clear that they were not interested in subjugating Finland within the Soviet Union and exceptionally, the Casablanca formula of 'unconditional surrender' would not apply to Finland.[8] These facilitations – including Swedish re-drafting of the initial Finnish response which Günther had likened to a suicide note – led to a Finnish delegation opening negotiations in Moscow in late March 1944.[9] The two difficult questions were what to do about the German troops on Finnish territory and the position of the post-war Finnish-Russian frontiers. The Finns were understandably sceptical of Russian 'clarifications' of their initial peace terms but the Swedes led them to believe that the Russians would later soften their terms. This forecast turned out to be misleading and by May the two sides remained apart.

FINNISH–RUSSIAN ARMISTICE, SEPTEMBER 1944

The Russians now decided to force the Finns to return to the negotiating table and on 9 June 1944 launched the first major offensive for two years. By late June the Finnish position was ever more desperate and Sweden's role at times resented.[10] Nevertheless, Swedish exertions continued and Ryti eventually stood down on 4 August to make way for Mannerheim. This change paved the way for further Swedish-mediated negotiations while rumours emanated from Berlin about a possible German occupation of the Ålands if Finland concluded a separate peace. Agreement was reached on 19 September 1944 and although the Russian conditions were stark, Boheman did not think that an earlier agreement would have softened them.[11] The Finnish army was to demobilise, the Germans were to be disarmed, Finnish access to the Barents Sea would be lost with the port of Petsamo, frontiers would return to those of 1940, Porkkala would be leased for fifty years as a Soviet base and $300m was to be levied in reparations. Finland would pay heavily, remain within the Soviet Union's influence but retain its independence. Sweden was satisfied with the result in that it largely returned Finland to the position following the Winter War yet still left the Ålands unfortified, demilitarised and without a Russian presence.

Sweden sugared the bitter pill for the Finns by providing a 150 million kroner trade credit and accommodating 50,000 refugees who fled from the retreating Germans. Sweden had again managed to broker a peace which secured Sweden's eastern borders while achieving a satisfactory relationship with the Soviet Union through its efforts to mediate. Even Stalin expressed his appreciation.[12] The retreating German army caused some instability on Sweden's northern borders and Swedish policy had to adjust to the new position of Finland in the approaching post-war world.

NEIGHBOURING OCCUPATION, OPPRESSION AND RESISTANCE, 1943–1945

Now that the war had turned, Swedish policy towards its occupied neighbours became increasingly active. Sweden had continually reminded the Allies that one important benefit of maintaining a relationship with Germany was some ability to influence the Nazi regime in positive ways. As concerns about occupied Norway and Denmark grew, Sweden also sought to assist their populations in various ways including the creation and training of Norwegian and Danish paramilitary units, so-called 'Police Troops' in Sweden from 1943.

Norway

Per Albin still considered that the Germans remained a potent military and trade threat to Sweden while a growing 'Norwegian lobby' in the country increasingly differed. The lobby's primary target was ending German transit, resulting in a huge protest meeting in Stockholm in spring 1943. Yet even under pressure, Per Albin continued to resist a hasty about-turn of Government policy on concessions to the Germans. He feared the effects of a cave-in not only on German opinion, but also on the now ascendant Western Allies, who could and would regard such a move as indicative of Swedish pliability even as they welcomed the ending of transit.

From 1943 to the first half of 1944, resistance in Norway was raised against Norwegian Government measures to conscript Norwegians into labour service for the Germans. Not only did Norwegians reject forced labour service, many saw it as a step towards Quisling's desire to introduce compulsory military service in the Norwegian Army. Opposition was widespread and people went into hiding rather than comply. After Stalingrad, Sweden's policy altered to Norwegian advantage. The legality of the government-in-exile in London was recognised, Swedish diplomatic contact was established, and the Norwegian envoy in Stockholm was accredited despite German protests. From 1944 onward, resistance became more military and the Norwegian military resistance, *Milorg*, became better equipped and trained. This was the final period of the war for which they had been waiting. There could be no freedom for Norway without the defeat of the German army on the main battlefields of Europe but the Home Forces (as *Milorg* also became known) increasingly harassed the Germans, *Nasjonalsamling* and *Hird* members, and other collaborators. Reprisals continued until the end of the war and many Norwegians questioned the value of the sabotage actions when set against the high price which civilians had to pay in retaliation killings. The repression of the Norwegians began to take on an increasingly desperate character against this rising tide of armed resistance. By the end of 1944, 6,000 Norwegians were in prison in Norway while 8,000 had been deported to Germany. Shortages of food caused an epidemic of malnutrition and illness, particularly among the young and the old. There were 14,000 cases of diphtheria in 1944 compared with seventeen in 1940. Sweden was able to persuade the Germans to permit supplies of food, clothes and household goods raised from collections by Swedish charities such as *Svenska Norgehjälp* and many Norwegian children were nourished by so-called *Svensksuppe.*

During the 1944 retreat by the German army from north Norway, pursued over the Finnish-Norwegian border by the Russians, Sweden permitted secret imports of weapons and other supplies from Britain to Stockholm and then onward transit by American aircraft to north Norway to support Swedish-trained Norwegian 'Police Troops' who joined Norwegian forces landed in Finnmark from Britain. This transit was a concession as inconsistent with strict neutrality as German transit had been earlier. By the end of the war, Sweden was sufficiently concerned about the potential for a German last-ditch resistance on Norwegian territory – and the consequential effect on the civilian population that it authorised staff talks with the Western Allies.

Up to 1942, Sweden had adopted a passive policy towards Norway due to German pressure but increased its humanitarian support following the Jewish deportation in November 1942. Despite German protests, it attempted thereafter to support and assist the Norwegian government-in-exile while maintaining a neutral stance that it was prepared to abandon in principle and practice to aid its oppressed neighbour.

Denmark

1943 was the year in which previously minor Danish resistance exploded into violence and widespread civil disorder whose effects spilled over on to the shores of Sweden. Britain had begun to take a tougher line with Denmark's lack of resistance. The group of Danish army officers who represented the military resistance in Denmark (code-named 'The Princes') saw their role as preparing to fight only when the Allies were about to win. The SOE-supported resistance groups often disagreed with them and there were disputes over policy. Finally, an RAF air-raid of a shipyard in Copenhagen in January 1943 forced the choice – more British bombing with indiscriminate civilian casualties or more sabotage attacks against German targets – which of course carried the risk of German reprisals. The Danes chose sabotage and this determined the course of the occupation and the fall of the Government now led by former Foreign Minister Erik Scavenius. The 'Princes' were also told by the SOE that action was required now, not in the future. This all coincided with the German defeat at Stalingrad and Danish realisation about who would win the war. During spring and summer 1943, sabotage operations were followed by strikes which the Scavenius Government vainly attempted to stifle. Following unsuccessful encouragement to crack down on the participants, the Germans lost patience and in late August deposed the Government, disarmed the Danish forces and introduced direct rule under General Hermann von Hanneken and *Reichskommissar* Dr Werner Best of the SS.

Danish soldiers and sailors fled to Sweden to join an already well-organised resistance group but a much more significant flight was about to take place across the Sound in October 1943 – that of about 7,000 Danish Jews escaping a planned round-up and deportation action by the Gestapo. Von Hanneken was opposed to the action because of the burden on his troops and the likely Danish reaction, while remarkably one of the German marine attachés, Georg Duckwitz, not only warned the Danes to alert the Jews but also travelled to Stockholm to alert Günther and Per Albin who agreed to give them refuge. The 7,000 escaped deportation to the death camps which swept up the 500 or so who did not flee. By December 1943, there were 11,000 Danish refugees in Sweden, mainly accommodated in Skåne, of whom 4,500 were employed. In a superb example of Swedish official ingenuity, the Swedish government, unwilling to go to the *Riksdag* through normal channels and draw German attention to the level of financial support required for the Danish refugee contingent, instead authorised the Danish representative in Stockholm to withdraw five million kroner for distribution to his countrymen – as a personal loan.[13]

The resistance movement continued to grow under military rule and the reprisals also began. Hitler had decreed a five to one ratio of reprisals – that is five Danes for every German killed. The Danish Army intelligence organisation continued to function after the arrests because most of its members fled to Sweden. Many in the former Army organisation feared that the Danish Communists with their active saboteurs were planning to take over after liberation and so a new Command Committee was set up to coordinate all resistance activity under the Danish Freedom Council. This meant that by 1944, resistance groups were able to benefit from more frequent arms drops by the SOE from Britain and small scale actions against the Germans increased. Reprisals against Danish resistance were often carried out by Danes in the Schalberg Corps, a disbanded group of Danish SS veterans. The reprisals were met in June 1944 by more strikes and riots in Copenhagen. The Germans threatened to cut food, power and water and so a deal was brokered by which the Germans would withdraw the Schalberg Corps if the strikes ended. The main casualty of this agreement was the 7,000 strong Danish police force who had failed to curb the unrest. They were disbanded, 2,000 were arrested and sent to camps in Germany in September from where they were later rescued by a Swedish expedition in 1945.

DANISH AND NORWEGIAN 'POLICE TROOPS' IN SWEDEN, 1943–1945

The recruitment and training of Danish and Norwegian paramilitary units, so-called 'Police Troops', in Sweden were significant departures from neutrality. These were concrete actions from 1943 by Sweden to help prevent loss of life in Denmark and Norway. The intention was that the 'Police Troops' would be sent to Denmark and Norway to maintain order, subject to Swedish Government consent, when the German occupation ended. [14]

The Danish 'Police Troops' were formed in Sweden from the military refugees who had fled there at the suggestion of former Danish Prime Minister Buhl. Once German transit had ceased, Per Albin pressed for 7,500 Danish 'Police Troops' to be given material assistance and training, a proposal which was resisted within the Cabinet but agreed in early December 1943. In November Danish recruitment offices were opened and shortly thereafter, three camps were created.[15] There were 3,000 trained recruits by 1945 in what came to be known as the Danish Brigade who naturally concentrated more on improving military expertise rather than police work.[16] Their equipment was considerable and even included a squadron of Swedish *SAAB* B17 fighter-bombers with Danish pilots trained by the Swedish airforce at Såtenäs in the autumn of 1944.[17] During the closing stages of the war, the Swedish Government restrained the Danish Brigade from intervening too early in order not to complicate the German forces' surrender in Denmark.[18] The Brigade embarked on Danish ships released from Swedish custody, landed at Helsingborg on the same day that the Germans in the country laid down their weapons, and civil order was maintained. 'Police Troops' were also recruited from the 30,000 Norwegian refugees and later armed by Sweden. The Norwegian recruits had had less previous military training and so their initial build-up, from May 1943, focused more on actual police work. However, from the summer of that year, they were supplied with light weapons by the Swedish army and their numbers continued to increase until by 1945 over 12,000 men had been trained and equipped in fourteen different Swedish locations.[19]

The Germans of course objected to this and in April 1944, complained that the 'Police Troops' were incompatible with Sweden's neutral status. Sweden responded that since they were being trained only for police rather than military duties, and that as they would not be deployed until the occupation had ended, their presence conformed to international law. By the end of 1944, the 'Police Troops' were equipped with grenade launchers, anti-tank weapons, boats and other distinctly unusual police equipment.[20] This remarkable arrangement on neutral territory, made possible by the fiction that these were 'police officers', was consistent with Sweden's objective to avoid civil disorder – which could favour Communists – on the borders of Sweden. The existence of Norwegian and Danish 'Police Troops' would also blunt any demands, which the Norwegians eventually made, for Swedish intervention in the war to protect fellow Scandinavians. Another motive may have been to provide an outlet for the energies of a potentially disruptive and disorderly group of refugees bent on revenge against the Germans. Swedish support for 'Police Troops' also improved relations with their neighbours and demonstrated Scandinavian solidarity to politicians at home and abroad.

Further material assistance was provided to Denmark when Sweden permitted the transit from the Swedish coast to resistance groups in Denmark of Swedish pistols manufactured by Husqvarna and British-sourced weapons brought into Lysekil by British MTBs. This smuggling began in early 1944 with the full knowledge and support of a limited number of Swedish officials, albeit under convoluted circumstances in case of intelligence reaching the Germans. Over 4,000 pistols, four million bullets, 5,000 grenades and other military equipment made the crossing.[21] Swedish support had ensured that Danish resistance was armed and the 'Police Troops' trained, while giving refuge to the thousands of Danish nationals who fled there and rescuing the Danish Police officers who had been interned in Germany in late 1944. In addition, the Swedish Army Staff had made plans to invade the Danish island of Bornholm in a joint-services operation should the population there be threatened by the German garrison. In the event, the garrison surrendered after being bombed by the Russians and the operation was not necessary.[22]

MORE PRESSURE ON SWEDEN, SEPTEMBER 1943–JANUARY 1944

The diplomatic pressure which the Soviet Union had applied to Sweden in order to underline the new war situation following the Allied victories at El Alamein and Stalingrad was also increasingly applied by Britain and the United States. The mid-1943 trade negotiations with the Western Allies had resulted in Sweden being forced to end the transit concession to the Germans, while successfully negotiating a continuation of the strategically important 'Safe-Conduct Traffic' supply route which brought oil and other materials to Sweden from the west. Sweden was now, in September 1943, more neutral in terms of an absence of concessions to either side than at any time since June 1941. The Western Allies were not satisfied with strict neutrality; they wanted to ratchet up pressure to end all trade with Germany and for Sweden to favour the Allies in a number of military and trade areas. Aggressive United States diplomacy was increasingly setting the tone for the Western Allied relationship and replacing the more empathetic approach represented by the British Minister in Stockholm, Victor Mallet, and to a notably lesser extent his masters in the Foreign Office in London. This aggressive tone was echoed to a lesser degree by the Russians whose antipathy was tempered by their need to have Swedish support for their peace feelers to Finland. Prior to the Allied Foreign Ministers' Conference in Moscow in October 1943, the Soviet Union had been arguing for Sweden to be forced into providing airfields on Swedish territory for Allied use to support the eastern offensives by the Red Army. This proposal, despite extensive and prolonged discussion among the Allies, never came to the attention of Sweden before being dropped after the Teheran Conference in order to concentrate on the coming invasion of France. By January 1944, the Red Army had also succeeded in pushing back the *Wehrmacht* over the Polish and Estonian borders which reduced the need for Swedish airfields.

Sweden took advantage of the German reverses to negotiate stricter limits on Swedish-German trade that the Anglo-American trade negotiators had pressed Hägglöf for in June 1943. Sweden also wanted to secure guarantees from the Germans to maintain the 'Safe-Conduct Traffic' which had again been suspended in October 1943 by the Germans on a pretext. Germany's attitude to Sweden was that of resigned bitterness in the face of military reverses but sensing German weakness, Hägglöf successfully concluded a trade agreement for 1944 which reduced Sweden's exports to Germany, particularly in the key materials of ball-bearings and iron ore, now limited to 7.1 million tonnes, that met and even exceeded the Allied demands made in 1943 for a 7.5 million tonnes maximum.

THE BALL-BEARING OFFENSIVE, MARCH 1944–JUNE 1944

Despite the Western Allies having concluded the 1943 London Tripartite Agreement (LTA) which reduced Swedish exports to Germany, their trade negotiators urged on by Washington's military, returned to the offensive in the spring of 1944 with further reductions in prospect for iron ore and more particularly, ball-bearings. This was against a background of the slow progress of the Allied offensive in Italy and stronger than expected German resistance. The supply of these strategic components also took on the character of one of Günther's feared 'prestige issues' as Washington stimulated a high-profile press campaign against Sweden.

Sweden tried to avoid diplomatic escalation by attempting to restrict discussion to the 'Joint Standing Commission' which had been set up to oversee the operation of the 1943 LTA and endeavouring to emphasise that the trade was in accordance with that Agreement. Not for the first time, the United States acted in an overbearing and opportunist manner by simply asserting that Sweden should further reduce her exports to Germany with no reference to the 1943 Agreement except to claim that Sweden had broken its terms. Boheman and his colleagues tried in vain to dampen the tone but the Americans were in the ascendant. An Allied note of 17 March 1944 demanding lower exports was answered on 6 April without conceding any reduction and referring to the 1943 Agreement. Ball-bearings now dominated the 1944 Allied agenda in the same way that iron ore had preoccupied their 1939–40 relations with Sweden. The Pentagon targeted these components ahead of the invasion of France believing them to be strategically important to the continuing German war effort and the *Luftwaffe* in particular. Britain also had been importing Swedish ball-bearings since 1942 using the civilian air service between Stockholm and Scotland and would supplement these imports by MTB from Lysekil to Hull.[23] Another Allied note of 13 April 1944 stiffened demands for further ball-bearings reductions requiring an immediate ban for the next three months. This note had been preceded by a broadcast by the United States Foreign Minister, Cordell Hull, attacking Swedish exports to Germany as well as a widespread press campaign in American newspapers. Sweden responded formally again by reference to the existing 1943 Agreement but Boheman informally advised the Allies that the Government would seek to reduce shipments within existing *Svenska Kullagerfabriken (SKF)* contracts.

These continued demands for Sweden to break existing agreements with Germany were seen in Sweden and Berlin primarily as part of an overall drive to force Sweden into the Allied camp before the invasion of Europe, with the secondary benefit of depriving Germany of some strategically important materials and components.[24] The Swedish Foreign Ministry now feared that such high-profile demands from the Allies would provoke the Germans into similar counter-demands, so-called '*Gegendruck*', and possible retaliatory measures, not excluding military action.[25] The Coalition Government now moved to eliminate the contentious issue of ball-bearings from the agenda. One American negotiator had even hinted at a bombing raid on the *SKF* plant in Göteborg.

Two days after the invasion of Normandy, the Allied negotiators met in Stockholm to request a reduction in exports of ball-bearings to Germany with compensatory orders from the Allies. At the Cabinet meeting on 8 June, Per Albin said that he feared that such an agreement would contribute to Sweden's weakness towards the Allies while it would probably make little difference to relations with Germany. The Cabinet decided by a majority (the Conservatives and the Agrarians dissenting) that *SKF* should be encouraged to take up the Allied offer of compensatory orders. This decision broke not only the existing agreements with Germany but also with the Allies. Per Albin stated resignedly that 'he certainly wanted to keep to the agreement but it really was not always so easy . . . we must take account of the situation.' This reference to the Allies breaking previous assurances acknowledged the American view that any agreement was temporary and that the 1943 London Tripartite Agreement had in Hägglöf's American counterpart's words 'served its main purpose.'[26] On 12 June 1944, *SKF* agreed to reduce the following four months' exports to Germany by 60 per cent and make up the difference by an increase in delivery in late 1944. Thus Sweden both met Allied demands and the contractual obligations to the Germans. The Western Allies, primarily the United States, had succeeded in driving Sweden into actions which it had not wanted to take and they would again force the pace in the autumn of 1944.

This episode demonstrates that although the decisions were taken in principle by the Cabinet, the practice was left to the negotiators to work out in detail. While the Western Allies had established their foothold in Normandy, Swedish politicians were equally concerned about the Russians, who they knew were monitoring carefully any sign of Sweden going over to the Western Allied side. The Russians were not involved in the ball-bearings pressure and indeed in August 1944 declared themselves satisfied with Sweden's conduct. [27]

ENDING GERMAN TRADE, JULY 1944–JANUARY 1945

The Normandy invasion of 1944 had been preceded by an elaborate Allied deception exercise, *Fortitude North*, which was intended to mislead the Germans into thinking that an Allied attack on Germany would be made through Norway and Sweden. Another deception plan, *Operation Graffham*, was intended to support *Fortitude North* by misleading the Germans into thinking that Sweden was being approached to support a Scandinavian invasion. Despite the extensive preparation, there is only minor evidence that either Sweden or the Germans took the deceptions seriously although credence was given to a diplomatic hint on 8 June that the Allies might invade Norway.[28]

With an Allied presence in France and the Russian armies cutting off the German armies in Estonia and Latvia, Sweden pressed on with reductions in German trade. From the end of July 1944, no coal, coke or cement would be allowed to transit Sweden to Norway, which the Germans accepted without much protest. A further sign of German weakness was their agreement to release the small Swedish-speaking population from Estonia to prevent them falling into the hands of the Red Army. The Allies next demanded that all Swedish shipping to Germany be suspended. This led to Sweden withdrawing war-risk insurance from Swedish vessels, effectively cutting the shipping capacity to Germany by half as Swedish owners withdrew their ships. The Americans continued to push for a complete cessation of exports to Germany and pressed the British to join them in presenting a demand on 24 August 1944 to end all commercial ties with Germany. Sweden responded in measured terms on 4 September in order to avoid a rupture with Germany but also to reassert the country's neutrality at a time when the end of the war was clearly close at hand. Taking the Russo-Finnish armistice as a pretext, Sweden did close her territorial waters to German shipping from 27 September. This was well-received as an indication that Sweden had heeded the Allies but the United States remained intent on stopping Swedish trade with Germany altogether.[29]

Swedish neutrality was now flexed to meet the contingencies of the final phase of the war. The Germans aimed to ensure that Sweden did not fall into the Allied side and so they attempted to maintain good relations through gestures like suspending the transfer of Norwegian prisoners from Norway to Germany. Even when confronted with the final ending of all ball-bearings exports to Germany on 12 October 1944, a momentous and obvious outcome of Allied pressure, Minister Thomsen merely sent a note to Berlin reviewing the events of the previous few months which were unfavourable to Germany without suggesting retaliation. The Allies no longer pushed for a complete break with Germany but on 20 October 1944 requested that all Swedish metal and ore exports should now cease. Sweden was still trying to maintain the 'Safe-Conduct Traffic' and told the Allies that it would need to continue ore exports until December and that furthermore they needed Allied agreement to the delivery of much-needed rubber imports from the United States on board the 'Safe-Conduct Traffic' ship, the *Saturnus*.

The *Saturnus* was now held as the bargaining counter by the Americans to support their demands for a Swedish guarantee to stop *all* exports to Germany, a guarantee which was given on 24 November 1944 but had to be concealed from the Germans until the *Saturnus* cleared through the German blockade of the Skagerrak. When the *Saturnus* arrived in Sweden on 1 January 1945, Sweden informed the Germans of the export ban while hoping that they would permit the 'Safe-Conduct Traffic' to continue. In fact the German near-collapse in policy and coordination was such that the Traffic continued on a case-by-case basis, totalling ten ships, even after the Germans withdrew formal permission on 31 January.[30] Further wrangling continued with the Allies over the interpretation of the *Saturnus* guarantees. The Americans claimed that the export ban extended to Norway and Denmark but as Sweden's trade with both Germany and the Allies had now effectively ceased during the final stages of the war, attention had shifted to concerns about damage limitation in occupied Norway and Denmark, post-war geopolitics, and trade matters.

MEDIATION AND INTERVENTION, FEBRUARY 1945–MAY 1945

While there had been continuing unrest in Swedish public opinion about German atrocities, arrests and reprisals in the neighbouring lands since April 1940, these had been muted in the media which largely followed the Coalition Government advice not to antagonise the Germans by unduly publicising such acts. The Coalition Government preferred to attempt to influence German behaviour by other means where at all possible. Yet, as the German success turned to failure, both the press and the Coalition Government became more vocal in their criticism and furthermore, the Coalition Government permitted concrete measures of assistance to their neighbours.

The Norwegian 'Police Troops' were used in October 1944 in north Norway to occupy territory abandoned in the wake of the retreating Germans fleeing the Red Army advance through Finland. The American OSS and the British SOE were permitted to organise air transport for the 'Police Troops' from south Sweden to the north Norwegian border areas. They also established forward intelligence posts on the Swedish side of the Norwegian border to monitor the activities of the Germans in one of the several instances of intelligence cooperation between Sweden and the Western Allies at the end of the war.

In February 1945, Sweden responded to an opportunity offered by the Germans to send a rescue mission to Germany to collect Norwegian and Danish prisoners from captivity in Germany. This response was organised by Count Folke Bernadotte who also took all the credit for an exercise in which Foreign Minister Günther was the main inspiration and driving force. Through this action in which the prisoners were rescued in 'White Buses', Sweden perhaps rescued over 7,000 Scandinavians and between 6,000 and 7,000 Jews although the statistics are not reliable.[31] Less successful were attempts to broker a separate peace between Germany and the Western Allies. Certain members of the Nazi leadership were keen to use Swedish mediation to avoid the 'unconditional surrender' policy of the Allies which would mean surrender to the ruthless Red

Army rather than yield to the Americans and British. As in the case of Finland's peace with Russia, Sweden was wary of becoming entangled in a process which could rebound on Sweden's standing and neutral position. The Coalition Government was particularly pessimistic about the chances of success and refused to lend any official weight to peace feelers by German Foreign Minister Ribbentrop which nevertheless took place. Surrender was a different issue as the Coalition Government was particularly concerned about achieving a bloodless end to the occupation in Norway and Denmark and was prepared to become involved, if necessary, to achieve this. In scenario planning, the Western Allies had, in their concern for the liberation of Norway from German occupation, planned to involve Sweden despite her neutral status. More surprisingly, Sweden agreed to military staff talks, that is preliminary coordination discussions, to promote these plans. These were never actioned due to the eventual German capitulation in Norway in May 1945. In the opinion of one knowledgeable commentator, this is one of the most remarkable decisions taken by the Coalition Government during the war.[32]

The Allied Joint Planning Staff had been instructed to develop plans based on the realistic scenario (dismissed, however, by Churchill) that the *Wehrmacht* would fight to the last in 'Festung Norwegen' after the main German armies had surrendered or been annihilated in Europe. As it was undesirable that the Red Army should be involved in such an operation, the planners reckoned on deploying two Allied divisions, supplemented by four Swedish divisions and Swedish help with sea transport. The Norwegian government-in-exile was encouraged to approach the Coalition Government to sound out their preparedness to help in the liberation of Norway which they did on 12 April 1945. Not only did the Coalition Government reject this, it also considered from its own intelligence sources in Norway and Denmark that the Germans were likely to surrender anyway without Swedish sabre-rattling and told the Norwegians not to encourage 'rash behaviour'. The Coalition Government joined in Churchill's scepticism of the '*Festung Norwegen*' scenario and replied that any Swedish military mobilisation could provoke the *Wehrmacht* in Norway into resistance. The request was left open while the planners continued their diligent preparations. Despite Norwegian Foreign Minister Lie wanting no Swedish contribution to the liberation of Norway, the planners believed that the best solution would be a joint Allied-Swedish force under the Allied Command. On 25 April Eisenhower now concurred in the view that

Swedish help was essential for bases, harbours and transport to mount an invasion of Norway and requested that discussions be opened without delay with the Swedish authorities. This was agreed by Washington on 30 April and that day the British and American Ministers in Stockholm received instructions to persuade the Coalition Government to agree to staff talks without delay. Surprisingly, this was agreed the same afternoon. They had met Günther at 12 a.m. and received a positive answer within a few hours. The chain of events does not indicate any deep discussion within the Coalition Government about an issue that could have led to the ending of neutrality and a possible confrontation with the Soviet Union which had not been informed of the approach, a point that Mallet indiscreetly disclosed to Günther and which may have been a decisive reason for Günther's positive response. The other person who would have been consulted was Per Albin who probably considered that agreeing to non-binding staff talks about a hypothetical situation which he considered unlikely to develop might gain some benefits from the Allies at this stage of the war. In the event, the German capitulation in Europe which also included the armies in Denmark and Norway released Per Albin from the undertaking to hold the talks. However, there were indications that he had begun to prepare the *Riksdag* for such an event when in secret session, he carefully referred to altered circumstances which might lead to engagement in neighbouring countries, a decision to which the *Riksdag* constitutionally had to give its assent. Mallet also reported to London that Per Albin later told him that the Coalition Government had been ready to play a part in Norway.

The possible outcomes are pure speculation but the episode demonstrates that Per Albin and Günther were prepared to lead the country into a more 'activist' situation than they ever countenanced during the whole previous five years. Western involvement would have changed the entire character of Sweden's post war security, representing as it did a clear step away from the carefully preserved neutral position of which the Russians approved. If this had been put into effect, 200,000 Allied troops would have been landed in Sweden to cross the Norwegian border with the support of the Swedish army. Swedish neutrality was to be suspended in order to save Norwegian lives.[33] The presence of victorious Western Allies in Europe and humanitarian necessity in Norway, not to mention the danger of hostilities spilling over the Swedish border if the *Wehrmacht* held out, were powerful incentives for the two most cautious men in the Government to agree to such an important step. In this, however, they would have undoubtedly been supported by Swedish public opinion.

Through Bernadotte, Heinrich Himmler passed a message to the Western Allies on 23 April offering to surrender Germany, Norway and Denmark to Western Allied troops. Three days later, the offer was refused and Himmler was rebuffed. Notwithstanding, he again tried though his intermediary, SS General Walter Schellenberg, on 30 April to arrange for a peaceful surrender in Norway provided German troops would be allowed to be interned across the border in Sweden. The suicide of Hitler and the accession of Admiral Dönitz to the German leadership changed the aim of Schellenberg's mission which was now to negotiate with Sweden, under Dönitz' instructions, for the end of the Norwegian occupation. Günther sought Allied responses to this initiative and when Schellenberg arrived in Stockholm on 5 May the Coalition Government passed his message on to the Allies. Events were beginning to overtake Schellenberg as the army in Denmark had surrendered the previous day. Also, on the afternoon of 5 May Churchill responded to the message by warning Sweden off from becoming involved. At this, the Swedish mediation ended and the Norwegian surrender was arranged through Eisenhower's European headquarters (SHAEF) in France as part of the overall European surrender to the Allies.

The war now ended on 9 May 1945 with Sweden intact as an independent and neutral state. The battle for independence against Hitler was now ended. The struggle to resist the Soviet Union would continue for some time.

Notes

1. Rothwell, *War aims*, pp. 144–5.
2. President of Czechoslovakia, Emil Hacha, was summoned to Berlin in March 1939. Hitler told Hacha that he was going to occupy Czechoslovakia and called on Hacha to sign a proclamation requesting the establishment of a German protectorate.
3. Meinander, *Finlands historia*, pp. 217–18.
4. Carlgren, *Svensk utrikespolitik*, p. 220, n. 123.
5. Ibid. p. 452, n. 4.
6. Ibid. p. 460.
7. Boheman, *På vakt*, p. 246.
8. Ibid. p. 249.
9. Ibid. p. 254.
10. Carlgren, 'Sverige och Finlands utträde ur kriget', pp. 68–9.
11. Boheman, *På vakt*, p. 262.
12. Ibid. p. 263.

13. Dahlberg, Hundra år i Sverige, p. 305.
14. Carlgren, Svensk utrikespolitik, p. 557.
15. Frost, Dansk soldat i Sverige, p. 13.
16. Tennant, Touchlines of war, p. 169.
17. Norrbohm & Skogsberg, Att flyga är att leva, pp. 90–1.
18. Christensen, Lund, Olesen & Sørensen, Danmark besat, p. 619.
19. Lindqvist, Drömmar och verklighet, p. 555.
20. Gyllenhaal & Gebhardt, Slaget om Nordkalotten, p. 122.
21. Friberg, Stormcentrum Öresund, pp. 183–99.
22. Bojerud, 'Hur skall vi komma i land?', pp. 192–223.
23. Nilsson, Sandberg, & Nilsson, Blockade runners, p. 80.
24. Grafström, Anteckningar, May 1944.
25. Hägglöf, Svensk krigshandelspolitik, pp. 299–300.
26. Carlgren, Svensk utrikespolitik, p. 448.
27. Johansson, Per Albin och kriget, p. 340.
28. Grafström, Anteckningar, 8 June 1944.
29. Hägglöf, Svensk krigshandelspolitik, p. 30.
30. Carlgren, Svensk utrikespolitik, p. 551.
31. See Persson, 'Vi åker till Sverige', pp. 432–8, for a review of the disputed statistics.
32. Leifland, General Böhmes val, pp. 155–7.
33. Ibid. pp. 65–158.

6

Trading with Germany and the Allies – Blackmail and Brinksmanship

Swedish trade policy and Swedish foreign policy were closely linked by the Swedish policy makers. They were painfully conscious that decisions in one could have – and often did have – significant consequences on the other. The standard history of Sweden's trade policy was written by one of its main participants, the diplomatic negotiator Gunnar Hägglöf. Hägglöf made clear that Sweden's policy was to secure vital supplies through negotiated trade agreements with both sides and so one of the requisite skills to achieve this was a delicate balancing act with both parties – referred to as 'double-negotiation' – taking care not to disclose or concede perceived advantages to which the other might take exception.

The vital supplies on which Sweden was so dependent were primarily coal, coke, and oil imports because the country has few carbon resources despite extensive forestry. Before the war, coal and coke were imported from Britain which was Sweden's primary trading partner, and oil from the United States. Germany was also an important trade partner.[1] Germany relied on Sweden for about 40 per cent of its supplies of iron from ore which was extracted in the huge Norrland mines of Gällivare and Kiruna. The ore was transported by rail to the port of Luleå on the coast of the Gulf of Bothnia in the ice-free months, and to the port of Narvik on the coast of Norway in the winter months for shipment by sea to ports in Germany.[2] Iron ore was correctly anticipated by the UD to be one of the most contentious issues in a European war.

Swedish technological development in special steels had also made one of its companies, *Svenska Kullagerfabriken* (or *SKF* as the global brand is still called), a major supplier of ball-bearings. Like oil, ball-bearings were essential for military operations. No truck, tank or aeroplane could function without ball-bearings at the rotating heart of its power system, while wheels carrying troops, supplies, guns and landing-gear all rotated on ball-bearings. Machine tools like lathes and drills which produced military components such as gun barrels also rotated on ball-bearings. Without ball-bearings, a country's war effort would grind to a halt. SKF had both the technology and the manufacturing resources to supply these sophisticated components – a strategically important source which would also become contested by the belligerents.

Sweden's trade war fell into three main periods when conditions were partly dictated by the respective military ascendancy of the belligerents and partly by Sweden's access to the west. These phases will be covered here as *Double negotiations 1937–1940; Axis ascendancy 1940–1943; Allied ascendancy 1943–1945.*

Sweden's Negotiators

The men who grappled with the challenge of obtaining Sweden's vital supplies and maintaining the country's economic independence were exceptionally able and experienced. Broadly speaking, they were charged by the politicians to make the best deal that they could secure for Sweden. There were always going to be stresses between delegates and principals and these tensions were strikingly evident at times.

Gunnar Hägglöf was the most prominent of the full-time diplomats dealing with trade throughout the war but Marcus Wallenberg Senior's two sons, Marcus Wallenberg Junior and Jacob Wallenberg, became closely involved in trade negotiations during the Second World War for the Swedish government. The family name of Wallenberg appears repeatedly in histories of Sweden and remains a force in contemporary Swedish public life. A banking dynasty (founders of *Stockholms Enskilda Bank – SEB*) their prominence runs through Sweden's twentieth century history. Since 1934 Jacob had been a member of the Swedish-German Trade Commission, the primary trade regulatory body, and his extensive German connections reached even into the right-wing opposition movement to Hitler. Jacob's close confidante, former mayor of Leipzig and Bosch company executive, Carl Goerdeler, was executed following the July 1944 bomb-plot. Marcus Wallenberg Junior was equally well connected in

Britain and the United States. He was an urbane Anglophile who had lived in London and had been married to a Scot, Dorothy Mackay (who later became the wife of Charles Hambro, head of the Scandinavian Section of the British SOE and later of the entire SOE). The third leading businessman to supplement the Swedish team was Gunnar 'Spitfire' Carlsson, head of Sweden's leading merchant fleet, the Transatlantic Shipping Line. Carlsson was a veteran negotiator who had been instrumental in 1917–18 in helping Marcus Wallenberg Senior to settle the London shipping negotiations which ended the blockade of Sweden by the Western Allies. On being thanked by George V for his 'good services . . . to my country' he responded 'Sire . . . the work I have done, I have done for my country and not for yours'.[3] Carlsson's First World War regal retort encapsulates the principle underlying Second World War trade policy and its implementation by Swedish negotiators.

The profile that emerges is of a group of Sweden's senior businessmen and trade negotiators, tasked with safeguarding national interests during the changing circumstances of a developing conflict. There was a strong alignment of self-interest alongside national interest, particularly in the case of the Wallenbergs. Furthermore, *SKF* interests seem to have been particularly well represented.

DOUBLE NEGOTIATIONS, 1937–APRIL 1940

The initial Swedish tactic in 1939 was to secure a comprehensive trade agreement with the Western Allies before concluding a similar agreement with Germany, but in the lead-up to war, there had been some significant preliminaries.

By Spring 1939, the British treated Swedish iron ore as a blockade issue and in April a British delegation attempted to 'warn off' Sweden, concluding with the statement that in the event of being unable to stop German-bound ore-carriers in the Baltic 'I'm afraid that we have to destroy your mines.'[4] Sweden, however, believed that the British would be willing to accommodate continued exports to Germany if controlled by an agreement. When war was declared in September 1939, the British lost no time in presenting proposals to Sweden that would limit re-export of Swedish imports onwards to Germany but otherwise countenance trade continuing at 1936–8 averages. To Britain, Sweden maintained the pre-war stance that iron ore shipments were essential in order to maintain German supplies of coal and coke, while Germany made it clear that continuity of iron ore supplies was the key to any agreement. Despite British bluster, for example to 'cripple Swedish trade', the War Trade Agreement (WTA) was concluded in London on 2 November 1939 to the intense relief of the Swedish negotiators who were about to begin their negotiations in Berlin. The WTA confirmed the British view that it was an 'impractability' to persuade Sweden to end ore exports to Germany.[5] The negotiations with the Germans resumed with the Swedish objectives of safeguarding the import of four to five million tonnes of coal and coke and 350,000 tonnes of steel per annum. The tonnage of iron ore supplies proved to be the main bargaining point. Buckling under German pressure, Sweden offered ten million tonnes as a maximum, which could be explained away to the British by adding occupied Czechoslovakia and Poland to the 'normal' German supply tonnage. The ten million tonne offer was accepted by the Germans.

Within four months of the start of the war, Sweden had succeeded in achieving agreements with both belligerents which, if maintained, would preserve Swedish exports, supply Swedish needs for fuel and continue Sweden's ability to remain independent. With Britain, Sweden had been able to establish the principle of continued exports of iron ore to Germany. Sweden's satisfaction with the trade agreements with both Britain and Germany was, however, short-lived because the invasion and occupation of Denmark and Norway in April 1940 changed the whole trading position for the remainder of the war, right up to May 1945.

NEGOTIATING WITH BRITAIN AND GERMANY – AXIS ASCENDANCY AND WESTERN ACCESS, 1940–1943

Due to the British navy's less than impressive performance during the German invasions of Denmark and Norway, Sweden was cut off within twenty-four hours from its western trading partners who had provided two-thirds of Swedish trade in peacetime. Swedish trade policy was now in some disarray with double-negotiation being replaced in practice by a dominant partner, Germany. Prudently, the preceding seven months had been used to build up reserves of imported goods and raw materials so there was a limited breathing space to create new agreements to match the dramatically altered situation.

The Swedes persisted in seeking to re-open trade with the west and Marcus Wallenberg successfully proposed that Sweden should confirm its adherence to the WTA with Britain even after the blockade as 'one of the main bulwarks against German pressure.'[6] This was put to the British on 7 May 1940 and acted as a signal that Sweden was seeking to limit its economic ties with Germany despite being now surrounded and almost completely dependent on Germany for imports. The British Admiralty, like its German counterpart, was unsympathetic to Swedish pleas to re-open sea-routes to the west. Sweden was now almost totally dependent on Romania for oil, which supplied only a fraction of Swedish requirements; 6,300 tonnes in 1940 rising to 26,100 tonnes in 1941.[7] The intractability of the situation spurred Swedish consideration of alternative sources of oil, one of which was the Soviet Union.

On 15 May 1940, a tentative approach to Soviet Trade Minister Mikoyan seemed promising but at subsequent meetings he reduced the oil on offer and increased the reciprocal demand for railway truck wheels. An agreement was signed on 7 September 1940 that envisaged 100 million kroner of Swedish exports in the form of railway material, steel, ball-bearings, tools, machine tools, electrical machines, steam turbines and so on. In return, the Soviet list of exports included kerosene, gas oil, grease, flour, and seed cake up to a value of 17 million kroner. This agreement was not fully implemented in the nine months preceding the German invasion of the USSR and was of no real significance to the Swedish supply problem. Only 10,000 tonnes of oil were imported from Russia in 1941.[8]

Meanwhile, the victorious Germans were setting out their vision of the Reich-centric 'Greater German Economic Area' (*Großraumwirtschaft*) to reorganise the European economy with Germany at its heart and satellite nations as suppliers. The Swedes feared that this plan would engulf them. While the Germans made it clear that they were now in a dominant position, political considerations of avoiding antagonising Russia by pressurising Sweden and the easing of iron ore supply with the acquisition of the French ore fields, meant that the German negotiators did not fully exploit their ascendancy. The Swedish negotiators stubbornly kept to practical questions of trade when dealing with the agreement for 1941 rather than responding to theoretical German positions, for instance stone-walling German feelers on Swedish involvement in *Großraumwirtschaft* while rejecting suggestions that the WTA with Britain could be nullified in the new circumstances. The Germans did succeed in forcing Sweden to increase exports to Germany, in contravention of the WTA, in order to pay for the additional imports from Germany which the blockade now necessitated. Given the situation, the British fully expected Sweden to make concessions, and Hambro's view in September 1940 was that they were 'so small as to be incredible.'[9] In October and November the British began to moderate their previously hard line about reopening access to Göteborg which the Swedes had maintained was in the spirit of the WTA and would prevent Sweden being completely isolated and dependent on Germany. In return for Sweden accepting British rationing of oil quotas, the British agreed in principle on 28 November to allow access to Göteborg permitting four Swedish ships a month in and out, provided navicerts and control port procedures were followed.[10]

German objections now had to be overcome. Some flexibility was shown in late 1940 when four ships were allowed through the German blockade as a special case but it was not until 7 February 1941 that Swedish arguments prevailed and the Germans agreed to what became known as 'Safe-Conduct Traffic'. Securing permission from the two belligerents was a triumph of persistence over probability. 'Safe-Conduct Traffic' provided Sweden with access to essential supplies from the west and gave the country an alternative to Germany and *Großraumwirtschaft*. The Swedish case to the Germans was that the importance of Swedish-German trade meant that it was in Germany's interest to maintain Swedish production and purchasing power. The case to Britain was that it was in the Allied interest to prevent Sweden being totally isolated within German control, reinforced by continual Swedish insistence that they had not made any essential economic concessions to Germany.

'Safe-Conduct Traffic' quickly became important to the overall Swedish supply position. During 1941, 120,000 tonnes of goods, primarily paper-pulp, paper, iron and steel, and machines were exported. Although a fraction of normal trade, they contributed to overseas earnings. Much more importantly, of 200,000 tonnes of goods imported in 1941, about 50 per cent comprised food supplies while of the remainder, 55,000 tonnes of oil went to military use and the balance such as wool, cotton, machine parts barely kept the country ticking over.[11] The contribution to morale is difficult to quantify but the resumption of trading contact with the world outside the totalitarian ring round Sweden promoted a flicker of hope in an otherwise bleak encirclement. Germany was the first to suspend 'Safe-Conduct Traffic' in April 1941 so as to pressurise Sweden as a prelude to securing Swedish compliance prior to the *Operation Barbarossa* invasion of Russia. It was not until the Engelbrecht Division had passed through Sweden that Germany allowed its resumption in July. Given its weak position, Britain

FIGURE 6 The oil tanker *Sveadrott*, 1940. This was the first Swedish tanker permitted through the British and German blockades of Sweden in 1940 bringing vital fuel to Sweden from the United States. These shipments became known as the 'Safe-Conduct Traffic' and suspending them presented an attractive blackmail instrument to both Britain and Germany.
(PA Photos)

unsurprisingly had been generally more accommodating with regard to Swedish concessions to Germany, but in the autumn of 1941 the question of the Norwegian ships in Göteborg began to emerge as an issue in the Anglo-Swedish discussions on 1942 quotas.

With American and Japanese entry into the war in December 1941, Sweden's trading position became more complex, and as far as its relationship with the United States was concerned, more exposed. The 'Safe-Conduct Traffic' westwards became more restricted both in destination and composition of cargo. The entry of the United States into the war had of course exacerbated the already tight supply position of certain commodities, such as hides for leather products, and Swedish negotiators had difficulty in accepting these new restrictions.[12] British inability to intervene successfully with the Americans on Sweden's behalf to prevent previously agreed quotas being cut indicated the shape of the future relationship with the Allies in which the United States had the controlling interest. The feeling grew amongst Swedish policy-makers that an early resolution of the issues raised by the new situation in the form of an Allied-Swedish trade agreement was desirable and Swedish diplomacy began to reflect this aim. On 4 May 1942 in Washington, the Swedish Minister submitted a memorandum inviting the United States to join the Anglo-Swedish WTA having previously in April requested a doubling of oil imports from 15,000 to 30,000 tonnes a quarter to maintain Swedish defences. The British added their conditional support on 11 June, subject to a modification of Swedish concessions to Germany, in particular the 'Leave Traffic' to Norway. Oil supply in return for the ending of concessions to Germany remained the main trade issue between the Allies and Sweden, and the issue of concessions festered until the end of the war.

Pentagon-based hawks were gradually gaining ascendancy in Washington throughout 1942 and began to regard the 'Safe-Conduct Traffic' with concern as contributing indirectly to the German war effort.[13] In fact in spring, 1942, Sweden was having great trouble in holding Germany to the maintenance of the volumes of coal, coke and steel products which had been agreed with such difficulty in 1941. The Germans agreed to supply armaments to help redress the balance and Hägglöf also believed that Sweden was achieving a stronger negotiating position vis-à-vis Germany. When negotiations for the 1943 agreement started on 17 November 1942, he took a tough line and told his German colleague that the time had come to end Swedish trade credits which were attracting Allied disapproval. His firm handling paid off when the Germans renewed a five million tonne coal and coke quota for 1943 without credits. Sweden had regained the initiative with Germany but that firmness crumbled when confronted by the Western Allies' demands. By late summer, 1942, the Swedish government regarded its diminishing oil reserves and the relationship with the Allies over future supplies as having reached the stage where high-level direct discussion was required. Although the Germans had been supplying Sweden with significant quantities of oil from Romania, an alternative supply was essential to reduce dependence on Germany.[14] Boheman was dispatched to London in October 1942 with the remit to get the oil imports underway again. The British, as anticipated, offered understanding but it was the Americans who had the oil.

After encouraging preliminary discussions with British officials and an ego-boosting but inconclusive one-to-one meeting with Churchill, Boheman had to travel over the Atlantic to make his case to the senior authorities there with a letter of introduction from Churchill to Roosevelt. He had a difficult time with many blunt-speaking officials. Under-Secretary for War, Robert Paterson opened a meeting with 'how did you get Hitler's permission to come here?' They, unlike the gentlemen of Whitehall, had no long-term relationship with Sweden and even less understanding of Sweden's exposed geopolitical situation.[15] What they saw was a neutral that supplied goods and materials to an enemy of the United States and they did not neglect opportunities to spell this out to Boheman, whose legendary urbanity and deft advocacy was put to its severest test. Boheman gradually prevailed and secured an agreement in principle that an increase in the oil quota would be made in return for the right to charter a further twenty Swedish merchant ships for Allied service and for permission for the two remaining Norwegian ships trapped in Göteborg, *Lionel* and *Dicto*, to leave for Britain with their cargoes. This would break a rare written undertaking by Günther to the Germans.

Faced with the loss of oil imports, the previous Swedish position went quickly into reverse and to Hägglöf's disapproval, the government conceded the release of *Lionel* and *Dicto* to the Allies by 14 January 1943 while attempting to minimise the damage to Swedish-German relations. *Lionel* and *Dicto* never in fact left, due to the increased risk of sinking by the Germans, but the affair had served its purpose: the Allies had demonstrated that Sweden recognised their stronger bargaining position. These events took place during the final death-throes of the German Sixth Army at Stalingrad and ushered in the next phase of Sweden's trade policy to deal with an increasingly confident and predictably victorious Allied side. Hägglöf's view was that the Swedish government, swayed somewhat by Boheman's political arguments in favour of accommodating the Allies, had conceded *Lionel* and *Dicto* too readily. Hägglöf may have been tactically correct, but that was now strategically irrelevant in view of Germany's approaching defeat after its failure in Russia. But the Swedish leadership still faced German encirclement and the task of a country to feed, heat, employ and re-arm.

NEGOTIATING WITH BRITAIN, AMERICA AND GERMANY – ALLIED ASCENDANCY AND WESTERN ACCESS, 1943–1945

Boheman's discussions in Washington had provided an ominous indication of probable Allied demands in 1943. Hägglöf added to the gloom by setting out the problems to be dealt with in the forthcoming negotiations. Washington would demand direct limitation of 'Leave

Traffic' and effective limitation on the transit of war material to Finland and Norway, which would mean rescinding these concessions to Germany. The United States clearly envisaged swingeing reductions in Swedish exports to Germany and occupied lands during 1943 but Sweden had already concluded an agreement with Germany for the whole of that year.

The worsening military situation for Germany made the withdrawal of some concessions less risky for Sweden while in the opinion of the British military there was no risk of invasion whatsoever. However, Per Albin wanted to limit perceptions of the pliability of Swedish foreign policy under pressure, arising from the reversal over *Lionel* and *Dicto* in January 1943. He now refused to cave in to Allied demands over concessions to Germany. 'Sweden has its line and it will follow it.'[16] Hägglöf and his colleagues were then sent to London in May with a tortuous, face-saving remit thrashed out with their political masters. If the Allied negotiators pushed Sweden hard on 'Leave Traffic' and transit questions, then the Swedes could propose a complex mechanism. This stipulated that if concessions were not ended before 1 October 1943, the Swedish side would accept that any newly negotiated WTA with Britain and the United States would be rendered invalid. This controversial remit exposed the weakness of the Swedish position; having defended their concessions to Germany using the threat of potential German invasion and occupation, they lacked a coherent response when that threat was diminished. Furthermore, a domestic campaign had emerged in the Swedish press calling for an end to the unpopular concessions.

The Swedish delegation arrived in London on 9 May when the Allies were celebrating the German surrender in North Africa. The British Blockade Minister, Lord Selborne, opened the negotiations with the rejoinder to the Swedes that there was in Britain 'sometimes a feeling . . . that we get all the sympathy while the Germans get all the goods.'[17] During the following week Sweden was forced to agree to ending concessions by 1 October. The Allies did not want to take the risk that Sweden would receive the imports and then, from 1 October say that it could not end the concessions. Such apparent lack of Allied trust offended Hägglöf but demonstrated the tougher Allied stance from their new position of strength which forced Sweden to agree on 2 June 1943 to a settlement based on ending transit. The agreement which they thrashed out contained significant concessions to Allied interests. For 1943, Sweden would reduce the value of its total exports to Germany by 130 million kroner compared with 1942. Sweden also undertook to refuse trade credits to Germany and limit them for Finland. For 1944, a slashing of iron ore export volume by 25 per cent would be introduced to hold Germany to seven and a half million tonnes with each tonne of Swedish ore exported being recompensed by a half tonne of German coal imported.

Back in fortress Sweden, the negotiators were met by a barrage of criticism for operating independently. Bagge remarked that: 'Sweden had now appeared to have got its London government'.[18] Even Boheman expressed dissatisfaction at the extent of the concessions describing them as 'the biggest blunder during my time in the foreign service'[19] Hägglöf conceded to his government critics at a Cabinet meeting on 28 June that the provisional agreement was economically unfavourable but asserted that it was politically shrewd to adjust to a future Allied victory and improve the prospects of securing a share of post-war European reconstruction. The Cabinet decided not to approve the agreement, something which had happened before in 1915 and 1917 when the Hammarskjöld Government rejected their negotiators' efforts. But the war situation was changing weekly, with the Allied landing in Sicily having a particular impact on the Government's outlook. Boheman took these changes as his theme in an influential brief to the Cabinet urging a speedy resolution that would be unlikely to affect the 'Safe-Conduct Traffic' so that Sweden would get the oil import benefit from the agreement. This helped to tip the Cabinet into bold approval on 24 August 1943. Further minor Swedish changes were accepted by the Allies on 17 September and the subsequent agreement became the fragile reference point for Sweden in the coming onslaught of increasing Allied demands. The 1943 Swedish-British-American London Tripartite Agreement (LTA) represented a 'win' for the Allied economic warfare policy. How would the 'losers' react?

The nervous Swedish diplomats had to deal with the German reaction to the ending of concessions and the tightening of trade. The Germans kept the 'Safe-Conduct Traffic' open until the end of October 1943, when the blockade was reinstated to deter the break-out of *Lionel* and *Dicto*. Despite Per Albin's worst fears, Sweden had succeeded in ending 'Leave Traffic' without significant damage to Swedish trade. Nevertheless, when the negotiations for 1944 opened in Stockholm in November 1943 the Germans complained that the Swedish proposal to reduce iron ore exports to seven million tonnes was inspired by Allied pressure. In December 1943 Schnurre turned up to further pressurise Sweden on 'Safe-Conduct Traffic'. He failed to make any impact and the Swedish–German agreement for 1944 was concluded in January 1944 on terms which the Swedes considered favourable. They had succeeded in meeting the Allied requirements to reduce exports to Germany while still maintaining adequate incoming supplies from Germany. They had also secured an undertaking on the 'Safe-Conduct Traffic' which delivered the benefits from the LTA in the form of essential oil and food imports from the west. This 1944 agreement enabled Sweden to build up substantial stockpiles of coal and other goods which would bridge the anticipated interruption in supplies arising from the defeat of Germany.

In the United States, and in the Pentagon in particular, the 1943 London Tripartite Agreement (LTA) was seen as too ineffective and moderate, particularly with regard to iron ore and ball-bearings. The Allied backlash came in January 1944 with strong protests which Boheman attempted to parry. He offered to reduce the 1944 iron ore exports by the excess tonnage over 'normal' trade and set off to London to reduce tension. There he met a hostile reception and it was clear that sentiment was running high against Sweden in both London and Washington. The LTA negotiators were now being bypassed in favour of stronger, direct protests between governments instigated by powerful Allied military chiefs who dismissed the negotiators as too conciliatory. On 17 March 1944 the Allies submitted a demand to limit iron ore exports to 2.583 million tonnes for the first half of 1944 instead of the LTA figure of 3.75 million tonnes, an effective reduction of just over 30 per cent. Sweden gave no assurances which could weaken the Swedish position based on the LTA.

The vexed question of ball-bearings now took centre stage as the Allied policy of pressure and purchase pre-emption was now increasingly applied to Swedish exports to Germany. For the Allies during 1943, because of revised economic warfare evaluations, ball-bearings acquired the status similar to that of iron ore three years earlier as the Achilles heel of German war production. In their December 1943 discussions for the Swedish-German agreement, the Swedish negotiators had discovered that this was one of the Germans' most sensitive areas when they proposed reductions in line with Allied requirements, yet demonstrable cuts were made by Sweden despite attractive German counter offers of arms and aero-engines. On 3 March 1944, the Allies responded with additional demands for further severe reductions for the following four months, in preparation for the coming D-Day invasion. Despite apparent Swedish willingness to discuss how this could be done, the stakes were increased by a diplomatic demand on 13 April 1944 that

Sweden cease *all* exports of bearings, machinery, tools and special steel for bearings to Germany: this in concert with a high-profile press campaign in the United States against Swedish exports to Germany. Notwithstanding Boheman's evident distaste for American methods, which extended to threatening bombing Göteborg, blacklisting, and alleging *SKF* impropriety in the USA (an accusation which would also taint the Wallenbergs), a complex agreement was reached with the Allies six days after D-Day in June 1944 to reduce *SKF* exports to Germany by 60 per cent for June–October 1944 and accept pre-emptive Allied orders in return.[20]

The end was now in sight for trade with Germany. From August 1944, Sweden progressively ended exports to Germany on Swedish ships. When coal imports from Germany ceased in the autumn of 1944, the Fuel Commission had been able to build up their stockpile to not less than five million tonnes, well over a year's wartime imports. By the end of 1944, trade with Germany had been ended and ironically the only remaining shipping trade was with the west by 'Safe-Conduct Traffic', permitted by both navies.

COMPULSION OR COOPERATION?

The trading record is undoubtedly one of the most controversial aspects of Sweden's wartime history. In recent accounts, it has been portrayed as sustaining a genocidal regime with supplies long past the time when it could afford to end such trade without fear of invasion or military retaliation. Such retro-simplistic assertion ignores three facts which Sweden's policy makers had to face up to and which are starkly evident from their actions during the period. Firstly, Sweden remained surrounded by German forces until May 1945 and not even the most optimistic contemporary Allied military assessments envisaged that they could come to Sweden's aid if, for example, some of the 300,000 strong *Wehrmacht* force in Norway were ordered to attack. Ending iron ore exports at the height of German hegemony would have been seen by Germany as a symbolic and hostile act that would increase the possibility of German military retaliation. Secondly, following the closure of all other sources, Sweden was unable to support itself with sufficient fuel to maintain even basic heating and industrial production. German supplies of coal and coke prevented the country from sliding into the starvation, poverty, unemployment and civil disorder experienced during the '*Hungerskjold*' years of 1916–18. As Martin Fritz wrote: 'Thanks to a continued foreign trade, Sweden's population could go to work, support itself, not starve and not freeze', to which should be added, could re-arm and defend itself.[21] Also, the supply of vast quantities of coal and coke to Sweden was a burden to the fragile German war-economy. As early as 1941, Goebbels noted in his diary 'serious coal situation in Berlin. We have to find coal or close down essential factories.' [22] This burden was also recognised by the Allies as discounting the advantage that Germany gained from Swedish iron ore supply. Thirdly, Sweden was determined to maintain its independence against all great powers: these had fully demonstrated their contempt for the rights of the neutrals and were clearly capable of subordinating Swedish interests to those of their own. As Boheman commented about the Allied repudiation of the LTA 'an agreement between a great power and a small country is not worth particularly much'[23] Soviet submarines and mine-layers targeted iron ore shipments to Germany in the Baltic and Gulf of Bothnia after June 1941 in an undeclared war against Swedish trade. The Western Allies clearly ignored the concerns of Sweden regarding the USSR and it was in Sweden's interest to demonstrate independence from the Western Allies when it came to brokering Finland out of the war. Stalin's suspicion would surely have rested on a lap-dog Sweden which rolled over to Western Allied demands. Sweden's trading relationship with Germany reflected the country's economic dependence and not its political sympathies. The avoidance of *Großraumwirtschaft* and the desperation to negotiate 'Safe-Conduct Traffic' to re-connect with the west is evidence enough. Rather, following April 1940, the relationship reflected the survival needs of its population when no alternative beckoned. The anxious attempts to trade with the Soviet Union and through Petsamo show the lengths to which Stockholm would go to avoid the embrace of Berlin.

Curiously though, most of the Germans involved in negotiating with Sweden appear to have enjoyed at least as good a working relationship with the Swedes as did their Allied peers. They were trade professionals doing a job in strange circumstances and with a few exceptions, ideologues and lightweights were excluded. Culturally, the Swedes seem to have preferred the predictable Germans to the rogue Americans.[24] It is evident that for the Swedes, the Germans kept their agreements while the Allies did not, a strange inversion of most diplomatic experience and perception of Nazi Germany. But of course it was in the best Nazi interest to do so – while others paid the price in the bleak mines, factories, and the starving, frozen occupied territories of the Third Reich, far from the comfortable meeting rooms and dinners in Berlin and Stockholm. Did Swedish post-war memoirs and histories fail to acknowledge the forgotten victims of Nazi trade out of embarrassment or from indifference? The testament of a British army prisoner of war in a German coal mine in Marionschaft highlights the brutal origins of German coal.

> I had joined the army to escape the mine at home, and here I was going to work down in one for the Germans, as slave labour. The workforce included about 50 civilians, along with SS Officers as bosses to make sure we got our work out every day . . . Your quota was six tubs per nine hour shift. The penalty for not getting your quota out was another nine hours down the pit, till you did . . . With us not getting good food, if we got a knock in the mine the coal dust turned the wound septic and ulcers used to form on our legs and arms.[25]

THE WALLENBERG BROTHERS

As Sweden's modern Medici, Wallenbergs were (and remain) important in the symbolism of Swedish wartime relations and like the Medici, they gained influence and unimaginable wealth through taking risks, staying close to powerful political figures and appearing to support and provide services to all of them. It is no exaggeration to say that the Wallenberg dynasty had the greatest non-political influence on Sweden's profile during and after wartime. The two brothers, Jacob and Marcus Junior discreetly exerted enormous (and frequently controlling) influence over most of the big names in Swedish industry like *SKF*, *SAAB* and *ASEA* through the family bank, *Enskilda*. The two brothers had established an extensive network of business and political contacts throughout Europe and America between the wars and in 1939 they placed their international expertise, rare in Swedish circles at that time, at the disposal of the Swedish state. They travelled tirelessly for Sweden, primarily as negotiators on the various trade agreements but also acted as unofficial representatives and channels of communication – even for sensitive political and military intelligence. Marcus focused on the Western Allies while Jacob was a habitué of the German corridors of power – and they also used their contacts, travels and associates to preserve and extend their business interests, which were of course threatened by the widening conflict.

Their father (Marcus Senior) had been involved in negotiating at

Versailles to exempt Swedish assets in Germany from being seized for reparations and also had experience of the disguising of German business assets in Sweden. From this the brothers were fully aware of the opportunities which Germany offered and the corresponding risks to their own business empire when the Second World War began. One opportunity was that in return for large fees, the Wallenbergs disguised and concealed the overseas assets of German companies, Bosch and I. G. Farben, using false ownership by their *Enskilda* Bank or an associate. The American Bosch Company (ABC) was a case in point when Marcus personally arranged the transfer of its shares in July 1940 to *Enskilda* to shield the German asset from the United States' Alien Property Custodian (APC). Unfortunately for Marcus, the meticulous Germans retained all documents related to the deal and when found in 1945, they revealed the fees charged by the Wallenbergs for the transfers and concealment.

The risk to the Wallenbergs' interest in *SKF* arose from the deep involvement of the German arms industry in the decisive *SKF* acquisition by Marcus Senior of the ball-bearings business of Hess-Bright in Philadelphia in 1917 prior to the USA's entry into the war. This United States presence was followed by the purported acquisition of the German ball-bearings company, *VKF* in 1929, master-minded by *SKF*'s boss, Björn Prytz, later Swedish Minister in wartime London. The German and Swedish ball-bearings industries were intertwined through technology, patents, markets and manufacturing equipment. Control of the combined *SKF* probably remained in Germany but the company was Swedish as far as the Versailles Treaty was concerned. When the Second World War started, *SKF* represented most major Swedish companies through its 185 global sales organisations. When the Germans refused to export ball-bearings to South America, this shortfall was replaced by *SKF* Philadelphia, which in turn reduced the supplies available to US manufacturers making armaments for the Allies. Some of these South American imports found their way back to the Germans in 1943.

The Wallenbergs enjoyed very high-level connections within the United States administration (as well as inside the British Ministry of Economic Warfare, Foreign Office, the American and British Legations in Stockholm, and with Boheman in the *UD*) but their activities had been under scrutiny in America since January 1942 with regard to *Enskilda* Bank and the ownership of the American Bosch Company (ABC). In May the FBI became involved and in October the Alien Property Custodian (APC), in a rejection of the Wallenbergs' assurances about ownership, took control of ABC and allowed other

United States companies to use the valuable ABC patents, some of which concerned strategically important equipment for airplanes and diesel engines.

As the war drew to a close, the United States, concerned about the flight of Nazi assets abroad, particularly stolen property such as gold and art from occupied Europe and Jews, set up the *Safehaven* programme to prevent it. In April 1945, the OSS representative in Stockholm, outside the Wallenberg circle of connections, prodded the United States Treasury to investigate the Wallenbergs at the same time as the American Bosch documents linking the Wallenbergs to the concealment of ABC were discovered in Germany. By August they had been placed on the United States Treasury's unpublished 'black-list' which limited their ability to carry out transactions. Marcus arrived in the United States followed by Jacob and immediately began a frenzied attempt to remove *Enskilda* Bank from the 'black-list'. Their connections were used to defend them, particularly when the British Government was in danger of presenting a prestigious award to Marcus simultaneous with his personal 'black-listing'. Even Herman Eriksson, the wartime Trade Minister, was sent a text to sign and issue to the Americans in support of the Wallenbergs. He refused.

There was clear evidence that the Wallenbergs had misled the United States authorities. They finally admitted doing so in late autumn 1945 in the case of ABC while their State Department allies battled on against the Treasury hawks over the 'black-listing'. The British Foreign Office decided in February 1946 not to 'black-list' them and after Jacob accepted the blame for concealing ABC and 'resigned' as head of *Enskilda*, the Wallenberg connections succeeded in May 1946 in keeping them off the list. The United States' *Safehaven* programme to trace and restore looted assets now took priority and the United States wanted the Wallenbergs to oppose Swedish trade credit for the Russians. Later, never to be out of pocket, *Enskilda* sued the APC for ABC compensation and received in 1950 the original amount invested in ABC. The Cold War and their network of connections saved the Wallenbergs from public humiliation while they went from strength to strength in post-war Sweden.

In 1982 Marcus gave a unique interview to Swedish Television about his life and experiences. In reply to a soft question about mixing Wallenberg business with state business during the war, the old man fixed the interviewer with a penetrating stare and replied: 'Not a bit . . . absolutely not done.' He was next asked if he had ever influenced a Swedish politician. Replying in the negative, the veteran of five years of trade negotiations (and who later in the same interview described how he convinced a reluctant Wigforss to accept the 1943 LTA) said: 'I wouldn't know how.'[26]

Notes

1. Figures from *Sweden, a Wartime Survey*, pp. 93–100.
2. Fritz, *The Adaptable Nation*, p. 20, table 2.
3. Mattsson, *Redarna kring runda bordet*, p. 59.
4. Hägglöf, *Svensk krigshandelspolitik*, p. 27.
5. Medlicott, *The Economic Blockade*, Vol. 1, p. 617.
6. Hägglöf, *Svensk krigshandelspolitik*, p. 124.
7. Ekholm, *Det svenska jordbruket och folkförsörjningen*, p. 104.
8. Ibid. p. 123.
9. Hägglöf, *Svensk krigshandelspolitik*, p. 143.
10. Medlicott, *The Economic Blockade*, Vol. 1, p. 629.
11. Hägglöf, *Svensk krigshandelspolitik*, p. 181.
12. Medlicott, *The Economic Blockade*, Vol. 2, pp. 187–9.
13. Hägglöf, *Svensk krigshandelspolitik*, p. 223.
14. Boheman, *På vakt*, p. 242.
15. Ibid. p. 206.
16. Hägglöf, *Svensk krigshandelspolitik*, p. 253.
17. Medlicott, *The Economic Blockade*, Vol. 2, p. 465.
18. Hägglöf, *Svensk krigshandelspolitik*, p. 261.
19. Boheman cited in Arnstad, *Spelaren Christian Günther*, p. 364.
20. For details, see Medlicott, *The Economic Blockade*, Vol. 2, pp. 487–91.
21. Fritz,'Sveriges ekonomiska relationer med Nazityskland', p. 276.
22. Goebbels, *The Goebbels Diaries 1939–1941*, p. 306, 9 April 1941.
23. Boheman, *På vakt*, p. 268.
24. Ibid. p. 140.
25. Cpl Geoff Steer 1/4 KOYLI, The Second World War Experience Centre Archive, Horsforth, Leeds.
26. Swedish Television.

Part Two

7

Security, Subversion, Spies and Sabotage

One of the recognised benefits to Britain from Swedish neutrality and independence during the Second World War was the ability of agents based in Sweden to gather intelligence from, and support resistance in, occupied Europe.[1] Yet, all the belligerents maintained intelligence gathering in Sweden. The German *Sicherheitsdienst* (SD) and military *Abwehr* were there. British Secret Intelligence Service (MI6) and Special Operations Executive (SOE) were represented along with military intelligence. Following their entry into the war, the United States Office of Strategic Services (OSS, predecessor to the CIA) established themselves in Stockholm. The Soviet Union deployed the Russian Military Intelligence *(GRU)* and the State Security Section of the Council of People's Commissars *(NKVD)* – the instrument of Stalin's terror, which was reorganised constantly throughout the war and later became the *KGB*.

All of these organisations presented a threat to Sweden in one form or another. Most obviously, penetration of Swedish institutions by agents of these powers at best would reduce the ability of Swedish policy and decision-makers to conceal weaknesses and dissension. At worst, they could influence Swedish decisions in favour of their principals. Another risk to Sweden was that the belligerents would seek to destroy those assets in Sweden which they believed provided support to their enemy. Obvious targets were iron ore production, transit railways and military facilities. Military activity and resistance in adjacent Finland, Denmark and Norway raised the possibility of proxy conflicts on Swedish territory. In addition, there was the ever-present risk of Swedish citizens being recruited and directed by the belligerents to behave contrary to the interests of the Swedish state, including creating problems between Sweden and their opponents. Politicians no doubt recalled that eighteenth century Swedish history was characterised by decades of political weakness, sponsored by agents of France and Russia during the 'Age of Liberty'. More recently, in the early days of the First World War, Germany had been able to influence the Royal Family and attempt to bring Sweden into the war on the side of the Kaiser.[2]

This chapter will examine how the Swedish government and authorities, in particular the Civilian Security Service (*Allmänna Säkerhetstjänsten* or *AS*), were able, successfully, to prevent Sweden losing control of internal security and to maintain Swedish interests against those of the belligerents. The great powers were eager to exploit opportunities to damage their enemies through espionage, sabotage and counter-intelligence operations on Swedish territory. To combat this, Sweden operated two services: the counter-espionage *AS* which was an effective bulwark against the belligerents' intelligence-gathering and subversion, and Sweden's own military intelligence gathering organisation, *Centralen*, whose remit was to collect intelligence to protect and promote Sweden's interests.

Swedish Counter-Espionage

Sweden had been made acutely aware of the threat of external subversion when, following the Russian revolution in 1917, the Comintern began its efforts to foment external revolution. This naturally encouraged the predecessors of the *AS* to target Comintern activities in Sweden.

In the period following the First World War, the Swedish security emphasis was on supervision of foreigners and in 1923, a small group of officials was formed to continue that overview. Within Stockholm's criminal police another section was created to be responsible for investigations into threats to state security. In the mid-1930s the military, still fearing the Comintern, instigated the formation of a Committee to promote defence against external threats to the state. The Committee's report led to the approval by the Government in June 1938 to create the *AS*. The service came into force on the day Hitler invaded Poland in September 1939, under the controversial Eric Hallgren who previously had led the Stockholm criminal police group against communist and Nazi sympathisers.[3] Hallgren, on one occasion described as 'our blue-eyed Himmler' would soon be regarded with suspicion by the British in particular.[4] One characteristic which the new AS shared with the British security services was official silence about its existence. On the same day as the Government secretly decided to institute the AS, Social Minister Gustav Möller signed another secret order setting out AS guidelines.[5] Unsurprisingly, these gave the AS wide scope to prevent military intelligence leaks and to create both a surveillance and postal censorship organisation responsible to the government and to the military with dual reporting lines to each. The legal framework within which the AS operated was complex – a patchwork of different legislation related to foreign nationals, refugees, activity threatening to the state, internal security, espionage and sabotage. Some of this legislation pre-dated 1939 and was later sharpened and further widened with harder penalties. An example from 1942 saw one definition of illegality expanded from activity 'likely to risk war', to encompass actions likely to endanger 'friendly relations with a foreign power.'[6]

With these supporting laws and guidelines, the AS was launched in 1939 against Sweden's internal and external threats with an intricate central and local structure. This reflected the primacy of Stockholm in the oversight of foreigners and communications but recognised the importance of a local presence throughout the country. Compared with the earlier handful of security officials, the AS quickly grew to over 1,000 personnel in 1939. By 1944, Stockholm Section alone employed almost 200 people.[7] Nationally, there was surveillance of post, telegram, telephone, radio and communications in six national districts while Stockholm Section added censorship to these tasks. There were a further four Departments tracking respectively, Swedish and Soviet Communists: Germans and Nazi adherents: Allies, Norwegians and Danes: and Swedish citizens.[8] The statistics indicate the enormity of the effort. During the war in total, fifty million mail items and well over eleven million telephone conversations, as well as between 11,000 and 47,000 telegrams per week, passed under the eyes and through the earphones of the AS which by 1944 listed 80,000 individuals on their surveillance register.[9]

What did this huge, secret, state scrutiny result in? Again, the statistics are helpful. During 1939–44, almost 2,000 people were arrested for activity against the state with espionage and intelligence activity accounting for 60 per cent, sabotage forming just over 11 per cent and the remaining 29 per cent detained on miscellaneous associated charges.[10] Predictably, the deterrent penalties were not sufficient to prevent ideologically and financially motivated people from seeking to advance their cause or line their pockets and so deterrence relied on the effectiveness of the AS and its associates. The AS was later accused of partiality for its allegedly more relaxed pursuit of German cases in contrast to those involving Britain, Norway and Denmark. Before the turning point in 1943, this may indicate influence from the UD, nervous of Germany's reaction to any arrest and trial of its agents.[11] However Sweden, surrounded by occupied territory, permitting German transits and supplying German industry was always going to be more of a target for Allied espionage and sabotage than for the Germans. This viewpoint was endorsed by a senior German intelligence official.[12] The AS or 'Gustav Möller's secret police' as they later became known, increasingly fell under criticism from many quarters, despite their success in keeping the lid on a bubbling cauldron of spies and saboteurs.[13] Their priority was preventing what might happen rather than punishment after the event and in this, they were fairly successful. They of course won the enmity of people like the British SOE's Peter Tennant, whose energies were spent on outwitting AS surveillance in order to recruit Swedes.

BRITISH INTELLIGENCE AND ACTIVITIES

The British intelligence effort was directed towards several diverse objectives. The Allies wanted evidence which could give early warning of any German invasion of Sweden or information which could make Swedish iron ore shipments to Germany *more* vulnerable and shipments of bearings to Britain *less* vulnerable. Other valued intelligence included German transits to Norway and Finland, Swedish defence arrangements and assessments of the Swedish intention and ability to resist Germany. Furthermore, British efforts were aimed at recruiting agents from Norwegian and Danish refugees and assisting Allied propaganda in Sweden.

Each foreign legation was legitimately staffed with military attachés from all three services whose role was to gather information helpful to their nation. Specifically they used their service knowledge to form a better understanding of the military situation in Sweden and gather whatever intelligence they could regarding the wider picture. Officially, they formed two networks: firstly, they maintained contact with their corresponding Swedish service both formally and informally; secondly, they exchanged information on a mutually useful basis with other 'friendly' attachés. Unofficially, they sought and shared information with and from any useful source, Swedish or foreign, and utilised their diplomatic immunity to recruit agents and carry out espionage themselves. Military attachés had a somewhat ambiguous position: they were members of fighting services in wartime who nevertheless were supposed to operate within diplomatic rules. The British Legation had three very energetic attachés whose reports and contacts within the Swedish services contributed to the impression in London that an independent, neutral Sweden represented a vital window on Hitler's Europe but like all intelligence professionals, they occasionally over-estimated the value of what they produced, and the end results of their diligent endeavours.

The Naval Attaché, Denham, provided a good example of an effective attaché. In early 1942, he reported to his boss in Britain that his official connections with the eight other foreign attachés produced 25 per cent of his reports, excepting the USA's who suffered from 'lack of imagination and incompetence', but scathingly that his Swedish navy's official connection was of no value. This last may have been due to an anti-British sentiment prevalent in the Swedish naval officer corps and exacerbated by the British attempt to seize four Swedish warships en route to Sweden in 1940.[14] More useful was his nine-point 1942 list of 'unofficial' contacts ranging across Swedish businessmen, merchant shipping officers and senior military intelligence officials.[15] Such contacts ensured that Denham attracted the full attention of AS and his flat was watched and bugged.[16] Denham's intelligence contacts were frequently the cause of inter-departmental rivalry with MI6 and SOE but not with his fellow attachés. Denham was instrumental in arranging for the new Swedish Director of Combined Intelligence, Commodore Landqvist, to visit Britain in 1943 to counteract impressions gained during his visit to Berlin. Denham also valued his relationship with Petersén, head of Swedish Military Intelligence (Centralen), reporting in 1943 that: 'He has certainly been a good friend to me . . .'[17] Unfortunately, German intelligence had broken British naval codes and much of what Denham sent to Britain was read by the Germans.[18] Through their interception of German communications, the Swedes also knew this. It is understandable that many Swedish officials were quite guarded about what they said and to whom in such a leak-prone situation, particularly during 1940–3 when Sweden might be occupied by Germany. Also, as Minister Mallet observed in 1941, 'The

Swedish service departments are evidently under very strict discipline and have to be extremely careful what they say to foreigners. [Swedish] Foreign Office officials are much more indiscreet!'[19]

Denham's colleague, the combative Military Attaché, Reggie Sutton-Pratt, pursued a more dangerous course with his support for sabotage operations on Swedish territory. He also revealed the convoluted nature of confidential intelligence sources: 'The following report (on total and distribution of German formations) emanates from No. 36's opposite number in Finland. No. 36 hinted to me that No. 21's friends have had a hand in its compilation.'[20] The British Air Attaché, Thornton, established excellent relations with the Swedish airforce commander which resulted in him offering in 1944 in case of British invasion 'to receive 12 British fighter squadrons at the secret aerodromes and could take 3 more at the established aerodromes making 15 squadrons in all in the south of Sweden.'[21] These instances from the British archives of extensive and supportive connections do much to counter the impression that at an official level, Sweden was unhelpful to the Allies and overly predisposed to the Axis. For the *AS* however, their remit focused officials on safeguarding the interests and security of Sweden rather than any one of the belligerents. When criticism of *AS* started in 1943, the politicians quickly distanced themselves from any damaging allegations of complicity with Germany yet *AS* activities were known and approved by four Cabinet ministers, including a controversial Swedish visit to Gestapo Chief Reinhard Heydrich in Berlin in 1941–2.[22]

Two major British operations which did not at all rely on any official Swedish support were the heroic *Operation Performance* ship breakout in March 1942 and the questionably effective *Operation Graffham* pre-D-Day deception exercise. George Binney, the swashbuckling driving force behind *Operation Performance* had been sent to Sweden to procure supplies of special steels and ball-bearings and was accredited to the Stockholm Legation. In January 1941 following the occupation of Norway, Binney had organised and participated in a successful breakthrough of the German Skagerrak blockade in *Operation Rubble* with five Norwegian freighters loaded with 25,000 tonnes of war materials. He returned to Sweden in April but the Germans were now on alert. A further ten Norwegian freighters with Norwegian volunteer crews were loaded with cargo for Britain in *Operation Performance* but the fleet was delayed for months by legal action in the Swedish courts until March 1942 when they left to be attacked by the waiting Germans. Six were scuttled to prevent seizure, two returned to Göteborg and two reached Britain with their valuable cargoes. The cost was high with three crew killed and a further forty-three dying in a concentration camp in Germany. Binney had arranged for Lewis guns to be smuggled into Sweden in the diplomatic bags and covertly put aboard the ships, which as merchantmen were meant to be unarmed. This took a great deal of effort by SOE operatives with diplomatic cover and their Swedish agents.[23] For this, Binney was declared *persona non grata* and Sweden had to assure the Germans that the two returned ships, *Lionel* and *Dicto*, would not be allowed to leave. Minister Mallet who had not been told about the Lewis guns, any more than he had been told about a sabotage network organised by Sutton-Pratt's assistant, was summoned with Binney to be reprimanded by none other than Boheman. He told them that they had put the Swedish Government in a situation where 'they must either give the impression of being accomplices or "fools" [sic]'.[24] Binney went on to organise further shipments of ball-bearings to Britain from Sweden using MTBs crewed by civilians. This traffic was kept secret from the Germans with the connivance of Möller, Boheman and scores of less senior Swedish officials.[25]

Operation Graffham was one deception of the Swedish Government in which Mallet enthusiastically took part prior to D-Day from April to June 1944. Essentially, the operation was designed to lead the Germans (and the susceptible Hitler) to believe that the Allies would invade Europe through Norway and Denmark. Information about unusual behaviour by the British in Sweden would be picked up by the Germans from Swedish sources. This was intended to cause the Germans to maintain their large force in Norway and to mislead them about the likelihood of a landing in France. One ploy had the former Air Attaché, Thornton, openly entertaining high ranking Swedish airforce officers to make it appear that talks on cooperation were under way. In another, a British military railway expert was sent to discuss capacity and logistics issues with the management of Swedish Railways to hint at imminent troop transit through Sweden. It is debatable how successful this was in misleading the Swedes but Mallet, who had a key role in the deception, reported to London on 16 April that Günther's wife told a friend that Günther believed invasion would include Denmark and Norway and that the Swedish airforce chief believed that a British attack on Norway would lead to British planes using Swedish airfields.[26] Even on the eve of D-Day, Mallet was instructed 'to give the impression that this invasion is only one of several major assaults upon continent [sic].'[27]

The British did not only restrict their activities to intelligence gathering and deception but unlike the Germans also planned and carried out acts of sabotage on Swedish territory. Consequentially, it is perhaps not surprising that they attracted more *AS* attention than the Germans. The most famous attempt was one personally approved by Churchill.[28] Alfred Rickman was a British citizen and an MI6 agent from Section D, set up in 1938 for 'attacking potential enemies by means other than the operation of military forces'. His cover was the ownership of a dental product firm in Stockholm, but he had demonstrated an unusual interest in iron ore.[29] He was pointed out to *AS*, probably by the Germans, and *AS* surveillance led to his arrest on 19 April 1940, together with several associates. They had planned to blow up the iron ore loading cranes at the port of Oxelösund but had been caught through their own ineptitude.[30] The damage to British interests was greater than the failure of the operation and the sentences for the agents. The diplomatic difficulties that arose with Sweden went on for years. Interrogation had revealed a network of involvement by the British Legation, including Military Attaché Sutton-Pratt, and led to closer scrutiny by *AS* which limited intelligence gathering.[31] Two other incidents should be mentioned.

For July 1941, the SOE internal history states: 'A train with German goods which it was intended should have been sabotaged in Norway blew up prematurely in Sweden at Krylbe [sic] Junction.'[32] This operation had been organised by Malcolm Munthe, Sutton-Pratt's assistant, son of Axel Munthe (a Swede who had become a British citizen and author of *The Story of San Michele*) and an irritant to the UD.[33] Pencil bombs had been placed on a German ammunition train in transit and news of the Krylbo explosion, which injured twenty-four Swedes, broke timeously on the same day that Munthe left Sweden as *persona non grata*.[34] Despite a thorough police investigation, those responsible were neither identified nor arrested. This was perhaps a diplomatic rather than a police decision. The fears of the Swedish Cabinet of reprisals by Britain, expressed during their decision to allow transit, had now been realised.[35]

Actual loss of life occurred when less than two months after Krylbo on 17 September 1941, three Swedish navy destroyers exploded at anchor in Hårsfjärden near Stockholm. The destroyers were sometimes used to escort Swedish ships carrying iron ore and German troop carriers. Thirty-three sailors died and seventeen were injured. Again, there was no identification of the perpetrators or even if the cause was sabotage. Mishandling of torpedoes or accidental bombing have both been blamed, but the incident raised Swedish

FIGURE 7 SOE sabotage at Krylbo Station, July 1941. This scene of devastation followed the British SOE's sabotage of German ammunition in transit by rail to Norway when 24 Swedish civilians were injured, but the authorities found themselves unable to identify the perpetrators.
(PA Photos)

concerns regarding sabotage operations.[36] The fact that *all* the belligerents could be suspected for this incident strengthened the Swedish view that none was to be trusted. Even Sutton-Pratt believed that the Germans had done it to discredit the British or the Russians.[37]

One other SOE initiative in which British Press Attaché and SOE officer Peter Tennant was involved was the attempted creation of a chain of radio transmitters which could be activated in the event of a German occupation to support resistance sabotage activities. The organisation chosen for this task was the Tuesday Club (*Tisdagsklubben*), publicly an anti-Nazi group led by aristocratic eccentric Amelie Posse. In secret, Tennant supplied a small group of members with radio equipment and financed their activities although this operation was penetrated by *AS*. Another, separate group of Swedes was recruited by Tennant, primarily from Syndicalists, to develop a post-German occupation radio-communications network but this was disbanded during 1943 as the invasion threat diminished.[38]

Those four cases illustrate that Sweden could not afford to relax its defences against sabotage and subversion. Boheman was scathing about the effectiveness of the British intelligence effort and held a poor opinion of Munthe.[39]

DANISH AND NORWEGIAN NATIONALS

The benefits of Swedish neutrality played a major role in the British contribution to maintaining resistance activity in occupied Norway and Denmark.[40] Many of the vital communication channels were locally organised from the Stockholm Legation by the SOE.[41] With the resumption of the direct air service between Sweden and Britain in March 1941, those agents landed in Scandinavia by sea or parachute could be repatriated.[42] There were Danish and Norwegian sections in the SOE contingent in the Stockholm Legation attempting to recruit suitable refugees to return as resistance operatives, an activity which their governments did not always support. Restricted areas and restrictions on foreigners meant that when SOE started in late 1940 'it was necessary to concentrate organisation and planning inside the Legation itself and to use outside agents who had freedom of movement and who hoped to be able to escape the attentions of the Swedish police.'[43] Danish resistance was represented in Stockholm by journalist Ebbe Munck, who quickly established contact and a working relationship in February 1941 with SOE's Ronald Turnbull in the Legation. As well as playing a key role in the communications between SOE and the various parts of the Danish resistance, Munck established a regular flow of intelligence from Denmark to Britain.[44] Denham certainly benefited from this conduit.[45] The Norwegian resistance also kept close contact with the Legation and Assistant Military Attaché Malcolm Munthe was one of the earliest SOE organisers. The Norwegian Military attaché, well connected with *Centralen*, was also one of Denham's reliable sources.[46]

The Swedish authorities were initially extremely nervous about Danish and Norwegian nationals operating as agents on Swedish territory. Sweden rightly anticipated proxy conflicts on Swedish territory or being used as a base for unauthorised armed operations against German forces in occupied Denmark and Norway. There seems to have been a certain amount of clandestine warfare between German agents and Norwegian agents in Stockholm leading to death as well as injury.[47] One instance of assassination exemplifies the type of incident which the *AS* and their political masters dreaded and which somewhat justified their extensive surveillance. On 29 July 1944, a Norwegian national was shot and killed in the Norwegian Legation in Stockholm. The dead man was a suspected Nazi infiltrator, probably working for the notorious Norwegian Nazi agent, Henry Rinnan, and his executioner was a Norwegian SOE agent. The body was removed for burial in an unmarked grave in the countryside while the SOE man and a complicit associate were flown to England to avoid possible arrest. If it ever came to light, the Norwegians feared the ramifications for their Legation, for relations between the government-in-exile and Sweden, and the potential propaganda gift to the Germans. Fortunately for those concerned, it remained a secret.[48] Rinnan himself had also been the target of an earlier 1943 SOE-inspired operation to lure him to the Swedish border and to kidnap, interrogate and 'liquidate' him. Although the operation failed, it is only one example of Swedish intelligence 'facilitating' the passage for Norwegian SOE agents across the somewhat porous 1,300 kilometres-long Norwegian–Swedish border. In return, they received intelligence about the Germans in Norway. One drawback was that SOE agents could still be intercepted by Swedish military patrols that had not been informed of Swedish assistance for obvious security reasons.[49]

The Danes had established a 'Contact Committee' ('*Kontaktudvalg*') in Sweden in early 1944 at the behest of the Danish resistance as a link between them and the exiled Danish politicians. In addition to political communications, it also tried to optimise the use of routes to occupied Denmark and disburse funds to Danish groups in Sweden to best advantage. The routes originated primarily from small Swedish west-coast fishing ports over which were carried weapons, propaganda and resistance members. The many contacts between the Committee and the Swedish authorities at a high level, including with Gustav Möller and even Per Albin himself, meant that for the Swedes, the Committee became the representative organisation for the Danish resistance in Sweden.[50] It also provided a reassuring means for Sweden to influence and control Danish expatriate activities in Sweden.

RUSSIAN INTELLIGENCE AND ACTIVITIES

Fear of Sweden's historic enemy, Russia, and its agents was deeply rooted in the *AS* due to the activities of the Comintern in the interwar period and even earlier from Tsarist Russian spy-scares before the First World War.[51] During the Second World War, the Russians had almost the same intelligence objectives as the British but naturally with more interest in Swedish intentions and relations towards Finland. The *AS*, which did not discriminate between the Comintern and the Soviet Union, uncovered twenty-three cases of espionage and sabotage between 1939 and 1942 for which the Soviets had recruited Communists, anti-Nazis and Russian émigrés. The Winter War with Finland complicated Russia's relationship with Sweden which, as a non-combatant, was supplying Finland with equipment and permitting volunteers to fight. A Russian-trained Swedish communist agent, Bror Nyström, was caught by AS surveillance in early 1940 having received support from fellow Communists in Norrland, including the editor of the local communist newspaper, *Norrskenflamman*. This led to a hysterical reaction in the Swedish press, the unleashing of police raids on Communist Party offices on 10 February by Justice Minister Westman and an explosives attack on *Norrskenflamman* on 3 March that killed five people. This attack led to the arrest, trial and sentencing of a clutch of minor right-wingers, including army officers and Luleå's police-chief.[52] The case illustrates the corrosive effect of the type of subversive activity which the authorities were seeking to eliminate: Swedes killing Swedes, disproportionate responses leading to further disaffection, institutional infiltration and potential recruitment for subversion.

Action against Communists, who were felt to represent a threat to democracy and Swedish society, was widespread and intensive. From December 1939 in the labour movement, a general purge of Communists from positions of power at local level was accompanied by the slogan 'Swedish workers as representatives for Swedish workers!' The military also used conscription to isolate suspected party members and sympathisers in unarmed work companies, for example to build roads in remote Norrbotten as a form of internment. The navy even segregated their suspect ratings on a single ship in the Stockholm archipelago. There were between 600 and 700 held in ten companies nationally. Sköld initially defended these companies in the *Riksdag* in June 1940 but later abolished them in May 1943. There had been classification errors by the military leading to Social Democrats ending up in the work companies but what was perhaps more indicative of military attitudes was a distinct absence of Nazi sympathisers in these military camps.[53]

A second series of raids by the authorities involving about 1,000 Communists took place at the beginning of June 1941 as part of the continuing control of this potentially large opposition group in the country. The right-wingers, in particular Bagge, had been urging Per Albin to impose a ban on party membership but, fearing the result of driving the Communists underground, Per Albin steadfastly resisted that pressure and undoubtedly averted even more Swedes from becoming Russian agents.[54] Arrests of pro-Soviets diminished from their peak in 1941 to a handful by 1944.[55]

The Russians also used espionage to target iron ore shipments to Germany. From the United States' 'Venona' intercepts of *GRU* radio messages from Stockholm, it appears that the Russians had an agent within Swedish naval headquarters who was able to provide information on convoy dates, times and positions to assist Russian submarines to sink the transports.[56] Russian mines and torpedoes accounted for most of the sixty-seven Swedish iron ore ships which were sunk.[57]

GERMAN INTELLIGENCE AND ACTIVITIES

The Germans had infiltrated their own nationals as agents into Sweden long before the outbreak of war with cover identities as businessmen, journalists and tourists. In Stockholm, the German Tourist Office was used to conceal espionage activities. By the outbreak of war, the Germans had compiled extensive intelligence on Swedish industry. In its surveillance of the fractious Swedish Nazi groups, the *AS* and its predecessors had accumulated knowledge of German fellow-travellers as potential threats to state security equivalent to the Communists. German espionage objectives included information on exports to Britain, intelligence on enemy agents likely to interrupt Swedish exports to Germany, prior warning of Allied invasion of Sweden, assessments of potential landing areas for their troops, activities of Communists, Swedish attitudes to Germany, and intelligence about the country's defences.[58]

All countries used their diplomatically protected Legations as safe cover for agents and Germany was no exception. In February 1940 a doctor in the German Legation was caught acting with a Swedish Nazi to gather intelligence useful to Germany and was sentenced with four others in the network (the Michael-Strandberg case). The full result was six prosecutions and two expelled diplomats which the *AS* regarded as rolling up German espionage in Sweden. Given the hundreds of Swedish Nazis and the many remaining German diplomats, this seems unlikely. This rigorous action by the authorities against known German agents was not so evident after Sweden's encirclement in April 1940 when Sweden was keen to avoid difficulties with its new neighbour. The Michael-Strandberg case was used as an excuse for lack of action. Another feature of German espionage was that the *Abwehr* chief, Admiral Canaris, had in 1937 assured his Swedish opposite number that Germany would not undertake military espionage against Sweden. What this exclusion did not cover of course was German counter-espionage activity against German enemies on Swedish territory using Swedish nationals but the Michael-Strandberg case and the Canaris agreement provided *AS* with an explanation for their markedly lower success-rate in apprehending German agents. Not a single one was arrested between April and June 1941.[59] The available statistics show that during 1941–2, at the high point of German dominance, the AS arrested many more anti-German agents working for Britain and the Soviet Union than those working for Germany. It is difficult to avoid the conclusion that anti-Germans were targeted by the AS rather than the opposite.[60] Between 1939 and 1945, 420 Allied agents were sentenced compared with 180 German agents.[61] Certainly, people like Peter Tennant claimed that the 'Svestapo' (as he termed the AS) contained Nazi groups and assisted Germany.[62] However, the British Legation's Second Secretary, Archibald Ross, investigated espionage and sabotage statistics up to the end of 1942 and concluded in February 1943 that:

> The United Nations have in fact suffered more than the Axis . . . the law is more contravened by Allied agents than by Axis agents . . . may be due to the inferior skill . . . There is insufficient evidence for any conclusion on the question of partiality on the part of the authorities in tracking down offenders . . . There is no evidence of lack of impartiality on the part of the courts . . .[63]

This contemporary assessment does admit that easier communications and access to Sweden favoured the Germans and enhanced their ability to recruit a better class of agent. Added to this was the undeniable aim of the Swedish Government to minimise friction with Germany while it was in a position to harm Swedish interests. That presumably permeated the arrest policies of the AS but there is little evidence of overt interference from the UD. The AS endeavoured to ensure that they could make their cases stick and so there were fewer speculative raids on Nazi sympathisers compared with Communists. But when the war turned, German agents were apprehended for crimes committed years before and which had rested in AS files pending the appropriate juncture.[64]

However, one of the criticisms of the AS was its long-standing links with the German police. Official connections seem to have been arranged to humour the Germans, give them the impression of Swedish cooperation, and avoid being sucked into their 'crusade against bolshevism' while protecting Sweden against a real Russian security threat. The long-standing surveillance of Comintern-inspired activity by Sweden had increased in 1937 following a wave of pre-war sabotage against international shipping to Germany that used explosives of Swedish origin. This was organised by Ernst Wollweber, a communist German national, Comintern member and post-war chief of the *STASI* in East Germany. Sweden succeeded in arresting him in May 1940 leading to the downfall of his network, the 'Wollweber-League'.[65] Wollweber's earlier activities had encouraged the stationing of two *SS* officers in Stockholm on Gestapo Chief Reinhard Heydrich's initiative as part of a pre-war, pan-European German counter-sabotage operation. Swedish-German cooperation was renewed in March 1941 at the request of Heydrich to Gustav Möller, and three *AS* men subsequently visited the Gestapo in Berlin following agreement by the *UD*. In addition to information on the Wollweber case, they handed over various details relating to the Rickman case including photographs of the sabotage material.[66] In return, the Swedes received twenty-five names of 'dangerous' Communists in Sweden. Further trips to Stockholm took place in late 1941 through to February 1942 when two visiting Gestapo officers unsuccessfully attempted to extract details of German refugees in Sweden.[67] Despite these distasteful associations in order to contain the perceived communist threat, evidently approved at Cabinet level, the Swedes gave little away in these exchanges: not even Wollweber whom the Germans were attempting to claim. He was protected from extradition by a series of ingenious Swedish legal obstacles until he could be 'expelled' to Russia in 1944.[68] There was a single notorious consequence of Swedish-German rendition: a Norwegian Comintern agent of Wollweber was extradited to occupied Norway in February 1941without protesting (believing erroneously that he was protected by the Molotov–Ribbentrop Pact) but later transferred to Germany and executed in 1944.[69]

SWEDISH ESPIONAGE

Swedish military intelligence (as opposed to the counter-espionage activities of the *AS*) experienced enormous changes throughout the war, not least in name. Starting off as G-Section, it became C-Office in 1942 and more often was referred to as *Centralen*. It was led by the well-travelled Major Carl Petersén, a remarkable man who had taken part in the British invasion of Gallipoli in 1916 as well as the bloody and ruthless Finnish Civil War in 1918–19.[70] Petersén directed himself towards Allied contacts while his colleague Hellmuth Ternberg maintained contact with the Germans, particularly Admiral Canaris of the *Abwehr*.[71]

The Swedish military, Petersén's paymaster, had traditionally faced eastwards toward Russia where the threat to Sweden was evident. After April 1940, *Centralen* now found itself having to respond to demands for intelligence about the German threat on Sweden's borders. An agent network was quickly set up on the Norwegian border using 'reliable' volunteers such as customs officers to collect intelligence.[72] Unsurprisingly, given their proximity to the repression over the border, some also acted on behalf of the Norwegian resistance, for example delivering arms and explosives.[73] Petersén had few reservations about communicating with all the belligerents. Denham received his decisive intelligence on the Bismarck break-out from Petersén via the Norwegian attaché.[74] He also lunched with Petersén monthly throughout the war.[75] Denham recorded that 'the high grade and most valuable intelligence came from the Swedish staff, invariably . . . Chief of SSIS (Petersén) . . . and I had to find a quid pro quo' which was usually an 'appreciation' lacking in details.[76] Denham was also approached in August 1944 by Petersén offering to exchange 'complete and reliable information concerning (German rockets) V2, 3, and 4 in return for information of Allied plans for the re-entry into Norway.'[77]

Swedish service attachés abroad also attempted to gather and report intelligence but some of them experienced difficulties in doing so. The Swedish Naval Attaché in London was suspected by Britain of passing information to the Germans. The real source was a German agent who copied his reports in Stockholm and gave them to the 'Press Secretary' in the German Legation. In Moscow, the Swedish Ambassador was expelled in December 1943 on the excuse that the Army Attaché had disclosed Russian military secrets to the German High Command. There were other reasons for the expulsion but the attaché in question often complained that he relied completely on the 'Red Star' newspaper for his reports because he had no contact with the Russian military![78] In December 1944, the luckless Swedish Military Attaché in Berlin managed to lose a briefcase containing dozens of reports covering topics ranging from Hitler's health to intelligence on the V2 rocket. The Germans also had been getting his copied reports via their Stockholm agent but a Berlin contact had warned him of this, so there were perhaps few surprises for the Germans. However, his reports revealed that he had obtained some information from a source in Cologne and such disclosures could lead to death in Hitler's Germany.[79]

The networks which *Centralen* set up in Norway delivered extensive intelligence to the Swedish military authorities, as well as a selection for the Allies, but their value has been disputed. One criticism is that *Centralen* wrongly assessed the strength of the

Wehrmacht in Norway but it is also claimed that the otherwise detailed information collected would have saved Swedish lives *if* Sweden had been forced to intervene militarily in Norway, a far from remote possibility in 1945.[80] As the threat from Germany to Sweden decreased, *Centralen* and the British MI6 returned to their pre-war concern with the Soviet Union. The other major change was the entry of the Americans into the intelligence community in Stockholm in late 1942.[81] Like Mallet, Johnson, the American Minister, found the intelligence viper in his nest difficult to accommodate with his diplomatic work.[82] The British and Swedes had now to adjust to American OSS operations which were directed primarily at Norway and Finland. In *Operation Twinkle* the OSS set up and provisioned, with the assistance of the Norwegian resistance and *Centralen*, a series of military supply dumps along the Swedish–Norwegian border for use against the retreating Germans. In 1944, about five tons of arms and ammunition were flown monthly from London to Stockholm. Some was supplied to the 'Police Troops' and some to the Danish resistance, but the majority via supply routes to the secret border dumps.[83] Involvement in this operation placed *Centralen* firmly on the Allied side.

Regarding Finland, which held most intelligence on the Soviet Union, the OSS had agreed informally that MI6 would continue to operate there while they would cultivate contacts with the Finnish Legation in Stockholm.[84] In this, the OSS were extremely successful, securing Russian codes and other intelligence in September 1944 but they were ordered to hand all this over to the Russians by the American State Department to avoid Soviet accusations of collusion with the enemy.[85] Free from these conflicts of great power relations, *Centralen* and Petersén were more proactive and prior to the end of the Continuation War in Finland, they had brought most of the Finnish intelligence services personnel, equipment and records to Sweden as part of a deal to safeguard the officers and their families in case of Soviet occupation.[86]

This intelligence coup enabled *Centralen* to provide *FRA* (Swedish Military Signals Intelligence) with unparalleled access to Russian communications at a crucial period on the eve of the Cold War. Since 1905, *FRA* had been operating as a radio surveillance and code-breaking support to the military, and by 1939 had fifty officers. *FRA* had early success in the extremely complex and technically difficult task of intercepting German communications running through Sweden between Germany and Norway, Sweden and Denmark. The Germans had insisted on Sweden maintaining telegraph connections believing that their Siemens encoding apparatus, *Geheimschreibern*, based on the same type of technology as the Enigma machines (which the British decoded at Bletchley Park) would protect their communications. Mathematics professor Arne Beurling decoded the *Geheimschreibern* encrypts after studying only one day's signals in May 1940. A decoding machine was quickly developed and FRA was able to eavesdrop on the Germans between June 1940 and May 1943, the most vulnerable period of the war for Sweden.[87] In total, Sweden deciphered almost 300,000 German messages and intelligence of a special strategic or secret nature went direct to *Centralen*. Like Bletchley Park, such an intelligence advantage was a closely guarded secret but its existence was leaked to the Russians by a Swedish agent who was not arrested until early 1942. A second leak to the Russians was picked up by the Finns. They warned the Germans who changed all their codes in response. The intelligence which the FRA intercepted never had the significance of Bletchley Park's successes in, for example, the Battle of the Atlantic against German U-boats and of course never replaced human intelligence. Nevertheless, the Swedish Government derived reassurance about German intentions, attitudes to its policies and stance during the period when Swedish leaders feared for the future of their country.[88] They could also compare the differences between what they said to the Germans in Stockholm and the version that was reported by the Legation to Berlin.[89]

Another and more controversial area of cooperation between *Centralen*, the OSS and MI6 related to the Baltic states. Overrun successively by the Russians in 1940, the Germans in 1941, and the Russians again in 1944, the Baltic states had been an important source of Russian intelligence for MI6 before 1939. One commentator's view that: 'For many of the older MI6 officers . . . the war was merely an interruption in the battle against the Bolsheviks' echoed similar sentiments in Swedish military intelligence.[90] When the Baltic states were invaded, many refugees made their way to Sweden where some were recruited by *Centralen*. To start, Latvian agents were recruited and sent back in December 1943 to gather intelligence on the Germans and establish contact with the Latvian resistance.[91] In early 1944, similar operations were sent to Lithuania and Estonia from the Swedish island of Gotland. MI6 were closely involved in these operations, over sixty in all, and the remit extended to intelligence on Soviet held territory.[92] Ironically, these operations were reported to the newly appointed head of anti-communist Section IX in MI6, one 'Kim' Philby, the notorious and effective Russian spy.

From an early stage the Russians were probably made fully aware of Swedish involvement and that of the OSS in financing at least one of the operations.[93] For Sweden, the *Centralen* interest on behalf of the military leadership in recruiting Baltic states agents and cooperating with the Allies was to increase the flow of intelligence from a strategically important buffer area without being seen to be doing so.[94]

When the war was drawing to a close, there was a marked increase in the amount of intelligence and military cooperation between Sweden and the Allies. Particularly noteworthy was the 'blind eye' turned to the establishment of a radio beacon manned by RAF personnel in Malmö to guide Allied bombers on raids to Germany, Swedish permission in August 1944 to establish an RAF observation post on Öland to monitor German rocket testing from Peenemünde, and the handing over of V2 rocket wreckage to Britain following its landing in Sweden in June 1944. To these should be added the extraordinary behaviour of Petersén's colleague in *Centralen*, Curt Kempff when he met British military attaché Sutton-Pratt in November 1944. Chief of Staff Ehrensvärd had given him the signal for full co-operation with the Allies.

> I spent an hour firing questions at him and he flung open his files for me and gave me what they contained. I tackled Kempff as to possibility of Swedish intervention in Norway. He admitted (a) majority of senior Swedish officers and particularly Ehrensvärd and Douglas were most anxious to intervene in order that Swedes could hold up their heads and regain a prominent position in Scandinavia . . .[95]

POST-WAR CRITICISM AND OFFICIAL INQUIRIES

Criticism of the *AS* had begun in 1942 when a government committee was set up to assess the extent of Nazi sympathies in the nation's police forces. Predictably, they found some: in the May 1943 report, ninety out of 430 suspects were discovered to have Nazi associations. Revelations of further individual initiatives by two Nazi-oriented *AS* men who passed details of Danish refugees to the Germans led to a post-war inquiry, the all-party Sandler Commission, under the former Foreign Minister.

Robert Paulson had been convicted in 1945 for passing information about German refugees which he had acquired from his position in the Aliens Office (*Statens utlänningskommission*), the government agency responsible for registering foreigners in Sweden, issuing visas and working permits. It also had responsibility for the Swedish refugee camps, some of whose residents were of great interest to the Gestapo. Paulson, who had a background in secret police work and had fought for the Whites in the Finnish Civil War in 1918, was appointed in 1939. He had passed information on over 500 German refugees to a Swedish *Abwehr* agent which found its way to the Gestapo.[96] These revelations, together with a chorus of complaints from refugees about mistreatment in which Paulson featured heavily, created a political and public outcry. The Government responded by calling up Rickard Sandler in January 1945 to head an all-party Commission whose remit was to investigate AS activities and the treatment of refugees. Their remit was carefully drafted by future Prime Minister Tage Erlander to exclude any consideration of the activities of politicians, prosecutors, courts and military intelligence. It was only the AS who were to be the scapegoat. Erlander had been Möller's junior colleague ('*statssekretare*') in the Social Ministry and shared political responsibility for the activities of the secret police, had taken part in the organisation and arming of the 'Police Troops', yet expressed a surprising lack of knowledge of the AS contacts with the military perhaps in order to downplay his acceptance of a right-wing creation in Swedish society.[97] Specifically, the Commission was asked to consider whether the AS had abused their powers. Had they failed to act against German espionage with the same energy as that devoted against the Allies in the earlier years of the war? Should contact with the Gestapo have been maintained?[98] The Commission deliberated on these murky matters for two and a half years and published its findings in three parts in 1946 and 1948 covering treatment of refugees, information about refugees and finally the activities of the AS.

The Commission found that the treatment of refugees had been closely linked with Sweden's foreign policy and criticised the pre-1943 administrative detention which deprived refugees of their freedom.[99] As for sharing information with Germany, the Commission made a fine distinction between criminal and political information but noted that this sharing had been approved by the UD outside of the AS.[100] Finally, the Commission agreed with the rationale for and activities of the AS, as a necessary adjunct to normal policing in time of war and found that its extensive supervision of Swedish citizens was both essential and not generally abused. As to the partiality of the AS for anti-Allied activity, the Commission noted the arguments for this approach, clearly based on the political circumstances prevailing at the time.[101] AS chief Hallgren described the Government's neutrality policy as the guiding star for the application of the laws and as Janne Flyghed points out, this meant that the AS followed the policy of the UD to keep the country out of the war.[102]

In short, the Commission gave the AS its approval, ducked the partiality issue and only criticised the Government for keeping the existence of AS a secret which prevented political scrutiny and public awareness. The Commission had served its purpose when after blanketing debate for two and a half years years, it published most of its findings to general public and political indifference in a war-weary Sweden which had since January 1945, been exposed, through Auschwitz and Belsen, to greater human rights abuses than those carried out by a few snooping Swedish officials.[103] The Commission's findings on the relationship between Baltic refugees and Swedish military intelligence, *Centralen*, remained secret to avoid problems with the Russians.[104] Paulson's mistake was in not heeding the AS chief, Hallgren's warning against his connection with the *Abwehr* agent and then not passing information back to the AS on the agent's activities.[105] Had he done so, he probably would have received the same protection against prosecution afforded to the other Swedish officials whose activities were investigated by the Commission. Although the AS was guilty of naivety with the Gestapo, police contacts with the other German police authorities were in themselves not reprehensible. The many contacts between the police and the Western Allies were not examined by Sandler, nor was the linkage between AS and the military. Cold War considerations had superseded those of the hot war.

In addition to the Sandler Inquiry, Per Albin responded in May 1946 to widespread disquiet about police and army officers' Nazi sympathies by appointing a so-called 'Assessment Commission' (*Bedömningsnämnden*) to assess 'democratic reliability', including one of his foremost critics as a member; Ture Nerman, veteran left-winger and previously imprisoned editor of *Trots Allt!* This Commission investigated fifty-seven cases but failed to dent the patriotic arguments of those who appeared before it.[106] After six months, the Commission dissolved. As Anders Isaksson has pointed out, Nerman failed to back up his wartime accusations of Nazi infiltration of the military and the police.[107] This concluded the immediate post-war hunt for the 'guilty' which was to resume with a vengeance in the 1990s. There were to be other official inquiries much later, including notably the 1997 Commission on Jewish Assets but the impetus of the war years had faded. This has led many commentators to characterise the post-war period as a missed opportunity for the Swedish state to reveal all, but ignores the realities of the icy blast from the Cold War that was now enveloping Europe and Sweden.

Notes

1. Flyghed, Rättsstat i kris, p. 414.
2. Lindqvist, Drömmar och verklighet, p. 129 ff.
3. 'Han beskrevs så här av en av sina medarbetare: "politiskt var han borgerlig, nazismen var han rädd för – när den börjat visa sitt rätta ansikte, kommunister hatade han och socialdemokrater kunde han visa förakt för".' Lööw, Rättsväsendets historia: Då Säpo var ungt.
4. Grafström, Anteckningar, 25 March 1940 & Tennant, Touchlines of war, p. 158.
5. Flyghed, Rättsstat i kris, p. 277.
6. Ibid. p. 248.
7. Forsberg, Spioner, p. 59.
8. Flyghed, Rättsstat i kris, p. 281.
9. Ibid. pp. 302–19.
10. Ibid. p. 351.
11. Ibid. p. 448.
12. Ibid. p. 405 (Schellenberg).
13. Forsberg, Spioner, p. 142.
14. Denham, Inside the Nazi ring, pp. 60–2.
15. NA ADM 116/6267 Naval Attaché Reports 1941–1944 7 February 1942 Denham to DNI
16. Denham, Inside the Nazi ring, p. 141.
17. NA ADM 116/6267 Naval Attaché Reports 1941–1944 11 September 1943 Denham to DNI.
18. NA ADM 223/8 Scandinavia Naval Attaché 1940–1945.
19. FO 371 29684 Intelligence work by Legation 1941 N1106 19 March 1941 Mallet to Collier.
20. NA WO 208/683 German Army Manpower and Reserves 1943–1945 2 November 1944 C3 Sutton-Pratt to DMI.
21. NA FO188/446 Operation Graffham 22 May 1944 Maycock's Report on visit to Nordenskjiöld.
22. Flyghed, Rättsstat i kris, p. 448.
23. RA UD H 60 Ab Norwegian Ships Vol. 1644 April 1942 12 May 1942 Police Report by Pehr Synnerman.
24. RA UD H 60 Ab Norwegian Ships Vol. 1644 April 1942 12 April 1942 PM Boheman.
25. Mallet, Memoirs, pp. 130–1.
26. NA FO 188/446 Operation Graffham 1944 16 April Mallet to Foreign Office.
27. NA FO 188/446 Operation Graffham 1944 5 June Foreign Office to Mallet.
28. Churchill, The Second World War, p. 523, Appendix 3.
29. McKay, From information to intrigue, p. 46.

30. Tennant, *Touchlines of war*, pp. 126–32.
31. 'What are the facts regarding the British Legation? A clear involvement in the Rickman affair, when Sutton-Pratt himself apparently approved the explosives storage.' 26.5.42 Boheman to C.O. Gisle in London: RA UD HP 1 Ba.
32. NA HS7/190 SOE Stockholm Mission 1940–1945.
33. 'The assistant British Military attaché Munthe's activities in Stockholm have been irritating for a long time.' 24.4.41 Söderblom to Prytz RA UD HP 1 Ba.
34. Munthe, *I krig är allt tillåtet*, pp. 158–209.
35. Möller, *Per Edvin Sköld*, p. 227.
36. Forsberg, *Spioner*, pp. 92–7.
37. Flyghed, *Rättsstat i kris*, pp. 414–16.
38. Agrell, *Skuggor runt Wallenberg*, p. 77.
39. Boheman, *På vakt*, p. 298.
40. NA HS 2/10 SOE Policy in Scandinavia 1940–1945, Policy Paper 7 April 1941.
41. NA HS 8/151 SOE Clandestine Communication Lines.
42. Nilsson, Sandberg, & Nilsson, *Blockade Runners*, p. 155.
43. NA HS7/190 SOE Stockholm Mission 1940–1945.
44. Hæstrup, *Besættelsens Hvem-Hvad-Hvor*, p. 321.
45. Denham, *Inside the Nazi ring*, p. 131.
46. Ibid. p. 128.
47. Tennant, *Touchlines of war*, p. 75.
48. Moland, *Over grensen?*, pp. 134–6.
49. Ibid. p. 214.
50. Grundt Larsen, *Modstandsbevægelsens kontaktudvalg*, p. 140.
51. Forsberg, *Spioner*, p. 14.
52. Lindqvist, *Drömmar och verklighet*, pp. 430–2.
53. Möller, *Per Edvin Sköld*, pp. 206–11.
54. Johansson, *Per Albin och kriget*, pp. 287–90.
55. Flyghed, *Rättsstat i kris*, p. 371.
56. http://www.nsa.gov/venona/releases/13 December 1941.
57. Forsberg, *Spioner*, p. 137.
58. Forsberg, *Spioner*, p. 101.
59. Flyghed, *Rättsstat i kris*, p. 404.
60. Ibid. p 430.
61. Böhme, 'Svensk polis och Gestapo.', p. 59.
62. Tennant, *Touchlines of war*, pp. 110 & 151.
63. NA FO 371/37069 17 February 1943 Stockholm to London.
64. Flyghed, *Rättsstat i kris*, pp. 446–8.
65. Forsberg, *Spioner*, p. 124.
66. McKay, 'Iron Ore and Section D', pp. 975–8.
67. Böhme, 'Svensk polis och Gestapo.', pp. 65–6.
68. Boheman, *På vakt*, pp. 299–303.
69. Forsberg, *Spioner*, p. 129.
70. Ottosson & Magnusson, *Hemliga makter*, p. 80.
71. Ibid. p. 123.
72. Berggren, *Världskrig, kommunism och nazism*, p 96.
73. Ibid. pp. 98–100.
74. Denham, *Inside the Nazi ring*, p. 84.
75. Ibid. p. 130.
76. NA ADM 223/8 Scandinavia Naval Attaché 1940–1945.
77. NA FO 371/43509 German Secret Weapons and RAB Controversy 1944 N4807-865-42 V2 in Sweden.

78. Assarsson, *I skuggan av Stalin*, pp. 227–8.
79. Gäfvert, 'Militärattachéns borttappade portfölj', pp. 15–25.
80. NA FO 371/43500–0021 Selborne to Eden 14 December 1944
81. Ottosson & Magnusson, *Hemliga makter*, p. 124.
82. Agrell, *Stockholm som spioncentral*, p. 83.
83. Ottosson & Magnusson, *Hemliga makter*, pp. 128–31.
84. Agrell, *Stockholm som spioncentral*, p. 86.
85. Ibid. p. 91.
86. Ottosson & Magnusson, *Hemliga makter*, p. 135.
87. Ulfving,' Geheimschreiberns hemlighet', p. 199.
88. Boheman, *På vakt*, p. 152.
89. Ibid. pp. 153–4.
90. Bower, *Red Web* cited in Dorril, *MI6*, p. 270.
91. Ottosson & Magnusson, *Hemliga makter*, p. 103.
92. Dorril, *MI6*, p. 274.
93. Ibid. p. 274.
94. Ericson, 'Buffert eller hot?', pp. 127–50.
95. NA FO 371/43509 N6897/85/42 4 November 1944.
96. Forsberg, *Spioner*, pp. 113–16.
97. Flyghed, *Rättsstat i kris*, pp. 287–8.
98. Ibid. pp. 269–70.
99. Ibid. p. 217.
100. Ibid. pp. 331–2.
101. Forsberg, *Spioner*, pp. 246–8.
102. Flyghed, *Rättsstat i kris*, p. 441.
103. Ibid. p 270.
104. Zetterberg, 'Debatten om "övervakningssverige", 1945–1948', p. 473.
105. Forsberg, *Spioner*, p. 115.
106. Bojerud, 'Kryptonazister fick fribrev'.
107. Isaksson, *Per Albin*, p. 492.

8

The Battle for Sweden's Mind – Propaganda and Censorship

The Nazi propaganda offensive against Sweden opened long before the war started – and so too did Sweden's defence. Recognising the importance of influencing overseas opinion and neutrals, especially Sweden, Nazi Germany soon began to influence the German news agenda abroad through 'placing political and cultural articles according to the wishes of the (propaganda) minister.'[1] Germany's change of regime did not go un-remarked in Sweden. Right-wing liberal editor, Professor Torgny Segerstedt, famously reacted to Hitler's 1933 *Machtübernahme* with the editorial comment in his newspaper *Göteborgs Handels-och Sjöfartstidning (GHT)*: 'Herr Hitler is an insult.' This too did not pass unnoticed because a few days later, a protest telegram arrived from Göring.[2] It was to be the first of many German objections. This chapter looks at two aspects of information in wartime Sweden: firstly, the effort by the Government to control and manipulate what was written and broadcast and secondly, the attempts to influence the Swedish public.

MEDIA OVERSIGHT AND RESTRAINT

The 1933 *GHT* incident set a pattern which was to last over the next ten years: Berlin carefully scrutinised Sweden's press and radio broadcasts and protested about any item which it disliked. Not that this was a new experience for Sweden. During the First World War, Foreign Ministry officials had to endure almost daily complaints about Swedish press comment from all the belligerents' diplomats.[3]

It was, however, Germany that had maintained the most active 'press policy' which persisted even after the downfall of the Second Reich in 1918. One strand of German foreign policy in the 1920s was to resist the Versailles settlement while various German 'cultural' bodies like *Nordische Gesellschaft* (NG) promoted the anti-Versailles view abroad.[4] The Nazi takeover added organised impetus to these efforts and not all prominent Swedes were as antagonistic to them as Segerstedt. Sympathetic figures included Sven Hedin, the famous explorer; Frederik Böök, Professor of Literary History at Lund University; and Verner von Heidenstam, a poet and a member of the Swedish Academy with Böök. As Nazi Germany's power increased in the Thirties, Swedish Government concerns about the negative effects in Berlin from Swedish media comment also grew. As early as 1938, Per Albin (himself a former journalist) and Sandler together urged editors to avoid inflammatory reporting.[5]

When war broke out in 1939, the Germans increased the number of complaints about the Swedish press and also made it clear to Minister Richert in Berlin and through their Legation in Stockholm that they regarded the Swedish Government as responsible for curbing adverse press comment. The Germans insisted that they expected 'mental' as well as political neutrality from Sweden, '*Gesinungsneutralität.*' The seriousness of the issue can be judged by the fact that when Admiral Tamm met Hitler in April 1940 to reassure the *Führer* of Sweden's determined neutrality, Hitler spent some time expressing his irritation over the attitude of the Swedish press and even the radio. These were not threats to be taken lightly in 1940 and it was hardly surprising that the defiant utterances of Segerstedt and Nerman were nervously regarded by the Swedish Government as a risk to national security. As Boheman commented 'we could not judge with any confidence what went on in Hitler's confused brain.'[6]

Swedish Media

There were a large number of daily newspapers in Sweden whose coverage was both national and international. In addition, there were evening newspapers which were predominantly regional in their reporting. All but the largest drew their national and international news coverage from the national press agency, *TT* which gave *TT* enormous influence over external reporting. The newspapers projected their editorial views only in the leader columns and in local news but it was often in the content of the leaders and cartoons that the Nazis found fertile grounds for complaint. As well as newspapers in clear opposition to the Nazis such as GHT and Trots Allt!, there were others more favourably disposed, for example Norrköpings Tidningar and Nya Dagligt Allehanda.[7] Although it was difficult after 1933 to source accurate news from within Nazi Germany, reports by newspapers such as the prominent daily Dagens Nyheter left no reader in any doubt of the direction of Nazi policies.[8]

The Swedish Radio Service's (Radiotjänst) roots went back to 1922, the same year as the BBC was launched, when the Swedish Radio Club was founded in Stockholm and the impetus for a public service broadcaster gained momentum. In 1925, AB Radiotjänst was started as a company with joint press, news agency and radio industry ownership and by 1937 had one million licence holders. The State exercised control, partly by nominating half the Board membership and the Chairman, and partly by the Charter of Agreement with the State Telegraph authority which regulated their activities. In 1939 Radiotjänst, unlike its cousins in the newspaper industry, was in the firm grip of the state as State Telegraph boss Seth Ljungquist, was also its nominated Chairman.

New Authorities and Tighter Legislation

Prior to September 1939 the Government, anticipating the pressure from the coming conflict, had encouraged the press to show care when expressing opinions which could be regarded as offensive by foreign governments or bring into question Sweden's neutrality. This guidance was largely followed, with the exception of the GHT and Trots Allt!, but the Government did not intend on relying on encouragement alone. It toughened its policy and on the day of the German invasion of Poland, Per Albin sent out a strong signal to the press for self- restraint: 'We value our free speech highly and none of us wants to stifle it. So we much more have the right to demand responsibility and self-restraint in the administration of this valuable gift.'

An eponymous 'Three-man Committee' (Tremannanämnden) including the head of the TT news agency was created as early as 6 September 1939 to supervise the state information service that was charged with getting the Swedish Government message over to the people. A State Information Office (SIO) was introduced at the suggestion of Tremannanämnden on 15 September 1939. Much of

SIO's early work was aimed at preparing Sweden for wartime conditions, for example a campaign that attempted to point out to the newly mobilised conscripts and their relatives that careless talk regarding their activities was inadvisable. The SIO acted as the Government's mouthpiece and ensured that Government press releases were covered in the newspapers and also on radio. The *Tremannanämnd* was replaced on 26 January 1940 by the State Information Board (*Statens Informationsstyrelse* or *SIS*) whose remit was to inform, restrict, survey, and direct opinion as well as to combat foreign propaganda. Its Board was composed of representatives of *Radiotjänst*, *TT*, and the National Film Office (*SBB*). It was also responsible to the *UD*, whose press secretary regarded it as an information 'blackout of the Swedish people.'[9]

Since 1766, Sweden had recognised press freedom as a constitutional right but this was considered problematic by several in the Government concerned about the damaging effect on Sweden's relations with the major powers. Sensing that the press would need more than encouragement to restrain themselves, the Government set up a small investigative committee on 28 September 1939, under law professor Ragnar Bergendahl. It reported in November with the recommendation that Swedish press policy should be governed by the *perception* produced among foreign governments by the content of any publication, as well as the relative power position of the foreign governments concerned. This was an expression of *realpolitik* in dealing with Hitler's Germany and resulted in an alteration to Swedish press freedom. In 1940, the *Riksdag* agreed a change to the Constitution (Section 6) that, if confronted by war or the likelihood of war, directions could be issued to censor prior to publication, limit or halt publication.[10] In the event, this legislation was never used and the clause was abolished in 1945. It is, however, indicative of the mindset of the politicians in 1940 in their preparedness to abandon press freedom in a dangerous situation. Per Albin noted in his diary in September 1940 'we can't risk a conflict with another country so that one man (Segerstedt) can publish what he pleases.'[11] Also, its potential to be introduced quickly probably had some influence on press expression. The implied threat encouraged most, but not all Swedish newspapers into more anodyne treatments of news, particularly concerning Germany. Bergendahl's Committee cast a long shadow over Swedish press freedom.

The government had two other legal instruments at their disposal to rein in the press. Under the 1812 laws on press freedom making it illegal to publish articles which insulted, outraged or caused dissension with a foreign power, there was an un-repealed and arcane provision whereby the government could, without any preliminary legal proceeding, confiscate any publication if disagreement with a foreign power was likely to result.[12] Although not used since the mid-nineteenth century, the government grasped it like a drowning man reaching for a life-belt. Another chink in constitutional press freedom was the absence of an express right to physically distribute publications. Justice Minister Karl Westman regarded this as an opportunity for further Government control. In 1940, Westman proposed that publications with 'damaging tendencies' for Swedish society leading to risks to national security could be banned from being transported by road and rail, merely by an executive order. The *Riksdag* approved this measure on 1 March 1940 and in their debate, the members clearly envisaged its use in response to communist propaganda. It was indeed primarily used against the communist press but also occasionally against the Nazi press. The transport of *Trots Allt!* was also banned from April 1940 to January 1941. These two active executive measures, confiscation and the transport ban complemented the dormant threat of censorship and provided the Government with the means to support the new State Information Board (*SIS*) in its suppression of press articles judged incompatible with the Swedish national interest. To assist in this aspect of its work, the *SIS* introduced an official advisory system to publishers which took the form of memoranda on grey paper marked 'not for publication' – the notorious 'Grey Slips' which have been described by Janne Flyghed as a 'hidden threat' by the authorities.[13] A corresponding system of 'Green Slips' advised editors on what *should* be published.

Another body was created in autumn 1941 to foster good relations between Government and press. The *Pressnämnd* (Press Council) members were appointed by the Government on the recommendation of the press itself and also professional and political organisations. Their remit was to work for self-discipline and thereby avoid the necessity of legal interventions by the Government. The *UD* worked closely in advising the *Pressnämnd* of problems which it wanted to be addressed and the *Pressnämnd* members were diligent in communicating these to the publication concerned. The *Pressnämnd* was dissolved in July 1944, its function to guide the press having been fulfilled.

The effect of all these measures was a compliant but nevertheless seething press corps. The lid was now screwed onto wartime freedom of expression very tightly indeed – but Swedish government powers compared favourably with those of the belligerents. In Britain, comment was in theory free of censorship, but two newspapers that had attempted to stretch this point, The Daily Mirror and the communist Daily Worker, were disciplined by the Government.[14] British news was subject to self-censorship and 'advice' from the Ministry of Information.[15] In 1942, British censors were empowered, using terms similar to the Swedish 1812 law, to remove anything 'calculated to create ill feeling between the United Nations or between them and a neutral country.'[16] In Germany, the spider at the centre of the Nazi propaganda web, Josef Goebbels, exercised close and tyrannical control over the domestic press: 'The Berliner Zeitung has committed a serious political error for the second time. Editor dismissed.'[17] He also dealt with overseas publications: 'Again ban a number of foreign newspapers. They are ruining my entire mood. Even when they dress themselves up as pro-German'.[18]

From this viewpoint, it is not at all surprising that the Germans had difficulty accepting that the Swedish government could not control the national press output and that criticism of Germany did not indicate some official shift from Sweden's neutral stance. Grafström was even asked in Berlin in 1942: 'Could you not at least legislate harsh penalties for a journalist who on repeated occasions refuses to correct himself?'[19] It was precisely these perceptions to which the UD was ultra-sensitive, a sensitivity which pervaded the Government. In the uncertainty surrounding Berlin's intentions, it was difficult for Sweden to know how far hostile Swedish press comment could influence decisions to act against Sweden either in trade or in military matters. Those considerations applied also to Moscow's view. In July 1941, Russian Minister Kollontay complained to Per Albin personally that recent press articles had been 'so hostile to the Soviet Union in their tone that the (Russian) Legation felt that they portended serious events between our countries', hence the Government's interest in removing all doubts about Sweden's stance. In their pragmatic but debatable view, temporary restrictions on freedom of expression were a small price to pay to shore up the democratically chosen policy of remaining out of the war. Some in the UD, such as Boheman and Grafström, however, felt that Sweden could stand up to the German pressure more firmly.[20] Grafström nevertheless was assiduous in ensuring that visiting German journalists were not exposed to British propaganda.[21]

Punishment, Seizure and 'Advice'

As early as 1933 two communist newspapers, *Arbetaren* and *Ny Dag*, had been successfully prosecuted under the 1812 legislation by the authorities for insulting Göring and the publishers received three and four months' prison sentences respectively. Frequently there was little that the Swedish authorities could do within the legislation, even if they wanted, as the UD pointed out to the numerous pre-war German complainants. There had not been censorship since 1845 and despite the continual urging of the German diplomats to prosecute, the UD usually told them that there was little prospect of a successful prosecution but generally undertook to speak to the editor as a response.[22]

Once the war had started, the activities of the Swedish media took on new importance in forming opinion domestically and signalling policy abroad, so their output was scrutinised with even closer intensity. When the German Minister zu Wied protested to Boheman on 16 September 1939 about the bias towards Britain in the Swedish coverage, Boheman wearily told him that the Western Allied representatives had shortly before made their protests about the bias towards Germany.[23] The anxiety about the phoney war further south was soon eclipsed in Sweden by the proximity of actual fighting on the country's eastern border when Russia invaded Finland in late November 1939. This meant that the Government's policy came under intense pressure from the activists who wanted intervention on the side of the Finns and from the opponents of 'adventurism' who feared being drawn into an unmanageable and un-winnable war, as well as from the Communists who sympathised with Russia. The Government was again forced to press the 1812 legislation into service. This law was used to prosecute on nineteen occasions in 1939, primarily against communist newspapers for articles critical of Finland but also against Ture Nerman, editor of *Trots Allt!* who received three months' imprisonment in May 1940 for an article headlined 'Hitler's Hell-machine' published in November 1939. Nerman had met Westman following publication to apologise for creating problems for the Government, which he supported. Westman responded by telling him that in his ideological crusade, he ought to avoid undermining the political base from which he campaigned.[24] The press had been warned.

As a result of the Winter War, *Radiotjänst* was soon involved in the conflicting pressures from the activists and their opponents. This position was characterised by its Director, Carl Dymling, as being 'between the hammer and the anvil'.[25] The 'Daily Poem' slot became an expression of solidarity with Finland due to the selection of Finnish poets but a huge controversy took place over the proposal on 18 December from pro-Finnish activists that *Radiotjänst* should devote one hour to readings from the works of Finland's national poet, J. L. Runeberg whose epic poetry included one text, *Fänrik Ståls sägner*, celebrating military heroism against the Russians during the 1809 conflict. The activists' proposal was made at a time when Per Albin and the newly formed Coalition Government were trying to cool the overheated situation while avoiding any commitment to Finland. Dymling attempted in vain to get guidance from the Government and in the febrile atmosphere, the newspapers seized on the case. The press transformed the issue, alleging that the non-existent programme had been cancelled and proceeded to focus on who had cancelled it, rumoured to be Per Albin himself. Dymling took the principled yet practical stance that *Radiotjänst* could not adopt an approach which diverged from that of the Government but added that while those in *Radiotjänst* could have 'warm hearts', it was their 'duty to maintain a cool head at the same time.'[26] This approach kept the anti-*Radiotjänst* criticism running against Dymling in letters and newspapers but his careful position shifted to reflect a more sympathetic stance towards the activists.[27] Finnish-themed programmes in speech and music proliferated as the Government became more confident that its limited support policy towards Finland was succeeding in convincing the doubters.

Agrarian Party Justice Minister Westman was responsible for bringing all prosecutions which perhaps explains the early bias against communist and syndicalist publications. The most favoured instrument for press control was confiscation of the edition in question rather than imprisonment of the publisher. This not only restricted the spread of the material but it also lay directly within Westman's own control and could take place without reference to the courts. For printed media, statistics show a steady build up of confiscations of newspapers, books and magazines to a peak in 1942. Between January 1940 and November 1943, 315 seizures took place, predominantly from the far-left wing press, of which 147 were personally initiated by Westman.[28] Less than 10 per cent were directed at the pro-Nazi press. One of the most notorious confiscations was in March 1942 which covered seventeen newspapers. They had all published the same syndicated article which described Gestapo torture of Norwegian prisoners. Westman appears to have preferred pre-emptive action rather than reacting to complaints by the foreign power, usually Germany. As fellow Minister Andersson noted 'It was Günther who ordered the confiscations and Westman who delivered them.' The transport ban only affected periodicals rather than newspapers and was invoked against six titles, of which five were anti-Nazi. The measure may in fact have had the opposite effect of its intention by popularising the banned periodicals while ambiguously not actually banning their sale.[29] The confiscations and transport bans were in any case more effective than attempting to prosecute editors under the 1812 publication law. In 1940, there were fifteen prosecutions but only three convictions.[30]

More influential perhaps was the activity of the SIS in guiding editors on what could be published. Over 300 'Grey Slips' were issued in the period between February 1940 and May 1945, the first coming out on 12 April 1940, barely three days after the German occupation of Norway and Denmark. It is clear from the subjects of the 'Grey Slips' that they were not simply confined to excluding information critical of Germany. They also acted to protect Sweden's position in the country's contacts with the warring nations and to restrict information that could limit the UD's freedom of action in negotiations. A critical Swedish press comment could be quoted to support the other side's argument. Contrary to the targets of confiscation and transport bans, namely press comment on events outside Sweden, the 'Grey Slips' were mainly directed at limiting reporting of aspects of internal Swedish security or humanitarian actions. Their content varied with the events of the war years. Subjects included Swedish military secrets, 'Leave Traffic', the Engelbrecht Division transit, refugees including Jews, 'Safe-Conduct Traffic', the Norwegian ships in Göteborg and the rescue of Danish Jews (out of concern for endangering the rescue operation).[31] Further topics concerned the Norwegian and Danish 'Police Troops' in Sweden and the 1945 Red Cross rescue operation from Germany.[32] Later, as further regulations were issued covering what the press could *not* report, the requirement for 'Grey Slips' decreased: over 100 were issued in 1940 but less than fifty in 1941. Subjects which were forbidden in case they provided intelligence included troop mobilisation, military procurement, military accidents, espionage and sabotage. Care had to be exercised with reports about rationing and supplies in case hoarding was inadvertently encouraged. Sensitive military and political subjects were off-limits. For example, Swedish volunteers to Finland were not to be reported as were negotiations with the belligerents.[33] The British MTB ball-bearings collection from Lysekil in 1943 was also subject to a news blackout – by arrangement between the *UD* and Minister Mallet.[34]

The restrictive measures blanketed Sweden's freedom of expression and although they were applied to a relatively small number of publications, they caused a build-up of resentment among the press. When German pressure began to recede between 1942 and 1943, Günther came in for strong criticism in the *Riksdag* where the press was well represented among the members by editors and journalists. Westman had stoutly defended the Government actions in February 1942 in a meeting with 160 journalists but noted that when the discussion was opened, they offered only, 'insignificant skirmishes.'[35] The number of confiscations fell markedly during 1943 and after November none took place without a hearing. Westman had to retire due to ill-health in late summer of 1943 and with his replacement by Bergquist, the press moved towards a more self-regulatory basis in 1944. Yet many of the press themselves were intimately involved in the new bodies which were set up to influence press 'responsibility' such as the Press Committee (*Pressrådet* later *Pressnämnden*). In 1940, thirty-eight editors, of whom 75 per cent were Social Democrats, were members of the *Riksdag* that approved the transport ban and the censorship legislation. The large daily newspapers were also linked closely to the parties which composed the Coalition Government and so it was the communist press that bore the brunt of the prosecutions, confiscations, and transport bans.

The actual supply of foreign news to the Swedish press was the responsibility of the national press agency, *TT*, which also was solely responsible for the radio news items on the single-channel *Radiotjänst*. The State Information Board (*SIS*) closely monitored its output.[36] *Radiotjänst*'s chief Dymling also became a member of *SIS* which placed the radio medium under Government control, as '*SIS*'s hostage' according to Dymling's critics. Yet in February 1941, *Radiotjänst* hosted a discussion on press freedom that included not only Westman but one of his vocal critics.[37] *Radiotjänst* was officially independent but like its British counterpart, the BBC, it maintained open channels with Government. The *Radiotjänst* chief's membership of the *SIS* continued when Dymling was succeeded by Yngve Hugo in 1942. Although there are no recorded instances of *SIS* putting pressure on *Radiotjänst* to toe the Government line, membership of *SIS* may have promoted cautiousness, loyalty, and self-censorship in *Radiotjänst*. Hugo, more than Dymling, saw *Radiotjänst* as part of the national establishment and the *Radiotjänst* role as being a 'new weapon on the Home Front.'[38] This view was

FIGURE 8 Swedish newspapers, 1944. The Swedish press generally followed the Government's guidance on restraint and self-censored sensitive subjects likely to cause German protests. A small number of papers across the political spectrum were impounded by the authorities when that guidance was ignored, action which threatened the freedom of the press. These June 1944 posters cover the German evacuation of Rome, the Eastern Front, and a scare-story from *Dagsposten*, a German-financed mouthpiece, predicting a Soviet republic in bordering Lapland.

consistent with his presence on the *SIS*'s *Folkberedskap* ('Citizens' Cultural Mobilisation Section'). The radio weapon was a powerful one: in 1943, about 70 per cent of the Swedish population had access to a radio and when surveyed, 80 per cent of those listened to the 7 p.m. news. The other programmes secured 50 per cent of the audience who typically listened for between two and a half and three hours a day.[39] The Germans of course saw this successful radio medium as an opportunity to infiltrate and subvert the *Radiotjänst* news, current affairs and artistic agendas but here they were quite unsuccessful in gaining a foothold compared, as will be seen, with their attack on press and cultural life in Sweden. *Radiotjänst* remained cautiously neutral in its output during the period of German hegemony and gradually pro-western thereafter. Its adherence to Scandinavian solidarity in its programming throughout was remarkable considering the political minefield of its neighbours' circumstances, both to the west and the east.[40] However, some Danes regarded *Radiotjänst* broadcasts in mid-1941 as 'colourless'.[41]

As we have seen, the system of editorial 'advice' from a government information service coupled with measures against recalcitrant editors was not dissimilar to the British press. Interfering with the press is a risky venture for politicians at any time as the resentment which arises from any restriction, however well intentioned or based on national imperative, eventually surfaces in the very media which have been constrained. It is a feature of the Swedish wartime experience that some decisions to restrain the press were taken democratically while others were simply an extension of executive powers. The restraint of adverse press comment about Germany and the Nazis was a controversial addition to Sweden's concession policy towards Germany in the years 1940–4 and one which deeply affected one of the pillars of the country's democracy.[42] The result was summed up by *TT* chief Gustaf Reuterskiöld as: 'The truth, nothing but the truth, but not the whole truth.'[43]

German Propaganda Activity

On 14 November 1939, Joseph Goebbels noted in his diary:

> Dr Draeger (chief of the Nordic Liaison Office, *Nordische Verbindungsstelle*) and [. . .] report on their trip to Scandinavia. The mood there is one of slight desperation and increasing leaning towards England. London has a powerful attraction for these

peoples. Up there, one feels as if one is on English soil. We must produce much more propaganda against this. Particularly in the field of culture. I issue appropriate instructions.[44]

The Nazi Propaganda Minister recognised that as far as Scandinavia was concerned, the German message was up against powerful and deep-rooted Anglo-Saxon culture. The Germans had put a much higher priority on propaganda than the British as Press Attaché Peter Tennant observed first-hand when he arrived in Stockholm.[45] The organised nature of the pre-war impetus from Berlin to influence Swedish opinion contrasted strongly with the responses from both Germany's enemies and Sweden itself. The Swedish view of the German approach was 'smygpropaganda' – covert propaganda. This has been described by Åke Thulstrup as a concerted endeavour to secure and improve Nazi Germany's image and promote its messages in Sweden by influencing Swedish attitudes.[46] These actions included financial support to sympathetic newspapers, a torrent of publications, recruitment of high profile Swedes to the Nazi cause, creation of organisations to encourage Nazi sympathies – often disguised as cultural bodies, exchange visits between Germany and Sweden and specific media campaigns.[47] Thulstrup also noted that the difference between the pre-war German effort and the wartime one was of approach rather than intensity. During the war, Germans used every means at their disposal to influence the Swedes, from the familiar diplomatic protest against criticism to Swedish language radio broadcasts.[48] Their onslaught targeted Swedish hearts as well as Swedish minds but although German propaganda was prolific, it was fundamentally unsuccessful. German Minister Zu Wied's successor at the German Legation, Hans Thomsen, was forthright at the end of 1943 in blaming the influence of repressive German policy in Norway for alienating Swedes and nullifying German propaganda efforts.[49]

The Legation had been the origin of several press campaigns to influence Swedish opinion, for example to ensure Swedish 'strict neutrality' in order to maintain continuity of iron ore exports to Germany and in 1941 to stimulate interest in a racially and politically cohesive German commonwealth (*storrum*) in which Sweden would occupy a privileged position following the anticipated triumph over the Soviet Union. Later, there was a campaign to whip up support, and even participation, for the 'crusade against bolshevism' on the Eastern Front but the vigour of the propaganda effort declined in the later part of 1943 as bitter defeat stared Germany in the face. Less notable than the press campaigns was the massive volume of printed material which the Germans were able to transport to Sweden and distribute there. The bi-monthly picture magazine, *Signal*, one of the most important and successful German publications from 1941 to 1945 perhaps due to its military content, contained other articles which reflected the anti-semitic and propaganda objectives of its publishers.[50] In addition, there was a torrent of books with titles in the style of: 'The Führer and his people: Adolf Hitler in all areas of public life' and 'War Criminals – eighty Jewish confessions of war crimes.' None of these were likely to persuade Swedes to join the Nazi cause but they undoubtedly sustained those who already had.

German 'Front' Publications

There had been a scheme to buy into the Swedish press as early as 1933, an idea which was floated between the Stockholm Legation and Berlin unsuccessfully again in 1934 and 1936. More productive were German attempts to secure influence over editorial policy by covert financial support. There were concerted approaches using the German advertising firm *ALA* to channel advertising by German-connected companies towards certain titles and away from others. Unsurprisingly, the *GHT* was among the first to suffer. With *Dagsposten*, the newspaper of the extreme right-wing *SNF* Party, the Germans spent considerable sums in order to secure a dependable Swedish mouthpiece which printed under direction from the German Legation. In 1945, the publishers were tried in Stockholm for receiving foreign subsidies but only one was convicted.[51] Material favourable to Germany was also 'placed' in the form of articles and books. In 1939, the Legation succeeded in placing sixty-five articles in two months but this became more difficult as the nature of German intentions emerged. News agencies were targeted because their material fed into the Swedish newspapers and fact-based articles were easiest to get published. The Germans did not scruple to disguise the origin of these pieces in order to mislead the editors. German-inspired Swedish books were also camouflaged.

Cultivated Contacts

The Nazis placed a high value on developing their regime's contacts with prominent Swedes but the result was meagre. Goebbels wrote despairingly in his diary on 14 November 1939 that 'Only Bengt Berg (a pro-Nazi, prominent entomologist) and Sven Hedin are for us. The latter with reservations. Hedin fears our cooperation with Moscow'[52] Hedin was indeed his own man and being partly Jewish, his involvement with the anti-semitic regime was a triumph of his Russophobia and his Zionism over the evidence of Nazi persecution. Göring had promised him a national home for the Jews. It is difficult not to regard 'useful idiots' like Hedin as immaterial, but such prominent adherence to Germany surely strengthened public perceptions that the Nazis were on a rising tide of success.

The Germans particularly courted the Swedish officer corps in order both to overawe them with German might and to win them over to the inevitability of German victory. The Swedish military were treated to battlefield tours and other study trips during the early war years.[53] Somewhat higher profile was the award of the Great Cross of the German Order of the Eagle to the Commander-in-Chief, General Olof Thörnell in October 1940 with the scroll signed by Hitler and counter-signed by Ribbentrop. The resolutely anti-Russian Thörnell, in his speech of thanks expressed a hope for closer relations with Germany.[54] Such open recognition created dismay among the Swedish public. One concerned observer reported: 'That the highest commander of the German military is so familiar with our defences that he is prompted to award a distinction to *our* highest commander is something no one understands.'[55]

'Cover' Organisations

Alongside the shadowy *Nordische Verbindungsstelle*, the Nordic Liaison Office of Goebbels' Propaganda Ministry, there were other cover organisations which the Germans used to influence Swedish opinion.[56] Some pre-dated the Nazis like the *Svensk-tyska förening* (*der Schwedisch-Deutschen Vereinigung*, 1913), the Lübeck-based *Nordische Gesellschaft* (Nordic Society 1921) which later came under the wing of leading Nazi ideologue Alfred Rosenberg, and *Sveriges Nationella Förbund* (1915). Others were founded following the Nazi takeover like *Riksföreningen Sverige-Tyskland* based in Lund. *Nordische Gesellschaft* (*NG*) had been formed to promote German-Scandinavian relations, hold conferences and sponsor 'cultural evenings'. One notable member of *Riksföreningen Sverige-Tyskland* was the prominent national-romantic composer, Kurt Atterberg who was also a member of the International Composers Council founded by

Richard Strauss.⁵⁷ This was seen by the German Nazis as a bulwark against modernist music and Atterberg was a prominent critic of the modernity of Sweden-based Jewish composer Moses Pergament. The reality was that these German 'cultural institutions' mainly rallied those intellectuals who were already inclined to the Nazi regime and its values. Few converts were made but the existence of such bodies provided a focal point for fellow-travellers and was symbolic of a German Nazi cultural presence in Sweden. Perhaps the highpoint of this effort was the German exhibition of literature and graphic art which was staged in Stockholm in January 1941.

British Propaganda Activity

Publications proved one of the many areas in which the British and later the Allied propaganda effort were deficient. This was the result of transport difficulties that intensified following the Skagerrak blockade in 1940. Nor were the British as well prepared as Germany. Peter Tennant has described the chaos surrounding the belated establishment in spring 1939 of the British propaganda effort to Scandinavia.⁵⁸ What the British underestimated was the extent of Swedish media regulation which constrained the British propaganda effort because of the German reaction to unfavourable Swedish press coverage. British propaganda organisation was similar to that of Germany with central Ministerial direction and delivery through the Stockholm Legation. However material could not easily be sent from Britain after mid-1940 and so was slow to reach the Legation. Problems of resource existed despite priority at British Foreign Minister level. A senior Foreign Office official wrote to the MOI in May 1941 'that he (Eden) considers that the political situation renders it desirable to make every effort to combat German propaganda in Sweden'. In addition to resource problems, the Legation had to contend with the Swedish authorities. An early casualty was Harold Nicolson's book *Why Britain is at War*, withdrawn in July 1940, which Günther claimed was due to 'abusive statements' at variance with Swedish law.⁵⁹ But Günther himself was also under pressure to expel Tennant for distributing the key British propaganda publication '*Nyheter från Storbritannien*' (News from Britain).⁶⁰ This was despite Tennant's care to avoid action by the authorities.⁶¹ Boheman even tried to influence British Minister Mallet, saying propaganda 'was not needed to convince the public of Germany's iniquity and German propaganda was falling on the stoniest ground and having no effect whatever.' The Foreign Office found this line particularly unconvincing.[62] Mallet and the Foreign Office took a dim view of the new censorship proposals.[63] 'Press, not for the suppression of offensive anti-British attacks . . . but for the greatest possible freedom for both sides. The argument in favour of this policy is of course that HMG [His Majesty's Government] have more to gain from the exposure of German iniquities than they have to lose by the publication of anti-British material'.[64] British policy on Swedish censorship was clear.

British Publications

An assessment of delivery rather than content demonstrates the success of the Legation's activities. Tennant concluded that by late 1943: 'Our propaganda in Sweden would now appear to have achieved its main objectives.'[65] On a visit to London in November 1943, he agreed with the Foreign Office that he would now work through the Swedish press to end Swedish 'psychological neutrality' and to deliver 'black propaganda' to Germany for the PWE (Political Warfare Executive).[66] 'Nyheter från Storbritannien' resulted from Tennant's initiative and demonstrated the Legation's ability to influence Swedish opinion. N.-E. Ekblad of the SIS reported to the Riksdag's Konstitutionutskott (Constitutional Committee) in May 1942 that 'The most important Anglo-Saxon [sic] publication in Swedish is . . . the weekly 'Nyheter från Storbritannien': with its 250,000 copies, it is undeniably the most distributed foreign propaganda organ in Sweden'.[67] Tennant believed in 1942 that '(demand for) 'Nyheter' is an excellent barometer of public opinion in Sweden.'[68] The Foreign Office agreed.[69] By 1945 circulation had reached 500,000.[70]

British Council, Speakers and Visits

The 1943 SIS report referred to the British Council's 'remarkably effective British cultural propaganda in our country'.[71] The German exhibition of literature and graphic art mounted in early 1941 was a propaganda coup for the Germans yet a few months later when Bagge attended the opening of the British Council offices in late 1941, he was severely criticised by a Berlin spokesman. As well as demonstrating the propaganda importance of the British Council, the Swedish response to this criticism is significant. Richert, the Swedish Minister in Berlin, was instructed to protest about this attack on a member of the Government showing that the UD was not completely supine at a time when the Germans were firmly in the ascendant. Mallet wrote to the Foreign Office in early 1942 to 'remind' them of an earlier commitment to supply speakers to lecture in Sweden.[72] This started a hare running and the Foreign Office file notes illustrate the problems of wartime organisation and resources. 'We have had the most awful trouble trying to get Sir K Clark off to Sweden... the air service has been practically paralysed'.[73] Despite this, the MOI eventually succeeded in lining up T. S. Eliot and Leslie Howard; Eliot went but Howard did not.[74] Despite the difficulties, the Legation was able to support the British Council and maintain a flow of speakers who played an important role in influencing Swedish public opinion.[75]

Film and Other Media

Film propaganda, free photos for the press, and shop window displays were also organised by the Legation.[76] BBC radio broadcasts were made and Tennant ensured they were advertised in 'Nyheter från Storbritannien'.[77] Although reception was poor, by 1944, the BBC had 33 per cent of the 'listening market'.[78,79] By 1944, half a million cinemagoers saw British newsreels weekly.[80] Films were subject to interference from the authorities but one episode showed the Foreign Office unusually agreeing with a Swedish decision. In late 1941, the film 'Pimpernel Smith' was withdrawn by the Legation at Sweden's request. It starred Leslie Howard, cast as a professor turned spy, which ridiculed the Germans as 'uncultured, humourless, ungentlemanly and uncivilised.'[81] Grafström asked Montague-Evans not to show it again in public, conceding that it could continue to be shown in private. Montague-Evans thought that 'far more advantageous to us than persisting in a policy which might end [in] forbidding all private film entertainments'.[82] The continuation of private showings by the Legation led to one guest who saw 'Pimpernel Smith' telling his half-sister that he also would like to save people from the Nazis. His name was Raoul Wallenberg.[83] British propaganda from the Legation had reached out to influence a young Swede who went on to save thousands of Jewish lives in Budapest in 1944–5 before losing his own at the hands of Stalin's secret police.[84]

Sweden's Propaganda Response

When the SIS was created in early 1940 against the background of national military crisis and rumour, it was charged by the government with quickly organising a secretive *Sektionen för kulturell folkberedskap* ('Citizens' Cultural Mobilisation Section' or *Folkberedskap*) which would become one of the most controversial areas of SIS activity. The *Folkberedskap* was an easy target for the press already smarting over the main role of the SIS as a 'Censor authority' or 'Propaganda Ministry'. It was intended to work alongside and support other organisations, local authorities and government departments. One inspiration for this initiative was the Finnish response to the Russian invasion in 1939 and the role of the Finnish organisation, *Andliga Befolkningsskydd* (Citizens' Spiritual Defence) in providing human and practical support to a population struggling with the effects of the war.[85]

Moral Resistance

The *Folkberedskap* remit was to 'promote the Swedish people's intellectual and moral resistance' and to survey popular opinion on different topics: in other words, a citizens' Home Guard against external propaganda combined with Mass Observation.[86] A Board of eight figures from Swedish public life, including an army major, was appointed under Chairman Professor Sven Tunberg.[87] The *Folkberedskap* swiftly swung into action by appointing 2,100 district representatives, mainly teachers (52 per cent) and priests (16 per cent), to act as a communication channel and an opinion-monitoring group for the SIS.[88] These appointees were selected from nominations supplied by the chairmen of council educational committees and vetted by military security. *Folkberedskap* also nominated approximately thirty county representatives who convened every August or September from 1941 to 1944 to review the work of the district representatives. The district representatives were selected on the basis of their experience in education, being 'respected and trusted in the district' and their ability to represent pure Swedish interests rather than any evident talents as organisers or communicators. This meant that the appointees were of varied ability for the dual roles that the SIS and the government expected of them. The press were fairly hostile, with one leading article describing the initiative as: 'Nothing but pure drivel', but such comments also reflected a wider unease among those educationalists and others who felt excluded.[89]

The moral resistance work that they were expected to do was driven by *SIS* instructions to the representatives suggesting that they organise activities and events to strengthen national solidarity. The suggestions comprised lecture evenings, study circles, poster campaigns, competitions and other initiatives with local voluntary organisations and sports clubs.[90] Representatives were also encouraged to set up local 'Information Committees' ('*Upplysningsnämnder*'). They were not helped by the volume and content of *SIS* material which could be, 'worthless or purely derisory.'[91] One further limitation was that the representatives did not have a budget so they had to either make do with what resources they had or seek funds from unwilling and suspicious local authorities. One such rejected application to Västra Frölunda's local authority (near Göteborg) leaked out to the *GHT* which mercilessly lampooned the *SIS*. 'God protect us from more guardians than we already have.'[92] The unelected representatives were of course in an exposed position and despite their fervour to enthuse the nation, they found it difficult to gain attention and were often met with suspicion and condescension by more established community leaders and politicians who questioned the appointee's right to represent moral resistance.[93]

Their other main role, as monitors of public opinion, required somewhat less cooperation from the community but an equal amount of unpaid effort and commitment. The *SIS* surveyed opinion by sending out questionnaires for representatives to respond to and return. These responses were analysed and synthesised by *SIS* officials into reports which were then circulated to the government and military. There was, however, little remarkable or unsettling in these *SIS* reports. For example, in 1941, 1,194 representatives or 82 per cent responded that despite the war, the popular mood was calm and stable, 9 per cent thought that the situation was unsatisfactory (due to mobilisation and shortages) and only 1 per cent thought that the mood was poor. Reports from 1942 are notable for 'good mood' and 'exceptional solidarity' though one county representative thought that the public were ignoring the realities of the surrounding war. The few grumbles that were expressed in 1942 were due to food rationing and the same was also true for 1943.[94] Most of the representatives seem to have taken the task of responding to the *SIS* questionnaires seriously and these records, which Kurt Lindal has carefully analysed, present a fascinating insight to Sweden in wartime.[95]

Unsurprisingly, the issues which the representatives highlighted in their reports on public opinion concerned the concessions to the Germans, in particular German access to Swedish territory and exports. To these were added: grumbling about military conscription and rationing, trust in the government and its policies, increasing sympathies for the occupied Norwegians and Danes, and decreasing sympathy for Finland. At the senior level, county representatives agreed at their annual conference in 1941 that a calm mood pervaded the country. Some even thought that it was, 'unsettlingly calm' or 'completely peacetime oriented.' The main discord was over the rationing system, where the operation by the Government was thought by some delegates to have created conflict between farmers and the rest of the population.

SIS officials were not satisfied that they were getting a true picture from reports and that the representatives were sufficiently in touch with dissenting opinion. Neither did the authorities gain much from the SIS summaries except that the mood was calm across the country. This presumably confirmed the impressions gained by the Coalition Government members when they discussed the public mood with their local networks. There were two further subsidiary roles for the *Folkberedskap* representatives in the country. One was to identify and counter damaging rumours and the other was to act as a communication network in case of invasion and occupation.

Countering Rumours

Per Albin had openly criticised the 'devilish rumourmongers' in a radio talk in April 1940. He perhaps had in mind a damaging rumour then circulating in Stockholm, which was taken seriously by the authorities there, that a group of army officers were planning a coup.[96] Rumours were regarded as possibly originating from 'black propaganda' directed at Sweden by a belligerent to mislead the population and so were treated very seriously. The *Folkberedskap* representatives were speedily pressed into action and in August 1940, they were urged to report any rumour in their district which was then plotted on a map in *Folkberedskap* offices and if serious enough, countered with a briefing sent out to the representatives for them to disseminate. At the beginning, most rumours concerned rationing and the belief that scarce Swedish food was being exported to Germany. Next, there was a shift to military matters with rumours about deficiencies in Swedish defence, German decorations for Swedish officers and the presence of German troops in Finland.

The counter-rumour arrangements became more organised when in January 1941, the 'Inquiry Office' (*Frågebyrå* or *IFB*) was set up under the army major on the *Folkberedskap* Board, Arvid Eriksson. He had been the public relations chief for the armed forces and through his frequent radio broadcasts, he became known as the 'radio major'. One of Eriksson's broadcasts would shortly be at the centre of a diplomatic row with Germany but he mobilised the *IFB* into a rumour monitoring and response operation. The information on rumours from *Folkberedskap* representatives and others was analysed, reported secretly to the relevant authorities and then classified for urgency of response. Clarification and rebuttal responses were initially circulated in a briefing entitled, 'Why? – Because', for *Folkberedskap* representatives, community leaders, and selected officials, sometimes also extended to media representatives for radio and newspaper coverage. Two other briefing series aimed at different audiences: '*Complaints and Rumours*' and '*Questions and Answers*', soon followed and these created a certain amount of overlap and confusion because some of the material was classified for restricted circulation. Also, *Folkberedskap* representatives complained that slow and inappropriate responses from the *IFB* undermined their authority and role as community communicators.[97] Bureaucracy had strangled initiative in the rumour-filled spring of 1941 when the Swedish forces mobilised. Per Albin, Eriksson and even Defence Minister Sköld went on air to quell two rumours: ultimatums to Sweden from all sides and suppression of news of military action on Swedish territory. Eriksson criticised pointless speculation while Per Albin urged everyone to be on guard against rumour. These public pronouncements, particularly Eriksson's, were credited with calming nerves and rumours never again reached the same intensity.

If the War Comes

The remaining role of the *Folkberedskap* representatives was to act as a communications hub in the event of a communications breakdown due to invasion or occupation. This role was variously envisaged as 'social support' on the successful Finnish model, requiring representatives to inform stricken families about help that was available and how to get it, as well as calming panic and averting civil disorder. It was a tall order that some representatives understandably felt unable to fulfil. They had signed up to organise communication and were now expected to marshal panicky civilians.[98] Following further discussion in SIS, the idea was dropped in August 1941. Attempting to extend to a 'social support' dimension revealed some fundamental shortcomings in the *Folkberedskap* voluntary representatives' position and resources and probably contributed to its proponent, Yngve Hugo of *Radiotjänst*, departing from *Folkberedskap*.

Concern over how to respond to a military invasion rumbled on and by the end of 1942, the military had developed resistance plans which expected all citizens to assist in defence, whether as conscripts or civilians. This expectation was repeated on radio in January 1943 by Per Albin. Fearing that refugees would prevent military forces from moving freely as in the 1940 German offensives, it was decided to prepare guidance for civilians, which was published in July 1943 by *Folkberedskap* as a booklet entitled, '*If the war comes. Guidelines for the country's citizens in the event of war.*' There were over two million printed for extensive distribution to every household as well as to officials and authorities. *Folkberedskap* representatives were urged to assist in publicising the contents. With fighting talk, it defiantly warned: 'Every proclamation that resistance should cease is false. Sweden intends to defend itself, can defend itself, and shall defend itself.' Press reaction was positive and the booklet was studied carefully by its readership. One group which in vain sought enlightenment on its role during an invasion was the *Folkberedskap*. No directives came from the military to guide it.

At the end of 1940, alarmed by the amount of propaganda which poured into Sweden, *Folkberedskap* had surveyed its scope and content as well as asking the representatives for their views. Arising from concerns over the negative effect on Sweden's will to resist, Eriksson was encouraged by *Radiotjänst*'s Dymling to broadcast on the subject, and this was agreed by SIS chief Tunberg, not without concerns. The broadcast lambasted all propaganda, urging: 'Do not engage yourself passionately for German or British interests but act only with Sweden's interests before you.' Little wonder that an SIS colleague thought that one of the major's talks contributed more to Swedish counter-propaganda than the whole of the *Folkberedskap* effort.[99] Even Mallet in his report on the talk noted 'for every criticism directed against belligerent propaganda in general there are three or four shafts aimed solely at the Germans.'[100] The Germans were quick to respond and Military Attaché von Uthmann's protests to Commander-in-chief Thörnell led to Eriksson's removal to take up new duties on Gotland. The Major had occupied a comfortable grey area between military and civil control. Von Uthmann optimistically regarded the Swedish reaction to his protests as denoting the army's 'positive stance to Germany and its desire for cooperation between the two forces.'[101]

'Un-Swedish' Propaganda

Foreign propaganda continued to feature heavily on the SIS agenda and following Eriksson's talk, an SIS official, N-E. Ekblad, proposed a raft of preventive counter-propaganda measures: 'The public must be made aware that something is being done.'[102] SIS chief Tunberg took the initiative by suggesting the formation of a secret committee to deal with the issue which in June 1941 gave rise to the 'Coordination Section for Counter-Propaganda', commonly known as the Propaganda Office (Propagandabyrå) under Ekblad. There had been a mini-tussle over the control of the Propagandabyrå between SIS and Folkberedskap which resulted in Ekblad's group being semi-detached from both, rather like Major Eriksson's position. This detachment allowed a welcome degree of autonomy but with no one owning their activities, the Propagandabyrå became vulnerable to later criticism. The Propagandabyrå remit was to survey all 'un-Swedish' (osvensk) propaganda and passively report the comprehensive findings to authorities like the Justice Ministry and the military hierarchy. Ten reports were submitted between 1941 and 1944 for the authorities to note and act as they believed necessary. The tidy bureaucratic approach of sectioning each report by ideology and media, first Nazi then communist, then Western Allies, led to what Wijk describes as absurd categorisations when Swedish papers which criticised Nazi ideology found themselves categorised as 'propaganda supporting Western Allies'.[103] But the political and public mood in 1941 favoured strong action against propaganda which threatened Swedish interests.[104]

For the Propagandabyrå, defining 'un-Swedish' was the first problem. 'Un-Swedish' material could influence Swedish citizens to take a non-neutral position. The Propagandabyrå next classified propaganda into three categories: tolerable, politically undesirable, and morally offensive. The Propagandabyrå thought that the Swedish public should not be exposed to these last two categories, thereby arriving at a policy which conveniently responded to German sensitivities and disadvantaged British efforts to expose the Nazi racial agenda and brutal behaviour in occupied Europe. Ekblad continued to press for stiffer action against foreign propaganda and in autumn 1941 proposed that all propaganda not consistent with Swedish interests should be restricted. While he further proposed that organisations behind such propaganda, Nazi and communist, should be dissolved and banned, he also exposed himself by targeting the Western Allies. In a memo, he stated that Anglo-Saxon propaganda was comprehensive, effective and superior to the German. Western Allies were infiltrating their ideals to the Swedish people. The German propaganda was less effective and obviously cruder. Anglo-American propaganda was 'dangerous' because the Swedes did not notice how vulnerable they were to such indoctrination.

These conclusions were deemed so important that Ekblad was called upon to present his thoughts to the *Riksdag*'s *Konstitutionsutskott* in May 1942, then placed in an anonymous newspaper article in March 1943 and further published in Autumn 1943 in an anonymous pamphlet by 'Spectator' (actually Ekblad and a *Propagandabyrå* colleague). The row was immense and immediate, with Ekblad, by this time a diplomat in Venezuela, revealed as the joint author of opinions that were now at variance with the public mood of support for the Western Allies. The 'Spectator affair' grew into a full frontal press attack on *SIS* throughout 1944 focusing on issues such as why the *Propagandabyrå* had not been so determined in its pursuit of Nazi propaganda fronts like the German-financed *Dagsposten*. The row led to political support for *SIS* funding being withdrawn and it was wound up in December 1944.

Swedish Propaganda

With the Germans protesting about Swedish press coverage almost daily and the continuing controversies over foreign propaganda, the Swedish authorities had their work cut out in 1940–3 to contain threats and manage information in the country. However, there were three notable Swedish propaganda efforts which deserve recognition for what they set out to do. These were the creation of 'The Swedish Way of Life' course (1941), the publication in English of 'Sweden, A Wartime Survey' (1942), and the 'Mrs Loyalty' campaign (1944) to attract women into manufacturing industry.

'The Swedish Way of Life' (*Den svenska livsformen*) was a *Folkberedskap* counter-propaganda initiative born in February 1941 from its roots in the well-established national adult-education and correspondence school (distance-learning) movements. The *Folk-*

beredskap chief, Ragnar Lund wrote to Defence Minister Sköld proposing that a course could provide material to rebut defeatist and foreign propaganda which was felt to be damaging to the Swedish will to resist. Planning proceeded and in July 1941, the course structure was approved when the *Folkberedskap* representatives were asked to stimulate advance interest. It comprised five course modules in correspondence school format: examples of the development of the Swedish way in history; current democracy in political life; national organisations and movements; social security and responsibility; and finally the Swedish point of view and democracy. Over the next three years, just over 30,000 Swedes took this course which, for an SIS initiative, was well-received in the press. This was a conscious counter-propaganda endeavour which was perhaps too little, in that its uptake was disappointing, and too late to respond to the demands of the early war period. Also, its appeal to Swedishness was perhaps somewhat eclipsed by many of the more emotionally based campaigns, such as those for defence loans, which contrasted with the drier, academic content of the course. Yet in the view of the course director, despite the absence of clear success, it had been useful. [105]

Arid discourse certainly characterised 'Sweden, A Wartime Survey', published by the UD in 1942 that followed on from a similar publication aimed at Germany a year earlier. It was the most concrete instance of Sweden attempting propaganda aimed at the Western Allies. It boasted twenty-five chapters, some of whose titles would not appear misplaced in a Soviet Five-Year Plan. The titles of the '*Survey*' chapters covered three main Swedish features: institutions – for example 'King Gustav V', the economy – for instance 'Sweden's Fuel Supply' and culture and media such as 'Fine Arts and the Theatre'. The '*Survey*' was also meticulously even-handed, with twenty mentions of Germany compared to twenty-two mentions of Britain, most in connection with trade and cultural matters. From the content, the intention appears to have been to create a type of 'Swedish Way of Life' primer for English-speaking readers (presumably journalists, politicians and officials), which implied affinity with Anglo-Saxon institutions and values and a longing for a resumption of communication westwards. Tricky questions were partly touched on defensively (iron ore exports) or not at all (transit concessions). No comment on its reception has been found in British archives.

The '*Mrs Loyalty*' (*Fru Lojal*) campaign of 1944 was aimed at an altogether different audience, the Swedish married woman. Due to military conscription, the shortage of manpower in Swedish industry was acute and one solution was to recruit married women. It was judged important by the Employment Commission (SAK) and the unions to aim for married rather than single women to promote the smooth return to post-war 'normal employment' for the homecoming men. Married woman were patronisingly assumed to yearn humbly for home and family.[106] To promote this recruitment drive, a film was produced with a representative recruit, 'Mrs Loyalty' whose allegiance was primarily given to the nation as a reserve worker when the need arose. The film made it clear that she was temporarily replacing a man and would receive an initial training course to prepare her for work on the factory floor. The image of the diligent housewife swapping the cooker for the lathe was memorable but did not result in married women signing up so much as the unmarried younger woman who blended loyalty with emancipation and left home to secure an independent living. The 'Mrs Loyalty' campaign unwittingly promoted social mobility in wartime Sweden.[107]

MORALE AND PROPAGANDA

As the SIS had found, Swedish morale held up remarkably well during the war. The reality was that most of the durable features of 'The Swedish Way of Life' had been laid down years before with such measures as the universal vote, a representative Riksdag, the Social Democratic vision of Folkhemmet personified by Per Albin, the introduction of unemployment benefit in 1934 and pensions in 1935–7. These initiatives linked powerfully to an equitable rationing system as well as a constitutional monarchy that bonded the past with the present to provide a focal point for national sentiment. The lack of inter-war electoral success for the Nazi and Communist parties demonstrated that the seeds of foreign ideologies fell on stony ground due to an absence of widespread discontent and foreshadowed the fact that the fertiliser of their wartime propaganda primarily nurtured only those shoots which had already taken root.[108] The entrenched democratic ideals of Swedish political life related more easily to the western democracies than to the totalitarian states and the results of the three wartime Riksdag elections demonstrated confidence in the Coalition Government's conduct as well as a general rejection of totalitarianism.[109]

Despite press freedom being one of the icons of democracy, the Coalition Government's curbs on the most outspoken publishers seem to have been reluctantly accepted by most politicians and the general population as a humiliating price to be paid for restraining a potential cause of German aggression while they were in the military ascendant.[110] The reassuring signal that these curbs sent to the Germans was far from the capitulation of free expression to the Nazis that has since been implied by some commentators.[111] The Swedish public were fully aware of the threat which Hitler's and Stalin's ideologies posed to Swedish democracy and the brutality which their regimes imposed on their Balto-Scandinavian neighbours. Swedish interests would not have been served by press coverage which could have been interpreted as a Swedish policy shift against Germany or Russia by the unpredictable ideologues in Berlin and Moscow. The Government's primary duty was to protect its citizens from aggression and press freedom was correctly regarded as secondary. Sweden would not risk war only to defend a free press and its pragmatic politicians regarded public expression of views about the Nazis, which paradoxically they shared, as needless grandstanding from a position of vulnerability.

Ironically, given the resources which the State devoted to containing foreign propaganda, it appears that propaganda influence on Swedish attitudes was secondary to that of military victory and defeat in the theatres of war. The zenith of Nazi military success and the possibility of a long-term German hegemony in Europe caused even trenchant believers in democratic Sweden to re-evaluate their stance in order to adapt to a situation which Sweden could do nothing to influence.[112] This eventuality gave way to the expectation of German defeat after Stalingrad in early 1943 which removed some of the self-imposed press constraints but took little account of the capacity which an increasingly irrational German leadership retained to damage Sweden economically as well as militarily. The Swedish public looked for material which confirmed its preferences for a western democratic future and the cascade of well-produced Nazi invective could not stem that demand. The Swedish leadership in the meantime was turning to new opportunities to demonstrate its positive credentials to the world which the German retreat opened up. One of these was humanitarian assistance.

Notes

1. Quoted in Thulstrup, Med lock och pock, p. 19.
2. Lindqvist, Drömmar och verklighet, p. 362.
3. Quoted in Thulstrup, Med lock och pock, p. 14.

4. Ibid. p. 18.
5. Isaksson, Per Albin, p. 367.
6. Boheman, På vakt, p. 16.
7. Dahlberg, I Sverige under 2:a världskriget, p. 222.
8. Flyghed, Rättsstat i kris, p. 62.
9. Grafström, Anteckningar, 23 May 1940.
10. Flyghed, Rättsstat i kris, pp. 166–8.
11. Wahlbäck, Regeringen och kriget, p. 129.
12. Flyghed, Rättsstat i kris, pp. 173.
13. Ibid. p. 193.
14. Calder, The People's War: Britain 1939–1945, pp. 246 & 288.
15. Ibid. pp. 502–6.
16. Quoted in Time Magazine (New York: Time Inc.), 6 April 1942.
17. Goebbels, The Goebbels Diaries 1939–1941, p. 42, 8 November 1939.
18. Ibid. p. 45, 11 November 1939.
19. Grafström, Anteckningar, 5 November 1942.
20. Ibid. 26 July 1940.
21. Ibid. 29 January 1941.
22. Thulstrup, Med lock och pock, p. 93.
23. Ibid. p. 99.
24. Westman, Politiska anteckningar, 11.11.1939.
25. Lindal, Självcensur i stövelns skugga, p. 41.
26. Ibid. p. 51.
27. Ibid. p. 60.
28. Flyghed, Rättsstat i kris, p. 181.
29. Ibid. pp. 187–8.
30. Linder, Andra världskriget och Sverige, p. 160.
31. Grafström, Anteckningar, 7 October 1943.
32. Andolf, 'De grå lapparna', p. 326.
33. Ibid. p. 345.
34. Grafström, Anteckningar, 27 October 1943.
35. Westman, Politiska anteckningar, 21.2.1942.
36. Linder, Andra världskriget och Sverige, p. 159.
37. Westman, Politiska anteckningar, 26.2.1941.
38. Lindal, Självcensur i stövelns skugga, p. 259.
39. Feilitzen, 'A Historical Review of Radio Research in Sweden'.
40. Lindal, Självcensur i stövelns skugga, pp. 271–9.
41. NA FO 371/29292 Situation in Denmark 16 June 1941.
42. See also Johansson, Per Albin och kriget, pp. 204–8.
43. Isaksson, Per Albin, p. 458.
44. Goebbels, The Goebbels Diaries 1939–1941, p. 48.
45. Tennant, Touchlines of war, p. 157.
46. Thulstrup, Med lock och pock.
47. Richardson, Förtroligt och hemligt, pp. 149–284.
48. Thulstrup, Med lock och pock, p. 46.
49. Thulstrup, Med lock och pock, p. 51.
50. Böhme & Schön, Signal.
51. Berggren, 'Swedish Fascism: Why Bother?', pp. 395–417.
52. Goebbels, The Goebbels Diaries 1939–1941, p. 48.
53. Richardson, Förtroligt och hemligt, p. 152.
54. Cronenberg, 'Och får jag tag i den fan-', p. 243.
55. Lindal, Om kriget hade kommit, p. 116.

56. Maier, *Germany and the Second World War*, Vol. 2, p. 182.
57. Petropoulos, *Art as Politics in the Third Reich*, p. 68; Ständiger Rat für die internationale Zusammenarbeit der Komponisten.
58. Tennant, *Touchlines of war*, pp. 3–10.
59. RA UD HP 39 A I: Boheman (for Günther) to Mallet, 29 July 1940.
60. RA UD Handbrev Serie 3 Christian Günthers Privat Arkiv 1939–1945: Oskar Erich Holz to Günther, 15 April 1940.
61. 'The paper omitted most of those matters which were of a sensitive nature for the Swedes.' Tennant, *Touchlines of war*, p. 122.
62. NA FO 371/29660,1: Mallet to Foreign Office, 13 March 1941.
63. NA PRO FO 371/29673–4: Mallet to Foreign Office, 14 March 1941.
64. NA FO 371/33051: Collier to Bracken, 15 April 1942.
65. NA FO 371/37075: Propaganda in Sweden: Unsigned, undated note.
66. NA FO 371/37075: Foreign Office Minute, 24 November 1943.
67. SIS Den Osvenskan propagandan. Föredragning inför konstitutionsutskottet den 28.5.1942, p. 12.
68. NA FO 371/33051: Tennant to MOI, 23 January 1942.
69. Ibid.: 'Assuming that a family of four read each copy, about 10% of the population now read "Nyheter från Storbritannien" – a very good result for "amateur journalists" in 28 months.'
70. Tennant, *Touchlines of war*, p. 118.
71. SIS Den Osvenskan propagandan. Föredragning inför konstitutionsutskottet den 28.5.1942, p. 13.
72. NA FO 371/33055: Mallet to Foreign Office, 17 February 1942.
73. Ibid.: K. T. Gurney.
74. For a description of Eliot's attractiveness to the ladies of Stockholm, see Mallet, *Memoirs*, p. 143.
75. Ibid.
76. Tennant, *Touchlines of war*, p. 117.
77. Ibid. p. 118.
78. Ibid. p. 120.
79. Cole, *Britain and the war of words*, p. 153.
80. Ibid.
81. Aldgate & Richards, *Britain can take it*, p. 59.
82. NA FO 371, 33055: Montague Evans to MOI, 6 December 1941.
83. Aldgate & Richards, *Britain can take it*, p. 63.
84. Linder, *Andra världskriget och Sverige*, pp. 201–2.
85. Lindal, *Om kriget hade kommit*, p. 20.
86. Wijk, 'Censur- och propagandaministeriet', p. 34.
87. Lindal, *Om kriget hade kommit*, p. 39.
88. Ibid. p. 45.
89. Ibid. pp. 67–74: *Karlstads-Tidning*.
90. Wijk,'Censur- och propagandaministeriet', p. 34.
91. Lindal, *Om kriget hade kommit*, p. 85.
92. Ibid. pp. 60–2.
93. Ibid. p. 64.
94. Wijk,'Censur- och propagandaministeriet', p. 35.
95. Lindal, *Om kriget hade kommit*, p. 110.
96. Wahlbäck & Boberg (eds), *Sveriges sak är vår*, p. 81.
97. Lindal, *Om kriget hade kommit*, p. 128
98. Ibid. p. 312.
99. Ibid. p. 119

100. NA FO 371/29659–0004 Anglo-Swedish relations 21 April 1941.
101. Thulstrup, *Med lock och pock*, p. 50.
102. Lindal, *Om kriget hade kommit*, p. 258.
103. Wijk,' Censur- och propagandaministeriet', p. 38.
104. Wahlbäck, *Regeringen och kriget*, pp. 151–2.
105. Lindal, *Om kriget hade kommit*, p. 283.
106. Overud, *I beredskap med Fru Lojal*, p. 180.
107. Ibid. p. 218.
108. See also Berggren, 'Swedish Fascism: Why Bother?', pp. 395–417.
109. Hadenius, *Svensk Politik*, pp. 268–71.
110. Linder, *Andra världskriget och Sverige*, p. 157.
111. See for example Flyghed, *Rättsstat i kris*, p. 183.
112. For example, Alan Vougt: see Johansson, *Per Albin och kriget*, pp. 184–200.

Race, Rejection, Reception, Rescue and Redemption – Swedish Humanitarian Endeavours

In the second half of the twentieth century, Sweden adopted the mantle of a humanitarian nation, prominent in Red Cross and United Nations global activities. Earlier, during the First World War, there had been exchanges of war-wounded and displaced civilians across Swedish territory.[1] The persecutions of the inter-war years and the brutal horrors of the 1939–45 conflict provided further opportunities for neutral Sweden to contribute to relief for suffering humanity. In the era of the Holocaust, Soviet and German atrocities in occupied territories, how did Sweden respond?

RACE

> The enlightened example of the Swedish government in establishing the Swedish State Institute for Race Biology is one which other nations would do well to follow. The usefulness of such an institution was so well realized in Sweden that the *Riksdag* gave assent to its establishment without voting, on May 13, 1921.[2]

These approving remarks came from E. W. Gifford, Professor of Anthropology at the University of California in 1928, well before the Nazis employed racial difference as an instrument of state policy in Germany. Racial study had also been legitimised in Sweden by enthusiastic support across the spectrum from leading politicians including Social Democrat Hjalmar Branting and intellectuals such as Selma Lagerlöf. They were concerned about the long-term future for a Swedish population faced with a low birth rate, and excited about the possibilities of social improvement from eradicating disease and disability through scientific developments in eugenics. They failed to foresee the racial perversions of the Third Reich and in the years after 1900 this controversial research area seemed to offer possibilities for a better future.

The Institute can be regarded as a distraction from, rather than an indicator of Swedish anti-Semitism. It did not point a path to Auschwitz but rather towards an abhorrent form of social control practised globally at that time, namely sterilisation. The stated aim of sterilisation was to prevent mental illness and disease but that is a subject which lies outside the scope of this book.[3] The Institute's work and the publication of its director Herman Lundborg's publication, *The Racial Characteristics of the Swedish Nation* in 1926 certainly provided an intellectual underpinning for racial comparison. Those were unlikely to have created additional racial discrimination which was generally, but not exclusively practised by the less-academic. Swedish anti-Semitism long pre-dated the Institute but re-surfaced in the inter-war period to further add to a misleading impression that Sweden was at that time fundamentally racist. The Institute's real contribution was to highlight racial differences rather than to incite racist politics. Race had become a central theme in Swedish public attitudes towards refugees in the Twenties and Thirties.[4]

Rejection

Similar to the other democracies in the west, the Swedish Government watched the measures adopted by the Nazis against the German Jews after 1933 with distaste and concern but when the question of asylum was first raised by Ture Nerman in the *Riksdag* in April 1933, it was mainly dismissed out of hand by politicians claiming that Sweden's economic problems were too great to accommodate refugees from what was an internal German matter.[5] Swedish refugee policy was initially framed in a 1927 immigration law to be reviewed every five years. It was based partly on fear of unemployment caused by refugees and partly on maintaining racial integrity: visiting foreigners required permission to remain in Sweden.[6]

The 1932 review extended the 1927 law but before the 1937 review, the implications of Nazi persecution of the German Jews were evident. Some Social Democrats sought an easing of the restrictions: some right-wingers wanted tightening, while a small group of crypto-Nazis wanted to exclude all Jews specifically. Despite an inquiry, the restrictive policy largely remained in place but regrettably, racial persecution was excluded as grounds for asylum. While there was no quota, the twin concerns of the impact on employment and the effect on society effectively kept the numbers of Jewish immigrants at a low level in strikingly similar circumstances to British interwar immigration policy.[7] In the United States, open and powerful anti-semitic sentiment and job fears were exploited by the restrictionists to act as a brake on Jewish refugees.[8] Sweden's restrictive immigration policy was at that time within the western political mainstream.

A further change in the rules in September 1938 preventing entry to Sweden raised the barrier higher for those who could not return to their country, namely expelled German and Austrian Jews. Yet, pressure from refugee organisations was also growing and the restrictions were marginally eased after Nazi Germany's *Kristallnacht* pogrom of German Jews in November 1938. Anti-semitism in Sweden also grew and in spring of 1939, the news that a handful of German-Jewish doctors were to be given visas set off a chain of protest meetings addressed by doctors and other health professionals who felt their livelihoods threatened. Swedish doctors reflected a worldwide reaction. In Britain, apart from a nominal few, medically trained refugees from the Nazis were regarded with hostility as competitors by doctors and their entry into the British profession was resisted. The British Medical Association wrote to the Home Office after the 1938 pogrom in Germany to 'prevent the settlement here of these aliens to the detriment of British practitioners.'[9]

The torch of protest was taken up by the Uppsala Students Union in February 1939 which condemned the planned immigration. In the *Riksdag* Per Albin defended the restrictions, applied by his brother Sigfrid as chief of Sweden's Social Administration (*Socialstyrelsen*). In March another student meeting in Lund opposed immigration 'which brings about foreign elements among our people (that) are damaging and indefensible for the future.'[10] This inflammatory reaction was hardly justified by the pitifully small numbers of Jewish refugees actually choosing to remain in Sweden – estimated at 2,250 when the war started – possibly deterred by the hostile atmosphere.[11]

In 1938, the Germans attempted to collect information on Jewish employees in overseas firms with which they traded. This so-called

Arianisation project originated in Berlin in the *Reichsstelle für Aussenhandel* and was intended as a preliminary to the blackmailing of those firms by Germany to force them to terminate their employment of Jews. Foreign Minister Sandler criticised this openly in 1938 but public Government pronouncements ceased shortly after while the authorities tried to find out how business was responding to the German scheme. In fact, business organisations distanced themselves from German requests while some individual firms complied in order to derive some economic advantage. The Swedish response had been contradictory but even at the height of German influence over Swedish business from 1940 to 1942, German reports indicate that the initiative had failed to meet expectations. [12]

Even after the invasion of Poland and the stream of reports of atrocities, immigration policy continued to be restrictive. Jewish status was still not regarded as grounds for refugee admission to Sweden and it was not until the autumn of 1941 that this policy eased.[13] Yet, in February 1942, the authorities limited a Danish request for protective asylum for several hundred Danish Jews to only a few dozen following advice from the Chairman of the Jewish Congregation in Stockholm who feared creating anti-semitic reactions.[14] In another neutral country, the United States, the passage of the 1940 Alien Act increased the paranoia against German refugees and so further strengthened the restrictionists.[15] Tragically, while Sweden was easing entry for German Jews, the exit was being locked in the Third Reich and few could now escape from the oncoming Holocaust.

Reception

The flow of diplomatic and journalists' reports concerning the appalling treatment of Jews in German-occupied territories became a condemnatory torrent during 1941–2.[16] One notorious instance in August 1942 was the result of Berlin-based Swedish diplomat Göran von Otter meeting an SS officer returning from the Bełżec death camp in Poland who unburdened his conscience to the astonished official. Much has been made of the lack of response from the Swedish Government which von Otter had hoped would publicise the gassing atrocity and thereby pressurise the Nazis into stopping. He blamed Günther for suppressing the information but Günther may have had another reason for not taking the Nazis head-on. He was already involved in low-profile rescue efforts.

Gösta Engzell, the head of the *UD*'s legal section responsible for approving immigration applications had been one of the pre-war restrictionist bureaucrats.[17] However, he appears to have been influenced by the horrific reports after June 1941 and evolved what Paul Levine has termed 'bureaucratic resistance' against the Holocaust. This involved providing protective Swedish papers to Jews which the documentation-deferent Germans astonishingly respected. The technique would later be deployed in 1944 by Raoul Wallenberg in Budapest. The approach of working behind the scenes required the tacit cooperation of the Germans in going along with the Swedish documentary fiction and so strident Swedish exposure of the German genocide in the East might have jeopardised its acceptance. It is also significant that later condemnations by the Western Allies failed to slacken the Nazi enthusiasm for Jewish extermination and indeed may inadvertently have led to further deaths as the retreating Germans sought to cover up their ghastly crimes by executing surviving witnesses. This was not a regime that bowed to criticism – as the Swedes knew well and the empty record of successful censure demonstrates.[18] The German Foreign Ministry under Ribbentrop became progressively more chaotic and unprofessional as diplomats were replaced by Nazis supportive of the 'final solution' which made the task of any effective Swedish diplomatic representation on behalf of Jews increasingly difficult.[19] The Foreign Ministry's influence on the ideologically committed professionals in Himmler's *RSHA* (Reich Main Security Department) who organised the Holocaust was in any case minimal.[20] This formidable group including Reinhard Heydrich and Werner Best were unlikely to be significantly diverted by Swedish intercession. In the view of the respected Holocaust scholar, Donald Bloxham, such intercession would probably have served only to increase the 'siege mentality' of the *RSHA* and the Nazi leadership without saving Jewish lives and be regarded by both as confirming the influence of world Jewry on the Swedish leadership against the interests of the German people. Successful intervention to save large numbers only occurred in the last stages of the war with the Bernadotte initiative in 1945 which in any case circumvented the German Foreign Ministry.

The shadow of the Holocaust now fell on Norway in October 1942 when Jewish arrests began and the Swedish press boldly reported the fact. Those unfortunate enough to be arrested were loaded onto a German ship, the *Donau*, in Oslo and dispatched to Poland and death. Hundreds of others fled, many with the help of Norwegians, over the Swedish border. There was now no question of Swedish immigration restrictions for refugees. The UD interceded with the German Foreign Ministry with Günther's active support. Perhaps the Holocaust had touched the man who admired his Jewish daughter-in-law and feared for his grandchildren.[21] On 27 November 1942, Engzell sent a list of Jews with possible Swedish connections to the Oslo Legation for urgent review with the Germans. Additionally, the Swedish Legation in Berlin was ordered to protest to the Germans as well as to insist on an investigation, to ensure that no Swedish Jews were arrested. Meanwhile in Oslo, the Swedish Legation ignored the rules and issued Swedish citizenship papers to as many remaining Jews as possible. On 3 December 1942, Richert was instructed to communicate Sweden's offer, approved by Per Albin, to accept all remaining Jews from Norway, irrespective of origin.[22] As a result of these efforts and cross-border escapes, 900 Jews reached safety in Sweden. The UD (through the SIS) requested that these facts be suppressed in media reports to avoid jeopardising further rescue efforts. This led the Swedish public to believe that almost all Norwegian Jews had been deported to Germany.[23] Above all other wartime events in 1942, the Norwegian deportation galvanised Swedish opinion and forced Swedes to face up to their anti-semitic ambiguity expressed clearly in one observation published in a leading newspaper: 'I am no friend of Jews but I will not condone such horrors.'[24] The significant Swedish policy change did not go unnoticed in London: 'The Swedes have shown that their sympathy for the Jews is not only confined to words.'[25] Zu Wied commented acidly to Berlin that because these Jews would not be permitted to live in Stockholm or work, they would be 'new, unwanted ballast for the Swedish authorities' as they would also require to be supervised, a comment which may have echoed a misleading UD explanation about Sweden's reception difficulties in order to placate the Germans.[26]

The UD effort was spurred on by a German announcement in January 1943 that all foreign Jews in occupied territory were under threat. Engzell and Richert worked to press the Germans to provide exit visas to Sweden while warning them of the negative effect on Swedish public opinion. On 1 February 1943, the Swedish Government officially replied to the German announcement stating that Sweden assumed that despite the ultimatum, its citizens would continue to be allowed to travel to Sweden. This declaration meant that any Jew with Swedish papers would be protected and indicated that Sweden was standing up to Germany on the issue. Richert then personally intervened to save a small number of Jews with Swedish

FIGURE 9 The *Donau* loading for Auschwitz, Oslo, 1943, with 532 Norwegian Jewish men, women and children leaving Oslo on a bleak November day 1942 – beginning the journey which would deliver them to Auschwitz. This atrocity galvanised Swedish opinion into reversing the policy of limiting entry for Jewish refugees and by 1945, Sweden had welcomed many thousands from Norway, Denmark and Germany.
(PA Photos)

connections.[27] The German military zenith had passed and Sweden now felt more confident in its diplomacy. The public revelation of the Nazi extermination policy by Anthony Eden in the British Parliament on 17 December 1942 was well covered in the Swedish press and ensured that knowledge of the full horror of the Holocaust was now widespread among the Swedish public.

The escape to south Sweden from a planned Gestapo round-up of 7,000 Danish Jews between 30 September and 9 October 1943 is an event which remains controversial in the wartime history of Denmark. On closer analysis, a low-risk sea evacuation of the fleeing Jews by Danish fishermen was undertaken in exchange for payment by the Jews. Also, it now appears that its success was dependent on local German diplomatic and military complicity, firstly to warn of the impending round-up and secondly to allow the sea crossings to go unimpeded by 'looking through their fingers.'[28] One determining factor was the Swedish response when an anti-Nazi German Attaché in Copenhagen, Georg Duckwitz, met Per Albin in mid-September to request that Sweden accept the fleeing Jews.[29] Günther had previously approved automatic visas for fleeing Danish Jews but when the round-up started on 1 October Richert was told to protest to the German Foreign Ministry.[30] This protest was, unusually, publicised to the foreign press in Stockholm. The next day, *Radiotjänst* announced that Sweden would welcome all Danish Jews. The Swedish Government was now openly defying German racial policy but *Reichskommissar* Werner Best in Denmark had succeeded in making the country '*Judenfrei*.' What kind of reception did the refugees get in a country that only a few years previously had an immigration policy partly based on racial purity? One woman wrote about Malmö:

> Two men were selling newspapers and calling out: 'Out with the Jews' (I don't mind telling you the town is swarming with them – they come in crowds from Denmark every day). People flew at them [the vendors] and they had a pretty tough time until the police came and took the two paper-sellers off in a car. (11 October 1943)[31]

This observation is consistent with the continuing presence of organised anti-semitic agitators in south Sweden, previously a hotbed of such sentiment but also open abhorrence of their views.[32] Now, Nazi public meetings disappeared from the area as a consequence of the popular revulsion against the attempt to exterminate the Danish Jews. In Helsingborg, a reception centre was set up in the Ramlösa Hotel where the refugees received a medical examination, accommodation and support from the Swedish Red Cross, children's charities and innumerable private individuals and associations.[33] Swedish Jewish refugee policy had turned about, from rejection to rescue.

RESCUE AND REDEMPTION

The neutral status of Sweden, together with its access to Nazi Germany, both geographically and politically, attracted various missions attempting to rescue Jews from occupied Europe.

Adler-Rudel Plan

A representative of the Jewish Agency in London, Salomon Adler-Rudel, met leading Swedish representatives in February 1943 with the proposal that Sweden provide refuge for 20,000 Jewish children from occupied Europe, if they could be rescued. The Swedish Government initially rejected the plan but later agreed, subject to Britain and America exporting food to Sweden for them, paying for their accommodation and taking them in after the war.[34] This last apparently racist condition was suggested by the Swedes seeking to make the proposal palatable to the Germans, an example of Swedish double-negotiation tactics which simplistic analysis sometimes misinterprets.[35] This was the first rescue plan for non-Scandinavian Jews and was hotly discussed within the Cabinet. The plan's proponents were led by Möller who saw advantages in improving Sweden's position with the Western Allies as well as the humanitarian result while opponents including Per Albin and Bagge believed that it was a non-starter with the Germans and could lead to increased risk for Sweden.[36] The opponents' view of German attitudes proved correct. However Swedish diplomacy may not have pressed the point sufficiently in Berlin because they were faced by a competing British rescue plan to evacuate undernourished Norwegian children to Sweden, feed them there and then repatriate them.[37] 'What we wish to ensure is that the Adler-Rudel Scheme is not pressed on the Swedes to the exclusion of reference to any negotiations about the [British MEW] child-evacuation scheme.'[38] This absence of enthusiasm from Britain contributed to the failure of the Adler-Rudel plan while nine months elapsed before the British guaranteed the food. The British MEW was determined to maintain a restrictive blockade policy, even at the expense of seeking every opportunity to rescue Jewish children. A disappointed Adler-Rudel remained convinced that it was solely the Swedes who had dragged their feet.

Wallenberg Mission

While the Adler-Rudel plan was eclipsed by the momentous Danish rescue, the Germans continued to apply their 'Final Solution' ruthlessly in Europe despite military reverses and global condemnation. In March 1944 the Germans occupied Hungary, demonstrating their ability to take offensive military action at a time when they were in retreat elsewhere. This point was not lost on Sweden yet ignored by many critics of the Coalition Government's risk-averse foreign policy in 1944–5. Some 725,000 Jews in Hungary were now vulnerable and in April they were ghettoised. The risks were fully appreciated in

Stockholm and King Gustav personally appealed to the Hungarians in June to demonstrate humanity which may have postponed death-camp deportations.[39] The Swedish representative on the World Jewish Congress (WJC), Norbert Masur had earlier proposed that a suitable individual with *UD* cover be sent to Budapest, with funds, to facilitate the flight of Jews from Hungary by any means.[40] The chilling reality of Jewish vulnerability and the *UD*'s pessimistic assessment were later set out by the *UD*'s Erik Boheman, a 'Mischling of the second degree' (the Nazi classification for those with one Jewish grandparent), in a confidential press briefing in September.

> It would naturally be best if we could get these Jews over to Sweden. The possibilities of transporting home people from Hungary are however limited. They don't have any German travel permits except in a small number of cases . . . it can be seen that a measure is not always so easy when its effectiveness is taken into account. [41]

Despite these misgivings, the person selected was Raoul Wallenberg, nephew to the two Wallenberg brothers who were so prominent in Swedish trade negotiations.[42] He was in business with a Jewish Hungarian and was familiar with the country and its personalities. He was also an experienced sergeant instructor in the Stockholm Home Guard where his activities demonstrated his energy and initiative to some of his contemporaries.[43] United States President Franklin Roosevelt had established the War Refugee Board (WRB) in January 1944 and the Americans used this as a front for espionage. Unfortunately for Wallenberg, he had had contact with the WRB representative in Stockholm, Iver Olsen, before leaving for Budapest where he was installed in July as 'First Secretary' in the Swedish Legation.[44] To the advancing Russians, the funds for Wallenberg's activities came from the WRB and were linked to United States espionage.

Wallenberg's rescue actions fell into three categories. Firstly, with the assistance of another Legation diplomat, he issued thousands of Swedish protection passports (*Schutz-Pass*) to Jews which identified the bearer as a Swedish citizen awaiting repatriation. Amazingly, these documents were accepted by the German and Hungarian persecutors. They afforded actual protection against the transports to the death camps which Gustav V's appeal had helped to delay. Secondly, Wallenberg negotiated with and bribed German and Hungarian officials to allow those holding *Schutz-Pass* not to have to wear the Jewish Star and be treated as Swedish citizens. Thirdly, he used the funds he had received to rent thirty-two buildings to accommodate 10,000 of the new 'Swedish citizens', sign-boarded them as Swedish diplomatic territory to prevent raids and arrests, and provided funds for food. In these efforts, he was assisted by the Swedish Red Cross representative and the Swedish Minister. When the Russians occupied Budapest in January 1945, they found over 20,000 Jews under Swedish protection. Wallenberg's courage and determination in taking personal risks with the Germans did not prevent him being tarnished with espionage and falling into the hands of the Russians in January 1945. He was transported to Russia where he is believed to have died in 1947 while in the custody of the Russian security services. The Swedish authorities and his usually well-informed uncle Marcus had assumed that he was already dead.[45]

Red Cross and 'White Buses'

The Germans were now fighting the final struggle of the war but with their enemies' armies advancing on all sides, the Nazis still found the energy and resources to kill and torture Jews and opponents alike. The Swedish Government attempted humanitarian intervention by opening negotiations with the Germans in the autumn of 1944 with the objective of rescuing Scandinavians and later, non-Scandinavians held in camps in Germany. The idea was put to Günther by a Norwegian diplomat. He responded by involving Heinrich Himmler's masseur, Felix Kersten (a Finnish citizen) and Count Bernadotte of the Swedish Red Cross and King Gustav's nephew. They would sound out the idea of a Swedish-led rescue operation for Danish and Norwegian citizens with Heinrich Himmler, now more powerful than German Foreign Minister Ribbentrop. Himmler saw himself as the potential successor to Hitler and had attempted several times to use Sweden to open up secret negotiations with the Western Allies to seek a separate peace for Germany. Despite these talks coming to nothing, he maintained a partiality for Sweden as an 'Aryan' country and did not want Sweden to enter the war on the Allied side.[46]

Himmler's emissary, *SS* General and *Abwehr* chief Walter Schellenberg, had assured Richert in November 1944 that Himmler was well disposed to Swedish intervention on behalf of Norwegians – and to a lesser extent Danes – imprisoned in Germany which probably encouraged the Swedish initiative.[47] By January 1945 the *UD* was inundated also with requests for assistance with Jewish prisoners. The Americans pressed the *UD* on 27 January two days after the World Jewish Congress (WJC) had requested Boström, Swedish Minister in Washington to consider the use of Wallenberg's *Schutz-Pass* solution elsewhere in Europe and urge the Germans to cease the extermination. The pressure continued when on 3 February WJC Swedish representative Gillel Storch presented a list of rescue actions for the Swedish Red Cross or the Government to consider.[48] The *UD* directed Richert in Berlin to attempt to form a common approach with the Papal Representative and the Swiss Minister and protest to the Germans. On 7 February they declined to join in yet, despite Richert's pessimism regarding any successful outcome, the *UD* persevered.[49] Using Schellenberg as an intermediary, the Swiss President had succeeded in reaching an agreement with Himmler to receive 1,200 Jews a fortnight.[50]

The Swedish Government decided on 10 February to send Bernadotte, with Günther's approval, to negotiate the release of Norwegian and Danish prisoners with Himmler.[51] Kersten had earlier briefed Himmler by phone on the Bernadotte initiative. The choice of Bernadotte was partly cynical and partly practical: the Government could distance themselves if the attempt turned out badly while Richert lacked both resolve and the personality to negotiate in such an unstructured situation. Due to Hitler's violent reaction to the Swiss President's deal, the whole operation was kept low key. Bernadotte met Himmler on 19 February and secured agreement that the Red Cross would repatriate the weakest Scandinavian prisoners and some Swedish residents in Germany. There was no mention yet of Jews but hectic preparations began to assemble the requisite transport and personnel for the Scandinavians. This eventually amounted to about 300 Red Cross people and 100 repainted vehicles requisitioned from the Swedish army, the 'White Buses'.

On 12 March the column of vehicles entered Germany via Denmark after a week's delay caused by fruitlessly seeking Allied guarantees from attack. By 30 March the Swedes had assembled Scandinavian prisoners in the relative safety of Neuengamme camp in north Germany. They had transferred 4,500 out of other camps from as far away as Dachau in Bavaria by travelling at great risk across war-torn Germany. Bernadotte renewed his discussions with Himmler on 2 April and succeeded in securing the additional evacuation of 2,000 Danish police, who had been arrested in September 1944 and sent to Buchenwald.[52] He also agreed the inclusion of those surviving

Norwegian students who had been arrested and deported in November 1943.[53] One of the consequences of assembling these prisoners in Neuengamme was that the SS insisted on brutally dispersing the other nationalities housed there, sometimes using the 'White Buses'. The evacuations from Neuengamme to Sweden began on 3 April and the Swedes were joined by a parallel expedition from Denmark. By 20 April, 4,255 Scandinavians had been driven to safety. Pauly, the Neuengamme camp commandant was later hanged for war crimes which indicates the type of people with whom the Swedish mission had to deal in order to save lives. [54]

WJC's Norbert Masur again featured courageously in rescue attempts when as a Jew without a visa, he flew with Kersten from Sweden to Germany to meet Himmler on 19 April. On 21 April in Himmler's quarters, Masur succeeded in securing Himmler's agreement to the evacuation of 1,000 women from Ravensbrück Camp in addition to the 100 Scandinavians already evacuated. The important concession was that some of these 1,000 were Jewish, but to be designated as 'Polish'. In the end, at least 7,000 women were evacuated to Sweden and Denmark from Ravensbrück over the next few days: by train as well as by road. The last evacuation from Germany took place on 30 April by sea from Lübeck only days before the cataclysmic end of Hitler's Reich. The final total saved was over 21,000 of which an estimated 3,500–6,500 were Jews.[55]

OTHER HUMANITARIAN ACTIONS

While the history of Swedish humanitarian actions tends to concentrate on the headline events outlined above, there were a number of other contributions which receive less attention. These actions are quite apart from the reception and accommodation of the continual stream of escaping Norwegians and Danes from their occupied countries after 1940. By the end of the war, over 30,000 Norwegians and 11,000 Danes had been given refuge in Sweden. In some cases, Norwegians volunteered for the *Waffen-SS* in order, they told their Swedish interrogators, to be able to escape from the trains passing through Sweden.[56]

As the protecting power for Netherlands in Germany, Swedish diplomats, in addition to the International Committee of the Red Cross (ICRC), actively visited Dutch prisoners-of-war (PoWs) in German custody. Their reports on camps and their representation of prisoners in German disciplinary cases and eight formal protests on conditions, contributed to the welfare of the Dutch.[57] Sweden was less successful as the protecting power for the Soviet Union in Germany which in 1941 rejected the Geneva Convention provisions for Russian PoWs. In total, twenty-eight countries depended on Sweden to act as their protecting power.[58] The ICRC also pressed Sweden to assist in famine relief in occupied Greece which required the Allies and Germany to agree to Swedish ships, chartered by the Swedish Red Cross, loaded with grain from Canada, getting safe conduct through the blockades. On arrival, in August 1942 the cargo distribution was supervised by a joint Swedish-Swiss Commission and began an ICRC relief effort which continued until 1945 with ninety-one further shipments on Swedish vessels.[59] Later in early 1945, several ships loaded with aid were sent to the Netherlands. Four were lost on humanitarian service altogether including one vessel with twenty crew onboard.[60]

Closer to home and perhaps nearer to Swedish emotions were the tens of thousands of Finnish refugees, mainly children, who were sent for refuge in Sweden in two waves. When the Winter War started in 1939, several voluntary and charitable organisations from the Red Cross to the Salvation Army coordinated efforts in one body, Central Finnish Relief (CFR).[61] CFR organised 15,000 places in Sweden for children who were being encouraged to leave and 9,000 were actually sent. When the Continuation War started, CFR had been disbanded and so a new group, the Assistance Committee for Finnish Children was formed.[62] During the Continuation War and its aftermath when German troops were retreating, over 48,000 children were evacuated by official means and a further estimated 15,000 by private means. Formal reception in Sweden was medically necessary due to TB: sick children were sent to hospital and the healthy ones to Swedish homes and schools. As they were mainly under ten years old and spoke no Swedish, the evacuation caused a considerable amount of trauma and not all returned to Finland, with almost 5,500 remaining as adopted or fostered.[63] When the Germans retreated through Lapland in October 1944, harassed by the Finnish army, a further tragic stream of almost 50,000 refugees of all ages surged over the border into Sweden for temporary refuge. The influx had been anticipated in a request by the Finnish Government for sanctuary for up to 100,000 refugees that was approved in a record two hours by the Swedish Government.[64] Hasty plans were prepared and the Swedish authorities put refugees up in halls and churches as well as private homes. The thousands of cows and horses which they brought with them were also carefully housed.[65] As the retreat passed, these refugees began to go back and by July 1945, they had all returned to Finland.[66]

The Swedish army cared for the Finnish sick and wounded in 1944 but there had been an earlier humanitarian action to provide Swedish medical care for German wounded from the Eastern Front between 1941 and 1943. As many as 60,000 severely wounded German servicemen were transported on a Swedish hospital train from the Finnish border to Oslo. The operation was conducted in great secrecy, formally under the responsibility of the Swedish Red Cross (already heavily involved in relief work in Finland), and urged on by Per Albin. It clearly fell within the 1907 Hague Convention, Article 14, governing neutral aid to wounded servicemen. The proposal had come from the German Military Attaché and in August 1941 with the involvement of Prince Carl, Head of the Red Cross, the Swedish military organised the resources and made the arrangements, which of course had to be coordinated with the Germans who funded the train. So, a few weeks after the Engelbrecht Division had been permitted to cross Sweden eastwards, the trains carrying the wounded rumbled westwards back to Norway. On the first journey, Bernadotte's sister nursed the injured while Commander-in-Chief Thörnell and Prince Carl inspected the facilities.[67] This was a high-ranking Swedish presence for a low-profile Swedish humanitarian effort, reflecting both the impression of cooperation that Sweden wanted to give to Germany coupled with a fear of public anger if the aid became known. It is of course impossible to assess how much this cooperative Swedish Red Cross image assisted Bernadotte in 1945 in his negotiations with Himmler, but it probably helped. It was also included as item six on the thirteen item list of 'services' rendered, submitted to Schnurre in December 1941 during the 1942 Trade Agreement negotiation. [68]

One final category of Swedish humanitarian assistance in which Bernadotte later participated was PoW exchange and repatriation between the belligerents. One of the first repatriations was a group of British internees from the Norwegian campaign that the Germans permitted to embark from Petsamo in Finland in July 1940. This followed representations by the *UD* to Germany and the release of German internees, the first instance of Swedish PoW double-negotiation which was to characterise the stream of internee releases over the next five years.[69] The first large-scale exchange of wounded prisoners took place in October 1943 in Göteborg when 3,000 British PoWs were exchanged for 800 Germans (the remainder being freed in North Africa). [70] One small-scale prisoner exchange that failed was Bernadotte's approach to the Russian Foreign Minister Molotov to swap Stalin's son Yakov for Field-Marshal Paulus, recently captured at Stalingrad. Stalin refused saying 'War is war' and Yakov committed suicide in April 1943.[71]

Servicemen from most belligerent countries were among the military internees who found themselves in Sweden, either by mischance or design as Göran Andolf has described in detail.[72] In September 1939, 169 Polish sailors escaped in three submarines to Sweden's east coast. Norwegian, Danish and British military personnel flooded over the border during April and May 1940. Germans were shot down when they violated Swedish airspace over the Norwegian border or simply crashed. By the end of 1940, almost 5,000 different nationalities had been interned.[73] Military internees were a massive diversionary headache for the Swedish authorities. They required registration, accommodation, food and supervision from the overstretched Swedish state under Count Bernadotte as the Chief of Military Internment. In addition, internees' status was subject to continual representation by their countries. Britain and Germany wanted their servicemen returned and used all diplomatic devices to put forward cases for their repatriation. For example, within the Conventions, escaped PoWs were eligible for repatriation whereas those servicemen seeking refuge, shot down or washed ashore were not and so subject to internment. Germany in particular also wanted the return of their downed aircraft which was generally but not always refused, and even demanded the Polish submarines. From an early stage, exchanges of internees for repatriation were mediated by the *UD* acting as a referee for fair exchange on a case-by-case basis. Like all referees Sweden also was criticised by both sides when a decision was deemed unfavourable. As the Allied air war developed in Europe, the number of airmen downed in Sweden increased and they became a priority for repatriation efforts. After Barbarossa in 1941, a small number of Russian servicemen were interned. Their repatriation would be much more controversial because a number did not want to return to Stalin's gulags. A steady flow of escapees from occupied Europe also added to the variety reaching Sweden. In December 1941, the internee complement stood at 180 Poles, eight British, seven French Foreign Legionnaires, and 159 Russians: the Germans had all been repatriated though exchanges.

From summer 1943 as American airmen began to crash-land in Sweden in growing numbers, the British Air Attaché Richard Maycock found it difficult to keep track of the interned and repatriated Allied airmen. He agreed the tally with the *UD* in December as ninety-three, of whom seventy were Americans. In a significant shift away from exchanges, these now were to be repatriated in secrecy by agreement in unmarked Allied planes.[74] The numbers of internees involved grew significantly as European hostilities drew closer to Sweden. During 1944, 975 British and Americans, 121 Russians, twenty Poles and 328 Germans were freed.[75] One Swedish release of seventy-five British pilots took place in exchange for fifty British aircraft radio-sets for Sweden's under-equipped machines.[76] In addition, German deserters and Balts in German service began to arrive in Sweden. By May 1945, there were about 3,000 German servicemen in Sweden, many having arrived there in the final weeks of the war to flee the Russians.[77] As a postscript, in 1947 a Swedish bill was sent to Britain for 349,252.10 kroner covering salaries, food, clothing, quarters, medical treatment, transport and miscellaneous items incurred in accommodating British internees. In return, £24,136 5s 9d was paid from Britain's depleted post-war Treasury.[78]

In the autumn of 1943 and in 1944, Bernadotte organised an exchange of prisoners between Britain and Germany which resulted in 11,000 wounded and sick servicemen being exchanged through Sweden. Two Swedish ships, the *Gripsholm*, chartered by the Red Cross in Britain and the *Drottningholm* by the United States were both prominent in conveying exchanged prisoners back to Britain and the United States. Together, they carried 29,600 diplomats, PoWs, and wounded in thirty-six voyages between April 1942 and May 1945 with Göteborg as the exchange point in fourteen instances.[79]

It is ironic that one of the most publicised images of Sweden during the war is that of an armed Swedish guard pointing his rifle towards German soldiers milling around next to the goods wagons from which they have dismounted. It conveys an impression of close, armed Swedish supervision over Germans travelling by rail which the Swedish public have been allowed to assume reflected the conditions under which German soldiers transited Sweden to Norway between 1940 and 1943. The picture in fact dates from 1944 and is a transport of exchange prisoners.[80] The German soldiers in transit travelled through Sweden in comfortable carriages – while their Swedish counterparts were forced to travel on wagons. Photographs of those carriages are much harder to locate, due to the ban on press reporting of the traffic.[81]

BALT REFUGEES AND REPATRIATION

One humanitarian episode which was to cause Sweden some difficulty in 1944 and 1945 was the arrival in Sweden of thousands of Balts fleeing the advancing Red Army: 500 from Lithuania: 5,000 Latvians and 32,000 Estonians.[82] Of the Estonians, 7,000 were Estonian-Swedes whose forebears had settled in western Estonia during the early days of the Swedish Baltic expansion in the 15th century. The Swedish Government had considered taking them in 1939 but decided against, with Sköld complaining 'when it is not a question of Jews, then we do not want them.'[83] After the German occupation they had been favoured with the attention of the SS racial specialist Dr Ludwig Lienhard who declared them higher ranking racially than Estonians and also encouraged their links with Sweden. As the Russians approached, Lienhard and the SS organised their escape to Sweden, paid for by Sweden, the last arriving in September 1944.[84] The Russians, clearly angered by the flight of people they considered citizens of the USSR, began a campaign to brand all Balt refugees as fascists and collaborators, which some undoubtedly were, and demanded access to the refugee camps in Sweden. This access was conceded by the Swedish Government in December 1944 in order that the Soviet representatives could invite them back without reprisals. Eighty-six took up this unattractive offer. At the same time, to mollify the Russians, the Swedish authorities also investigated the non-Swedish Balt civilian refugees to identify possible criminals and soldiers in German service among the supposedly civilian refugees. One hundred were categorised as suspicious and removed to a special camp and in June 1945 the Coalition Government tried to decide whether to send them back with those who were classed as soldiers and interned on arrival, as the Soviets requested.

A long and bitter public debate took place in Sweden under Soviet pressure but Östen Undén, now the Foreign Minister, decided in January 1946 with Per Albin and the Social Democrats' approval, to repatriate those fit to travel. Per Albin stated 'There is no doubt that there are pure Nazis even among the civilian Balts.' Eventually, 146 Balts were taken under close arrest, several having attempted suicide, to a Soviet ship in Trelleborg on 25 January 1946 and repatriated to Stalin's Russia. Undén later excused the unpopular decision, similar to the handover by the British of Croats in German service to Tito in 1945, by pointing out that there was proof that some Estonians had been released on return.[85] In fact, although there is no comprehensive record of their fate, four were executed, two died under interrogation and over forty died in the Gulag.[86] For many Swedes however, this episode echoed Swedish wartime concessions to the Nazis and symbolised that they had exchanged one bullying neighbour for another.

RETROSPECTIVE

What did Sweden's wartime actions amount to? In terms of the enormity of the Holocaust, the statistics of Jews rescued are meagre yet meaningful. By these actions, Sweden fell clearly into the 'rescuer' category of Holocaust actors having been a 'bystander' up to 1942. No Swedish authorities delivered Jews into Nazi hands unlike some police collaborators in Norway. Through careful maintenance of the relationship with Nazi Germany, Sweden provided a unique haven for about 30,000 Jews, whether territorially for the Danes and Norwegians or diplomatically for the Hungarians. The opportunity of the 'White Buses' expedition to rescue Scandinavians was used to extend salvation to as many Jews as could be negotiated and liberated. It must be at least questionable whether all of this could have been accomplished had the Swedish Government adopted the high-profile – but almost certainly impotent – public condemnation of Nazi atrocities that critics demanded. Consciences would have been eased but possibly fewer Jewish lives saved. As for internees, PoW exchange, repatriation and foreign relief, Sweden attempted to derive as much kudos as possible from helpful assistance to the belligerents and their victims. This role was one that Sweden hoped would lubricate wartime and post-war relationships but was taken for granted and assumed rather than appreciated by the recipients.

Notes

1. Franzén, Undan stormen, pp. 232–5.
2. Gifford, American Anthropologist, pp. 493–5.
3. See Roll-Hansen & Broberg (eds), Eugenics and the Welfare State.
4. Svanberg & Tydén, Sverige och Förintelsen, p. 61.
5. Ibid. p. 89.
6. Ibid. p. 157.
7. See London, Whitehall and the Jews, 1933–1948.
8. Greear, 'American Immigration Policies and Public Opinion on European Jews from 1933 to 1945'.
9. Quoted in Decker, 'Divisions and Diversity', p. 856.
10. Svanberg & Tydén, Sverige och Förintelsen, p. 189.
11. Ibid. p. 295.
12. Nordlund, »En svensk tiger«?, pp. 303–4.
13. Svanberg & Tydén, Sverige och Förintelsen, p. 295.
14. Isaksson, Per Albin, p. 372.
15. Koblik, 'Om vi teg, skulle stenarna ropa', pp. 182–3.
16. Grafström, Anteckningar, 14 November 1941, 'mass deportations eastwards' & Koblik, 'Om vi teg, skulle stenarna ropa', pp. 186–7.

17. Cesarani & Levine (eds), 'Bystanders' to the Holocaust, p. 219.
18. Åmark,'Demokratin, neutraliteten och moralen, p. 60.
19. Seabury, The Wilhelmstrasse, p. 125.
20. Herbert, 'The National Socialist Political Police', pp. 105–8
21. Arnstad, Spelaren Christian Günther, p. 311.
22. Ibid. pp. 312–14.
23. Svanberg & Tydén, Sverige och Förintelsen, p. 249.
24. Dagens Nyheter 31.12.1942 cited in Svanberg & Tydén, Sverige och Förintelsen, pp. 260–1.
25. NA FO 371/37095 Reaction in Sweden to German persecution of Jews in Norway 29 December 1942.
26. NA GFM E035765 Juden im Schweden 4 December 1942.
27. Arnstad, Spelaren Christian Günther, pp. 341–2.
28. Grafström, Anteckningar, 7 October 1943.
29. Kirchoff, 'Denmark: A light in the Darkness of the Holocaust?', p. 465.
30. Koblik, 'Om vi teg, skulle stenarna ropa', p. 215.
31. NA FO 371/36866–0002 Intercepted correspondence report p. 5, 11 December 1943.
32. NA FO 371/33069–0005 2 May 1942.
33. Friberg, Stormcentrum Öresund, pp. 115–25.
34. Svanberg & Tydén, Sverige och Förintelsen, p. 263.
35. Sompolinsky, Britain and the Holocaust, p. 151.
36. Koblik, 'Om vi teg, skulle stenarna ropa', p. 163.
37. Engel, Facing a holocaust, p. 65.
38. Sompolinsky, Britain and the Holocaust, p. 154.
39. Carlsson, Gustaf V och andra världskriget, pp. 267–73.
40. Koblik, 'Om vi teg, skulle stenarna ropa', p. 216.
41. RA Justice Ministry F1 Vol. 2 1940–45, 30 September 1944.
42. Anger, Räddningen: Budapest 1944, p. 45.
43. Brink, Demokrat och krigsfrivillig, pp. 44–58.
44. Agrell, Skuggor runt Wallenberg, p. 172.
45. Aalders & Wiebes, The art of cloaking ownership, pp. 157–61.
46. Persson, 'Vi åker till Sverige', p. 111.
47. Ibid. p. 114.
48. Ibid. p. 122.
49. Koblik, 'Om vi teg, skulle stenarna ropa', pp. 256–7.
50. Halbrook, Target Switzerland, p. 234.
51. Koblik, 'Om vi teg, skulle stenarna ropa', pp. 257–8.
52. Hæstrup, Besættelsens Hvem-Hvad-Hvor, p. 194.
53. Singer, 'Norwegian Students Fight the War', p. 27.
54. Jackson, Battle of the Baltic, p. 191.
55. Svanberg & Tydén, Sverige och Förintelsen, pp. 370–1.
56. Frykholm, Protokoll vid riksdagens hemliga sammanträden, p. 139.
57. Smit, Onder de Vlaggen van Zweden en het Rode Kruis, pp. 156–65.
58. Ekman & Åmark (eds), Sweden's relations with Nazism, p. 64.
59. Lang, 'Red Cross Humanitarianism in Greece, 1940–45', pp. 71–88.
60. Lagvall, Flottans neutralitetsvakt, p. 147.
61. Innala, Finska krigsbarn, p. 9.
62. Ibid. p. 11.
63. Ekberg, 'Finländska krigsbarn i västerled'.
64. Boheman, På vakt, p. 264.
65. Forslund, Beredskapsdagbok 1939–45, pp. 81–8.

66. Dahlberg, *I Sverige under 2:a världskriget*, p. 279.
67. Hellström, *Sjuktransporter från norra Finland 1941–1943*, p. 70.
68. Documents on German foreign policy, 1918–1945, p. 928.
69. RA UD HP22D Internees Vol. 1, 1074 September 1940, Mallet to Günther & Mallet, *Memoirs*, p. 80.
70. Grafström, *Anteckningar*, 15 October 1943.
71. Sebag Montefiore, *Stalin*, p. 454.
72. Andolf, 'Militära interneringar i Sverige under de första krigsåren 1939–.'
73. Ibid. p. 205.
74. Andolf, 'Interneringen av britter och tyskar 1943–1944', p. 228.
75. Andolf, 'Amerikanska flygare i Sverige 1944–1945', p. 16.
76. Grafström, *Anteckningar*, 13 June 1944.
77. Andolf,'Amerikanska flygare i Sverige 1944–1945', p. 32.
78. RA UD HP22D Internees Vol. 1107, 9 April 1947 Grafström to Henderson.
79. Lagvall, *Flottans neutralitetsvakt*, p. 147.
80. Linder, *Andra världskriget och Sverige*, p. 63.
81. Jakobsson & Janson, *Sverige 1939–1945*, pp. 54 & 61.
82. Küng, *Sverige och Estland*, p. 96.
83. Westman, *Politiska anteckningar*, 16.10.1939.
84. Kranking, *Borderland Swedes*, pp. 338–9.
85. Undén, *Minnesanteckningar*, p. 160.
86. Silamikelis, *Baltutlämningen*, p. 394.

10

Military Matters

In 1939, the Germans were prepared for *Blitzkrieg*, the Allies for *Sitzkrieg* and the Swedes for *Fußkrieg*, that is pedestrian-paced warfare. Per Albin had made his notorious declaration in August that 'our preparedness is good', an assertion for which he was widely derided in the light of manifest deficiencies in military planning, organisation, equipment and training. Thousands of conscripts experienced this first-hand when they reported for duty: for example being sent to buy suitable replacement boots with the petty cash.[1] What was the real state of Sweden's military forces in 1939?

Pre-War Defence Planning

The Army's share of the defence budget of 146.2 million kroner was 54.5 per cent or 79.7 million kroner.[2] The interwar defence budget-cut decision in 1925 had reduced the army's peacetime and wartime planned strength to four Divisions which the 1936 re-armament decision increased to six wartime Divisions. The 1936 decision envisaged a ten-year build-up and transformation starting in 1937 with an interim reorganisation in 1940. European politics ran to a divergent timetable from that of the Swedish defence planners and by March 1939 Chief of Defence Olof Thörnell had realised that events were shaping up differently.

By 1937, the defence planners had developed four defensive war-scenarios constructed on three possibilities of Russian aggression and one potential attack from the resurgent German Reich. Their plans were deeply rooted in a fear of Soviet Russia while the likelihood of trouble with Germany was dismissed as possible rather than probable. The military had developed these scenarios and their resulting troop dispositions without the involvement of the politicians whom the senior military figures despised for their evident lack of interest in an 'activist' eastward-facing foreign policy. One of them – Scenario 1 – even committed Sweden to armed intervention in Finland.

Swedish occupation of the Åland Islands was central to military thinking, based on their view that Sweden was best defended on Finnish territory, alongside the Finns, against Russia.[3] This view held despite the political realities of great power opposition to the Stockholm Plan in 1939 that had envisaged joint Finnish-Swedish defence of the Ålands. For the first time but not the last, the firmly anti-Russian Thörnell tried to commit Per Albin and his colleagues to an interventionist strategy with a presentation of the four scenarios to a few of the Cabinet in March 1939. In this, he took advantage of the surprising lack of coordination between military strategy and foreign policy which existed in 1939. Not even the tectonic shift of the Molotov–Ribbentrop Pact in August occasioned a joint discussion.[4] This meant that on the eve of war, Swedish defence was unprepared; strategy, direction, organisation as well as attitude, logistics and equipment were all deficient for the task ahead but it was in equipment that the problems were most evident.

An analysis of the three services by Stellan Bojerud showed that in 1939, infantry rifles dated from 1896, machine guns were in short supply, uniforms dated from 1886 or 1910, and so on.[5] The reliance on 'oat power' for horse transport of field artillery, of which almost 400 of the 600 pieces pre-dated the First World War, at least allowed the infantry to pace their artillery support in a *Fußkrieg*. The Swedish landscape was believed to hamper tank warfare so there was almost no development of either tanks or anti-tank weaponry before 1941. At sea, the three Swedish battleships were between fifteen and twenty years old and there was a six-vessel deficit in the essential submarine fleet, but it was in the air that Sweden was weakest. In the mid-1930s, Sweden had only 150 aircraft as against a planned 250 and these were elderly and slow compared with Russian or German machines. The Swedish air-defence doctrine of that time was to attack the enemy's bases rather than his aircraft in the air so bombers were fatally favoured over fighters, almost the opposite of the British approach. The planned rearmament from 1936 had only been partly implemented causing shortages of equipment. The conscript forces in 1939 joined a regular army which was more at home in barracks than out in the field.[6] Still, the military leadership relished the prospect of sorting out the Russians and looked to the *Wehrmacht* for their military if not their political inspiration. Swedish military preparedness on the eve of the war could only be considered good in comparison with Denmark and Norway's depleted and disorganised defences.

THE WINTER WAR, 1939

Barely three months after Poland was over-run, the Russian invasion of Finland had provided the Swedish military leadership with its anticipated excuse to become involved in Finland. However, its ambitions were curtailed by the politicians, despite heavy pressure from an emotional public response to Russian aggression against their neighbour. Two army Divisions were mobilised in December 1939 and January 1940 for the defence of the Swedish-Finnish border in Norrland province. Thörnell was appointed national Commander-in-Chief in early December. Per Albin had relieved some of the public pressure for intervention by declaring Sweden as non-combatant in the Winter War rather than neutral. This allowed material support to be given to the hard-pressed Finns but this would have to come from Sweden's meagre resources. Defence Minister Sköld was willing to provide planes, rifles and ammunition to a country whose resources were even more slender, particularly in comparison to the enemy's. For example the Finns had thirty-two light Renault First World War tanks against 1,600 Soviet machines.[7] Sweden imported, assembled (with British assistance) and supplied 142 British and American planes to Finland during the Winter War.[8] The Government now sought to remedy multiple equipment deficiencies with an urgent procurement mission to the United States led by Gunnar Hägglöf. An earlier effort to Berlin had failed in December 1939, partly due to the Germans trying to avoid difficulties with the Soviet Union by supplying Finland's armourer.[9] This later trans-Atlantic attempt was somewhat burdened by an abortive effort to purchase a prestige battleship to operate in the Baltic but was successful in placing orders for modern fighter aircraft to replace the outmoded biplanes in service.[10]

In addition to the Western Allies threatening to intervene in the Winter War, Sweden's military leadership, in particular Thörnell, Axel Rappe, Archibald Douglas, and Carl August Ehrensvärd were also naively or mischievously seeking to place Swedish troops in North Finland 'without breaking the peace with Russia.' Rappe, Douglas, and Ehrensvärd had fought for the Whites in the Finnish Civil War in 1918 under Mannerheim with *Wehrmacht* assistance. Thörnell and Rappe gave the Coalition Cabinet an overview of the situation in February 1940 and outlined the four scenarios with Rappe strongly urging a military intervention in Finland by four Swedish Divisions.[11] Per Albin is supposed to have muttered: 'Bloody nonsense!' ('*Djävla skitprat!*') and the politically insensitive and conspiratorial Rappe, who had openly discussed a coup with colleagues, was transferred within a year to a military backwater.[12] Per Albin had earlier eased the interventionist pressure by permitting a volunteer force organised by Rappe and Ehrensvärd, including Army servicemen taking special leave, to fight in Finland in 1939. The predominantly working class force amounted to over 8,000 and fought bravely in the appalling conditions of the Finnish winter, losing thirty-three dead, four missing and 130 frost-bitten.[13] The Swedish-sponsored peace, when it came on 13 March 1940 was a relief to the Coalition Government but the cost in materials had been significant for Sweden as subsequent military events were to demonstrate.[14]

The threat of Allied intervention in Finland as a pretext to seize the iron ore mines in Norrland had receded with the peace but Sweden had been prepared to defend these important strategic assets. The conscripts in Norrland had also suffered the freezing winter quartered in farms where Sköld had visited them in January 1940. Having achieved their territorial objectives at enormous cost, the Russians stood down on the Finnish front and Sweden could both enjoy a lull and began to send conscripts in Norrland on leave. The respite lasted three weeks until somewhat contradictory intelligence reports indicated a massive German build-up of an invasion force along the Prussian Baltic coast aimed at Scandinavia, but where? In Berlin, Minister Richert thought on 31 March that it was directed towards Sweden but on 7 April altered his forecast to Norway and Denmark instead. [15]

MOBILISATION MISFIRE, APRIL 1940

On 4 April Thörnell proposed a significant mobilisation of the three Divisions not in Norrland and a deployment in Skåne province in south Sweden where a German landing would be easiest. The coast had been fortified by a series of fixed defences referred to as the 'Per Albin Line'. Even though Thörnell discounted the likelihood of invasion from Germany, he viewed a mobilisation as providing both some territorial security and a negotiating position for Sweden in an obviously threatening situation. When Sköld rejected the proposal on the grounds of insufficient intelligence of an attack directed towards Sweden, Thörnell unwisely suggested an improvised and more limited mobilisation without the three Divisions. Even this was rejected, on Saturday, 6 April, by the Cabinet whose concentration was distracted somewhat by consideration of Allied criticisms of Swedish conduct. Instead, only a small staff group and officers without troops were to be deployed. There were evident party tensions in the four-month old Coalition over Ministerial prerogative: when Westman urged further mobilisation if the intelligence continued to be disturbing, Sköld replied: 'You can bet your bloody life that if I consider it necessary, I'll mobilise – whatever you think about it.'[16] Thörnell took the day off on Sunday, 7 April and the airforce went on to a war footing on 8 April but retained Sweden's only fighter squadron in Stockholm.[17] The navy deployed destroyers on high alert in the Kattegat to defend Göteborg and a battleship with two destroyers put to sea off the east coast.[18] Eleven torpedo seaplanes lay frozen near Stockholm – without ice skis.[19] The disorganised and irrational troop deployment resulting from Thörnell's botched proposals meant that on the night of 8 April while the Germans were heading to Norway and to Denmark, lying only a few miles to the west of Skåne over the Öresund, the 'Per Albin Line' on which millions had been spent was garrisoned with a few barely-trained conscripts who had only 50–80 per cent of the required weaponry of machine-guns and anti-tank guns that most did not know how to operate.[20]

The shock of this inadvertent exposure galvanised the Swedish authorities and by 3 May an additional 230,000 men had been mobilised and deployed in west Sweden and along the Norwegian border. Nevertheless, the failures of 9 April came in for sustained criticism.[21] Sköld later defended his decision not to mobilise by citing the deterrent effect of the defences surrounding the iron ore mines in Norrland on a German attack, and secondarily the need to conserve agricultural labour on the farms.[22] Günther's more subtle defence that a mobilisation with troop redeployment from Norrland could increase the possibility of a German attack found little favour with later critics of the deficiencies in military and political leadership on the grounds of his inconsistency and irrationality.[23] The evident failure was seen as indefensible.

Sweden now could experience *Wehrmacht* effectiveness by proxy over the border, with the small and ill-equipped Norwegian army, lacking essential air cover, fighting a rearguard action in the south, tardily joined in the north by inadequately equipped and poorly coordinated British and French expeditionary forces, also lacking sufficient air cover.[24] After barely two weeks fighting, the British decided to evacuate mid-Norway and by 30 April only Narvik was contested with an outnumbered German force eventually retreating towards the Swedish border on 28 May. For Hitler, the Norwegian campaign was a personal prestige operation as he had personally involved himself in its planning and so maximum diplomatic pressure was exerted on Sweden to allow reinforcing troops and military supplies to cross Sweden by rail to Norway. The Swedish argument was that military transit was unthinkable while the Norwegians were fighting, but following the final Allied evacuation with the Norwegian King on 7 June Sweden no longer had that excuse, and the pressure for transit was maintained in order to provide increased protection for German supplies and troops from Allied attack.[25]

In Stockholm, May's determined rejection of transit gave way to June's equivocation as the likelihood of the German military threat became evident. At the key Cabinet meeting on 17 June to discuss the latest German demand from Ribbentrop, Sköld stated that a war with Germany would be 'hopeless' but conceded that transit could lead to British bombing raids. The Cabinet yielded against the background of Allied failure and the defeatism of the Swedish military leadership. Even British Minister Mallet conceded that a discouraged Sweden 'could not resist for long' without a 'proper airforce'.[26] In February when Mallet had been approached by Günther seeking help against the *Luftwaffe*, Günther told him that: 'The Germans would be able to obtain immediate and complete domination in the air and could destroy every city in Sweden.'[27] The lack of airpower was a decisive factor in the Government's sense of military weakness. The Swedish military now dug in for a prolonged four-year period of defensive duty with intervals of high tension. The Government was resolved to resist any Norwegian-style invasion by Germany.[28] The emphasis in the armed forces was on strengthening their equipment and training.

Procurement Problems

The dependence on foreign suppliers for military equipment had proved an Achilles heel for Swedish defence capability, particularly in airpower, but the problem extended across the entire procurement spectrum. There were four main areas of difficulty arising from foreign procurement. Firstly, because most of Sweden's equipment was supplied from overseas, this meant that standardisation was a nightmare, for example in ammunition calibres. Secondly, domestic arms production was under-developed except for artillery manufacturers *AB Bofors*. Thirdly, delivery was uncertain with experience of Italy, United States, Holland, Britain and Germany as unreliable suppliers. It was now evident that in a world at war, the priorities of the supplier would be met first. Sweden had demonstrated this in 1940 when guns ordered from the Bofors for Argentina, the Dutch East Indies and Thailand were simply appropriated by the Government through an export embargo and diverted to Swedish army use, leaving the two Asian countries less well-defended when the Japanese invaded two years later. Similarly, Germany in 1939 had denied Sweden the opportunity to purchase arms. The United States had been willing to supply guns, machine-guns, MTB's and planes in early 1940 but Sweden had to take its place in the queue behind Britain and France. That change of priority had its most damaging effect on the massively under-equipped Swedish airforce. An order for 300 planes from the United States was simply not fulfilled.

Italy was prepared to supply Sweden after the outbreak of war but this led to the fourth difficulty for Sweden, namely convincing the belligerents that permitting arms supplies to Sweden was not arming a presently neutral country which might end up on the other side of the conflict. Before the invasions of Norway and Denmark in early 1940, Sweden had purchased four second-hand destroyers of two different classes from the Italians and they sailed in late March for Sweden. After a prolonged voyage the little Swedish fleet was at anchor in the British-controlled Faeroe Islands on 20 June when their commander was told by the British navy to surrender his ships to them to prevent them falling into 'enemy hands'.[29] Outgunned and outmanoeuvred, he did so and it was only following two weeks of intense diplomatic effort, overshadowed by the German transit concession, that the ships – plundered of equipment – together with their crews were released. Sweden had been humiliated, Britain had acted illegally and high-handedly and the Swedish navy bore a grudge for its dishonour. This would overshadow future operations by Britain, for example the *Operation Performance* break-out in 1942.[30] The reason for the seizure was of course a British Admiralty fear that the destroyers could become part of the German *Kriegsmarine*, a perception which the Swedish Government resented.[31] The

Admiralty's stance showed how rapidly Sweden's external procurement situation could change with the fortunes of war. Only a few weeks earlier in April the British War Cabinet had supported the Swedish attempt to purchase the 300 aircraft from the USA.[32]

Lighter Equipment

By 1941, Swedish defence thinking had altered substantially due to experience and observation from over two years of successful German military operations. The effectiveness of speedy, mobile armour, closely supported by aircraft as well as the new trend of tank battles, paratroops, and the use of assault artillery had been carefully noted by a Government Commission set up by Sköld which reported in February 1942. An annual defence budget of about 560 million kroner had already been agreed the previous year to support a five-year plan.[33] Essentially, the Commission recommended greater mobility for the army with lighter weaponry backed up by airpower. For the navy, heavy battleships were abandoned for lighter craft such as destroyers, minesweepers, MTBs and submarines. Naval ship building proceeded with some urgency in the yards in Sweden, particularly in those of *Götaverkan*, and over seventy new ships were built in the five years between 1940 and 1945 while twenty-five obsolete vessels were scrapped.[34] By 1945, the Navy were able to deploy almost double the vessels, 148 compared with seventy-six in 1939, but with less than half the increase in tonnage.[35]

Other military procurement was also under way. Fortunately for Sweden, it suited the Germans to rectify their balance of payments deficit with exports of armaments. Germany had also supplied the Soviet Union on the same basis up to 1941. In the spring of 1942, the Germans supplied artillery and shells, hand-grenades, machine guns with ammunition, and radio equipment.[36] In addition, anti-tank guns came from Switzerland in 1941 and even grenade-throwers from Finland in 1942–3. The greatest change was, however, in domestic design and manufacture: large civilian manufacturers such as *Husqvarna*, *Ericsson* and *Volvo* had all become significant suppliers of military equipment comprising tanks, armoured vehicles and terrain vehicles, often based on foreign designs. *AB Bofors* continued to increase its output of artillery, supplemented by German deliveries.

The real breakthrough was in domestic aircraft design and manufacture for the airforce, primarily by *SAAB* (*Svenska aeroplan aktiebolaget*). In 1940 *Piaggio* engines were ordered from the Italians for a new, Swedish monoplane light bomber and reconnaissance aircraft, the *SAAB* 17. These supplemented emergency orders for *Fiat* and *Reggiane* fighters as well as *Caproni* bombers.[37] The Italians eventually supplied 216 aircraft and 180 engines.[38] The *SAAB* 17 bomber was joined in service in 1943 by the Swedish *SAAB* 22 fighter. *SAAB* 18 twin-engined bombers entered service in 1944 but the air force remained under-resourced.[39] Despite the development of domestic designs and production of aircraft, the air force was under strength relative to its plans perhaps partly due to a lack of earlier interest by the elderly Thörnell.[40] As late as 1942, the Cabinet was told that a new squadron could not be created due to a lack of machines and men.[41] Nevertheless by May 1945, the core of 200 fighters, now supplemented by United States Mustang fighter-bombers and 200 bombers, contrasted with the meagre strength in 1940, and an eight to ten-fold increase on 1936.

POST-1940 ARMY STRATEGY AND DEPLOYMENT

Following the near chaos of April 1940, the Swedish armed forces were confronted with a radically altered geopolitical situation which required different defensive strategies as well as tactics. Although unlikely, an attack on two fronts was not impossible but the immediate threat was now Germany. It was this factor which drove the politicians' policy of accommodation and concession to German interests. Militarily, the situation for Sweden was poor in terms of equipment and training but the strategy remained defensive: to resist any invasion of Sweden from any quarter. Against the threat of German invasion from Norway, the Swedish army was deployed primarily along the border area with a new emphasis on opposing paratroop landings elsewhere. The appearance of German troops in Finland in early 1941 was an additional factor to be taken into account for defence planning. The navy's coastal units would seal off entry into the Gulf of Bothnia and attack any sea-borne invasion on the east coast. The exception to the overwhelmingly defensive strategy was an offensive plan to take Narvik and so again secure a western seaport.[42]

The developments on the Russian Eastern Front in 1942 led the Swedish Command to plan in the summer for the possibility of an Allied pincer attack in northern Sweden in which the Western Allies would land in north Norway and the Russians would attack from Murmansk. In July the navy was directed to protect Åland and the northern coasts while the air force was instructed to attack any invasion across the Finnish borders. In October 1942, Swedish national defence was somewhat decentralised into seven military districts and by November a new, more offensive strategic plan was developed. Most of its operational objectives remained in force until the end of the war. One exception was the possibility of a Russian attack over the Finnish border in 1944 until this was ruled out by the Finnish-Russian armistice.[43] Primarily, the military districts were to oppose the Germans along the length of the Norwegian and Finnish borders in case of war – even envisaging attacking Norway in the Oslo area in the event of a German assault. These orders were accompanied by an instruction that they were to be followed even if Headquarters no longer functioned. The spirited instruction added: 'Every announcement that resistance should cease is [to be regarded as] false.'[44] Swedish fighting spirit was evident. As the Germans began to retreat in 1943, Swedish defence planning now had to confront the possibility of the advancing Red Army in Finland and north Norway threatening northern Sweden while the Germans remained a threat to the south and west. Fortifications in the north were strengthened and plans for a delaying action made. By 1944, Swedish planners now believed that a Western Allied attack was unlikely but that the Germans remained a potent threat in the short-term and the Russians in the long-term. This led to minor changes to army planning with a strengthening of the eastern defences. By mid-1944, however, new Commander-in-Chief Helge Jung could advise that the invasion threat was over for Sweden. Attention could now shift to dealing with the German end-games in Norway and Denmark.

Sweden's conscript army was expensive to mobilise both in direct costs for wages and fuel and in indirect costs to the economy and production through the loss of labour on farms, in forests and in factories. There was resistance to mobilisation within the Government partly for these reasons and partly from fear of increasing tension with the Germans. Hence mobilisation was ordered infrequently, primarily for defensive purposes but occasionally for training.[45] There were four significant mobilisations from 1940 onwards which were triggered mainly by concerns of a German invasion in response to Swedish political decisions or tensions in the relationship. The first mobilisation was the defensive response to the assaults on Denmark and Norway in April 1940 which continued during the period of threats from Germany over transit in early summer. The next instance of mobilisation was during the 'March

Crisis' of 1941, when tensions arose in Berlin over unfavourable Swedish press comment coupled with Swedish dismissal of a German request to transport heavy artillery to Norway by Swedish rail. In addition, Hitler had been unnerved by the British commando attacks on the Lofoten Islands. He thought that they foreshadowed a more substantial British landing in Norway. Thörnell requested and was given approval to call up 130,000 additional troops as a demonstration of strength with Per Albin's support.[46] The transit of the 15,000 troops of the Engelbrecht Division to Russia in June 1941 proved a political 'Midsummer crisis' rather than a military challenge for the Swedish army. Mobilisation was not undertaken in order to signal acquiescence.[47] In the 'February Crisis' of 1942, Hitler's renewed fears of a British invasion through Norway led to a build-up of German forces there directed against Sweden. Sweden mobilised 300,000 men in the third, large-scale mobilisation of the war.[48] Some evidence suggests that this mobilisation may have discouraged German intentions of 'liquidating' Sweden.[49] Finally in August 1943 the Government, fearing an adverse German reaction from the ending of troop transit, instructed the largest and final demonstration of force with 367,000 men mobilised. Germany accepted this decision without military response, partly due to simultaneous distractions in Italy and partly due to the *Wehrmacht's* inability to undertake an offensive response.

CONSEQUENCES OF GERMAN RETREAT

Although no further large-scale mobilisations would take place, Thörnell warned early in 1944 that even though the risk of Sweden being drawn into war on the Allied side had disappeared, a retreating German army in Finland in the short-term could launch an attack on Sweden to improve its tactical position. In the longer-term, the advancing Red Army would also be in a position to threaten Sweden and he recommended three divisions being mobilised to address these threats. The Government instead in March ordered a state of alert in Norrland and some strengthening of coastal defences in the Gulf of Bothnia. Later on, Günther's concerns about the Germans caused limited mobilisation. With the September 1944 armistice between Russia and Finland, the immediate threat to Sweden from Russia had now waned but not without a last twist. In their negotiations with the Finns, the Russians demanded the area around Porkkala for a military base which was dangerously close to Helsinki.

Finland attempted to substitute Åland for Porkkala and if they had been successful, then Sweden would have had a direct border with the Soviet Union.

Despite the reduced possibility of German attack, over 300,000 Germans remained as an army of occupation in Denmark and Norway until the end of the war, posing a threat to Sweden as well as to the approaching Allies. If the Germans chose to resist, the threat would also extend to the populations of all three countries. With this in mind, Sweden prepared militarily for the end of the war in three ways. Firstly, Danish and Norwegian 'Police Troops' were recruited, quartered, equipped and trained on Swedish territory for deployment into their countries to secure order and protect the civilian population. Secondly from 1943, the Swedish Defence Staff had been planning military intervention aimed at safeguarding lives and property in Norway and Denmark from a potentially destructive and lawless *Wehrmacht* as defeat drew nearer. The two operations 'Save Denmark' and 'Save Norway' not only envisaged a massive operation involving 500,000 men but also a combined forces landing on Bornholm. These operations were of course offensive rather than defensive. Thirdly, during the very last days of the war in Europe in April 1945, in the event of the German forces fighting a last-ditch defence in *Festung Norwegen*, Ministers approved an Allied request for military staff talks with Swedish officers to prepare for the deployment of Allied troops through Sweden to invade Norway. In the event, none of these operations were required. The Germans surrendered peacefully and the 'Police Troops' entered their countries with only light opposition, mainly from their collaborationist countrymen. Only in Danish Bornholm was there a rearguard action when the Russians supplanted the Germans as occupiers for almost a year. The devastation that had been a feature of the German retreat from Northern Norway was not repeated.

SEA WAR

At sea, the fleet's defensive duties were to safeguard shipping and prevent incursions into neutral waters using patrols, mine-laying and escort vessels.[50] In case of war the fleet's duties were coastal protection and harassment of enemy landings, primarily in the east, in cooperation with the air force. The Molotov–Ribbentrop Pact had galvanised the partly decommissioned navy into standby to prevent Russian incursion in the Baltic but it was the German *Kriegsmarine* that initially in 1939–40 aggressively challenged Swedish merchant shipping with attempts to search or seize Swedish vessels in international waters. The Germans forced Sweden to reduce its territorial limit from four to three miles thus restricting Sweden's three battleships to the Baltic and compelling Swedish shipping to reduce cargo to lessen draught for the shallower five metre depth passages.[51] More than forty cases of German interception were reported, some even in Swedish waters. The German arrogance was noted.[52] After the occupation of Norway and Denmark, the Skagerrak was blockaded and Swedish shipping cut off from the west which forced the navy to cut back on its operations due to a shortage of imported oil.[53] Naval planning now turned towards the prevention of invasion on the east coast and anti-submarine operations against the Russians in the Baltic.

Oil shortages restricted naval operations even further in autumn 1941 but the navy was detailed by the Government to escort German troopships within territorial waters as part of the settlement which defused the 'March Crisis'.[54] Following *Barbarossa* in June 1941, there were further concessions to the Germans when they confined Swedish naval operations to narrowly delineated areas, insisted on the Swedish completion of a mine field across the entire Baltic in order to restrict Russian submarines, and demanded the expulsion of Russian ships from Swedish ports. The Swedish navy chafed in the German collar. Even so, it was a German supply convoy which ignored Swedish warnings on 9 July and steamed directly into a Swedish minefield losing three ships and over 150 crew.[55] Further escort duties were ordered for German troop transports to Finland in territorial waters while Swedish merchant shipping went unprotected.

The freezing winter of 1941–2 restricted all seagoing in the northern Baltic and parts of the west coast until spring when the Russians prepared to launch their submarine offensive against shipping in the Baltic. These submarines were first detected in June 1942 but due to Finnish dilatoriness in laying a minefield, they had penetrated Bothnian waters by August. The torpedoing of shipping started in June against Finnish, German and Swedish ships with some success. By early July Sköld secretly had ordered retaliatory measures to warn off and if necessary, attack submarines near Swedish escorts. In mid July the navy believed it had sunk two submarines but the attacks against iron ore shipping continued during August. Swedish measures compelled the Russians to shift their operations further south and east into international waters. Oil shortages continued to hamper patrol and escort duties through the winter into 1943. In April a German mine sank the Swedish submarine *Ulven* and a nervous German ship opened fire on its sister submarine *Draken*. Both incidents took place within Swedish waters. Sweden now withdrew coastal access to the German navy in April and new shipping controls were introduced in July. In addition further minefields were laid in the Baltic in preparation for the Swedish withdrawal of transit in August and important harbours were blockaded to prevent any German attack.

Autumn and winter 1943–4 were relatively quiet but with fears of Russian advances in Finland, the fleet was on higher alert. This was in case of a preventative Swedish occupation of Åland being required and also to increase defences against a possible German attack on Skåne in March 1944. In late March and April 1944 fears of an invasion force created nervous reports about German shipping in the Baltic and regular reconnaissance continued. But with D-Day, the likelihood of a German invasion on mainland Sweden diminished. Nevertheless, the Swedish navy sank one of Aristotle Onassis' requisitioned tankers in the entrance to Göteborg harbour to provide a blockade defence.[56] This contributed to a farcical collision that same week when the disputed Norwegian ships, *Lionel* and *Dicto*, moved up the coast to Lysekil.[57] In the Baltic, the Russian advance had again brought the prospect of submarine attacks in Swedish waters aimed at German troop evacuation ships. Foreign merchant ships were forbidden passage in September and the Germans declared most of the eastern half of the Baltic to be a German operational area. Despite Swedish counter-measures, the Russians torpedoed the Gotland ferry in November 1944 with eighty-four civilians lost. Although naval escorts were intensified, even Swedish fishing boats were now attacked.

By the end of the war, the Swedish navy had lost 163 men due mainly to mines but also through accidents, particularly the explosions causing the sinking of three destroyers in Hårsfjärden in 1942. The navy undertook a massive building and re-equipment programme throughout the war but was hampered in its operations and training by a lack of oil rather than a dearth of seamanship or courage.[58] Its role in providing concessions to the Germans, carefully concealed from the Allies, was the responsibility of the politicians and not the officers. Its presence contributed significantly to the overall deterrent effect of Swedish defence.

Air War

The air force's wartime remit was to contain or disrupt the operations of enemy formations and to limit their effectiveness. In 1939, its ability was compromised by weaknesses apparent in equipment and training. Its aircraft mainly comprised bombers to attack enemy bases and it lacked fighters, modern or otherwise.[59] Due to equipment and manpower limitations, defence was severely limited to critical potential targets and even then, without night fighters throughout the war, it was accepted that the enemy bomber would always get through to destroy and kill. Fighters were initially placed around Stockholm and Skåne but anti-aircraft batteries were probably more effective in defence. In the early months of the war, the emphasis was on protecting Swedish airspace through preventing incursions by enemy aircraft rather than fear of intentional attack. During the Winter War, the focus shifted north from Skåne to Stockholm and a Russian plane was downed by anti-aircraft in December 1939 in Norrland. Rules of engagement were changed to include warning shots and exclude medical and damaged aircraft from fire.

Increased German activity in April 1940 led to the deployment of the air force in the west but following the occupation of Denmark and Norway, the duties varied between reconnaissance and patrol from rapidly changing locations. The presence of the *Luftwaffe* and the RAF in close proximity to the Swedish border during the Norwegian campaign from April to June 1940 created incidents, primarily incursions, of which there were 830 during those months with thirty-six planes fired at and ten shot down by Swedish defence forces. The *Luftwaffe* fired twice at Swedish targets and the RAF bombed Sweden three times in 1940: at Vassijaure on the Norwegian border, near Malmö and Helsingborg. The new phenomenon of crash landings which was to continue throughout the war now began. Fifteen planes made forced landings in 1940 while twelve escaping Norwegian planes also landed. Extensive patrol operations severely stretched both machines and personnel and the air force switched to a lower alert after the transit concessions reduced German-Swedish tension in mid-1940. Swedish fighters were considered to be so inferior to those of the belligerents that they were held in reserve, with the main job of policing the frontiers left to the anti-aircraft gun regiments.

Fears of air attack in 1941 by the Western Allies or Russia as the Engelbrecht Division was transported across Sweden saw anti-aircraft batteries stationed at key points on their route. The 1941 transit concessions also included over-flying permission to German aircraft. In conjunction with over-flying rights, repeated German pressure led to an easing of the orders to fire warning shots at planes encroaching on Swedish territory which in effect meant that single German or Finnish planes would not be fired on. There were almost 1,000 incursions in 1941 and only on fifty-six occasions were shots fired. No planes were shot down but a British bomber crash-landed, an occurrence which would increase as Bomber Command began to target Germany. In 1942 greater numbers of RAF bombers intruded over Swedish airspace on their way to and from Germany but from May all single planes were exempt from warning shots. Again, about 1,000 instances of incursion were recorded in 1942 but 1943 saw an increasing number of Allied machines involved. Sweden could do little to intercept them while they flew at night. German over-flying rights were severely compromised when a German courier plane which made a forced landing was found to have uniformed and armed servicemen onboard in contravention of the over-flying agreement. The outcome was stricter rules.

In spring, 1944, the possibility of German action against Åland led also to increased alertness and reconnaissance by the air force. Three Swedish reconnaissance planes were shot down over the eastern Baltic in May, almost certainly by the Germans. Incursions and crash-landings continued over Swedish territory but an increasing number were being brought down by Swedish anti-aircraft batteries. During July and August alone, three planes were downed, fifty-seven force-landed and eleven crashed. Incursions continued right up to the end of the war, primarily by Allied bombers but joined now by German deserters fleeing the imploding Reich. Sixty-three German planes landed between September 1944 and May 1945.

Despite the fact that the main duty of deterring incursions into Swedish airspace fell on the anti-aircraft batteries rather than the slender resources of the air force, the air force was gradually able to shoulder an increasing amount of the defensive load with better equipment and training. The air force was primarily held in reserve in the event of enemy attack and its capability in this role was never put to the test.

Service Leadership and Attitude

The Swedish military caste during the war changed fundamentally in both leadership and attitude but there were significant differences between the three service branches.

The army was in 1939 characterised by Prussian military values at the top. For example, Thörnell was described by a close associate as 'having and retaining a rather considerable admiration for the old German officer corps', an admiration which pre-dated 1914.[60] This admiration was strengthened additionally by the early success of the *Wehrmacht* which gave way to a general conviction that Germany would dominate Europe through military victory. It was further buttressed after June 1941, by a widespread belief that Germany was safeguarding Sweden and Finland with its 'crusade against bolshevism'. Chief of Staff Samuel Åkerhielm hoped that the Russians would bomb the Engelbrecht Division during its transit to bring Sweden into the war, questionably 'the best thing that could happen.'[61] Thörnell, unlike some of his officers, exhibited total loyalty to the Government, despite disagreeing with many of its decisions.[62] As Westman noted, Thörnell would, 'do his duty to the limit, even if he did not believe in success.'[63]

The impact of mass-conscription was to change those Prussian attitudes. A reform group of senior officers in the 1930s had set out an agenda for change in the military journal, *Ny Militär Tidskrift*. The army was characterised by poor training, rigid discipline and an officer corps out of touch with changing Swedish society. Between 1940 and 1942, Sköld set out a challenging vision for the leadership which envisaged a democratisation of the army's duties towards its soldiers without weakening their requirement to obey commands. Officers should be less selectively recruited to promote closer identification with their men and enhance their leadership.[64] These statements found concrete expression in the formation of the Defence School in 1942.[65]

Sköld was reflecting views held in wider circles.[66] Westman noted that when an acquaintance of his had discussed politics with senior officers in early 1941, they were so out of touch that they believed – or hoped – that if Russia again attacked Finland, the Swedish Government would split and civil war would break out.[67] Grafström believed that almost the only source of Nazi support in Sweden was the military – in ironic contrast to the situation in Germany.[68] The well-known German tendencies of the officer caste had created unease and distrust in both the Government and the country which became focused on the loyal but indiscreet Thörnell. He had of course contributed to these concerns by his profound conviction that Germany would succeed while a German defeat by the Soviet Union would shackle Sweden to bolshevism.[69] Never one to miss an opportunity, he and his like-minded colleague Åkerhielm formally proposed to the Cabinet in June 1941 that, following the Engelbrecht concession, Swedish military and material support for the German attack on Russia should be provided indirectly. In doing so, they both completely misread the sentiments of the Government in which two members, Wigforss and Bagge, were determined to unseat Thörnell.[70] Thörnell's position had been secure during the long period of German ascendancy as a visible indication of Swedish inclination. With the change in the war situation in 1943, opposition to him grew but his departure was delayed by the unexpected support of Per Albin who did not wish to confront Germany with a clean sweep of German sympathisers at a time when the Germans could still damage Sweden. Instead, Thörnell was even further marginalised in Government thinking and discussion.[71] Eventually, the Government changed the leadership on 1 April when Helge Jung and CA Ehrensvärd replaced Thörnell and Åkerhielm after much discussion of the candidates' characteristics by the Cabinet. The Germans realised that this signalled a significant change in Swedish attitude, particularly as a raft of their other service contacts had seen German-oriented officers replaced by Allied-oriented individuals.[72]

Per Albin's comments about the German connections in his armed forces reveals an important strand in the Swedish containment of the German threat to Swedish institutions, policies and personalities. When challenged by the *Dagens Nyheter* political editor that such associations gave the wrong impression, he responded:

> 'Don't say that,' said Per Albin with a sly look. 'I think it's rather good for us that the Germans mainly come into contact with people like Thörnell and Åkerheim and Kellgren in the High Command. Uthmann (the German Military Attaché) values them.'[73]

This insight reveals a conscious effort to delude the Germans into thinking that they were making inroads into Swedish influential circles while they were in the ascendant. Per Albin ensured that the right-wing military's political influence was strictly limited and in 1944 he kicked the loyal and elderly General upstairs – never 'a long-term arrangement'.[74]

Heading up the Navy for the duration of the war was Thörnell's supporter, Admiral Fabian Tamm who had famously, with Thörnell, presented a bust of Karl XII to Hitler in 1939. He had also been dispatched to Germany in April 1940 to reassure both Göring and Hitler of Sweden's determination to resist being drawn into the war. The Navy was suspected of pro-German tendencies by the British, possibly due to their humiliation at the hands of the British over the Italian destroyers' seizure in 1940. Naval Staff Chief, Commodore Strömbäck was quoted in early 1942 as having been 'convinced of a German victory and [that] a victory for the Russians would be Europe's misfortune' [75] A year later, the same Commodore blamed the German sinking of the Swedish submarine 'Ulven' on its Captain.[76] Vice Admiral Claës Lindsström is alleged to have personally ensured that German transports to and from Finland using Swedish territorial waters through the Stockholm archipelago were exempt from stop and search and that information regarding their passages was strictly limited to a few officers, all due to his Nazi sympathies. An alternative explanation might be that this was what the UD wanted and Lindstrom was so instructed, irrespective of his sympathies. This concession had been agreed with the Germans in August 1941 to avoid German pressure for further rail transit through Sweden.[77] Lindsström was in any case retired in 1942.[78] The Navy actively engaged Russian submarines that menaced Swedish shipping in the Baltic and since it escorted German shipping within Swedish territorial waters it had necessarily close operational ties with the Germans. The British Naval Attaché still regarded the navy as pro-German as late as December 1944.[79]

The air force demonstrated the most pro-Allied attitudes from the top down.[80] Air chief Nordenskiöld was greatly admired by the British, who noted in 1944 that as a result of him and his predecessors:

> In comparing [with] the Swedish Army and particularly the Swedish Navy, it can be said that in the latter service [the air force] pro-German sympathy is practically non-existent[81]

That the youngest service should differ from the other two is perhaps not surprising as recruitment to its officer corps was based on meritocracy rather than class and heredity. It also modelled itself on the RAF rather than the German military establishment. The impact of a large influx of conscripts altered the regular military establishment culture away from rigid hierarchy to a more open and flexible organisation. It is clear that Sköld had these aspects in mind when he reflected on the change in attitude in 1945 and spoke of the voluntary defence organisations as 'folk-movements' and the importance of generating a positive 'defence mentality' together with the conscripted officers. The Home Guard even selected their own leaders, reflecting the new democratising influences.[82] How did these changes, added to the vast sums spent on re-equipment and training, improve the effectiveness of Swedish defence?

SWEDISH DEFENCE CAPABILITY

The strength of Swedish defence increased substantially as resources poured into the three services after 1940. These changes had an effect on the observers who continually assessed Sweden's defensive capabilities in order to consider to what extent Sweden could stand up to Allied or German invasion. These opinions contributed to each side's policy towards Sweden. In the Government, Swedish ability to resist a German invasion was perhaps overestimated in comparison to the views of the belligerents.[83] By November 1941, an impressed German Military Attaché could report the Army's strength at 220,000 men, deployed around Sweden but in particular along the Norwegian-Swedish border where two Divisions could be deployed east of Narvik at forty-eight hour's notice to defend the iron ore mines.[84] By mid 1942, the British assessment was less generous. Churchill was surprised to learn that the War Office had estimated Swedish resistance against a German attack at only two weeks. This view was rejected by the Stockholm attachés who estimated that with current reserves of material and fuel, resistance could hold out for three months. [85]

A more detailed assessment had been carried out by a representative of the German High Command in October 1943. He concluded that Swedish defence capability had been boosted by impressive rearmament and the placing of the country's supplies on a war-footing. There were still specific areas of weakness in weaponry such as heavy anti-aircraft guns, obsolete tanks and artillery, but the army was particularly well trained in rifles, operations in forests and rough terrain in adverse weather. Those battle skills had badly disadvantaged the Russians in Finland in 1939. The assessment went on to contrast these strengths with growing German difficulties in Norway. The navy and air force also came out well from this assessment.[86] German perceptions of Swedish strength were further boosted in April 1944 when their Attaché overestimated Swedish mobilised troop dispositions due to a misunderstanding about mobilisation organisation.[87] Sweden had succeeded in further deterring the Germans.

The Allied assessments in autumn 1943 were less positive than the German view but still recognised that Swedish forces formed an adequate defence. Swedish resistance was estimated to last about a month in south and central Sweden but the greatest value to the Allies lay in Sweden's strategic position as a base for striking at German forces.[88] This Allied view was less complimentary during the planning for a possible Allied-Swedish relief mission to Norway in 1945 which accurately identified the great Swedish weakness, despite five years of training and re-equipment, as a lack of combat experience.

> It is unlikely that the Swedish military can become a particularly effective force due to their not having any fighting experience and because they have mainly been trained for defensive duties. They ought however to be extremely useful in following-up, reserve and L of C (lines of communication) roles.[89]

It is clear that Sweden's defensive capability did increase considerably during the war but that significant weaknesses remained, particularly in air power and tanks. Still, the belligerents did factor Swedish resistance into their appraisals. In early 1940, the Allies had to face the fact that they could not land troops and transport them to Finland without Swedish cooperation. Similarly, the Germans looked for evidence of military muscle to back-up the Government's repeated assurances that Sweden would resist any invasion from any quarter. Although the Cabinet suspected German motives and feared German military action throughout the whole wartime period, only one German plan was ever developed – in 1943.[90]

THE VON SCHELL INVASION PLAN, 1943

Hitler's fears of an Allied invasion landing in Norway were stimulated further by Allied deception *Operation Tindall*. Its objective was to mislead the Germans into thinking that a European invasion was aimed at Norway and not Sicily and led to panzer-expert Lieutenant-General Adolf von Schell being sent there in 1943. He was to prepare plans for an attack on Sweden which could be launched if an Allied landing threatened to bring them into the war on the Allied side.[91]

The careful intelligence assessments by the Germans assisted von Schell when he began planning in April 1943. The ingredients that he used for his daring plan were German strengths and Swedish weaknesses. He believed that a German *Blitzkrieg* using a relatively small panzer force and infantry, striking hard with surprise and speed supported by air attacks, could overcome a Swedish defence twice its size. The attack should utilise open country to minimise the Swedish advantage of forest warfare and favour German advantages in tank gunnery, assault artillery, motorised infantry, and fighter-bomber aircraft with air superiority. Fixed defences would be circumvented as was the Maginot-line and in echoes of the Low Countries in 1940, the speed and success of a German advance would rout Swedish resistance.

The attack would be in two main operational areas: in the north, *Operation One* would invade with the support of paratroops from the Trondheim area to take Sundsvall on the Bothnian coast and join forces landed from Finland. Further south in mid-Sweden, *Operation Two* envisaged cracking the Swedish defensive lines running north-south through open country between the Norwegian border and Stockholm with forces landed on the coast north of Uppsala. The Swedish fleet would be bottled-up in port by the *Kriegsmarine* through mine-laying while the Swedish air force with its outmoded equipment was not felt to be a factor, unlike the well-equipped anti-aircraft defences which were anticipated to be effective. Overall, the Swedish forces would be caught napping and quickly collapse, allowing the Germans to move north against the invading Allied forces. The von Schell plan had the additional advantage of not requiring an Allied invasion to trigger the attack: Germany could equally move against Sweden without it.

As with all good plans, implementation is the difficult part and von Schell set about it intensively, holding the necessary staff discussions and military exercises between April and August 1943, which of course came to the notice of the nervous Swedes through excellent military intelligence from *Centralen*. Sweden was in the process of terminating the transit agreement and in July mobilised all services in anticipation of German retaliation. For von Schell, the military situation deteriorated with the failure of expected reinforcements to arrive while the Eastern Front was disintegrating at Kursk. In particular, the 25th Panzer Division which was key to the success of the plan may have been at only half-strength with mixed weaponry and was in any case diverted on 23 August to counter an possible Allied landing in France, *en route* quelling civil unrest in Norway and Denmark. Von Schell's daring plan was never tested due to the increasingly chaotic military task facing the German High Command while growing Swedish defensive strength raised the cost of invasion even further for the Germans.

Home Defence

Von Schell had envisaged a swift military defeat of the Swedish army in the field followed by occupation whereas Sweden had taken steps to supplement conventional forces to ensure that this was not going to be a walkover. At an early stage in the war, a number of irregular local defence volunteer initiatives had sprung up, stimulated by the prospect of the Winter War spilling over into Sweden. There had been a long tradition in Sweden of voluntary paramilitary organisations such as rifle-clubs with 200,000 members nationwide. These overlapped with the *Landstorm* (Territorial Army or TA) and certain women's groups to provide additional military reserves for Sweden. This spontaneous popular movement converged with some military thinking in 1938–9 which envisaged locally organised civilian groups supporting reservists; for example in dealing with a paratroop attack. During the winter of 1939, the army responded to popular clamour by announcing in January 1940 that a study would investigate the feasibility of a national organisation. The study quickly resulted in a recommendation to plan the formation of a Home Guard (*Hemvärn*) force and during that planning process, volunteers registered with the dozens of unofficial groups which had formed throughout the country.[92] Defence Minister Sköld, perhaps seeing an opportunity to broaden democratic involvement in the armed forces and respond to popular pressure, moved quickly and in the nervous and urgent atmosphere of May 1940, the *Riksdag* passed the required legislation.

Early in June the *Hemvärn* started to recruit from among the volunteers, whose numbers had increased to 85,000. The broad-based recruitment by district representatives reflected all groups in society with about one-third over forty, one-third under twenty and the remaining one-third being untrained men of conscription age. The local commanders who occupied these politically sensitive posts were also broadly selected and reflected over 220 occupations, demonstrating that leadership was not the exclusive preserve of old soldiers and right-wing reactionaries. An additional feature was the formation of work-place units which complemented the district-based organisation, falling under the national leadership of Colonel Gustaf Petri. The *Hemvärn* task was to guard local installations and deal with airborne attacks for which initially they were poorly equipped and trained. The shortages of weapons, particularly rifles, had forced the Government to limit *Hemvärnet* numbers, and volunteers were encouraged to provide their own guns. They brought in about 18,000, further supplemented by 15,000 from the hard-pressed army stores. Automatic weapons arrived later in 1941. Like the regular army, uniforms were in short supply but again, improvements took place later. Training initially focused on rifle practice but later, innovatively using the distance-learning techniques of study circles, correspondence schools and public radio broadcasts, about 75,000 volunteers learned at home about field-craft, weapon handling and dealing with airborne landings. Despite the *Hemvärn* being locally organised, it was gradually brought in to the regular army structure for defence planning and from October 1942 became integrated as part of Swedish defence organisation. Like its equivalents among the belligerents, the force suffered in its early days from a shortage of equipment and training but they gradually transformed into a stable and respected reservist fighting force that took part in exercises with the regulars.[93]

One of the women's groups which acquired heroine status during the war was the so-called '*Lottor*' (Lottas) emulating the Finnish women's Lotta Svärd Corps. The Corps was named after Finnish writer, J. L. Runeberg's redoubtable heroine and the concept of a women's group to support the male military was transposed into Sweden in 1924 to provide non-combatant auxiliaries to the *Landstorm*. In 1940, the *Hemvärn* began to incorporate them in their operations and at the end of 1942, they separated from the *Landstorm* to become an independently organised defence force ('*Sveriges Lottakårer*') organised into 500 different local corps which reflected their much-increased range of duties and numbers.[94] Their contribution spanned catering, nursing, communications, administration, logistics, air defence and civil defence while their numbers grew from 26,000 in 1939 to 110,000 in 1945.[95] By 1945, just over 5,000 of these served the Navy in roles such as issuing uniforms and laundry. Many a hungry conscript or Finnish refugee had cause to welcome the catering *Lottor* and many of them combined a demanding job, either as housewife and mother or in employment with their 'spare time' duties as a '*Lotta*'. The Government had initially relied on patriotic zeal to form the Corps but as the war progressed and the demand for their services increased, patriotism had to be supported by payment and better conditions.[96] Despite women playing an active role in the volunteer movement, the roles which they were allocated tended to reinforce traditional attitudes and did not represent any liberating breakthrough away from domestic duties or simple tasks. To further release men for military duties, the Swedish Woman Drivers Association (*SKBR*) was created in 1942 following earlier initiatives. The *SKBR* women drivers made a major contribution to refugee evacuation.

'FREE WARFARE' BEHIND ENEMY LINES?

While von Schell was planning his attack in early 1943, the Swedish army was developing, in great secrecy, a force intended to operate behind enemy lines to attack and disrupt communications and supplies. The secrecy was due to two factors: the main enemy would be Germany and the force would necessarily operate offensively across Swedish borders in Norway and Finland. The idea for such a force arose in 1942 from earlier war experience and Swedish exercises. It was championed by Viking Tamm, who had himself served as a volunteer in the Winter War and was designated 'Free warfare' ('*fria kriget*'). Six of the seven national military district commanders were instructed in October 1942, to carry out two preparatory actions: first to plan for a number of uniformed commandos ('*jägartrupper*') at the outbreak of war to get behind the enemy front with arms for the local population and organise attacks on enemy support lines: secondly to create a number of secret dumps of armaments and food to support these commandos, assuming that the enemy front had advanced into Swedish territory.

The required personal characteristics for the commandos who would operate without regular army contact, emphasised robust fitness to cope with challenging terrains and weather, excellent weapon skills, and appropriate field-craft for orientation and concealment. Preferred backgrounds included ski-sport, hunting and forestry. Their commanders required initiative and cunning as well as outstanding leadership skills. In some ways, they were the antithesis of the earlier Swedish army traditions of obedience and structured response to detailed plans, and reflected the recent infusion of flexible thinking which was filtering through. They were equipped with light weaponry, grenades and explosives together with high calorie rations.

The plans for the commandos were to support the military district's objectives by crossing the borders and attack a defined number of points up to 100 kilometres inside Norway and Finland, for example airfields, bridges and radio stations. Fifty of the targets lay inside Norway and two districts planned to involve and arm the Norwegian resistance. Only seven of the targets were in Finland. These plans were approved in December 1942 and the effort now focused on recruitment and training, activities which continued until the end of the war. By August 1944, when they were integrated more closely with the regular forces for more effective deployment, there were fifty-eight commando formations but these retained the ethos of independent cross-border operations. The Germans would have found these well-trained and fully equipped men a formidable opponent in their rear when their best troops were forward on the advance. Sweden may not have had combat experience but the formation of the commandos demonstrates a determination to go on the offensive to hamper a German attack with high-calibre troops recruited, equipped and trained to kill Germans. Von Schell and his planners were wise to avoid taking on Swedes in forests and rough country. The *Wehrmacht* was probably no match for them and the German fear of surprise attacks in the forests had been well noted by the Swedes.[97] The earlier fate of the Red Army in Finland had served as a potent warning.

Military Conclusions

The contribution of Swedish forces to the maintenance of Swedish independence is now largely overlooked while interest in Sweden's war has moved towards simpler polemical issues. Yet there are points worth emphasising that arise from their record. It is evident that the politicians were firmly, if at times inexpertly, in charge of the country's defences. Furthermore, the political will to resist invasion was apparent from swelling defence spending, conscription, mass-mobilisations and the creation of irregular forces. Whether an Allied force would have been resisted with the same vigour as a German or Soviet formation was never tested. What is certain is that Sweden would not have been a pushover for either the *Wehrmacht* or the Red Army. Commander-in-Chief Thörnell's loyalty overcame his misgivings about the wisdom of his Government's instructions and their reluctance to share his enthusiasm for supporting Germany against Russia. Yet he proved an appropriate and disposable symbol of Swedish cooperation that in essence conceded little to strengthen the German military position. Thörnell also symbolised a class of right-wing militarism that the Social Democrats had had in their sights for decades. The army's interest in pre-1914 coups, its inter-war behaviour in shooting strikers dead and its leaders' naked ambitions to involve Sweden in a Finnish war with Russia made it a target for reforms that duly took place during the war. The post-war services characterised a citizens' force rather than a class elite. The two greatest weaknesses were in equipment and training. Defence against Blitzkrieg and total warfare depended heavily on the skilful use of aircraft and pilots that Sweden clearly lacked right up to 1945 despite desperate efforts to acquire modern machines. Added to this was the understandable absence of combat experience in all services. However, it is notable that the period of resistance that foreign observers believed the Swedish forces would offer an invader increased during the war and this increase reflected the effort expended on addressing the weaknesses. Still, airpower allowed Germany to threaten Sweden with a Rotterdam or Warsaw-type bombing to cow the Government into the 1940 transit concessions in the absence of fighter defence. A major legacy of the failed procurement policy was the development of a domestic defence equipment manufacturing industry which would sustain Swedish armed neutrality in the post-war period. Another legacy was the significant mass-engagement of the Swedish population as a result of conscription and volunteers for military service. The experience changed the lives of many individuals and as we shall see, the post-war national psyche. But for some, however, the experience was traumatic. An estimated 50,000 servicemen were invalided as a result of injuries, accidents and the appalling conditions in which many were billeted and deployed.[98]

Notes

1. Forslund, Beredskapsdagbok 1939–45, p. 11.
2. Norrbohm & Skogsberg, Att flyga är att leva, p. 64.
3. Cronenberg, 'Kapplöpning med tiden', p. 114.
4. Carlgren,'Den stora överraskningen', p. 148.
5. Bojerud, 'Mundering modell 39', pp. 123–41.
6. Cronenberg, 'Kapplöpning med tiden', p. 120.
7. Meinander, Finlands historia, p. 190.
8. NA FO 371/24833–0005 9 June 1940.
9. Hägglöf, Möte med Europa, p. 227.
10. Hägglöf, Svensk krigshandelspolitik, p. 101.
11. Möller, Per Edvin Sköld, p. 190.
12. Johansson, Per Albin och kriget, p. 125.
13. Lindqvist, Drömmar och verklighet, p. 428.
14. Möller, Per Edvin Sköld, p. 196.
15. Wahlbäck & Boberg (eds), Sveriges sak är vår, pp. 55–61.
16. Möller, Per Edvin Sköld, p. 213.
17. Norrbohm & Skogsberg, Att flyga är att leva, p. 73.
18. Sundell, 9 April, p. 100.

19. Lagvall, *Flottans neutralitetsvakt*, p. 160.
20. Cronenberg, 'Krigsfall Tyskland', p. 242.
21. Möller, *Per Edvin Sköld*, p. 215.
22. Wahlbäck & Boberg (eds), *Sveriges sak är vår*, pp. 64–5
23. Sundell in Wahlbäck & Boberg (eds), *Sveriges sak är vår*, pp. 69–71 & Cronenberg, 'Krigsfall Tyskland', p. 252.
24. Petrow, *The Bitter Years*, pp. 82–4.
25. Documents on German Foreign Policy, Vols 8–13. The War Years, 1939–1941, p. 563, No. 427, June 1940 Keitel to Ribbentrop.
26. NA FO 371/24861–0004 8 July 1940 Mallet to FO.
27. NA FO 371/41934 8 February 1940 Mallet to Halifax.
28. Grafström, *Anteckningar*, 20 February 1942.
29. Lagvall, *Flottans neutralitetsvakt*, p. 132.
30. Tennant, *Touchlines of war*, p. 218.
31. Lindqvist, *Drömmar och verklighet*, pp. 471–2.
32. Medlicott, *The Economic Blockade*,Vol. 1, p. 619.
33. Möller, *Per Edvin Sköld*, p. 257.
34. Wangel, *Sveriges militära beredskap*, p. 322.
35. Lagvall, *Flottans neutralitetsvakt*, p. 109 (78,000 tonnes compared to 109,000 tonnes).
36. Hägglöf, *Svensk krigshandelspolitik*, p. 235.
37. Norrbohm & Skogsberg, *Att flyga är att leva*, p. 77.
38. Beredskapstid 1939–1945.
39. The aircraft category type numbers have been simplified.
40. Grafström, *Anteckningar*, 13 June 1944.
41. Westman, *Politiska anteckningar*, 5.3.1942.
42. Wangel, *Sveriges militära beredskap*, p. 468.
43. Gäfvert, 'Det fria kriget', p. 267.
44. Wangel, *Sveriges militära beredskap*, p. 472.
45. Kellgren, *Sex krigsår i Skölds skugga*, p. 33.
46. Westman, *Politiska anteckningar*, 14.3.1941.
47. Scott, 'The Swedish Midsummer Crisis of 1941', p. 378.
48. Möller, *Per Edvin Sköld*, p. 267.
49. Boheman, *På vakt*, p. 294.
50. This description is based on Wangel, *Sveriges militära beredskap*, pp. 546–74.
51. Lagvall, *Flottans neutralitetsvakt*, p. 27.
52. Ibid. p. 24.
53. Wangel, *Sveriges militära beredskap*, p. 555.
54. An instruction which appears to have been overlooked in a recent popular allegation of naval nazism. See 'Spioner, seglare, flyktingar och sjöräddare' in *Stångmärket*.
55. Lagvall, *Flottans neutralitetsvakt*, pp. 50–1.
56. Mattsson, *Redarna kring runda bordet*, p. 187.
57. Mattsson, *Redarna kring runda bordet*, p. 196.
58. Lagvall, *Flottans neutralitetsvakt*, p. 112.
59. Wangel, 'Luftsförsvaret under beredskapsåren', pp. 514–15.
60. Kellgren, quoted in Richardson, *Förtroligt och hemligt*, p. 181.
61. Quoted in Ekman, 'Skilful realpolitik or unprincipled opportunism?', p. 189.
62. Möller, *Per Edvin Sköld*, p. 241.
63. Westman, *Politiska anteckningar*, 18.2.1942.
64. Möller, *Per Edvin Sköld*, pp. 232–6.
65. Böhme, 'Upplysning om och inom försvaret', p. 252.

66. Zetterberg, 'Storkriget går mot sitt slut', p. 30.
67. Westman, Politiska anteckningar, 14.3.1941.
68. Grafström, Anteckningar, 30 January 1941.
69. Möller, Per Edvin Sköld, p. 265.
70. Zetterberg, 'Storkriget går mot sitt slut', p. 38.
71. Ibid. p. 37.
72. Ibid. p. 32.
73. Cronenberg, 'Och får jag tag i den fan-', pp. 278–9.
74. Johansson, Per Albin och kriget, p. 224.
75. Grafström, Anteckningar, 21 April 1942.
76. Ibid. 24 April 1943.
77. Westman, Politiska anteckningar, 1.8.1941.
78. Sobéus, 'Admiral Claës Lindsström'.
79. NA FO 371/43529 'Survey' of Pro-German sympathies and attitudes 17 December 1944.
80. Mallet, Memoirs, pp. 115–16.
81. NA FO 371/43529 'Survey' of Pro-German sympathies and attitudes 17 December 1944.
82. Brink, Demokrat och krigsfrivillig, p. 58.
83. Boheman, På vakt, p. 293.
84. Zetterberg, '1942: storkriget vänder, Sveriges utsatta läge består', p. 121.
85. NA FO 371/33068 Estimates of how long Swedish resistance could hold out, 1 June 1942.
86. Zetterberg, 'Storkriget går mot sitt slut', pp. 46–9.
87. Ibid. p. 43.
88. Zetterberg, 'Svensk säkerhetspolitik 1943, pp. 97–8.
89. Quoted in Leifland, General Böhmes val, p. 98.
90. Westman, Politiska anteckningar, 19.4.1940 'En sådan plan måste har funnits utarbetad'.
91. See Zetterberg, 'Svensk säkerhetspolitik 1943, pp. 55–80.
92. Brandberg, 'Hemvärnet', pp. 381–92.
93. Möller, Per Edvin Sköld, p. 220.
94. Brink, Demokrat och krigsfrivillig, p. 9.
95. Grafström, 'Frivilligförsvaret', pp. 396–7.
96. Lagvall, Flottans neutralitetsvakt, pp. 158–9.
97. Berggren, Världskrig, kommunism och nazism, p. 93.
98. Forslund, Beredskapsdagbok 1939–45, p. 127.

11

The Front at Home – *Beredskapstiden*

One striking feature in Swedish accounts of the war years is the frequent use of the term, *beredskap*. There is no direct equivalent in English but it combines the characteristics of preparedness, readiness, stand-by and emergency. Its usage to describe the state of the country during 1939–45 is significant because it allowed the authorities to portray their military and civil measures in a passive, defensive manner. This suited a neutral that officially regarded the belligerents on an equal footing and studiously avoided any implications that war was likely with any one of them. Swedish *beredskap* was what Per Albin famously claimed was good in August 1939 but *beredskapstiden* – the stand-by period – was the defining term for the Home Front. As the Second World War raged outside its borders, Sweden experienced a calmer *beredskapstid* within. Yet while it is true that relatively few of its citizens died while on active military service or even as civilian casualties, it would be grossly misleading to characterise the everyday life of Sweden as unaffected by the Second World War. The population experienced significant social, political and economic disruption as a result of wartime conditions and emerged in 1945 as an altered society in attitude and aspiration. Furthermore, governmental institutions and the economic infrastructure had been strengthened through adaptation to wartime conditions. The political turmoil of the 1920s and 1930s had by late 1939 stabilised somewhat with the formation of the wartime Coalition Government. There seems little doubt that political unity – at least outwardly – coupled with Per Albin's *Folkhem* vision, created a stronger foundation for the social and national cohesion which was a remarkable feature of the war years in Sweden. How did the country function politically and socially during the years of relative isolation, with trade to the west controlled by Germany? What was life like for ordinary people in the towns, villages and countryside of Sweden?

Observers familiar with the British experience on the Home Front during 1939–45 might discern distinct parallels between everyday life in Sweden and in Britain. Of course most – but not all – Swedes were spared the dreaded telegram announcing death or disappearance of a close relative. For Sweden, the toll was about 2,200 fatalities, due mainly to mines and torpedoes at sea. Unlike urban Britain, Swedes did not live in constant dread of the *Luftwaffe* and V-weapons. These apart, Swedes did experience real fears of invasion, with disruptive conscription, air raid precautions and for some, casualties from military action. Almost everyone suffered from shortages, economic hardship, rationing, black marketeers and official surveillance while refugees flooded into the country. These shared experiences together with an active media and growth of popular entertainment contributed to a lowering of class barriers and an expectation of a fairer post-war society.

WARTIME POLITICS

The necessity during the war for an outward display of cross-party and political unity which dampened open debate and stifled criticism of foreign policy in the *Riksdag* did not extend across all political issues. Defence spending had been a contentious issue in Swedish politics for the previous thirty years. Per Albin had played a prominent role and Conservatives had been pitted against the Social Democrats and liberals. This debate had been sidelined in the ominous atmosphere of late 1939 by cross-party agreement that defence spending should be increased as far as technical and economic resources allowed. This agreement was a complete break from earlier traditions in Swedish defence policy.[1] Unsurprisingly, given the bitter debates of the 1920s and 30s, dissident groups had to be reminded that outward unity on defence was expected, but it was clear that this unity rested on unstable foundations. In the 1941 *Riksdag* debate on increased conscription, a few Social Democrats expressed the view that the expansion of defence was only temporary and that 'sensible thinking' would prevail at the end of the war. Again in 1942 when a new five-year defence budget was debated, a number of People's Party and Social Democrat members wanted to cancel the building of three cruisers arguing that, while they were prepared to support fully immediate measures for the country's defence, they were not willing to tie future governments to long-term commitments. Although this minor attempt to rein in expenditure in 1942 was unsuccessful, by spring 1944 when the Germans were in retreat on all fronts, a significant group of Social Democrats in the Lower Chamber, particularly women members, succeeded in forcing the Government to limit the duration of a measure to increase civilian conscription. With echoes of the interwar debates, the Conservatives complained of Social Democratic 'disinterest in defence'.

Those earlier debates had been driven by a number of factors which remained as party differences. For the Social Democrats, there remained a profound distrust of the military whose upper-class conservatism and self interest was anathema to the *Folkhem* idealists while officers' predilection for anti-communism and anti-socialism was disguised as support for Finland and for some, support for German ambitions in Russia. The Conservatives shared some of these opinions and since military influence in wartime politics was strictly proscribed, those views tended to find expression through Conservative politicians like Bagge and to some extent conservative newspapers. The Conservatives regarded some of the Social Democrats with distrust, particularly those subscribing to Marxist economic tenets and a continuing dedication to the class struggle.

These undercurrents of conflict rarely surfaced in foreign policy debates due to the imperative of national unity. Clashes sometimes arose in defence debates but only infrequently for the same reason. However, disagreement occurred more regularly in economic and social debates regarding distributive policy. In these, exchanges often reverted to traditional party lines. In November 1939, the Social Democrats, Wigforss in particular, had difficulty accepting a proposal by the Agrarians for higher agricultural prices for farmers since these would cause problems for their working class support.[2] Conservative leader Bagge recorded his clash with Social Democrat Finance Minister Wigforss, when following a Cabinet meeting on the level of subsidy for fats and milk, Wigforss told him that this proposal concerned 'taking from the rich and giving to the poor'. When Bagge told him not to be so 'demagogic' on the issue, Wigforss retorted that there were deep divisions between their respective outlooks. The longest running Government crises occurred over domestic policy, in particular the farmers' demands for higher sugar prices in 1941. These claims ran counter to Wigforss' economic policy and tested the loyalty of the Agrarians to the Coalition Government.[3] Another crisis involving farmers and prices was a threatened milk-strike in Dalarna in December 1942.[4]

Wigforss was closely concerned, as Finance Minister, with the issues arising from the worsening economic conditions due to the war. The blockade after April 1940 reduced imports by half and exports by one-third of 1936–7 volumes. There was a drastic reduction in food imports which increased reliance on labour-intensive domestic production at a time when conscription was claiming most able-bodied men. Farmers took advantage of this to close a perceived gap between town and country living-standards which increased inflationary pressures. The agreement on re-armament saw defence expenditure rise from 248 million kroner (1938–9) to 2,000 million kroner (1944–5) and so, despite successful war loans, tax rises and falls in living-standards were unavoidable.[5]

The war brought a number of social problems to a head. The political problem of allocating tax and living-standard burdens within adverse economic circumstances challenged the political parties' interests and ideologies. While there was little common ground on these issues, the parties were nevertheless reluctant to demonstrate open divisions. Wigforss was an exception and in 1942, he published a pamphlet arguing that social justice required that the better-off should bear the burden of the war expenditure and necessary subsidies. That directly challenged the Conservatives' view that sacrifices should be borne equally and that those unable to get by should receive specific, means-tested support. This difference in principle was evident in discussions regarding a proposal that civil servants should receive salary supplements to compensate wartime inflation. Wigforss wanted this supplement to be paid only to the worst-paid groups while Bagge stressed that all civil servants should be treated equally. The difference was resolved through a Cabinet compromise but in the *Riksdag* there were mutterings that the principle of the burdens being borne by those most able to bear them should have been followed.

Taxation was another policy area which split the Coalition Government. Marginal income taxation had been gradually increased between 1910 and 1938 up to a range of 2 per cent – 31 per cent.[6] In 1940 income and wealth (*förmögenhet*) tax was raised by 50 per cent thereby sharpening progressive taxation. This differential treatment was accepted by the middle classes and it was of course difficult for the Conservatives to oppose taxes which strengthened defence through rearmament. However, a proposed 25 per cent increment to the 1940 tax rates in the spring of 1942 caused protests. The Conservatives opposed higher taxation levels on wealth, which when combined with income tax, could amount to more than some peoples' annual incomes or even cause capital loss. Wigforss had introduced some measures to prevent this but did not succeed in stifling protests. The Social Democrats, with support from the People's Party, succeeded in outvoting the objectors. The argument spilled over into the 1942 election campaign with a Social Democrat proposal for a 'one-off' capital tax. Under attack from the Conservatives who argued that it would ruin the country's small savers, the Social Democrats abandoned the proposal.

The Conservatives had early on in the war argued for a wider distribution of the tax burden to the working classes. This became an issue in June 1940 when Wigforss introduced a proposal for a 5 per cent sales tax, and subsidies on essential goods for the poorest. They would be worst affected by the tax because a greater proportion of their income would go on taxed-goods expenditure like food and clothing. These sales taxes were accepted by the *Riksdag* but there remained a substantial group of dissenters among the Social Democrat members, notably women, who succeeded in voting down the Government proposal in a debate on subsidies in the Lower Chamber in June 1942. This defeat forced the Government to take this dissident group into account in future debates on the issue.

The most extended economic and social dispute related to the role of budget deficit financing in the value of the Swedish krona. The Conservatives took the view that the deficit was a prime cause of corrosive inflation while Wigforss believed that high prices were the main driver. The Conservatives wanted lower state spending, particularly by reductions in subsidies, to reduce the deficit and so curb inflation while Wigforss saw price control as the target. This difference in viewpoint had significant policy implications because in Wigforss' view richer people would eventually pay for the subsidies to the poorer. Unusually for the Coalition Government, Bagge attacked Wigforss openly in the *Riksdag* in June 1942 but, in a significant characteristic of Swedish political discourse during the war, he did not attack taxation directly but addressed it obliquely in connection with the budget deficit and its serious effect on the currency value. The only vote on the issue resulted in a division between the Social Democrats and the right wing parties.

The restraint evident in foreign policy debates when compared with sharper domestic policy debates was due to the need to demonstrate political unity, both internally to the Swedish people and externally to the belligerents who were always ready to exploit differences to their own advantage. In foreign policy, the relatively low-key discussions which took place in the *Riksdag* or in abstract terms in public did not necessarily mean full support for the Coalition Government's foreign policy – or what was known about it. The absence of challenge was more a vote of confidence in the Coalition Government to act in the best interests of Sweden when responding to the events of the war. That confidence was conspicuously absent when it came to social and economic aspects of domestic policy and while defence expenditure issues were sidelined for the duration of the war there were sufficient markers laid down to indicate that these would resurface. But trust in the Coalition Government was tested in democratic elections throughout the war.

WARTIME ELECTIONS

Sweden held three *Riksdag* elections in the war years 1940, 1942 and 1944. The Coalition Government had considered postponing the September 1940, Lower Chamber election until a calmer period. As the situation stabilised, Per Albin insisted that it was held and that each party should compete rather than offer the electorate a Coalition Government party-list candidature. The result reflected not only a strong vote of confidence in Per Albin but a major success for the Social Democrats who gained an absolute majority in both Chambers while the Agrarians lost seats. This success was somewhat pyrrhic: while it could not be used to promote Social Democrat policies that might force out the Conservatives and split the Coalition, it landed the Social Democrats with an unwanted political responsibility for all the unpopular measures which, as the largest party, they could not avoid. The disappointed Agrarians had to be wooed by both the King and Günther to remain in the Coalition Government but their clumsy attempt to extract concessions from Per Albin for doing so was unsuccessful. The 1940 election campaign itself was not unnaturally somewhat restrained in its conduct by all parties, coming so soon after the prolonged period of German threats. Per Albin worried that his party's success would be seen as a negative signal to a menacing Nazi Germany whose leaders had earlier crushed the German social democrats.

In contrast to the 1940 election, the September 1942 Upper Chamber and Municipal campaign was marked by a sharper party contest. The 'one-off' capital tax proposal from the Social Democrats had energised the Conservatives who portrayed it as a 'capital confiscation'. The other issue was food supply and rationing in which the Communists exploited discontent over Government food aid to Finland which followed on from the shortages caused by two bad harvests in succession. Defence expenditure was off the parties' agendas. The result was little different from that of 1940 except that the Agrarians regained some of their losses and despite the Conservatives' campaign, the Coalition Government continued without major dissension.

The 1944 Lower Chamber election was coloured by the expectation of peace and the promise of new opportunities and challenges. At the Party Congress, the younger Social Democrats carried a manifesto commitment for a post-war programme but the political responsibility which the Social Democrats assumed by default in the 1940 election came back to haunt them. The electorate was set to punish them as a party and Per Albin as its leader for the growing dissatisfaction with the Coalition Government. In the 1944 election, the Social Democrats lost 7 per cent of their 1940 vote and it was the Communists, free of any association with Government policy, who gained by doubling their share of the vote to 10 per cent. A post-election survey by the Social Democrats indicated that the main reasons for their losses were the wages freeze, conscription and the Coalition Government. [7] The electoral setback also put paid to the optimistic hopes that Per Albin nurtured for a Coalition Government continuing in peacetime with him as its leader. He was somewhat isolated within his own party on this issue and it was clear that the younger members looked forward to a pure Social Democratic agenda. The discontent which the Communists exploited in the election also contributed to the damaging engineering industry strike of spring 1945 that halted much of Sweden's manufacturing industry but it did not prevent the Social Democrats being able to carry on when the Coalition Government was dissolved in July 1945.

The wartime elections demonstrated that, although Swedish citizens were subject to many restrictions during the war, the democratic right to vote was not one of these restrictions and that between 66 per cent and 70 per cent of the electorate voted in the three wartime elections. Also, despite dissatisfaction with the Coalition Government, the elections highlighted the fact that the more extreme elements in the Swedish political landscape never made any real impact on the mainstream parties. The Coalition Government had succeeded in the aim of preserving a democratic, independent Sweden.

SHORTAGES AND RATIONING

As in the diplomatic arena, the authorities were determined to avoid the mistakes of 1914–18 which left the country vulnerable to social and economic disruption. Although many of the problems of post-1940 trade and national security could not have been reasonably anticipated, what was well-planned was the national supply strategy. As early as 1928, a state Commission for Economic Defence Preparation (RKE) had been formed to plan measures to enable the Swedish economy to adapt to war or an interruption of supplies. To avoid the 1914–18 shortages, they planned a system of rationing of essential goods materials and food to be introduced when appropriate. In addition, they set up strategic reserves of essentials (*Statens reservförråd*) to cushion disruptions in supply chains.

These well planned measures were undoubtedly in Per Albin's mind when he made his much derided speech on 27 August 1939, in which he stated 'Our preparation is good.' For the hastily assembled conscripts lacking complete uniforms or equipment, this seemed like a joke in poor taste but supply preparation *was* in fact good. At least 165 million kroner had been spent on the strategic reserves and the 1938 harvest had delivered a surplus of 390,000 tonnes of grain which was equivalent to one year's demand. Sweden was self-sufficient in sugar and potatoes, with supplies of fats and coffee also satisfactory. The main problem which would increasingly concern the Government throughout the war was the shortage of fuel oil reserves. In this strategically important commodity, there were only three months' reserves or perhaps ten months' with strict rationing.[8] Lack of fuel for vehicles, warships and aircraft could hamper the country's defence. This explains the Government's later concerns to keep the 'Safe-Conduct Traffic' from the west open which would become the main source of fuel oil after April 1940 until May 1945.

To implement the system of rationing, a state Food Commission (*Statens Livsmedelskommission*) was created. It formed thirty-three county Emergency Boards (*Kristidsstyrelserna*) that in turn mobilised 2,523 Emergency Committees (*Kristidsnämnder*) which from September 1939 overviewed and coordinated rationing in every parish. As in Britain, there was an explosive growth of state bodies at the beginning of the war but the speed with which the Swedish authorities acted to implement rationing was impressive. This reduced people's fears of a repeat of the shortages, starvation and inequalities which had afflicted Sweden in 1917 and 1918 as the Allied blockade gripped Europe. To complete the system, national control of resources was overseen by a new Ministry of Supply formed in October 1939, initially under Hermann Eriksson and from March 1941 headed by Axel Gjöres, an experienced and respected administrator from the Cooperative movement whose contribution to its effectiveness was significant.

One of the issues realised by the Social Democrats and the Agrarians as early as September 1939 was that as a result of the raft of planned measures, the war's impact on Swedish daily life would be both considerable and unpopular. Westman pointed out that:

> The Swedish peasant had not changed since Gustav Vasa's time and he [Vasa] knew them well when he said that if the Hanse increased the salt-price or the annual harvest was poor, they blamed this on the government like everything else.

The two Coalition parties' fears of the political consequences of excessively narrow representation contributed to early consideration of an all-party Coalition Government.[9]

The first rationing measures, excluding those taken earlier for petrol, took place in March 1940 to preserve foreign currency reserves. The German blockade of shipping to the west in April 1940 after the occupation of Norway and Denmark meant that real shortages of soap, cocoa, bread, pork and butter began while sugar was also rationed to prevent panic buying. As the labour shortages in agriculture and food processing due to conscription and war production began to have an effect, rationing was extended in 1941 to oats and flour (already included in the bread ration), most meat, eggs and cheese. In the summer of 1941, personally identifiable ration cards and coupons were introduced to combat fraud and misrepresentation. By 1942, the supply situation had deteriorated. Soap became scarce and a utility bar of soap was introduced. Due to shortages in animal feed, meat was further rationed to 150 grammes per person per week – the lowest in Europe at that time – while a heavily criticised egg ration was limited to one per person per week. Hoarding had almost disappeared due to the shortage of goods yet small change coinage was squirrelled away causing a scarcity in late 1942 and even toilet paper was stockpiled in households.

Milk, fish, and potatoes were never rationed but consumption increased dramatically to compensate for dietary shortages in meat and other dairy products whose dearth was partly due to scarce fodder being diverted to milk-cows. Queues at fish stalls had to be supervised to deter multi-purchasers. The pressure to find other protein foods saw an increased interest in chicken, turkey, deer, and elk. The situation improved slightly at the end of 1942 but Christmas that year was a lean time with newspapers carrying recipes for rabbit, fish or offal sausages. Harvests in 1940 and 1941 had been poor but supplies improved in 1943 with the 'Safe-Conduct Traffic' under way again and better weather. About 50 per cent of import tonnage consisted of foodstuffs mainly from South America that eased the hard-pressed Swedish food reserves.[10] A month-long sugar-worker strike caused immediate reductions in sugar rations and demonstrated that margins for error were small. By mid-1944, renewed German blockade of the 'Safe-Conduct Traffic' caused rations of meat and other foods to be reduced so that even at the beginning of 1945, the bread ration was again reduced to the 1942 level.

The exigencies of wartime rationing affected every Swedish mealtime. Even the British Air Attaché in one of his dispatches complained that the interned British airmen whom he had visited ate better in their camp than he did back in Stockholm. In the same way as throughout Europe, townspeople with access to rural supplies fared better than those without connections. In restaurants and shops, coupon-free foods were correctly regarded with suspicion, as badgers, squirrels, seagulls and rabbit made an appearance as ingredients and food manufacturers' ingenuity extended to surrogate foods. For example, 155 different types of coffee substitute, sixty-two types of egg substitute and forty-three types of fat substitute were approved during the war by the Food Commission in consultation with the Public Health Institute.

Despite the shortages and changes in diet, Swedes became healthier during the war years, apart from those whose health had suffered due to military service.[11] Many people gave up the struggle to get meat, becoming vegetarians, and the inability of civilians to obtain petrol led to many more people cycling instead. Other dietary changes were positively beneficial, for example the greater consumption of wholemeal grains, fresh vegetables, fruit, and unrefined sugar. Starting in August 1942 practical demonstrations and advice at a travelling exhibition 'Housekeeping in the Crisis' (*Folkhushållning i kristid*) showed housewives how to achieve a good diet from cheap and available foodstuffs. A survey finding in 1942 that school children had never been so healthy was put down to less fat and sugar together with more exercise and lower house temperatures due to heating restrictions. Parents were encouraged to give the better food to the young in order to nourish their growing bodies. As one doctor put it 'Father can manage on porridge and potatoes.'[12]

With rationing, despite the authorities' vigilance, 'black-market' activity increased during the war. Thefts of rationed goods such as food and clothing as well as ration cards also soared as did cycle parts and hard-to-get rubber tyres and tubes. Much of this stolen property ended up in the hands of black marketeers.[13] For most of the population, however, despite the inevitable grumbling and bureaucracy, consumer rationing was a successful measure that achieved better shares for all while reducing rather than eliminating unfair advantages arising from wealth or position. No one suffered malnutrition due to food rationing unlike the experiences in 1917 and 1918 but, as elsewhere in Europe, rationing continued long after the war had ended. This contributed to a feeling of popular anger and disappointment as austerity seemed endless. The Food Commission (*Livsmedelskommissionen*) became known in a popular pun as the 'Lifetime Commission' (*Livstidskommissionen*).

While Sweden was reasonably self-sufficient in foodstuffs, the same was not true of fuel, particularly oil. To preserve the slender reserves of fuel oil, private vehicle use was banned days after war broke out. Next, tyres were requisitioned and many cars spent the war on bricks in garages. Essential users were initially allowed petrol coupons but from December 1940, this too was stopped. Over 30,000 vehicles had already converted to GenGas, a technique which extracted combustible gas from burning wood or charcoal and delivered it to the vehicle engine in place of petrol. By the end of the war 40 per cent of all motor traffic operated on GenGas which was estimated to require only up to 20 per cent of Sweden's annual timber production. The technology was also extended to small inshore shipping like fishing boats but the space required aboard for the wood or charcoal made it an impractical substitute. It was, however, ideal for slow-moving agricultural tractors and there were 5,000 of them by 1940.[14] Horsepower or 'Oat Engines' also experienced a resurgence in the cities as well as the countryside but the main change was the switch to public transport, particularly railways, as a result of the oil shortage. Even here, difficulties were experienced as there was insufficient coal to power all steam locomotives, despite 45 per cent of the rail system being electrified by 1942 to take advantage of domestically generated hydro-electricity. Even with fuel rationing, the social effect was significant because the rich, the powerful and the less well-off shared the same problems of finding a seat on the crowded trains or cycling to work.[15]

The increase in rail passenger traffic contributed to a decrease in unemployment at the beginning of the war when to cope, rail staffing was increased by 25 per cent to 10,000 employees. Even senior officials like Boheman and Wigforss used two wheels instead of four.[16]

A Society in Flux

While rationing and transport difficulties contributed to a feeling of a fairer society, there were other forces at work which were assisting in the reduction of class barriers, not to mention bastions of privilege in Swedish society.

Military and civilian conscription was one of the more obvious measures leading to a levelling of class in Sweden. As one social historian has remarked 'Mass war, involving a high proportion of the total population tends to a levelling in social class differences.'[17] Military conscription initially affected hundreds of thousands of Swedish men. In spring 1939, 50,000 were called up, to be followed shortly after in September by a further 50,000. Between May and October 1940 when the threat from Germany was at its height, there were (including the Home Guard) about 400,000 men in service out of a total population of 6.3 million. Although women were never subject to official military conscription despite legislation being in place to do so, they nevertheless volunteered in their thousands to serve in other military and civilian roles. An astonishing 800,000 women put themselves forward for a variety of full and part-time jobs. The Swedish war was a citizens' war as these statistics show and the shared hardships of wartime cold, hunger, shortage, separation from home and family, and uncertainty made inroads into many of the remaining Swedish class barriers. Country-folk mixed with towns-people, reducing mutual distrust and isolation while the use of the formal 'you' decreased along with undue deference to upper classes. This represented an acceleration of the processes that ethnologist Orvar Löfgren defined as 'informalisation' that released Swedes from formalised rituals in behaviour and social interactions.[18]

In the forces, the conscription experience could be harsh but that was true for all conscripts. Swedish television's 1970 dramatisation of Jan Olof Olsson's novel about life during wartime 'Somewhere in Sweden' (*Någonstans i Sverige*) successfully captured many of the undercurrents of adjustment as a motley group of conscripts tackled the challenges of military service in north Sweden. Most were away from home, families, friends, lovers and familiar surroundings. All were subject to the same military discipline and harsh conditions of service. All suffered economically as well as emotionally during conscription – farms were neglected and advancement was frozen – wives were unfaithful and lovers were tempted to stray. Military service also built on teamwork and mutual dependency. That alone reduced class differences and re-defined an individual's worth as contribution rather than background. Sweden's post-war meritocracy was reinforced by the wartime conscription experience which provided a model proving ground for many of Per Albin's *Folkhem* ideals of social levelling.

Women's Changing Role

Alongside external hostilities, a domestic struggle for status was conducted by the nation's women that deserves greater coverage than space here permits.[19] As far as women were concerned, one of the early casualties of the war was poorly rewarded and exploitative domestic service. This remnant of class dominance was subject to state scrutiny in 1939 but when a new law regulating hours of work and other conditions was introduced in 1944, the numbers of servants had been reduced through more attractive employment opportunities. Most servants had been single, unmarried women and as Johanna Overud shows, it was precisely this category who responded most to the opportunity of independence through employment. In contrast, the state had hoped to attract married housewives into wartime employment to replace the manpower conscripted into the forces and other war work because it was thought that their married status would make them amenable to giving up their employment when the men returned.[20]

Women became more popularly appreciated as workers alongside men when replacing the conscripted absentees. They were recruited into a variety of occupations from lorry-drivers to bus-conductors. Yet for women postal workers, the *Svenska Dagbladet* in 1940 reflected the somewhat patronising view that: 'We'll certainly get our post with the same unerring precision as their male colleagues have accustomed us to.'[21] This dismissive attitude towards women led to such instances as being allowed to take fares on buses but not being permitted to drive them. Before the war, women's groups had anticipated that they might be allotted a secondary employment role in wartime due to concerns about male unemployment and they had determined to act. Married women were considered unable to serve two masters, one in the workplace and one in the home. As part of a women's political campaign to secure employment for them, an official Women's Employment Committee was created in 1938, with support from Wigforss. This proposed forbidding employers to discriminate on grounds of marriage or pregnancy and became law in 1939.[22] Still, women remained unhappy that they were excluded from wartime employment planning and the opportunity to contribute to the Swedish war effort.[23] In November 1938 the Women's Associations' Standby Committee (*Kvinnoföreningarnas beredskapskommitté* or *KBK*) was formed to unite Swedish women's groups in demonstrating their 'resolve to defend their nation.'[24] Within the *KBK*, there was a diverse range of organisations and objectives, not always reconcilable or consistent. There was a mix of aspirant ideal housewives with career-oriented working women; middle-class attitudes and working-class culture. [25]

The *KBK* organised women nationally and compiled a register of 800,000 volunteers who wanted to 'do their bit' for the country. The State Employment Commission (*SAK*) was the Government body responsible for labour market planning but when offered the *KBK* register, they declined to accept it with the explanation that they preferred volunteers rather than conscription. This camouflaged a conservative view that women should not be compelled. Military and industrial conscription was never applied to women despite conscription legislation in December 1939 providing for both sexes. There was a widespread and deep-rooted fear of female dilution among the male work-force, for example in Bofors and Domnarvets steelworks. Unions pursued equal pay to prevent employers from driving down men's rates by using cheaper women's labour.[26] This resulted in agreements which provided for 80 per cent of male rates and a commitment to maintain a man's job on his return from service.

While the *KBK* was pressurising the Commission (*SAK*) for a greater role outside the home, the State Information Board (*SIS*) instigated an information section called Active Housekeeping ('*Aktiv Hushållning*' or *AH*) whose objective was to enable Swedish households to better use the limited and rationed resources at their disposal, a task that fell primarily upon women. *AH* promoted the women's role paradigm of housewife over that of the *KBK*'s women reserve worker and perhaps better reflected the all-male Government's role preferences. The housewife's contribution as the economic planner in her kitchen was elevated at the expense of her less acceptable contribution as an equally paid industrial worker. The

KBK had failed to persuade the government to accept fully a new gender contract of providing female reserve workers in return for greater economic, social and political influence. Predominantly, the male was the provider while the woman remained the homemaker and mother. Nevertheless, the participation of women during the war meant that they were able to lobby to be included in the long-term as well as the short-term post-war planning agenda in 1943 through the SAK and in 1944 with the Myrdal Commission.[27] Notable examples were Alva Myrdal's influence in SAK, Karin Kock's role in AH, the SAK's training of women for industry, and the 'Fru Lojal' engineering industry recruitment campaign. These instances support Arthur Marwick's view that although cultural attitudes towards women remained unchanged by the war, their progress in the labour market and increased self-confidence were important advances.[28] The war had provided an opportunity for women that they exploited as far as possible, but the rewards were deferred until the post-war period.

Farming for Food

One sector of Swedish society and economy that lagged behind the urban-oriented industrial changes of the 1920s and 1930s was farming. Even with, or perhaps because of the accelerating exodus from the countryside, farming remained labour-intensive and backward at the beginning of the war, and the demands of conscription worsened the situation when men and horses were called up, leaving the women, the old and young to work the land without adequate labour or motive power. The authorities were forced to balance the needs of national defence with food supply when granting leave to conscripts. Campaigns were mounted to attract volunteers to provide extra hands in the summer months and many women and school students from towns responded. As the stream of displaced people arriving in Sweden grew after 1943, they were initially directed into agricultural labour. Refugees accounted for 16 per cent of the workers placed in agriculture and forestry by the labour offices.[29]

These wartime visitors found that despite the progress of modernisation in urban Sweden, many farming families lived in simple circumstances, often without electricity and running water, and worked the land in back-breaking conditions largely unchanged from the previous war. The nineteenth century's *'FattigSverige'* (Poverty-Sweden) which had driven over a million Swedes to emigrate by 1930, cast a long shadow over the twentieth century. One particular group whose circumstances were an affront to a modern society were the 'statare', a category of landless labourers who were hired by larger farmers on an annual basis and provided with basic accommodation. The drawback was that they mostly received payment in kind rendering them unable to escape their servitude while the whole family was expected to work on the employer's farm. Despite a long and incisive campaign by writers such as Ivar-Lo Johansson, this iniquity survived throughout the war years and the practice did not end until 1945 when remuneration was introduced.

The task of substantially increasing Swedish farming output failed due to problems in adjusting to wartime circumstances but there was partial success: Sweden remained 90 per cent self-sufficient in food. Arable land only increased by 1 per cent and many outputs actually fell: meat by 16 per cent, milk 10 per cent and most grains, whereas potatoes increased by 10 per cent.[30] Numerous small farmers were subsistence only and supplemented their meagre income with forestry work. Larger farms (over 50 hectares) accounted for only about 20 per cent of the total but they proved capable, in combination with rationing and other measures, of delivering close to national self-sufficiency in food. Livestock were slaughtered to reduce their numbers to a level commensurate with the lower supplies of animal fodder, reduced partly due to adverse weather causing poor harvests and partly to shortages of labour. Additional acreage including parkland was put under cultivation and substitutes such as reeds, leaves and cellulose were used to bulk out animal feed.

Harvests and agricultural production were carefully monitored by the authorities because of the upward effect on food prices caused by shortages. This could cause inflationary problems in the wider economy and hardship among the population. The authorities also tried to set production targets to match demand for particular produce but in this they were mainly unsuccessful, despite a mixture of incentive payments and propagandist exhortation. Voluntary action was preferred over enforcement. The country literally had to tighten its belt with a wartime population increasing faster than food production and there was a shift in diet from animal to vegetable dishes to match the changes in availability.

The sector largely succeeded in overcoming the problems caused by labour shortage, fuel rationing and poor harvests. Agricultural output remained vulnerable throughout the war and was anxiously scrutinised by the Cabinet, its importance ranking alongside major foreign policy decisions. For example, in January 1942, after a crucial

Cabinet discussion about the policy that Sweden should adopt for the release of the Norwegian ships, Westman carefully noted from the meeting the following meat storage and animal slaughter statistics: 'Rationing approx. 2,200 tons a week, that is stocks for 8 weeks' consumption.'

CIVIL DEFENCE

The fear of the bomber and of poison gas dominated pre-war Swedish civil defence as in the rest of Europe. When Air Defence (*luftskydd*) was organised in 1937 with responsibility at county level, there was an emphasis on sirens, shelters and gas masks. Plans were made also for observers, removal of combustibles in attics, nursing, and maintenance of civil order by volunteers. Urban evacuation planning was entrusted in 1939 to yet another Commission (*Utrymningskommissionen*) to which one of the women's movement's (KBK) leaders was appointed. Children in districts considered vulnerable to attack were registered for possible compulsory evacuation. Following the outbreak of war, the tempo of preparation increased with blackout measures to screen lighted areas from air attack. Blackout paper was attached to windows and the streets patrolled by vigilant wardens. Public transport crawled around with covered headlights while on moonless nights, pedestrians had to avoid walking into parked bicycles. In spring, 1940, the authorities stipulated that every rented block of flats should provide an air-raid shelter in addition to public provision. By the end of 1941, Stockholm could boast 8,000 shelters in flats for 400,000 people and public shelters for a further 60,000, in addition to workplace provision.[31]

The effectiveness of Air Defence measures was tested repeatedly throughout the war and the exercises became increasingly realistic. For example, a voluntary children's evacuation was staged in June 1940. In autumn, 1940, Swedish radio (*Radiotjänst*) broadcast a play featuring the sound of a bombing raid and its consequences, to accustom listeners to conditions with which Londoners were already familiar. In Stockholm in September 1941, the air force carried out mock-attacks, both day and night over the capital with defenders responding with searchlights and anti-aircraft fire. Over three nights, firewatchers communicated incidents and residents sat in shelters while Air Defence leaders organised simulated first aid and rescue. The initial night was well lit by the moon but the subsequent two nights were darker and rescue results less successful. In

FIGURE 10 Preparing for the *Luftwaffe*, 1940 – a realistic simulated air-raid exercise to recover wounded civilians. The Swedish civilian population experienced evacuation, shelters, blackouts and gas masks – but very few actual bombs.
(PA Photos)

December 1942 another even more realistic exercise was held in Uppsala when a condemned house was detonated to provide a test site for salvage teams while 200 people checked their gas masks in a simulated attack. Exercises continued until spring 1945 but as the war progressed without attack, enthusiasm receded and people increasingly refused to interrupt their normal life to sit in shelters during drills, despite clear orders from officials. In 1943, the organisation of civil defence was reviewed and the following year the various organisations responsible for air defence, evacuation, accommodation, fire prevention and wardens were streamlined into a new Civil Defence Board which replaced volunteers with civil defence conscripts aged between sixteen and sixty-five who received payment for their service.

SURVEILLANCE

The Home Front in Sweden was at times under actual attack from the belligerents in the form of espionage and sabotage activities as well as minor military action that potentially endangered many Swedes. An increasingly active internal security policy of preventive surveillance was supported by a raft of legislation which had been passed before 1939 and supplemented in 1939, 1940 and 1942. The work of the Civilian Security Service (Allmänna Säkerhetstjänsten or AS) included monitoring post, telephone eavesdropping, censorship, observing political parties and coordination with the criminal police. While this represented an unprecedented and largely secret intrusion into Swedish civilian life, it also produced results in the form of arrests and successful prosecutions.[32]

Other preventative measures which challenged pre-war concepts of civil rights and the rule of law in Sweden concerned the 600–700 conscripts that the military deemed as 'unreliable' due to their political affiliations (mainly Communists or other left-wingers) who were dispatched to what was effectively administrative detention. So instead of defending their country, they were disarmed and forced to labour for it until these special 'closed' camps were disbanded in 1943. The other group of detainees were refugees who had been interned by the Aliens Office, whose numbers rose to 1,600 by 1945.[33] Some of these were refugees of dubious provenance, such as Quisling supporters from Norway who had seen the writing on the wall and were attempting to save their skins in Sweden.[34]

One particular aspect of espionage and sabotage was the tendency of the belligerents to attempt to recruit Swedish citizens to carry out their espionage and sabotage operations. To forestall the risk of Swedish citizens inadvertently revealing information useful to foreign services, the State Information Board, SIS mounted the famous *En Svensk Tiger* campaign in 1941 which was a pun on the Swedish word *tiger* which means both to 'keep silent' and also the animal 'tiger'. The artist Bertil Almqvist was commissioned to design a poster with a marvellously solemn tiger whose blue and yellow stripes replicated the Swedish national colours. The tiger remains today as one of the iconic images of the Swedish Home Front during the Second World War.

ENTERTAINMENT AND CULTURAL LIFE

Radio, cinema, theatre and books all flourished during the war as people tried to keep abreast of the latest news and events while seeking escapism in films and plays but it was the State-sponsored radio, *Radiotjänst*, which became anchored as the dominant daily medium and came of age during the war.

Radio

Determining a neutral broadcasting policy in a public authority was not without its problems. Germany in particular analysed output for bias and reacted ferociously when it believed it was being disadvantaged. The broadcasters also had to contend with their own government which expected support for its policies, particularly the fostering of national unity, conformity with 'guidance' from the UD and a readiness to act as a mouthpiece for its announcements. These multiple burdens could have made for exceedingly dull programming but *Radiotjänst* rose to the task of entertaining as well as educating and informing. Socially, *Radiotjänst* was instrumental in bringing the war into Swedish homes and workplaces through its news and reporting, while increasing the awareness of national crisis and the need to respond. The news from the national press agency *TT* was the lynch-pin for daily programming and was read at 12.30 a.m., 7 p.m. and 10 p.m. In September 1940 Sweden (like Switzerland) agreed to end transmissions at 10.15 p.m. instead of at 11 p.m. which gave *Radiotjänst* programming difficulties. The Germans alleged that

Swedish broadcasts assisted British night-bombers to navigate. They had also to fit in morning-gymnastics, a religious spot, weather, school broadcasts, the daily poem, talks for housewives, farming programmes, radio plays, music (45 per cent of output) and 'Dagens Eko' (Daily Echo), the current affairs newsreel.

It is difficult to determine if the frequent controversies over entertainment programme content as opposed to current affairs were symbolic or real. The left-leaning intelligentsia chafed at the restrictions placed on content by the cautious *Radiotjänst* leadership as a result of the *UD*'s concern about adverse German reaction. These conflicts covered the choice of daily poem, contributors and content in 'Dagens Eko', and radio plays. The nineteenth century poem *Det eviga* (The Everlasting) by national poet Esaias Tegnér, was broadcast on no fewer than nine significant occasions during 1939–1945. Its theme rejected strong, warlike Napoleonic leadership and violence in favour of truth, beauty and justice, sentiments that resonated with listeners wearily familiar with the cult of Stalin and his terror, Hitler's *Führerprinzip*, the Nazis and the *Wehrmacht*.[35] This poem expressed a low-profile Swedish repudiation of such ideologies and its broadcast typified the understated way in which a Swedish institution maintained national morale and identity without creating friction with the totalitarians. As *Radiotjänst*'s Carl Dymling recalled: 'The question was always . . . how far could we go, how far dared we show our colours?' [36]

'Dagens Eko' in the early years of the war was stripped of any comment on foreign policy and even about life and culture in occupied Norway and Denmark. When it covered the hardships of military life in 1939, it attracted criticism for doing so. A new request programme called 'Attention . . . At ease!' (*Giv akt! . . . Lediga!*) was hastily produced for the thousands of conscripts and their hard-hit families at home. At Christmas 1939, the national conscience was stirred so thoroughly that donations poured in for distribution. This was the first appearance of the 'Radio Major', Arvid Eriksson, whose later broadcasts included appearances on 'Dagens Eko'. Those broadcasts were felt to contribute to stiffening national resistance but his comments on propaganda in early 1941 fell foul of German complaints to the Army. He was re-assigned to Gotland and silenced.

Radiotjänst was fortunate to have the noted writer, poet and playwright Hjalmar Gullberg as its director of radio theatre. Gullberg was a cultural constant in a wartime world of changing ethics. His personal mission was to promote collective national identity and values (the 'inner front') as a cultural patriot: his own work avoided extremes of military resistance and armed attack on the surrounding 'barbarians', sentiments which he left to others like Pär Lagerkvist.[37] His contribution to *Radiotjänst* was in the choice of plays, readings, and 'cabaret' entertainment. For example, during the Winter War, he supported a Finnish-Swedish play. Following Norway's occupation he sponsored an Ibsen play in autumn 1940, promoted a Danish discussion in March 1941, and invited Lagerkvist to give the 1941 New Year's Eve traditional address. These were bold initiatives in testing times. As examples of his programming, Gullberg broadcast work by Swedish writers and Nazi critics Vilhelm Moberg and Bertil Malmberg, and by Denmark's poet-priest Kai Munck, later murdered by Danish collaborators in 1944. On a lighter cabaret note, he also promoted the famous revue artiste Karl Gerhardt whose satirical songs about the (un-named) Germans – the 'Trojan Horse' – attracted attention from his targets as well as the UD who attempted to close him down. Gullberg went some way to bridge the gap between committed opponents of totalitarianism and a Government which was attempting to promote national unity, optimism and resistance but which regarded provocative productions as needlessly damaging to the country's interests.

These concerns about *Radiotjänst* programmes may well have been confined to a relatively small group of politicians and intellectuals. For many, the radio was an entertainment medium to escape weightier subjects. One young listener later recalled:

> What was most listened to at ours' was news, certainly . . . other popular programmes were old-time dance music, certain revues, talks in the style of the Optimist and the Pessimist [a popular programme dealing with current events]. Sport and other reports from Sven Jarring [a famous radio reporter] who was excellent: another radio voice was researcher and traveller Sten Bergman who was a delight to listen to.[38]

Cinema

The second mass-medium after radio was film. Swedish productions vied with foreign imports to attract burgeoning audiences. Cinemas had deferred sensibly to the primacy of the 7 p.m. radio news, relayed on loud speakers in their foyers, and started films at 7.15 p.m. instead. Sweden had been devouring English language film from America and Britain since the 1930s and the demand for this output increased rather than decreased during the war. This meant that Anglo-American cinema had a head start in cultural influence over Germany and also over local productions.

Swedish output consisted of a mixture of light-weight escapism such as musicals, military farces starring popular comics like Edvard Persson and Nils Poppe and heavyweight epics such as *General von Döbeln* (1942) based on a novel by Sven Stolpe about the eighteenth century Swedish hero. These so-called 'Emergency-films' (*beredskapsfilmer*) were entertainment with a purpose, that of strengthening national solidarity and the will to resist. Critics complained that increased output meant decreased quality but a canny choice of subject could overcome dramatic weaknesses. One example from 1943 concerned the travails of an unidentified, occupied, foreign land in *Det brinner en eld* (*A Fire Burns*) which formed the basis for box-office success with a public eager to empathise with what was happening in Norway. Ivar-Lo Johansson's seamy classic, *Kungsgatan* (1944), was also a runaway success but many of the forty features released that year, including Ingmar Bergman's first scripted production, slipped into obscurity.[39]

Foreign films, particularly French melancholy, were high on the list of classics in 1939 but Hollywood and England soon supplied a stream of hits such as *The Hunchback of Notre-Dame* and the *Wizard of Oz* (1940), *Gone with the Wind* and *Mrs Miniver* (1942), *Dr Jekyll and Mr Hyde* and *Casablanca* (1943), *Gaslight* and *For Whom the Bell Tolls* (1944). These last four were also notable for performances by a Swedish actress from Fjällbacka, Ingrid Bergman. Zarah Leander, another famous Swedish actress, chose Germany rather than Hollywood. Her name permeates the diaries of Germany's ultimate film mogul and womaniser, Josef Goebbels.[40] Unsurprisingly, given her insensitivity regarding her film projects, public opinion turned against her in Sweden and her career never recovered. German film productions ranged from crude, threatening propaganda films like *Feuertaufe* (1940) and *Sieg im Westen* (1941) about the German campaigns in Poland and the Low Countries to more sophisticated output like *En drottnings hjärta* (1940) with Leander portraying the tragic Queen Mary Stuart and the fantasy *Baron von Münchhausen* (1943) which reflected the growing real-life Nazi delusion that Germany, like the Münchhausen character, could overcome all set-backs.

Film was another contested battlefield in the propaganda war and the Germans attempted to ensure that their output from Goebbels' studios was distributed and Allied films restricted. All films had to be approved pre-release by the State Cinema Office (*Statens biografbyrå* or *SBB*) so the Germans knew that they could apply indirect pressure through the *UD*. The German effort to scupper critical films began in 1933 and continued intermittently up to 1939 when Charlie Chaplin's anti-Nazi satire, *The Great Dictator*, was subject to German representations and the *SBB* did not approve it until November 1945. The showing of foreign films was not subject to major German criticism but from time to time, lists of films that the Germans considered to be provocative or insulting were submitted and frequently not approved. Yet, the German anti-semitic film, *Jude Süss*, also failed to be approved in 1941. The *SBB* was criticised in the German press for being 'anti-German' and despite German protests, the British film *Manhunt* was passed by *SBB*. Directed by Fritz Lang and released as *Nattexpress*, it was an adaptation of Geoffrey Household's 1939 novel *Rogue Male* about the attempted assassination of 'a dictator', clearly Hitler. The film adaptation of Bertil Malmberg's openly anti-Nazi play *Excellensen*, which *Radiotjänst's* Gullberg had broadcast as a radio production in 1944, was attacked by German Minister Thomsen who even unsuccessfully complained directly to King Gustav – but it was released without hindrance.[41]

Theatre

Theatre was a significant provider of wartime entertainment primarily for urban audiences. The performances reflected a public appetite for more criticism of Germany and also digs at the Government, along with the work of staple playwrights and out-and-out escapist spectacles.

Two significant productions on the critical edge were Moberg's *Ridd i natt!* (*Ride tonight!*) and Karl Gerhard's revue, *Gullregn* (*Laburnum*). Moberg's 1942 play, based on his 1941 novel, dealt with the analogous oppression of Swedes by a German bailiff in the seventeenth century and was enormously popular. Moberg had intended that his overtly political message should reach a wide audience and it became a Swedish film the same year. Gerhard's revue placed the action in classical Greece and he poked fun at government restrictions there. In a song he portrayed Hitler's *Mein Kampf* as a Trojan horse in Sweden, which led the authorities to order the song's removal. Despite his clear sympathies, Gerhard remained a frequent performer on *Radiotjänst*.

Some plays attracted critical attention for poor content while others drew Government attention because of their message. One example of both in 1943 was the Norwegian play, *Om ett folk vill leva* (*If a nation will survive*) whose limited dramatic merit was compensated by its depiction of Norwegian resistance. It was then controversially banned for its anti-German content after two performances. The UD defended its pre-emptive strike – no German complaint had been received – by reference to an 1868 public order statute.[42] In 1944 the fate of the Jews in the Holocaust was acknowledged by Stockholm's *Dramaten* Theatre production of Shakespeare's *Merchant of Venice* in which Shylock, the eponymous Jew, was portrayed as a fundamentally good man forced into his meanness by the attitudes and expectations of his tormentors.

Meanwhile, in open air parks (*Folkparken*) in summer-time Sweden, travelling troupes kept families entertained with a mixture of lighter revue material from the likes of Nils Poppe, popular songs and music from the versatile Alice Babs, and plays starring Ludde Juberg in so-called 'bush-theatre' (*buskis*). Solid Swedish pre-war entertainment traditions were maintained to provide light escapism during a dark period, a long way from serious books and libraries.

Literature

The hunger for diversion extended to reading material and the period saw record levels of book production, both in real and relative terms.[43] Bookshops were busy and libraries saw increases in membership and loans. The numbers of book circles which circulated ten books among their membership began to be significant. As in cinema, quality did not always improve with quantity.

Contemporary Swedish writers were engaged intellectually in the gigantic struggle between ideologies represented by the war. Vilhelm Moberg, Hjalmar Gullberg, Selma Lagerlöf, Harry Martinson, Eyvind Johnson, Olof Lagerkrantz, Elin Wägner and Karin Boye produced relevant work or contributed personally to causes. Lagerlöf gave up her Nobel Prize medal for auction to help Finland while Martinson's talks roused Swedish volunteers there in 1939. A bleak, polemic style characterised Eyvind Johnson's trilogy, *Grupp Krilon* (1941–3). This rehearsed contemporary political thinking through the declamatory discourse of the group's phonetically allegorical characters (for example, 'Staph' was code for Gestapo) while reflecting drab wartime Stockholm and the loneliness of the human condition.

In addition to the challenge to totalitarianism by fiction such as

Johnson's, writers like Boye and Lagerkvist described dystopian analogies to current violence and servitude in their works *Kallocain* (1940) and *Dvärgen* (1944). Perhaps the poem which best captures human frailty and powerlessness in modern warfare was Karl Vennberg's 1944 *Om det fanns telefon* (*If there was a telephone*). Such serious literary work co-existed alongside best-sellers such as *Tänk, om jag gifter mig med prästen!* (*Imagine if I married the vicar!*, 1941), about a young teacher in rural Sweden who has a secret love-affair with the priest. This was a runaway success when filmed, perhaps due to its romantic escapism. Another popular book in 1941 was anti-Nazi Frans G. Bengtsson's Viking epic, *Röde Orm*, which in translation as *The Longships* remains a world classic and one of the most widely read Swedish novels. Another debut author was the children's writer Astrid Lindgren whose famous character, *Pippi Långstrump*, first appeared in early 1945. Children's literature was generally sanitised when it dealt with the war but a literature survey has revealed a distinctive bias against the Soviet Union in the adventures of many of its youthful characters.[44]

Foreign-language books, primarily English translations, also ranked high in Swedish best-seller lists and reflected the Swedish-language mix of high and low-brow works. The works of the now unfashionable British best-selling novelist, Howard Spring, such as *Fame is the Spur* vied for sales with classics from Ernest Hemingway such as *For Whom the Bell Tolls*. Sweden's evident cultural preference was Anglo-Saxon and reflected the majority's political sympathies. Swedish writers and producers provided books, films and theatre which often reflected their distaste for totalitarians, in particular Nazism. This was laced with the everyday output of entertainment to leaven the ever-present worries and put a spring in the step of Swedes faced with rationing, shortages, and hard work.

AT WORK

While inter-war unemployment had been declining in Sweden, the reduction in joblessness caused by conscription in 1939 was offset by increased layoffs due to wartime disruption of export markets and imported raw material supplies. These, together with a collapse of house-building and reductions in the transport sector, left 100,000 still unemployed in 1940. A major shift in labour deployment was required and in 1940 the new State Employment Commission (*SAK*) under Arthur Thomson replaced the former Unemployment Commission. It was charged with national labour planning supported by the 1939 Civil Conscription law which permitted the authorities to deploy labour as required. It also took central control of the previously independent county Labour Offices (Arbetsförmedlingar) and created twenty-five County Employment Committees (Länsarbetsnämnder). The new service dealt with thousands of requests for deferment of military conscription and offered removal and travel expenses for new starts, filling of vacancies, vocational training and conversion courses to match skill shortages, as well as finding work for refugees, particularly Norwegians. Many of SAK's labour market measures were untested but the situation demanded experimentation and new solutions.

The vocational training courses which began in 1940 were aimed at filling skills shortages in the engineering sector and had been quickly created by the SAK in cooperation with both employer and union organisations. The training opportunities ranged from simple welding to bench-work and turning on lathes and lasted between eight weeks for welders and up to six months for some other skills. The total trained between 1940 and 1944 was 10,000 and the highest output was in 1941 with almost 3,000. This was timely as the reserve of unemployed had virtually disappeared by 1942.[45] As well as shortages in the engineering sector, the requirement for workers had soared elsewhere. Farming had been hard-hit by conscription and in the labour-intensive forestry sector, the drive to replace scarce imported coal with wood had increased demand. To address the wood shortage, SAK ended the inter-war road-building programmes which had given employment to the workless and encouraged them to go on forestry courses and then on to logging camps where a life in barracks awaited them. The meagre benefits system encouraged experienced foresters to move continually from county to county and sign on as new recruits, creating 'Sweden's poorest tourists' as one participant joked.[46] These volunteer trainees, 57,000 by 1943, were supplemented in the forests in 1942–3 by 30,000 young conscripts, the only time the 1939 civilian conscript law was used. Norwegian refugees also came to the rescue in the forests, directed there by the Labour Offices. Norwegians had filled 20,000 vacancies by 1943, mainly in the forestry sector, with 3,000 in industry, and the refugees' contribution enabled Sweden to field a larger military force than would otherwise have been possible. For farmers, the solution was seasonal volunteers, school and college students and women, who exchanged desk and home for backbreaking toil on the land and basic accommodation. In 1942, 86,000 volunteers came forward to contribute their labour.

Despite strains on labour relations caused by erosion of spending power due to inflation, the union-backed Government wage and prices freeze provided industrial peace during the war years. In 1945 the Metal-workers' Union, which had become influenced by the Communists, disassociated itself from the national settlement and struck for higher wages in February. The stoppage failed to achieve its aim and strikers were forced to settle for the original offer in July, a set-back which lost the politically resurgent Communists a great deal of support.

Swedish industry came through the war with its production and output intact – in some sectors strengthened – and faced the post-war world with more optimism than its economists, who feared a collapse in demand due to dislocation. For Swedish workers, the 'harvest years' were about to begin.

Sport

Amazingly, sport remained high on the agenda of the Swedish public, despite an inevitable reduction in foreign fixtures. This led to an increased sporting exchange with those countries which could be reached, including Germany. From early 1940, Minister Richert in Berlin proposed a resumption of sporting contacts with the ever-sensitive Germans to demonstrate Swedish good-will. This eventually led to a three-nation athletics meeting with Germany and Finland in Helsinki in September 1940. Participation by Germany was approved personally by Hitler who saw the event as a strand in the closer ties which he aimed for with Finland.[47] Further fixtures between Germany and Sweden followed, from bowling and boxing to ice-hockey and fencing. In October 1941, Sweden thrashed Germany 4–2 in Stockholm at a football match attended by King Gustav and Per Albin. The German team stood with raised right arms as the Swedish national anthem was sung. The Swedish Ski Federation became embroiled in a controversial decision by its president to hold a replacement for the 1941 World Ski Championships in Italy as an 'International Competition' after the Norwegians had boycotted the event. Worse, the Swedish army sent a team which boasted of its success against a severely restricted, unrepresentative opposition – a shameful performance in the view of Swedish post-war public opinion.[48] The Swedish Sports Association (Riksidrottsförbundet) sensed public disquiet at Axis-oriented fixtures and in April 1941 proposed to hold a Scandinavian tournament the following February.

Enthusiasm was expressed for an event which would provide: 'A welcome break from daily routine and monotonous competitions'. However, the proposal collapsed under the weight of practical wartime difficulties, as well as criticism of the probability that occupied Norway would use the occasion to promote Quisling participation. The UD and the Government deemed it unwise to proceed.[49]

Not all Swedish sporting endeavours were a consequence of Swedish foreign policy. Domestically, the football league (*Allsvenskan*) continued, despite conscription affecting team strength, with Elfsborg, Helsingborg, Göteborg, Malmö and Norrköping providing the *Allsvenskan* winning teams during the war years. Athletics records were hotly contested and a duel emerged between two distance-runners, Arne Andersson and Gunder Hägg, who caught the public imagination with their world record-beating performances. In 1943, Hägg managed to travel to the United States and won seven of the eight races in which he competed, cheered on by sleepless Swedes glued to their radio sets despite the time difference. Again in the winter of 1944, Hägg toured the United States but lost three indoor races. His opponent said generously: 'The war was on, he had to travel two weeks on a freighter zigzagging across the Atlantic and he arrived two days before our first race.'[50] Hägg's 1945 world record for the mile was not broken until 1954 by Britain's Roger Bannister.

One particularly Swedish blend of sport and mass-engagement was the emergence of the *Riksmarsch* ('National March') phenomenon in 1940 organised by the Swedish Walking Association to improve the health of the nation as well as to heighten national unity by promoting an event which included all sections of society. Against the clock, men walked 15 kilometres, women and children 10 kilometres, and medals were awarded to the fastest finishers. The spectacle of even *Riksdag* members striding out contributed to its popularity and in May 1941, just over one million Swedes took part in a solidarity match with Finland. The Finns won with one and a half million participants and better times in an event in which even Finnish President Ryti and Prime Minister Rangell competed. After 1941, Sweden continued the annual *Riksmarsch* alone with decreasing interest yet participants wore their badges with a strong element of national pride. Sport for wartime Sweden combined entertainment, diversion, fitness, national unity, and at times foreign policy, in a virtuous circle which only partly anticipated the later controversies about its role in foreign policy.

After the War

Socially, Sweden had probably become an even more homogeneous society as a result of the wartime experience. Social levelling was an inevitable consequence of two wartime measures: conscription and rationing. Conscription propelled people from different backgrounds into meritocratic organisations which required them to operate in groups, irrespective of class or origin. Rationing forced women, predominantly, to stand in the same queues and experience the same shortages and make the same adjustments as the next person, a levelling which promoted affinity and shared values. Yet, these levelling mechanisms did not seem to lead to a feeling of a less class-conscious society. In a survey in 1948, 52 per cent of respondents regarded Sweden as a class-divided society.[51] The newly found improvements in living standards and social security did not translate into a feeling of equality in society. This may have arisen from a lack of social mobility into the Swedish power elites.[52] The largest group for whom barriers tumbled after the war was women, who were emancipated by the changes in social provision as well as access to jobs and careers. For them, admission to politics was a slow progression but even in this arena, almost 10 per cent of *Riksdag* members in 1950 were women, the highest parliamentary percentage in Europe at that time.[53] Karin Kock had been the first woman Cabinet member in 1947 but remained a lone representative there until 1950. Inequality had diminished in Sweden but not disappeared entirely. Glass ceilings had replaced the previous barriers to progress for many outside the traditional upper classes.

As well as promoting homogeneity in society, the war enhanced the level of civic engagement, already promoted by the labour movement, which supported the introduction and development of *Folkhemmet*. The mobilisation of the population equalled similar levels of engagement to those of the belligerent countries, whether as military conscripts, *Hemvärn* (Home Guard), *Lottor* (woman auxiliaries) *Fru Lojals* (woman replacement workers), or *Folkberedskap* representatives (Citizens' Cultural Mobilisation). This personal experience of wartime conditions and adaptation to changes in daily life consequently increased post-war levels of civic participation in Swedish society to levels experienced by the victorious Western Allied and the defeated Axis countries.[54] Sweden gained societal benefits from war without suffering the same loss of lives and property as the belligerents and occupied nations. Although in 1939 Per Albin rued the diversion of resources from peace to war, the Swedish wartime experience worked in his favour to forge consensus and promote levelling in Swedish society which, together with institutional changes, facilitated the introduction of his *Folkhem* vision.

Notes

1. Molin, 'Riksdagspolitik under andra världskriget', p. 288.
2. Westman, *Politiska anteckningar*, 8.11.1939.
3. Westman, *Politiska anteckningar*, 17.4.1941.
4. Westman, *Politiska anteckningar*, 11.12.1942.
5. Molin,'Riksdagspolitik under andra världskriget', pp. 280–1.
6. Roine & Waldenström, *Top Incomes in Sweden over the Twentieth Century*, p. 36.
7. Johansson, *Per Albin och kriget*, p. 387.
8. Ibid. pp. 61–2.
9. Westman, *Politiska anteckningar*, 11.9.1939 & 13.9.1939.
10. Ekholm, *Det svenska jordbruket*, p. 94.
11. Forslund, *Beredskapsdagbok 1939–45*, p. 127.
12. Dahlberg, *I Sverige under 2:a världskriget*, p. 71.
13. Tham, 'Crime in Scandinavia during World War II', pp. 415–28.
14. Dahlberg, *I Sverige under 2:a världskriget*, p. 160.
15. Westman, *Politiska anteckningar*, 22.6.1940.
16. Mallet, *Memoirs*, p. 85.
17. R. M. Titmuss cited by Summerfield, 'The Levelling of Class', p. 255.
18. Frykman, 'Between rebellion and champagne', pp. 40–1.
19. See for example Almgren, *Kvinnorörelsen och efterkrigsplaneringen*: Overud, *I beredskap med Fru Lojal*: Frangeur, *Yrkeskvinna eller makens tjänarinna?*
20. Overud, *I beredskap med Fru Lojal*, pp. 228–9.
21. Dahlberg, *I Sverige under 2:a världskriget*, p. 125.
22. Frangeur, '30-talets kvinnorörelser och dagens: svensk feminism i medgång', pp. 1–3.
23. Overud, *I beredskap med Fru Lojal*, p. 17.
24. Ibid. p. 75.
25. Frangeur, '30-talets kvinnorörelser och dagens: svensk feminism i medgång', p. 4.
26. Almgren, *Kvinnorörelsen och efterkrigsplaneringen*, p. 54.
27. Ibid. p. 261.
28. Ibid. p. 27.
29. Ekholm, *Det svenska jordbruket*, p. 123.
30. Ibid. p. 185.
31. Dahlberg, *I Sverige under 2:a världskriget*, p. 106.
32. Flyghed, *Rättsstat i kris*, pp. 343, 351 & 520.
33. Ibid. p. 214.
34. Dahlberg, *I Sverige under 2:a världskriget*, p. 295.
35. Lindal, *Självcensur i stövelns skugga*, pp. 270–1.
36. Ibid. p. 269.
37. Landgren, *Hjalmar Gullberg och beredskapslitteraturen*, p. 260.
38. Persson, 'Beredskapsminnen'.
39. Dahlberg, *I Sverige under 2:a världskriget*, pp. 198–9.

40. For example, 'Brief discussion with Frau Leander about her new war film'. Goebbels, *The Goebbels Diaries 1939–1941*, 22 June 1941.
41. Thulstrup, *Med lock och pock*, pp. 114–15.
42. Dahlberg, *I Sverige under 2:a världskriget*, p. 181.
43. Hägg, *Den svenska litteraturhistorien*, p. 413.
44. Boëthius, *I barnböckerna var ryssen värre än tysken*.
45. Almgren, *Kvinnorörelsen och efterkrigsplaneringen*, pp. 51–2.
46. Dahlberg, *I Sverige under 2:a världskriget*, p. 139.
47. Richardson, *Förtroligt och hemligt*, p. 237.
48. Ibid. p. 241.
49. Ibid. pp. 245–6.
50. *New York Times*, 2 December 2004.
51. Zetterberg, 'Klassamhället och jämlikheten'.
52. Samuelsson, *From great power to welfare state*, pp. 283–6.
53. Wide, *Kvinnors politiska representation i västeuropa 1950–2000*, Tabell 1.
54. Kage, *War, mobilization, and social learning*, Table 2, p. 40.

12

Looking Back in Anger? The Assault on 'Small-State Realism'

It is sometimes said that if you want to discover how a country's establishment wishes its history portrayed, then the place to go is a college text-book. Just over twenty years after VE-Day, the author of 'Swedish History' (*Svensk historia*), a text book whose aim was to 'ensure that events in our country are correctly understood', entitled the chapter on 1939–45 'The Second World War threatens our freedom and supplies.' The text continued:

> Several times, Sweden came into the danger-zone when its peace and freedom were exposed to great risks ... Under pressure from Germany's threatening power-situation, the Swedish Government was forced to concede the demand [for transit] but on conditions that were thought to prevent these transits leading to risks for our country's security or to harm the Norwegian people ... in this case a deviation from strict neutrality ... The great dangers that threatened compelled the Swedish people to national unity ... In the western powers' interests, Swedish exports to Germany were cut back and discontinued completely in autumn 1944.[1]

This excerpt contains most of the elements of what came to be known as the 'small-state realism' interpretation. This rested on the following propositions: national independence, the welfare and survival of the Swedish people were at stake; German military hegemony over Sweden was unchallengeable; concessions were limited and only given where they were essential: neutrality was bent but not broken; national unity was paramount; and the neutral right to trade with

Germany was legitimate. The factor significantly absent from the book is any mention of the Holocaust, perhaps because the author wanted to distance Sweden from its perpetrators. This interpretation would dominate discourse until the 1990s, evolving in post-war historiography and reinforced by memoirs and diaries.

SMALL-STATE REALISM

Immediately before the war ended, politicians and officials in Sweden and Britain were beginning to feel the hand of history on their shoulders and responded accordingly. Following criticism of Günther in August 1944, Grafström noted 'Günther's real interest . . . is his own obituary in Swedish history' and further regarding Günther's future reputation: 'I think probably that he will just pass the judgement of history. It is only that he has such huge ambitions. Perhaps these huge ambitions will be fulfilled, at any rate by some historian later on.'[2] In October 1944 Günther had been invited to discuss Sweden's wartime foreign policy at a dinner with journalists present. He accepted, perhaps unwisely, and spoke guardedly off the record about the Prytz Telegram and the importance of the impression which British defeatism made on the Swedish Cabinet in 1940, much to the fury of the British Foreign Office which responded in kind. 'It is of course most undesirable that this misrepresentation of British policy in 1940 should gain credence among the Swedish intelligentsia as it is now doing, and we cannot allow Monsieur [sic] Thermaenius . . . to incorporate it in his official history of Swedish Foreign Policy'[3] The telegram affair then disappeared until Prytz referred to it in a broadcast in 1965. Boheman had published his memoirs the previous year but had not been permitted to mention its existence.[4]

Günther's early revelation was made as part of the official defence to counter the negative impression that the 'Leave Traffic' concession had created in Norway and Sweden.[5] A rather anodyne book aimed at Norwegians as well as Swedes in a 'Questions & Answers' format – 'clearing up' points of difference such as transit from the perspective of 'small-state realism' – was published in late 1945.[6] It was followed by a Scandinavian history in English by Rowland Kenney published in 1946 that was among the first to describe the wartime events in Scandinavia. Kenney had been based in Norway as Press Attaché after which he had dealt with British propaganda to Scandinavia in the Ministry of Information where he evidently detested

Björn Prytz and the Swedish policy on transit.[7] Kenney highlighted the divergent view from 'small-state realism', for instance 'The Swedes who were most guilty of what was in effect a pro-German policy will soon be claiming that Swedish neutrality gave the Allies the victory!'[8] These early publications were the first of an accelerating output during the post-war period of which the following are a selective summary.[9]

The Government decided as early as 1943 to instruct Edvard Thermaenius of SIS, a diplomatic political historian, to compile the UD's wartime history. In February 1945 he headed a small Committee to assemble and publish a collection of documents from the UD archives which resulted in the release in 1947 of three volumes of the so-called 'White Books' covering the communications prior to the invasion of Norway and Denmark, the transit issue and reactions to it by the belligerents in 1940.[10] These documented German pressure and the hopelessness of the military situation, thereby validating 'small-state realism' as it affected 'Leave Traffic'.

There was then a post-war gap in wartime Swedish historiography which was scathingly commented on by Krister Wahlbäck in 1967: 'little has been written... There are no official histories... not even its military aspects'. Wahlbäck ascribed this partly to stringent state secrecy rules which limited access to archives and partly to low academic interest in modern Swedish history at that time.[11] The gaps were partially filled, however, by the publication of diplomatic memoirs, for example by Assarsson (1963), Boheman (1964), and Hägglöf (1972). Added to these were political memoirs from Wigforss (1954), Andersson (1955), and military memoirs from Kellgren (1951).[12] Hägglöf contributed his history of Swedish trade policy in 1958 and Åke Thulstrup revealed the essentials of the German propaganda assault in 1962.[13] Wahlbäck himself added to the growing body of primary material (with Göran Boberg) in a ground-breaking document collection in 1966 and a selection from wartime politicians' diaries in 1972.[14] The memoirs neither question the contribution of Swedish trade to the German war-effort nor do they mention the Holocaust. Collectively, they support the 'small-state realism' interpretation and exude an air of smugness and self-congratulation for a job well done in difficult circumstances while showing little sympathy for the abuses and suffering that the war inflicted elsewhere.

In the meantime, a realisation that gaps required to be filled generated the semi-official but academically driven historical research project, 'Sweden during the Second World War' or SUAV

('*Sverige under andra världskriget*'). This started its work in 1969 financed by the Bank of Sweden Tercentenary Foundation and was both sponsored and controlled by the Military Academy. *SUAV* produced twenty theses and was widely publicised. However, despite its status, some *SUAV* researchers faced official obstacles when pursuing their research in the mid-1970s. One, Leif Björkman, was asked by his professor to take over an abandoned *SUAV* subject concerning Finland's and Sweden's controversial roles in *Operation Barbarossa*. He met a blank refusal from the archivist Wilhelm Carlgren when seeking access to the *UD*'s files for the period. When he at last submitted his thesis in January 1971, the Defence Staff and the *UD* demanded that whole passages be excised that revealed unpalatable Swedish and Finnish attitudes to the Germans as well as the Russians. The row reached the Swedish Cabinet before Björkman's professor, Sven-Ulric Palme contacted his cousin, Prime Minister Olof Palme, who personally took the responsibility for publication of the thesis with deletions on the grounds of security only.[15] Twenty-five years after the end of the war, the subject of wartime policy evidently remained extremely sensitive in official circles.

No such issues troubled the well-connected Wilhelm Carlgren whose later extensive history of Swedish foreign policy in 1973 benefited from access to the *UD* archives and enjoyed official cooperation. His book set out an exhaustive and lengthy account of the diplomatic engagements with the belligerents and Sweden's neighbours. It also placed the *UD* and Günther rather than the politicians at the centre of events and can be regarded as the ultimate testament to 'small-state realism'. Carlgren's concluding chapter is entitled, 'Neutrality and practical policy'. It cites the events surrounding the 'Leave Traffic' concession in 1940 as exemplifying 'small-state realism' in response to the German threat while stretching neutrality status to defend the 'practical policy' of remaining out of the war.[16] An abridged version omitting the archival sources and much interesting detail was published in English in 1979.[17]

Following this diplomatic justification, there was a steady increase in historical output including the *SUAV* publications, covering specific but somewhat technical aspects, for example military organisation, strategy and equipment.[18] Prominent among later books was Alf Johansson's excellent 1984 study of Per Albin and wartime politics, the publication in 1982 of a collection of economic essays edited by Martin Fritz revealing the extent of Swedish-German trade and Jan Flyghed's 1992 research questioning the basis of the wartime legal framework governing subversion and secret police activities.[19] Two other valuable insights into the Coalition Cabinet and the UD were provided by the publication in 1981 of the complete diaries of Justice Minister Westman and in 1989, those of UD diplomat Grafström (edited by historians Wilhelm Carlgren and Stig Ekman respectively).[20] But in 1991 it was a journalist rather than a historian who threw a large stone into this relatively tranquil pool of interpretation.

From 'Small-State Realism' to Moral Interpretation

Maria-Pia Boëthius' 1991 book 'Honour and conscience' (Heder och samvete) exploded like a grenade in the heavily defended and tight fortification of 'small-state realism' and caused extensive injuries to the reputation and standing of post-war Swedish academic historians.[21] Boëthius is a campaigning writer who up to 1991 had been regarded as more interested in gender politics than foreign policy. Her selective polemic attack on Swedish conduct was deprecated by 'serious' historians and commentators, not least those who had toiled in the SUAV source-mines and whose worthy but sometimes dull output she dismissed as: 'burying Sweden and the Second World War in oblivion.'[22] She questioned for instance the basis of Swedish relations with the Nazi regime, concession policies and limitations on civil liberties. In doing so she broadly attacked the *moral* basis of 'small-state realism', for example alleging: 'One country that did not lift a finger to stop the Nazis' war and conquests was Sweden.'[23] Her opponents responded with comments like: 'one-sided, tendentious, and full of odd perspectives and interpretations' but failed to land a blow on her moral case, one which they had not previously considered as important or relevant.[24] Their own focus had been on political and economic rather than moral justification for Swedish policy.

It was not until 1995 that historian Alf Johansson responded with his essay on modern Swedish national identity that charted the discourse after the end of the war.[25] He conceded that in an attempt to distance Sweden from the concessions and relations with Germany during the war years, insufficient weight had been given to evaluating alternatives to the dominant 'small-state realism' interpretation, exemplified by Carlgren, that condoned flexible interpretations of the rules of neutrality together with the necessity of trade and other links with the Nazi regime.[26] Johansson traced the moral argument back to the closing days of the war. Per Albin had stoutly defended the Coalition Government's policies in the same way as some Danish politicians in 1945 had attempted to seize the initiative over the interpretation of wartime events in Denmark.[27] Yet, Per Albin was not able to draw on the useful myth of widespread national resistance that was employed in Denmark and Norway in order to exculpate those nations from the reality of extensive collaboration and trade with their German occupiers alongside civil and military resistance. The shift in emphasis from 'small-state realism' interpretation to moral interpretation meant that the Coalition Government could be portrayed as 'running errands for a tyrannical butcher', as Johansson put it.[28]

In 'Honour and conscience', Boëthius admits her suspicion that 'it will never be possible to establish if Sweden 'did right' or 'did wrong' during the war, claiming that the conclusion depends on 'which attitude to life one has.'[29] She pejoratively categorises attitudes into those of 'freedom people' or 'survival people'. These labels of course ascribe an implicit moral judgement to both categories which is unhelpful when attempting an impartial assessment. There are two paradigms, however, which may be more useful in clarifying the 'attitude to life' problem that lies at the core of the argument on 'right' or 'wrong'. The first is the ontological distinction between cosmopolitanism and communitarianism which can help to illuminate how to think about and justify policy.[30] The second is the pioneering work by psychologist Abraham Maslow in his 1943 paper 'A Theory of Human Motivation'.[31]

Cosmopolitanism is an ethical view that individuals form part of a universal moral community that accords inclusiveness and egalitarianism to every other person. This implies an obligation to extend, universally, consideration of the effects of policies to all those affected by them. In this view, the effect of Swedish policy on Norwegians and European Jews for example, would rank equally with its effect on Swedish citizens. By contrast, communitarianism emphasises restricting moral obligations to community members 'in terms of established traditions, felt relations and shared values.'[32] This stance relies on constant reference to the moral community from which it draws its justification and accords with 'small-state realism' and Swedish self-interest reinforced by the Folkhem and 'Swedish way of life' ideals propounded during the war. Per Albin and the Cabinet appear to have been generally communitarian in their outlook by placing Swedish interests first and justifying this by reference to the needs of the Swedish people whereas Segersted's campaigning journalism reflected cosmopolitanism through its identification with democratic forces outside Sweden and concern for the effects of Swedish policy on occupied neighbours. Ethically, there are justifications for each viewpoint but both cannot easily be held simultaneously or reconciled. While not opposites, the emphases in cosmopolitanism and communitarianism are very different.

The second paradigm, Maslow's 'hierarchy of needs', postulates a five-level categorisation of human needs that motivate individuals to satisfy them. According to Maslow, an individual cannot proceed to the next level of motivator before satisfying the previous need. These levels can be summarised as:

1. *Basic* human needs such as food, drink, warmth and shelter.
2. *Safety* needs such as order, stability, security and law.
3. *Social* needs such as community, family and work-group.
4. *Esteem* needs such as confidence, achievement, respect of others and prestige.
5. *Self-actualisation* needs such as self-fulfilment and realisation of potential.

If Maslow's hierarchy is applied to wartime Sweden as a whole, it helps to clarify why the post-war generation has had such difficulty understanding the rationale of a concessionary wartime policy that was approved by most Swedes. Sweden in the 1930s was a relatively poor agricultural country with a predominantly rural population on the periphery of Europe. For many farming and industrial workers and their families at that time, attaining Maslow's first level would have been a major step. It was to meet those needs that Per Albin's *Folkhem* welfare state and Social Democracy was directed. The second level, safety needs, emerged following the outbreak of war in 1939 and the importance of safety increased after April 1940 for all Swedes. As the war progressed, safety and security needs were increasingly met as the Government's concessionary policy eased the German threat but the need for security from German aggression remained in place until 1945 when the threat posed by Germany was replaced by the Soviet Union. Level three's social needs began to be met by the wartime collective sense of national unity and community engagement in the war effort.

After the war, the growth of the *Folkhem* welfare state and a burgeoning economy allowed most Swedes born from 1945 onwards to enjoy higher standards of education and material comfort from the state. Together with security and a certain moral superiority from non-alignment in the Cold War era, this privileged generation was able to concentrate on satisfying esteem (level four), and aspire to self-actualisation (level five), with little concern for the lower levels of need that had so pre-occupied the preceding generation and the wartime Government.

The problem for the post-war generation to which Boëthius belongs is that it was failed by the historical community who, taking their cue from the political community, on the whole neglected to debate the ethics of the Coalition Government's concession and trading policies before the 1990s. As a result, the morally conscious and increasingly cosmopolitan post-war generation was wrong-footed when progressively more Holocaust-centric interpretations of the Second World War implied that *any* contact with Nazi Germany was immoral and questioned Sweden's wartime actions. This vulnerability of 'small-state realism' was compounded by the gradual overtaking of the communitarian view of the state by a cosmopolitan perspective which by the 1990s supported a view that Swedish wartime 'small-state realism' was ethically flawed. The post-war generation in the twenty-first century has been further disadvantaged by their understandable inability to regress their analytical model from a cosmopolitan state, integrated in Europe and no longer peripheral, and from a society in which people now strive to meet their needs for esteem rather than Maslow's basic needs. Instead, they prefer to transfer: 'The presence of the present to the past', as a leading historian of Nazi Germany, Jill Stephenson puts it, and seem unable to comprehend the grip of the persistent spectre of poverty, starvation, insecurity and ill-health on the Swedish communitarian politicians of the 1930s and 1940s. Most were focused on delivering support to Swedish citizens struggling to meet basic human standards of diet, warmth and shelter while attempting to protect the nation from very real Nazi and Soviet threats to life and liberty.

Swedish esteem has further been challenged by being classed as a state that was involved with stolen Jewish assets. Post-war Swedes became accustomed to occupying the moral high ground and were proud of belonging to one of the world's most advanced democracies with a notable record of humanitarian and political intervention. But they found themselves on the moral defensive, inadequately prepared by their historians and politicians to deal with criticism of Sweden's past, for example from Stuart Eizenstadt in 1998:

> whatever their motivations, and however acceptable by the standards of the time for neutrals, the cumulative trade of the World

War II European neutral countries helped to sustain the Nazi war effort by supplying key materials to Germany essential to their conduct of the War – in many cases well past the point where, from the Allied perspective at the time, there was a genuine threat of German attack.[33]

Small wonder that public resentment soon raged against historians and politicians, with the forum shifting from academic discourse to newspaper columns.

'REVELATIONS', THE HOLOCAUST AND STATE INQUIRIES

Following Boëthius' book, which implied an establishment cover-up surrounding Sweden's wartime actions, there was a new, revelatory wave of disclosure about those aspects of Swedish-Nazi contacts which had previously been ignored. The publication in 1996 of Gunnar Richardson's detailed study of the extensive non-diplomatic, cultural and sporting contacts between Sweden and Nazi Germany during 1940–2 followed Maj Wechselmann's 1995 revelations about similar contacts.[34] These disclosures met a new interest in Holocaust-oriented interpretation which had begun with Steve Koblik's masterly 1987 examination of documents between 1933 and 1945 relating to official Sweden's early ambivalence towards Germany's treatment of Jews and the post-1942 phase of active intervention. This was followed in 1996 by Paul Levine's study of the diplomacy of the 'activist' phase including an important examination of *what* the UD knew about the Holocaust and *when* they knew it. In 1997, Svanberg and Tydén followed Koblik in publishing another collection of Swedish Holocaust documents with a commentary. The collaborative economic activity between Nazi Germany and Sweden was then intensely scrutinised by two Dutch researchers, Aalders and Wiebes, whose 1997 study of the role of the Wallenberg brothers and *Enskilda* Bank in protecting German overseas assets significantly damaged the brothers' reputation. Alongside the Holocaust-oriented texts, research had continued on many of the mechanics of Swedish foreign policy, diplomacy, politics and defence which was published as sixty-nine essays in a first-rate six-volume series between 1989 and 1995.[35]

The Swedish state became involved in 1997 when a high-powered State Commission including Wahlbäck, Johansson and Levine amongst others was charged with investigating the ownership of

Jewish assets which were transferred to Sweden before and during the Holocaust; the Commission published its findings in 1999.[36] Aalders and Wiebes' disclosures and their attempt to link the disappearance of Raoul Wallenberg in Budapest to the activities of his uncles stimulated another inquiry in 2001 to establish the actions of the UD. It published its findings in 2003.[37] The Government was now thoroughly committed to rooting out the facts of the wartime period and in 2000 instructed the (then) Swedish Council for Social Research (HSFR) to sponsor a wide-ranging research programme under the direction of respected historians, including Klaus Åmark and Stig Ekman, to investigate Sweden's relationship to Nazism, Nazi-Germany and the Holocaust. This 'SUAV 2' trod where 'SUAV 1' did not or could not tread when it looked at controversial topics such as race and eugenics, arianisation in Sweden, and German ownership of Swedish business. The scale of the funding (20 million kroner) reflected the Government's concern to get every aspect of the remit out into the open and the distribution of research throughout Swedish academic institutions galvanised dozens of researchers to cover the ground thoroughly. Publications, conferences (including one in 2000 which was attended by the Prime Minister, Göran Persson), lectures and presentations rained down on a mainly Swedish audience with the aim of promoting debate. Along with overseeing additional research and inspiring academic and public debate, 'SUAV 2' in 2003 sponsored an invaluable and exhaustive review of all research related to Sweden, Nazism and the Holocaust that ran to over 350 pages with an edition in English, reflecting perhaps the project's intention to reach the audience outside Sweden as well as domestically.[38] Later, in 2007, the project sponsored a collection of eighteen essays focusing entirely on aspects of the morality of Sweden's wartime actions.[39] As well as familiar positions from Zetterberg ('small-state realism') and Boëthius ('new moral paradigm'), there were a number of contributions providing fresh and contrasting insights from less well-established contributors. Together, they exhaustively address moral aspects of the issues of neutrality policy, refugees, trade and post-war judgement.

Per Albin and the Communitarian Ethic

Through diaries, letters and reported discussions as well as official documents, historians now have a reasonably detailed picture of how the wartime Coalition Government's policies evolved and were applied. What is striking is Per Albin's deliberate personal displacement of moral authority based on cosmopolitanism in favour of political authority based on communitarianism. His stance generally reflected majority public opinion and he was single-mindedly resolved to keep Sweden out of the war. By doing so, he was able to stand above ideologically charged conflicts in Cabinet and country and play to his undoubted strengths, developed during twenty-five years at the top of domestic politics, to create sufficient consensus and unity despite opposing internal and external forces. Recent Swedish critics have tended to focus on the cosmopolitan deficit rather than the communitarian advantages.

That is not to say that Per Albin lacked a cosmopolitan outlook completely but rather that he sublimated its promptings to the political requirements of being a neutral leader of a neutral country during a war involving totalitarian ideologues, national interests and territorial ambitions. His rational, common-sense approach contrasted with those of more emotionally charged individuals like Segerstedt. Per Albin's colleagues on the other hand were freer with their opinions and ideas. The Cabinet appeared at times to be more of a debating club than a decision-taking group. Individuals could safely indulge in grand-standing and express fanciful views on foreign policy sometimes based more on wishful thinking rather than reality. These views were never tested in the real world thanks to Per Albin's firm grip on outcomes rather than on policy formulation. He did not hesitate to sweep policy proposals to one side if he felt that they added to the vulnerability of Sweden's position or if they failed to meet the communitarian objective of keeping Sweden out of the war.

There was a qualified place for the cosmopolitan position in wartime Sweden as one observer noted. 'The Swedish Line' represented by Segerstedt is read and admired . . . The great majority read Hjörne (*Göteborgs Post*) and Segerstedt, but put their trust otherwise in Per Albin.'[40] While cosmopolitan Swedish hearts were with Segerstedt, their communitarian heads were with Per Albin, a stance reflected in the wartime election results. Diplomat Sven Grafström, a dedicated admirer of Segerstedt, personally experienced the conflict between idealistic cosmopolitanism and practical communitarianism. 'I am neither an anglophobe nor an anglophile', wrote Grafström in April 1940 as the Germans invaded Norway, 'I only know what this gigantic fight means for mankind.'[41] But only a week later when placed in a unique position to prevent supplies reaching the Germans fighting there, he faltered.[42] His bitter tears of shame contrasted with the steelier resolve of the leaders whose actions he frequently scorned but who fulfilled their undertaking to the Swedish electorate.

Concluding Comments

A frequent blind-spot in non-Swedish historiography is Russia, the ever-present elephant in the room of Swedish foreign policy. From 1917, Bolshevism simply encapsulated the latest Russian threat to Sweden and that threat was no less chilling than the Nazis. After all, it was Stalin's state that killed Raoul Wallenberg, not Hitler's. Yet while Stalin's thirteen million victims during 1941–5 exceed Hitler's on numbers killed, the industrialised genocidal crimes committed by the Nazi régime during its conduct of the war now also place it outside any human morality.[43] Through its relations with that régime, Sweden has been judged complicit in those policies, and sensationalist 'revelations' about 'Sweden's secret Nazi past' are now a frequent event. Where Sweden *was* complicit after 1945 was in a policy of minimal disclosure, avoidance of moral issues, occasional concealment and propagation of a new, non-aligned humanitarian image on the world stage in the hope that the damaging wartime association would gradually be forgotten by the international community and perhaps its own citizens.

As the principals in Watergate found out, it is not so much the actions themselves as the slow extraction of the facts that is most damaging to image, reputation and trust. Jenny Björkman related the story of a Swedish student who considered that the Second World War was the last war in which Sweden participated because she thought 'we had supported Germany and our neutrality policy made us morally guilty for the war and the Holocaust', a consequence that Björkman considered was due to the historiography of the 1990s.[44] However, as Bergquist has pointed out, the sanctification of the defence of Sweden's neutrality in many earlier semi-official accounts was bound to attract revisionist attention.[45] Andersson and Tydén added that superficial, moralising, and sensational viewpoints have gained attention because of historians like Carlgren having left the moral assessments to others.[46] Many Swedes now reluctantly believe that their wartime government's neutrality policy was compromised by pro-German, possibly anti-semitic, Nazi sympathisers and war-profiteers who failed to help their occupied Scandinavian

FIGURE 11 The transit myth, 1944. An armed Swedish soldier supervising German soldiers on transit through Sweden in uncomfortable goods trucks. This 1944 photo often appears as an illustration of German troop transit but is actually of PoWs *en route* to be exchanged.
(PA Photos)

neighbours, who favoured trading with Germany to be paid with looted gold while Swedish armed forces covertly supported their German counterparts and allowed these forces free access within the country's borders. What fewer appreciate is that this small, democratic country felt so threatened militarily that it was forced to concede transit rights to Germany, and so isolated economically that it had to trade with Germany to survive and defend itself as a neutral until the Allied successes enabled it to withdraw from these concessions and join the other democracies in celebrating victory over the Nazis. 'It was no heroic policy but it was in Sweden's extremely poor situation, a calculating and sound policy.'[47]

One of the objectives of this book is to provide sufficient material and background to allow the reader to form his or her own conclusions regarding the moral aspects of the country's policies. In addition to the suggested paradigms of cosmopolitanism, communitarianism, and Maslow's hierarchy, there are five significant features which should influence any assessment.

FIGURE 12 The transit reality, 1941. This is a rare photo of an actual German troop transit through Sweden showing that German soldiers normally travelled comfortably in carriages without close Swedish armed supervision. Such photography was strictly discouraged by the Swedish authorities.
(SVT Imagebank)

Firstly, contemporary British sources, when understandable self-interest is factored out, were generally remarkably supportive of the actions and stances of the encircled neutral. One visitor to Stockholm in 1941 wrote:

I received the impression that conciliatory measures would have been adopted as long as possible ... but not indefinitely. Forced into a corner, I felt, the Swedes would be unable to stretch their desire for neutrality beyond a certain point and would eventually resist demands for transport and other facilities by Germany. Such resistance would have been short-lived if unsupported.[48]

The British Press Attaché, Peter Tennant, wrote after the war that 'Swedish neutrality was an act of survival carried out by a small cadre of highly competent officials'[49] and his Ambassador recorded 'Swedish neutrality was of far greater value to us than a Swedish act of suicide in 1940 would have been.'[50] In a Foreign Office briefing to Foreign Minister Eden in November 1944, an official noted British satisfaction with Sweden:

> Nor is a tough policy towards Sweden justified by recent Swedish behaviour. On the contrary, they have taken a stiff attitude towards the Germans . . . and have been ready to interpret their neutrality in as helpful a manner as possible to the Allies . . . Some little time ago we considered whether it would be to our advantage to press the Swedes to break off diplomatic relations with Germany, but this would seriously impair important sources of intelligence.[51]

Why this satisfaction? Could it be because there really was a general belief that Sweden was pursuing the sensible, though uncertain course which an exposed and vulnerable country should follow – according to what Andersson & Tydén call 'contemporary rationale'.[52] It is also extraordinary that a Government and its politicians should be pilloried for striving *not* to expose its citizens to the horrors of war. There was no appetite in the country for armed conflict and moreover, all the belligerents took great care to ensure that no real *casus bellum* was ever presented to Sweden.[53] Invasion of Swedish territory would have almost certainly been met with armed resistance but the Germans in particular crafted their demands with great care, adapting them to reach the limit of Swedish acceptability. The Allies were latterly less subtle. Sweden was justified in believing that they could not trust them either as a 1944 Chiefs of Staff telegram to Washington showed:

> Indeed we believe that tactics of keeping Swedes constantly in fear that we may at any moment lose patience if they do not take action in direction we desire are more successful than presentation of official ultimatum.[sic][54]

Secondly, all the critics, past and present, have focused their arguments on what the Coalition Government should *not* have done with few practical proposals on what the politicians *should* have done. Swedish options were in practice heavily circumscribed. When the UD warned Berlin in 1943 of 'serious consequences' in the case of the Danish Jews, the only suggestion for a sanction that Boheman came up with was to prevent individual Germans crossing through Sweden.[55] Stopping trade would have risked Swedish welfare and lives due to the stranglehold that Germany had on coal, fertiliser and oil imports and the very real likelihood of military attack. When it came to backing up remonstration, the Swedish tiger was in reality a paper tiger. To avoid making this obvious, the Government steered clear of pointless protests against German conduct. It is of course the prerogative of any political opposition to contradict those in charge of the country but with that power also comes responsibility. It is no coincidence that the strongest public critics were two newspaper editors, Segerstedt and Nerman, and one is reminded of British Prime Minister Stanley Baldwin's response to severe personal criticism in 1931: 'What the proprietorship of these papers is aiming at is power, and power without responsibility – the prerogative of the harlot through the ages'[56] The practical policy alternatives to attracting German military, trade or diplomatic retaliation were both few and unpalatable, and the Swedish electorate knew that when they supported the Coalition Government again and again throughout the war. The armed adventurism of the Karl XII era, apart from the 'activist' military circles, had been replaced by appropriate moderation – 'lagom', a fundamental characteristic of the post-war Swedish national psyche.

Thirdly, it is essential, though psychologically difficult, to place wartime Swedish indignation about the treatment of the Scandinavian Jews and the horrific post-war Holocaust images in the context of the period in order to make a valid and objective assessment. This was not a cosmopolitan war to safeguard vulnerable Jews and crush repugnant Nazism but a communitarian geopolitical struggle between five great world powers for hegemony and territory. Frontiers, not humanity, determined the actions and policies of the Allies. As Simon Sebag Montefiore has observed, neither Stalin nor Molotov, his Foreign Minister 'saw any contradiction between imperialist expansion and their Marxist crusade.'[57] Stalin's view of the post-war settlement was also clear. 'The question of borders will be decided by force.'[58] In 1939 the anti-semitic Stalin was also more than willing to torture and imprison Jewish officials in Russia in order to signal reassurance to Hitler. 'Purge the ministry of Jews.'[59] In contrast to Stalin's deliberate and murderous anti-Semitism then and after the war, one commentator's tenuous assertion that 'by trading with Germany . . . Sweden materially assisted the commission of genocide' lacks credibility.[60] By employing the same logic, it could be equally asserted that in supplying Stalin's Russia with aid to the Soviet war effort during 1941–5, the Western Allies materially assisted in the deaths of 530,000 people from national groups such as the Latvians in a series of ruthless wartime deportations – not to mention the many millions of Stalin's other victims.[61]

Sweden's diplomacy and trade policies were crafted initially to deal with the shortcomings evident from 1914–18 and only after 9 April 1940 did the Coalition Government discover that encircled Sweden was forced to have a much closer and more dependent relationship with the Third Reich than they had had with the Second. By then it was too late to alter course: the trading ties which bound Sweden to Germany could not be cut without a gamble on repercussions, so the chosen policy option was to disentangle slowly from the embrace of the ghastly regime while taking opportunistic initiatives that challenged German interests such as receiving Jewish refugees and supporting the formation of Norwegian and Danish 'Police Troops'. Boheman's confident 1939 forecast about Sweden's policy options failed to foresee Swedish isolation and German trade domination. Sweden was chained by its commercial dependency to the disintegrating corpse of Nazi Germany for far longer than it wished to be associated with that increasingly genocidal and criminal regime.

Fourthly, Sweden was an independent democracy in September 1939 and remained so throughout the conflict. The crucial, defining and contentious decisions taken by the Coalition Government on conceding, then ending transit, releasing the Norwegian ships, stopping ball-bearings exports and permitting staff talks with the Allies exemplified how Sweden's democratic political mechanisms functioned to arrive at policy decisions which were often hugely unpopular and from which some politicians sought to distance themselves in the post-war period. These decisions cannot be dismissed as undemocratic. The elected representatives of the Swedish people in the Coalition Government Cabinet and in the *Riksdag* believed that the nature and timing of these decisions was necessary in order to keep Sweden out of the war and provide for its people's welfare.

Finally, as for the hotly debated contribution of Swedish iron ore and ball-bearings to the sustenance of the German war-machine, the basis for that trade was established in 1939, before the Holocaust began to emerge and while the power-balance was stable. The cargo volumes were agreed, first with the British and then with the Americans, who both privately acknowledged the risks to Sweden from ending German trade. The Swedish negotiators of course flexed their positions to match the relative strengths of the great powers as the power-balance changed with military failure and success. The later Allied disputes with Sweden were about the timing of trade termination rather than about its morality. Morality only crept into the Allied cosmopolitan argument when they attempted to persuade Sweden to accept the Allied risk assessment of German military retaliation following trade termination rather than the Swedish Cabinet's own admittedly conservative assessment of the situation. There would be no military cost to the Allies if they were wrong as they had no intention of coming to Sweden's rescue. As the wartime history of Lithuania, Latvia, Estonia and Poland showed, the great powers were careless about the rights of small countries when it suited them. For the Baltic states, the Atlantic Charter would not apply and their populations again suffered Soviet oppression. Stalin's murderous crimes in Poland were ignored as inconvenient in the post-war settlement.

So Sweden prudently looked after its own interests and spurned the tutelage of the self-interested and evidently untrustworthy combatants. The responsibility for Sweden rested in Stockholm and nowhere else. Per Albin the card-player and Günther the race-goer were both avid gamblers but they were notably risk-averse when the lives and welfare of the people of Sweden were at stake. That was their over-riding responsibility and they discharged it for six long years without the luxury of personal security, conjecture, hindsight and time for extended reflection. Their reputations and that of Sweden could now be better served by those who enjoy those advantages. Current and future commentators would do well to remember what Sven Grafström of the *UD* wrote in 1940 before re-stating his credo as an anti-Nazi: 'It is easy for a little nobody ('*skit*') like me, without any vestige of responsibility, to conduct a discussion on how Sweden's policy ought to be formulated correctly.'[62]

Notes

1. Lindell & Lagerström *Svensk historia*, pp. 164–70.
2. Grafström, *Anteckningar*, 27 August 1944.
3. NA FO 371/ Montague-Pollock to Eden 18 November 1944 (author's file).
4. *The Times*, 9 September 1965.
5. NA FO 898/74 'Derby' Mission to Norway 1943–1945 PWE & SOE.
6. Kugelberg & Ihlen, *Grannar emellan*.
7. NA FO 371/29663 Kenney to Coote, 30 June 1941, 'I have never been enamoured of Prytz.'
8. Kenney, *The Northern Tangle*, p. 234.
9. See for example, Ekman & Åmark, *Sweden's relations with Nazism, Nazi Germany and the Holocaust: a survey of research*.

10. Bergquist, 'Revisionismens lockelser', p. 30.
11. Wahlbäck, 'Sweden: Secrecy and Neutrality', pp. 183–91.
12. Assarsson, I skuggan av Stalin; Boheman, På vakt; Hägglöf, Möte med Europa; Wigforss, Minnen. 3; Andersson, Från bondetåget till samlingsregeringen; Kellgren, Sex krigsår i Skölds skugga.
13. Thulstrup, Med lock och pock; Hägglöf, Svensk krigshandelspolitik.
14. Wahlbäck & Boberg (eds), Sveriges sak är vår; Wahlbäck, Regeringen och kriget.
15. Björkman, Sverige inför Operation Barbarossa, pp. 7–20.
16. Carlgren, Svensk utrikespolitik, pp. 585–93.
17. Carlgren, Swedish foreign policy during the Second World War.
18. Wangel, Sveriges militära beredskap.
19. Johansson, Per Albin och kriget; Fritz, The Adaptable Nation; Flyghed, Rättsstat i kris.
20. Westman, Politiska anteckningar: Grafström, Anteckningar.
21. Boëthius, Heder och samvete.
22. Ibid. p. 10.
23. Ibid. p. 134.
24. Kent Zetterberg quoted in Linder, Andra världskriget och Sverige, p. 6.
25. Johansson, 'Neutralitet och modernitet'.
26. Carlgren, Svensk utrikespolitik, pp. 13–14.
27. See 'Den politiske kamp' in Christensen, Lund, Olesen & Sørensen, Danmark besat, pp. 678–97.
28. Johansson, 'Neutralitet och modernitet', p. 212.
29. Boëthius, Heder och samvete, p. 152.
30. For a fuller explanation, see Atack, The ethics of peace and war, pp. 40–51.
31. For a fuller discussion of needs and ethics, see Lee, Toward a Sound World Order, pp. 25–44.
32. Dower, World ethics, p. 23.
33. Eizenstat, 'Testimony'.
34. Richardson, Beundran och fruktan: Wechselmann & Lindgren, De bruna förbindelserna.
35. Hugemark (ed.), Stormvarning: Sverige inför andra världskriget; Hugemark, & Gemzell (eds) Urladdning: 1940 – blixtkrigens år; Hugemark (ed.), I orkanens öga: 1941 – osäker neutralitet; Hugemark (ed.), Vindkantring: 1942 – politisk kursändring; Hugemark (ed.), Nya fronter?: 1943 – spänd väntan; Huldt & Böhme (eds), Vårstormar: 1944 – krigsslutet skönjes; Huldt & Böhme (eds), Horisonten klarnar: 1945 – krigsslut.
36. SOU 1999:20, Sverige och judarnas tillgångar: slutrapport.
37. SOU 2003:18 Ett diplomatiskt misslyckande.
38. Ekman, & Åmark (eds), Sweden's relations with Nazism, Nazi Germany and the Holocaust: a survey of research.
39. Andersson & Tydén (eds), Sverige och Nazityskland.
40. Cited in Wahlbäck & Boberg (eds), Sveriges sak är vår, p. 225.
41. Grafström, Anteckningar, 13 April 1940.
42. Grafström, Anteckningar, 20 April 1940.
43. Rummel, Lethal Politics, Table 7A.
44. Björkman,'Nollpunkten för vår tideräkning'.
45. Bergquist, 'Revisionismens lockelser', p. 33.
46. Andersson & Tydén, 'Historikerna och moralen', pp. 15–16.
47. Zetterberg, 'Eftergifter och motstånd', p. 120.
48. Weaver, On Hitler's doorstep, p. 192.
49. Tennant, Touchlines of war, p. 272.

50. Mallet, *Memoirs*, p. 174.
51. NA FO 371/43509 Warner to Eden, 20 November 1944.
52. Andersson & Tydén, 'Historikerna och moralen', p. 19.
53. Johansson, *Per Albin och kriget*, p. 325.
54. NA AIR 9/283 Chiefs of Staff to J. S. M. Washington, 28 August 1944.
55. Grafström, *Anteckningar*, 2 October 1943.
56. Quoted in Pearce, *British political history, 1867–1990*, p. 402.
57. Sebag Montefiore, *Stalin*, p. 308.
58. Ibid. p. 415.
59. Ibid. p. 310.
60. Ibid. pp. 600–1 and Levine, 'Swedish neutrality during the Second World War, p. 329.
61. Sebag Montefiore, *Stalin*, pp. 398n. & 482–3.
62. Grafström, *Anteckningar*, 5 May 1940.

Abbreviations and Glossary

ABC   American Bosch Company
Abwehr   German military intelligence
ACFC   Assistance Committee for Finnish Children
Allmänna Säkerhetstjänsten   Swedish Civilian Security Service
Allsvenskan   Swedish football league
APC   Alien Property Custodian, the United States organisation for enemy assets
AS   *Allmänna Säkerhetstjänsten*, the Swedish Civilian Security Service
Barbarossa   German operation to invade Russia in 1941
Bedömningsnämnden   Assessment Commission, a short-lived Swedish post-war investigation into alleged Nazi sympathisers in official positions
Beredskapstiden   The wartime emergency period in Sweden
Centralen   Swedish military intelligence
Comintern   Communist International, an inter-war Moscow-controlled organisation aimed at fomenting revolution
Continuation War   The second Russo-Finnish war, 1941–4
Den svenska livsformen   The Swedish Way of Life
DN   *Dagens Nyheter*, national newspaper
Engelbrecht Division   German Army Division permitted to travel from Norway to Finland across Sweden in June 1941 *en route* to join the invasion of Russia
Festung Norwegen   Fortress Norway
Final Solution   German policy to exterminate European Jewry
Folkberedskap   Citizens' Cultural Mobilisation Section of the *SIS*

Folkhemmet   The Swedish welfare state concept
Forhandlingspolitik   Denmark's policy of cooperation with the German occupation
FRA   Swedish Military Signals Intelligence
Frågebyrån (IFB)   Swedish Inquiry Office, to counter false rumours
Fußkrieg   Pedestrian-paced warfare
Gegendruck   Counter-pressure
Gessinungsneutralität   'Mental' neutrality
GHT   *Göteborgs Handels-och Sjöfartstidning*, a newspaper edited by Government critic Torgny Segerstedt
Grey Slip   Swedish Government guidance note to the media
Großraumwirtschaft   Greater German Economic Area
GRU   Russian military intelligence
Hemvärnet   Swedish Home Guard
Hird   Norwegian Nazi paramilitary organisation
ICRC   International Committee of the Red Cross
Judenfrei   Free of Jews
Konstitutionutskottet   Parliamentary Constitutional Affairs Committee
Kontaktudvalget   Stockholm-based Danish resistance organisation
Kriegsmarine   German navy
Kristidsnämnder   Emergency Supply Committees
Kristidsstyrelser   Emergency Supply Boards
Kvinnoföreningarnas beredskapskommitté (KBK)   Women's Associations' Standby Committee
Landstormen   Swedish Territorial Army
Länsarbetsnämnder   County Employment Committees
Leave Traffic   Transit of German troops by rail through Sweden on leave from the occupying force in Norway
Lionel and *Dicto*   Two Norwegian ships with their cargoes trapped in Göteborg by the German blockade
LO   *Landsorganisationen*, the Swedish Trades Union organisation
Lottor   Sveriges Lottakårer   A non-combatant women's auxiliary force
LTA   1943 London Tripartite Agreement on trade between Sweden, Britain and the United States
Luftskydd   Air Defence
Luftwaffe   German airforce
MOI   British Ministry of Information
Machtübernahme   Hitler's appointment as Chancellor in 1933
March Crisis   Mobilisation by Sweden in 1941 in response to fears of a German invasion

MEW British Ministry of Economic Warfare
MI6 British overseas espionage organisation also known as the Secret Intelligence Service
Milorg Norwegian military resistance organisation
MTB Motor torpedo-boat
Nasjonal Samling Norwegian Nazi party led by Vidkun Quisling
Nordische Gesellschaft (NG) German cultural and propaganda organisation
OKW German Military High Command
Operation Graffham Pre-D-Day British deception exercise
Operation Performance Norwegian ships breakout from Göteborg, 1942
Operation Rubble Norwegian ships breakout from Göteborg, 1941
Operation Tindall British deception in 1943 to mislead the Germans into believing that the Allies would invade Norway
OSS Office of Strategic Services, the United States wartime espionage organisation and forerunner of the CIA
Osvensk 'Un-Swedish'
Police Troops Norwegian and Danish paramilitaries trained and armed in Sweden
Pressnämnden Swedish wartime Press Council, previously known as the *Pressråd*
Propagandabyrån Coordination Section for Counter-Propaganda in the *SIS*
Radiotjänst Swedish Radio
Reichskommissariat German administrative body in an occupied territory
Reichsstelle für Aussenhandel German Authority for Overseas Trade, created to promote arianisation in overseas companies
Riksdagen Swedish Parliament
Riksidrottsförbundet Swedish Sports Association
Riksmarschen National March
RKE Commission for Economic Defence Preparation
RSHA German Main Security Organisation
Safe-Conduct Traffic Swedish cargo ships permitted by both Germany and Britain to pass through their blockades
SAK Swedish State Employment Commission
SBB *(Statens biografbyrå)* Swedish National Film Office for censorship
Schutz-Pass Protective passport
SEB *(Enskilda)* Stockholms *Enskilda Bank*, the Wallenberg family bank

SIS   Statens informationsstyrelsen, Swedish State Information Board
SKF   Svenska Kullagerfabriken, the Swedish ball-bearings manufacturer and exporter
Socialstyrelsen   The Swedish Social Administration Agency
SOE   Special Operations Executive, a British organisation promoting sabotage and espionage in occupied Europe
Statens informationsstyrelsen   Swedish State Information Board
Statens Livsmedelskommission   Swedish State Food Commission
Statens reservförråd   Swedish State Supply Reserves
Statens utlänningskommission   Swedish Aliens Office, responsible for refugees
Storting   Norwegian Parliament
SUAV   Sverige under andra världskriget: Sweden during the Second World War
SvD   Svenska Dagbladet, national newspaper
Tisdagsklubben   Swedish non-political, anti-Nazi group
Transito   Allied transit operation to supply Russia through Sweden during the First World War
Tremannanämnden   Three-man Committee created in 1939 to manage state information
Trots Allt!   A newspaper edited by Government critic Ture Nerman
TT   Swedish national news agency
UD   Swedish Foreign Ministry
Upplysningsnämnder   Information Committees, accountable to Folkberedskap
Utrikesdepartementet (UD)   Swedish Foreign Ministry
Utrikesnämnden   Advisory Council for Foreign Affairs
Utrikesutskottet   Parliamentary Foreign Affairs Committee
Utrymningskommissionen   Evacuation Commission
Utskott   Parliamentary Committee
Waffen-SS   Military wing of the German SS
Wehrmacht   German Army
Weserübung   German operation to invade Norway and Denmark, 1940
White Buses   Swedish mission to rescue Scandinavians in Germany, 1945
Winter War   The first Russo-Finnish war, 1939–40
WJC   World Jewish Congress
WRB   United States War Refugee Board
WTA   War Trade Agreement with Britain in 1939

Reference Sources and Bibliography

Aalders, Gerard & Wiebes, Cees, *The art of cloaking ownership: the secret collaboration and protection of the German war industry by the neutrals: the case of Sweden* (Amsterdam: Amsterdam University Press, cop. 1996)

Agrell, Wilhelm, *Skuggor runt Wallenberg: uppdrag i Ungern 1943–45* (Lund: Historiska Media, 2006)

Agrell, Wilhelm, *Stockholm som spioncentral* (Lund: Historiska media, 2006)

Aldgate, Anthony & Richards, Jeffrey, *Britain can take it: the British cinema in the Second World War* (Edinburgh: Edinburgh University Press, 1994)

Almgren, Nina, *Kvinnorörelsen och efterkrigsplaneringen: statsfeminism i svensk arbetsmarknadspolitik under och kort efter andra världskriget* (Umeå: institutionen för historiska studier, Umeå universitet, 2006)

Andenæs, Johannes Bratt, Riste, Olav, Skodvin, Magne, *Norway and the Second World War* (Oslo: Grundt Tanum, 1966)

Andersson, Gustaf, *Från bondetåget till samlingsregeringen: politiska minnen* (Stockholm: Tiden, 1955)

Andersson, Lars M. & Tydén, Mattias, 'Historikerna och moralen' in Andersson, Lars M. & Tydén, Mattias (eds), *Sverige och Nazityskland: skuldfrågor och moraldebatt* (Stockholm: Dialogos, 2007)

Andersson, Lars M. & Tydén, Mattias (eds), *Sverige och Nazityskland: skuldfrågor och moraldebatt* (Stockholm: Dialogos, 2007)

Andolf, Göran, 'De grå lapparna: regeringen och pressen under andra

världskriget' in Hugemark, Bo (ed.), Nya fronter?: 1943 – spänd väntan (Stockholm: Probus, 1994)
Andolf, Göran, 'Amerikanska flygare i Sverige 1944–1945' in Huldt, Bo & Böhme, Klaus-Richard (eds), Horisonten klarnar: 1945 – krigsslut (Stockholm: Probus, 1995)
Andolf, Göran, 'Interneringen av britter och tyskar 1943–1944' in Huldt, Bo & Böhme, Klaus-Richard (eds), Vårstormar: 1944 – krigsslutet skönjes (Stockholm: Probus, 1995)
Andolf, Göran, 'Militära interneringar i Sverige under de första krigsåren 1939–' in Hugemark, Bo (ed.), Vindkantring: 1942 – politisk kursändring (Stockholm: Probus, 1992)
Anger, Per (Intro.) Räddningen: Budapest 1944: Judarna skall deporteras: De svenska hjälpinsatserna: rapporter ur UD:s arkiv (Stockholm: Fischer i samråd med Utrikesdepartementet, 1997)
Arbetarrörelsens arkiv, Stockholm, Per Albins Brev
Arnstad, Henrik, Spelaren Christian Günther: Sverige under andra världskriget (Stockholm: Wahlström & Widstrand, 2006)
Assarsson, Vilhelm, I skuggan av Stalin (Stockholm: Bonnier, 1963)
Atack, Iain, The ethics of peace and war: from state security to world community (Edinburgh: Edinburgh University Press, 2005)
Åmark, Klas, 'Demokratin, neutraliteten och moralen: Sverige under andra världskriget' in Andersson, Lars M. & Tydén, Mattias (eds), Sverige och Nazityskland: skuldfrågor och moraldebatt (Stockholm: Dialogos, 2007)
Barker, Ralph, The Blockade Busters (Barnsley: Pen & Sword Maritime, 2005)
Beredskapstid 1939–1945 < http://www.silvervingar.se/Beredskapstid.html >
Berggren, Jan, Världskrig, kommunism och nazism i själva verket: aktörer, åsikter och aktioner inom statlig förvaltning under andra världskriget: exempel Tullverket (Stockholm: Carlsson, 2005)
Berggren, Lena, 'Swedish Fascism: Why Bother?', Journal of Contemporary History, Vol. 37, No. 3 (July 2002), pp. 395–417
Bergquist, Mats & Johansson, Alf W. (eds), Säkerhetspolitik och historia: essäer om stormaktspolitiken och Norden under sjuttio år: vänbok till Krister Wahlbäck (Stockholm: Hjalmarson & Högberg, 2007)
Bergquist, Mats, 'Revisionismens lockelser: debatten om Sverige under andra världskriget' in Bergquist, Mats & Johansson, Alf W. (eds) Säkerhetspolitik och historia: essäer om stormaktspolitiken och Norden under sjuttio år: vänbok till Krister Wahlbäck (Stockholm: Hjalmarson & Högberg, 2007)

Bergquist, Mats, Johansson, Alf W. & Wahlbäck, Krister (eds) *Utrikespolitik och historia: studier tillägnade Wilhelm M. Carlgren den 6 maj 1987* (Stockholm: Militärhistoriska förl., 1987)
Björkman, Jenny, 'Nollpunkten för vår tideräkning', *Populär Historia* 5/2005
Björkman, Leif, *Sverige inför Operation Barbarossa: ocensurerad: [svensk neutralitetspolitik 1940–1941]* (Stockholm: Hjalmarson & Högberg, 2006)
Boëthius, Maria-Pia, *Heder och samvete: Sverige och andra världskriget* (Stockholm: Norstedt, 1991)
Boëthius, Ulf, 'I barnböckerna var ryssen värre än tysken', *Svenska Dagbladet*, 28 October 2008
Boheman, Erik, *På vakt. Kabinettssekreterare under andra världskriget* (Stockholm: Norstedt, 1964)
Bojerud, Stellan, ' "Hur skall vi komma i land?": de svenska planerna på att i krigets slutskede invadera Bornholm' in Huldt, Bo & Böhme, Klaus-Richard (eds), *Vårstormar: 1944 – krigsslutet skönjes* (Stockholm: Probus, 1995)
Bojerud, Stellan, 'Kryptonazister fick fribrev' in *Hemvärnet*, nr 2 2001: p. 33
Bojerud, Stellan, 'Mundering modell 39: krigsmaterielfrågan och krigsorganisationens expansion inom armén' in Hugemark, Bo (ed.), *Stormvarning: Sverige inför andra världskriget* (Stockholm: Probus, 1989)
Brandberg, K. G., 'Hemvärnet' in Wangel, Carl-Axel (ed.), *Sveriges militära beredskap 1939–1945* (Stockholm: Militärhistoriska förl., 1982)
Brink, Lars, *Demokrat och krigsfrivillig: 1940-talets hemvärn – en brygga mellan krigsmakt och folklig kultur* (Göteborg Föreningen för Göteborgs försvar: Text & bild konsult, 2007)
Böhme, Klaus-Richard & Schön, Bosse, *Signal: Nazitysklands propaganda i Sverige 1941–45* (Stockholm: Bokförlaget DN, 2005)
Böhme, Klaus-Richard, 'Upplysning om och inom försvaret' in Huldt, Bo & Böhme, Klaus-Richard (eds), *Vårstormar: 1944 – krigsslutet skönjes* (Stockholm: Probus, 1995)
Böhme, Klaus-Richard, 'Svensk polis och Gestapo' in Hugemark, Bo (ed.) *I orkanens öga: 1941 – osäker neutralitet* (Stockholm: Probus, 1992)
Calder, Angus, *The People's War: Britain 1939–1945* (London: Pimlico, 1992)
Carlgren, W. M. *Swedish foreign policy during the Second World War* translated [from the Swedish] by Arthur Spencer (London: E. Benn, 1977)

Carlgren, Wilhelm M. *Svensk utrikespolitik 1939–1945* (Stockholm: Allmänna förl., 1973)

Carlgren, Wilhelm M. *Sverige och Baltikum: från mellankrigstid till efterkrigsår: en översikt* (Stockholm: Publica: 1993)

Carlgren, Wilhelm M., 'Den stora överraskningen: regeringen och Moskvapakten' in Hugemark, Bo (ed.), *Stormvarning: Sverige inför andra världskriget* (Stockholm: Probus, 1989)

Carlgren, Wilhelm M., 'Sverige och Finlands utträde ur kriget' in Huldt, Bo och Böhme, Klaus-Richard (eds), *Vårstormar: 1944 – krigsslutet skönjes* (Stockholm: Probus, 1995)

Carlsson, Erik, *Gustaf V och andra världskriget* (Lund: Historiska media, 2006)

Cesarani, David & Levine, Paul A. (eds), *'Bystanders' to the Holocaust: a re-evaluation* (London: Frank Cass, 2002)

Christensen, Claus Bundgård, Lund, Joachim, Olesen, Niels Wium, Sørensen, Jakob, *Danmark besat: krig og hverdag 1940–45* (København: Høst, 2005)

Churchill, Winston Spencer, *The Second World War, Vol. 1* (London: Cassell, 1948)

Cole, Robert, *Britain and the war of words in neutral Europe, 1939–45, The art of the possible* (London: Macmillan, 1990)

Cpl Geoff Steer 1/4 KOYLI, The Second World War Experience Centre Archive, Horsforth, Leeds

Cronenberg, Arvid, 'Krigsfall Tyskland': planering, mobilisering och uppmarsch in Hugemark, Bo, & Gemzell, Carl-Axel (eds), *Urladdning: 1940 – blixtkrigens år* (Stockholm: Probus, 1990)

Cronenberg, Arvid, 'Och får jag tag i den fan-: den militära oppositionen mot Olof Thörnell in Hugemark', Bo (ed.), *I orkanens öga: 1941 – osäker neutralitet* (Stockholm: Probus, 1992)

Cronenberg, Arvid, 'Kapplöpning med tiden: svensk krigsorganisation och krigsplanering' in Hugemark, Bo (ed.), *Stormvarning: Sverige inför andra världskriget* (Stockholm: Probus, 1989)

Dahlberg Hans, *Hundra år i Sverige: krönika över ett dramatiskt sekel* (Stockholm: Bonnier, 2000)

Dahlberg, Hans, *I Sverige under 2:a världskriget* (Stockholm: Bonnier fakta, 1983)

Decker, Karola, 'Divisions and Diversity: The Complexities of Medical Refuge in Britain, 1933–1948. *Bulletin of the History of Medicine*, Volume 77, No. 4, Winter 2003, p. 856

Denham, Henry Mangles, *Inside the Nazi ring. A naval attachéi in Sweden, 1940–1945* (London: Murray, 1984)

Documents on German foreign policy, 1918–1945: from the archives of the German Foreign Ministry. Akten zur Deutschen Auswärtigen Politik. Germany. Auswärtiges Amt. English. 8–13. The War years, 1939–1941. 1949 London: HMSO

Dorril, Stephen, MI6: fifty years of special operations (London: Fourth Estate 2000.)

Dower, Nigel, World ethics: the new agenda (Edinburgh: Edinburgh University Press, 1998)

Eizenstat, Stuart E., 'Testimony for Under Secretary Of State, House Banking Committee June 4, 1998' on the U.S. Government Supplementary Report on Nazi Assets

Ekberg, Henrik, 'Finländska krigsbarn i västerled' in Meinander, Henrik, Finlands historia. 4: inledning av Matti Klinge (Esbo: Schildt, 1999), p. 199

Ekholm, Gunnar, Det svenska jordbruket och folkförsörjningen under andra världskriget (Lund: Ekonomisk-historiska fören., 1976)

Ekman, Stig & Åmark, Klas (eds), Sweden's relations with Nazism, Nazi Germany and the Holocaust: a survey of research [co-editor for the English version of this survey: John Toler.] (Stockholm: Swedish Research Council [Vetenskapsrådet]: 2003)

Ekman, Stig, 'Skilful realpolitik or unprincipled opportunism?: the Swedish coalition government's foreign policy in debate and research' in Ekman, Stig & Eding, Nils, War experience, self image and national identity: the Second World War as myth and history (Stockholm: Bank of Sweden Tercentenary Foundation [Riksbankens jubileumsfond]: 1997)

Engel, David, Facing a holocaust: the Polish government-in-exile and the Jews, 1943–1945 (Chapel Hill, London: University of North Carolina Press, 1993)

Engle, Eloise & Paananen, Lauri, The Winter War. The Russo-Finnish Conflict, 1939–40 (London, Sidgwick and Jackson 1973)

Ericson, Lars, 'Buffert eller hot?' in Hugemark, Bo (ed.), I orkanens öga: 1941 – osäker neutralitet (Stockholm: Probus, 1992)

Estvall, Martin, 'Ett folk, ett rike, en åsikt?', in Andersson, Lars M. & Tydén, Mattias (eds), Sverige och Nazityskland: skuldfrågor och moraldebatt (Stockholm: Dialogos, 2007), pp. 306–23

Feilitzen, Cecilia Von, 'A Historical Review of Radio Research in Sweden.' Nordicom Review, Ulla Carlsson (ed.), No. 18 (1997) 1 (Göteborg: Nordicom, 1997)

Flyghed, Janne, Rättsstat i kris: spioneri och sabotage i Sverige under andra världskriget (Stockholm: Federativ, 1992)

Forsberg, Tore, Spioner och spioner som spionerar på spioner:

spioner och kontraspioner i Sverige (Stockholm: Hjalmarson & Högberg, 2003)

Forslund, Björn, Beredskapsdagbok 1939–45 (Täby: Larson, 1985)

Frangeur, Renée, '30–talets kvinnorörelser och dagens: svensk feminism i medgång' Paper framlagt vid NKKs nordiska kvinnorörelsekonferens på Island 10–12 juni, 2004, pp. 1–3 in Häften för kritiska studier. 2001(34):1, pp. 62–8

Frangeur, Renée, Yrkeskvinna eller makens tjänarinna?: striden om yrkesrätten för gifta kvinnor i mellankrigstidens Sverige (Lund: Arkiv, 1998)

Franzén, Nils-Olof, Undan stormen: Sverige under första världskriget (Stockholm: Bonnier, 1986)

Friberg, Göte, Stormcentrum Öresund: krigsåren 1940–45 (Stockholm: Natur och kultur, 1977)

Fritz, Martin, 'Sveriges ekonomiska relationer med Nazityskland' in Andersson, Lars M. & Tydén, Mattias (eds), Sverige och Nazityskland: skuldfrågor och moraldebatt (Stockholm: Dialogos, 2007), pp. 257–77

Fritz, Martin, The Adaptable Nation: essays in Swedish economy during the Second World War (Göteborg: Ekonomisk-historiska inst., Univ.: 1982)

Frost, Erik, Dansk soldat i Sverige 1943–45: den Danske Brigade – som jeg oplevede den! (København: Den Danske Brigadeforening (DANFORCE) på Frihedsmuseets venners forl., 1989)

Frykholm, Lars, Protokoll vid riksdagens hemliga sammanträden 1942–1945 (Stockholm: Riksdagens förvaltningskontor, 1976)

Frykman, Jonas 'Between rebellion and champagne' in Force of habit: exploring everyday culture edited by Frykman, Jonas & Löfgren, Orvar (Lund: Lund University Press, 1996)

Gifford, E. W., American Anthropologist, New Series Vol. 30, No. 3 (July–September 1928), pp. 493–5

Goebbels, Joseph, The Goebbels Diaries 1939–1941, translated and edited by Fred Taylor (London: Hamish Hamilton, 1982)

Grafström, Anders, 'Frivilligförsvaret' in Wangel, Carl-Axel (ed.), Sveriges militära beredskap 1939–1945 (Stockholm: Militärhistoriska förl., 1982)

Grafström, Sven, Anteckningar. 1938–1944: utg. genom Ekman, Stig, (Stockholm: Samf. för utg. av handskrifter rörande Skandinaviens historia, 1989)

Greear, Wesley P., 'American Immigration Policies and Public Opinion on European Jews from 1933 to 1945' (Master's Thesis, East Tennessee State University, 2002)

Grimnes, Ole Kristian, *Norge under okkupasjonen* (Aschehoug: 1983)
Grundt Larsen, Jørgen, *Modstandsbevægelsens kontaktudvalg i Stockholm 1944–45* (Odense: Odense universitetsforlag, 1976)
Gyllenhaal, Lars, & Gebhardt, James F., *Slaget om Nordkalotten: Sveriges roll i tyska och allierade operationer i norr* (Lund: Historiska media, 2001)
Gäfvert, Björn, 'Militärattachéns borttappade portfölj' in Huldt, Bo & Böhme, Klaus-Richard (eds), *Vårstormar: 1944 – krigsslutet skönjes* (Stockholm: Probus, 1995)
Gäfvert, Björn, 'Det fria kriget: från idé till krigsorganisation' in Hugemark, Bo (ed.), *Nya fronter?: 1943 – spänd väntan* (Stockholm: Probus, 1994)
Hadenius, Stig, *Svensk politik under 1900-talet* (Stockholm: Hjalmarson & Högberg, 2000)
Hæstrup, Jørgen (ed.), *Besættelsens Hvem-Hvad-Hvor* (København: Politiken, 1985)
Halbrook, Stephen P., *Target Switzerland: Swiss armed neutrality in World War II* (Cambridge, MA: Da Capo, 2003)
Hellström, Sven, *Sjuktransporter från norra Finland 1941–1943: humanitär hjälp och realpolitik* (Linköping, 2003)
Herbert, 'The National Socialist Political Police' in Mommsen, Hans (ed.), *The Third Reich between vision and reality: new perspectives on German history, 1918–1945* (Oxford: Berg, 2001)
Hugemark, Bo (ed.), *Nya fronter?: 1943 – spänd väntan* (Stockholm: Probus, 1994)
Hugemark, Bo (ed.), *Stormvarning: Sverige inför andra världskriget* (Stockholm: Probus, 1989)
Hugemark, Bo (ed.), *Vindkantring: 1942 – politisk kursändring* (Stockholm: Probus, 1992)
Hugemark, Bo (ed.), *I orkanens öga: 1941 – osäker neutralitet* (Stockholm: Probus, 1992)
Hugemark, Bo, 'Överraskning i teori och praktik' in Hugemark, Bo, & Gemzell, Carl-Axel (eds), *Urladdning: 1940 – blixtkrigens år* (Stockholm: Probus, 1990)
Hugemark, Bo, & Gemzell, Carl-Axel, (eds), *Urladdning: 1940 – blixtkrigens år* (Stockholm: Probus, 1990)
Huldt, Bo & Böhme, Klaus-Richard (eds), *Vårstormar: 1944 – krigsslutet skönjes* (Stockholm: Probus, 1995)
Huldt, Bo & Böhme, Klaus-Richard (eds), *Horisonten klarnar: 1945 – krigsslut* (Stockholm: Probus, 1995)
Hägg, Göran, *Den svenska litteraturhistorien* (Stockholm: Wahlström & Widstrand, 1996)

Hägglöf, Gunnar, Möte med Europa: Paris-London-Moskva-Genève-Berlin, 1926–1940 (Stockholm: Norstedt, 1971)
Hägglöf, Gunnar, Svensk krigshandelspolitik under andra världskriget (Stockholm: Norstedt, 1958)
Innala, Elin, Finska krigsbarn. (C-uppsats, historia, nr 2006:022. Luleå tekniska universitet, Avd för samhällsvetenskap)
Isaksson, Anders, Per Albin. 4, Landsfadern (Stockholm: Wahlström & Widstrand, 2000)
Jackson, Robert, Battle of the Baltic: the wars, 1918–1945 (Barnsley: Pen & Sword Maritime, 2007)
Jakobsson, Jakob & Janson, Erik, Sverige 1939–1945: svenska folkets egna bilder från krigsåren (Stockholm: LT, 1989)
Johansson, Alf W., 'Neutralitet och modernitet: andra världskriget och Sveriges nationella identitet' in Huldt, Bo & Böhme, Klaus-Richard (eds), Horisonten klarnar: 1945 – krigsslut (Stockholm: Probus, 1995)
Johansson, Alf W., Per Albin och kriget: samlingsregeringen och utrikespolitiken under andra världskriget (Stockholm: Tiden, 1988)
Kage, Rieko, War, mobilization, and social learning: civic engagement in the wake of World War II in thirteen countries. USJP Occasional Paper 06–04, Program on US–Japan Relations (Harvard University: 2006) < http://www.wcfia.harvard.edu/us-japan/research/pdf/06-04.kage.pdf >
Kellgren, Henry, Sex krigsår i Skölds skugga (Stockholm: Saxon & Lindström, 1951)
Kenney, Rowland, The Northern tangle: Scandinavia and the post-war world (London: J. M. Dent, 1946)
Kirchoff, Hans, 'Denmark: A light in the Darkness of the Holocaust?' in Journal of Contemporary History, Vol. 30, No. 3, p. 465
Koblik, Steven, 'Om vi teg, skulle stenarna ropa': Sverige och jude-problemet 1933–1945 (Stockholm: Norstedt, 1987)
Kranking, G. E., Borderland Swedes from Proceedings of INTER Conference, Norrköping, 11–13 June 2007, www.ep.liu.se/ecp/025/
Kugelberg, Bertil & Ihlen, Joakim, Grannar emellan: en bok om Sveriges förhållande till Norge under krigsåren 1940–1945 (Stockholm: Wahlström & Widstrand, 1945)
Küng, Andres, Sverige och Estland: äntligen goda grannar? (Göteborg: Akademiförl., 1991)
Lagvall, Bertil, Flottans neutralitetsvakt 1939–1945 (Stockholm: Marinstaben, 1967)
Landgren, Bengt, Hjalmar Gullberg och beredskapslitteraturen:

studier i svensk dikt och politisk debatt 1933–1942 (Uppsala: Univ.: 1975)

Lang, R. C. 'Red Cross Humanitarianism in Greece, 1940–45', *The Journal of Historical Review*, Vol. 9, No. 1, pp. 71–88

Lee, Donald C. *Toward a Sound World Order: A Multidimensional, Hierarchical Ethical Theory* (Westport, CT: Greenwood, 1992)

Leifland, Leif, 'They must get in before the end': Churchill och Sverige 1944 och 1945 in Bergquist, Mats, Johansson, Alf W. & Wahlbäck, Krister (eds), *Utrikespolitik och historia: studier tillägnade Wilhelm M. Carlgren den 6 maj 1987* (Stockholm: Militärhistoriska förl., 1987)

Leifland, Leif, *General Böhmes val: Sverige och det nazistiska Tyskland våren 1945* (Stockholm: Norstedt, 1992)

Levine Paul A., 'Swedish neutrality during the Second World War: tactical success or moral compromise?' in Wylie, Neville, *European neutrals and non-belligerents during the Second World War* (Cambridge: Cambridge University Press, 2002)

Levine, Paul A., *From indifference to activism: Swedish diplomacy and the Holocaust, 1938–1944* (Uppsala: Univ.: 1996)

Lindal, Kurt, *Om kriget hade kommit: Folkberedskapen och motståndsandan i Sverige under andra världskriget* (Stockholm: Carlsson, 2004)

Lindal, Kurt, *Självcensur i stövelns skugga: den svenska radions roll och hållning under det andra världskriget* (Stockholm: Carlsson, 1998)

Lindell, Thord & Lagerström, Herbert *Svensk historia. D. 2, Hur det moderna Sverige vuxit fram* (Stockholm, 1967)

Linder, Jan, *Andra världskriget och Sverige: historia och mytbildning* (Stockholm: Infomanager: 1997)

Lindqvist, Herman, *Drömmar och verklighet, Historien om Sverige* (Stockholm: Norstedt, 2000)

London, Louise, *Whitehall and the Jews, 1933–1948: British immigration policy, Jewish refugees and the Holocaust* (Cambridge: Cambridge University Press, 2000.)

Ludlow, Peter, 'Britain and Northern Europe 1940–1945', *Scandinavian Journal of History* 4: 1979, pp. 123–62

Lööw, Heléne, *Hakkorset och Wasakärven: en studie av nationalsocialismen i Sverige 1924–1950* (Historiska institutionen i Göteborg, Göteborg, 1990)

Lööw, Heléne, *Rättsväsendets historia: Då Säpo var ungt,* in Apropå 5/2001, (Stockholm: Brottsförebyggande rådet 2001)

Maier, Klaus A. [et al.], *Germany and the Second World War*, Vol. 2,

Germany's initial conquests in Europe (Militärgeschichtliches Forschungsamt (Oxford: Clarendon Press, 1991)
Mallet, Sir Victor, Memoirs (unpublished), Churchill College, Cambridge.
Mattsson, Algot, Redarna kring runda bordet (Göteborg: Tre böcker, 1996)
McKay, C. G., 'Iron Ore and Section D: The Oxelösund Operation', The Historical Journal, Vol. 29, No. 4 (December 1986), pp. 975–8.
McKay, C. G., From information to intrigue: studies in secret service based on the Swedish experience, 1939–45 (London: Frank Cass, 1993.)
Medlicott, William Norton, The Economic Blockade Vols 1 & 2 (London: HMSO, 1978)
Meinander, Henrik, Finlands historia. 4: inledning av Matti Klinge (Esbo: Schildt, 1999)
Moland, Arnfinn, Over grensen?: Hjemmefrontens likvidasjoner under den tyske okkupasjonen av Norge 1940–1945 (Oslo: Orion, 1999)
Molin, Karl, 'Riksdagspolitik under andra världskriget' in Koblik, Steven (ed.), Från fattigdom till överflöd: [en antologi om Sverige från frihetstiden till våra dagar] (Stockholm: Wahlström & Widstrand, 1973)
Munthe, Malcolm, I krig är allt tillåtet: som sabotör i Finland, Norge och Sverige (Stockholm: Hökerberg, 1954)
Möller, Yngve, Per Edvin Sköld: humanist och samhällsbyggare (Stockholm: Tiden/Athena: 1996)
NA: National Archives, London
Nilsson, Lars-Axel, Sandberg, Leif A., Nilsson & Eva H. Blockade runners: Sweden's lifeline in the Second World War (Svanesund: L.-A. Nilsson: 1996)
Nordlund, Sven, '»En svensk tiger« ? Svenska reaktioner på tyska ariseringskrav under 1930-talet och andra världskriget' in Lars M. & Tydén, Mattias (eds), Sverige och Nazityskland: skuldfrågor och moraldebatt (Stockholm: Dialogos, 2007)
Norrbohm, Gösta & Skogsberg, Bertil, Att flyga är att leva: [Flygvapnet 1926–1976] (Stockholm: Trevi: 1975)
Ogley, Roderick, The theory and practice of neutrality in the twentieth century (London: Routledge & K. Paul, 1970)
Olsson, Jan Olof, Någonstans i Sverige (Stockholm: Månpocket, 1989)
Ottosson, Jan & Magnusson, Lars, Hemliga makter: svensk hemlig militär underrättelsetjänst från unionstiden till det kalla kriget (Stockholm: Tiden, 1991)

Overud, Johanna, *I beredskap med Fru Lojal: behovet av kvinnlig arbetskraft i Sverige under andra världskriget* (Stockholm: Almqvist & Wiksell International, 2005)

Pearce, Malcolm L., *British political history, 1867–1990. Democracy and Decline* (London: Routledge, 1992)

Persson, Ragnar, 'Beredskapsminnen' in *Släkt och bygd*, Svalövsbygdens Släkt- Och Folklivsforskning, Nr 1 1997

Persson, Sune, *'Vi åker till Sverige': de vita bussarna 1945* (Rimbo: Fischer & Co, 2002)

Petropoulos, Jonathan, *Art as Politics in the Third Reich* (Chapel Hill, NC: University of North Carolina Press, 1996)

Petrow, Richard, *The Bitter Years. The invasion and occupation of Denmark and Norway, April 1940–May 1945* (London: Hodder and Stoughton, 1975)

Quensel, Nils, *Minnesbilder* (Stockholm: Norstedt, 1973)

RA: Riksarkiv, Stockholm

Richardson, Gunnar, *Beundran och fruktan: Sverige inför Tyskland 1940–1942* (Stockholm: Carlsson, 1996)

Richardson, Gunnar, *Förtroligt och hemligt: kunglig utrikespolitik och svensk neutralitet under andra världskriget* (Stockholm: Carlsson, 2007)

Roine, Jesper & Waldenström, Daniel, *Top Incomes in Sweden over the Twentieth Century* (Stockholm: Department of Economics, Stockholm School of Economics, 2005)

Roll-Hansen, Nils & Broberg, Gunnar (eds), *Eugenics and the welfare state: sterilization policy in Denmark, Sweden, Norway, and Finland* (East Lansing: Michigan State University Press, 2005)

Rothwell, Victor, *War aims in the Second World War: The war aims of the major belligerents, 1939–45* (Edinburgh: Edinburgh University Press, 2005)

Rummel, R. J. *Lethal Politics: Soviet Genocide and Mass Murder Since 1917* (New Brunswick: Transaction Publishers, 1990), Table 7A

Samuelsson, Kurt, *From great power to welfare state. 300 years of Swedish social development* (London: Allen & Unwin, 1968)

Scott, C.-G., 'The Swedish Midsummer Crisis of 1941', *The Journal of Contemporary History*, Vol. 37, No. 3

Seabury, Paul, *The Wilhelmstrasse: a study of German diplomats under the Nazi regime* (Berkeley: University of California Press, 1954.)

Sebag Montefiore, Simon, *Stalin: the court of the Red Tsar* (London: Phoenix, 2004)

Silamikelis, Valentins, *Baltutlämningen: under Baltikums flagga: dagboksanteckningar* (Stockholm: Contra, 1996)

Singer, Kurt D., 'Norwegian Students Fight the War,' *Journal of Educational Sociology*, Vol. 18, No. 1 (September 1944)
Smit, D.J., *Onder de Vlaggen van Zweden en het Rode Kruis. Het leven van Nederlandse militairen in Duitse Krijgsgevangenschap 1940–1945* (Den Haag: SMIT, D.J., 1997)
Sobéus, Urban, 'Admiral Claës Lindsström, Swedish Neutrality, and The Swedish Coast Artillery' in *The Royal Swedish Academy of War Sciences Journal*, No. 2, 2001
Sompolinsky, Meier, *Britain and the Holocaust: the failure of Anglo-Jewish leadership?* (Brighton: Sussex Academic Press, 1999)
SOU 1999:20, *Sverige och judarnas tillgångar: slutrapport.* Kommissionen om judiska tillgångar i Sverige vid tiden för andra världskriget (Stockholm: Fakta info direkt, 1999)
SOU 2003:18 *Ett diplomatiskt misslyckande: fallet Raoul Wallenberg och den svenska utrikesledningen.* Kommissionen om den svenska utrikesledningens agerande i fallet Raoul Wallenberg (Stockholm: Fritzes offentliga publikationer, 2003)
'Spioner, seglare, flyktingar och sjöräddare' in *Stångmärket: medlemsblad för Skärgårdsstiftelsen*, Nr. 2/2008, p. 13 (Stockholm: Fakta info direkt, 1999 Stockholm: Skärgårdsstift)
Strindberg, August *Det nya riket* (Stockholm: Bonnier, 1920) extract quoted in http://www.sub.su.se/forint/ksver2.htm
Summerfield, Penny, 'The Levelling of Class' in Emsley, Clive, Marwick, Arthur & Simpson, Wendy (eds), *War, peace and social change in twentieth-century Europe. A reader* (Milton Keynes: Open University Press, 1989)
Sundell, Olof, *9 April* (Stockholm: Sohlman, 1949)
Svanberg, Ingvar & Tydén, Mattias, *Sverige och Förintelsen: debatt och dokument om Europas judar 1933–1945* (Stockholm: Arena, 1997)
Sweden, a Wartime Survey: edited and published by the Press Bureau of The Royal Ministry For Foreign Affairs [sic] (Gebers: Stockholm, 1942)
Swedish Television < http://svt.se/svt/road/Classic/ 15 sept 1982. >
Tham, Henrik, 'Crime in Scandinavia during World War II, in *Journal of Peace Research*, Vol. 27, No. 4 (1990), pp. 415–28
Tennant, Sir Peter, *Touchlines of war* (Hull: University of Hull Press 1992)
The Times, 9 September 1965, p. 10, 'Compromise Peace mention in 1940'
Thulstrup, Åke, *Med lock och pock: tyska försök att påverka svensk opinion 1933–45* (Stockholm: Bonnier, 1962)

Time Magazine (New York: Time Inc.)
Ulfving, Lars, 'Geheimschreiberns hemlighet: Arne Beurling och den svenska signalspaningens framgångar' in Hugemark, Bo (ed.), I orkanens öga: 1941 – osäker neutralitet (Stockholm: Probus, 1992)
Undén, Östen, Minnesanteckningar (Stockholm: Bonnier, 1966)
Wahlbäck, Krister, 'Sweden: Secrecy and Neutrality', Journal of Contemporary History, Vol. 2, No. 1 (January 1967), Historians on the Twentieth Century, pp. 183–91
Wahlbäck, Krister, & Boberg, Göran (eds), Sveriges sak är vår: svensk utrikespolitik 1939–45 i dokument (Stockholm: Prisma: 1966)
Wahlbäck, Krister, Regeringen och kriget: ur statsrådens dagböcker 1939–41 (Stockholm: Prisma: 1972)
Wangel, Carl-Axel (ed.), Sveriges militära beredskap 1939–1945 (Stockholm: Militärhistoriska förl., 1982)
Wangel, Carl-Axel, 'Luftsförsvaret under beredskapsåren' in Wangel, Carl-Axel (ed.), Sveriges militära beredskap 1939–1945 (Stockholm: Militärhistoriska förl., 1982)
Weaver, Denis, On Hitler's doorstep [An account of the war in Russia from October 1941, as reported from Sweden] (London: Hodder and Stoughton, 1942)
Wechselmann, Maj & Lindgren, Stefan, De bruna förbindelserna (Stockholm: Ordfront, 1995)
Westman K. G., Politiska anteckningar september 1939–mars 1943: utg. genom W. M. Carlgren (Stockholm: Samf. för utg. av handskrifter rörande Skandinaviens historia, 1981)
Wide, Jessika, Kvinnors politiska representation i västeuropa 1950–2000. Vad förklarar variationen i tid och rum? Statsvetenskapliga Förbundets Årsmöte i Växjö, den 6–8 oktober 2002. < http://www.pol.umu.se/personal/Wide_Jessika/vaxjo.pdf >
Wieslander, Hans & Molin, Björn, Sverige efter 1900: en modern politisk historia (Stockholm: Bonnier, 1988)
Wigforss, Ernst, Minnen. 3, 1932–1949 (Stockholm: Tiden, 1954)
Wijk, Johnny, 'Censur- och propagandaministeriet: en översikt av Informationsstyrelsens verksamhet 1940–45 utifrån dess efterlämnade arkiv.' in Historisk tidskrift 1990 (110), pp. 21–49 (Stockholm: Svenska historiska föreningen)
Wilhelmus, Wolfgang, 'Det tyska anfallet mot Skandinavien' in Hugemark, Bo, & Gemzell, Carl-Axel (eds), Urladdning: 1940 – blixtkrigens år (Stockholm: Probus, 1990)
Zetterberg, Hans L., 'Klassamhället och jämlikheten', Indikator, SIFOs Nyhetsbrev, Stockholm, augusti 1969

Zetterberg, Kent, '1942: storkriget vänder, Sveriges utsatta läge består' in Hugemark, Bo (ed.), *Vindkantring: 1942 – politisk kursändring* (Stockholm: Probus, 1992)

Zetterberg, Kent, 'Storkriget går mot sitt slut: Sveriges läge förbättras' in Huldt, Bo & Böhme, Klaus-Richard (eds), *Vårstormar: 1944 – krigsslutet skönjes* (Stockholm: Probus, 1995)

Zetterberg, Kent, 'Svensk säkerhetspolitik 1943: en balansakt på slak lina mellan de krigförande' in Hugemark, Bo (ed.), *Nya fronter?: 1943 – spänd väntan* (Stockholm: Probus, 1994)

Zetterberg, Kent, 'Debatten om "övervakningssverige" 1945–1948: krigsårens långa skugga och debatten om Sandlerkommissionen' in Bergquist, Mats & Johansson, Alf W. (eds) *Säkerhetspolitik och historia: essäer om stormaktspolitiken och Norden under sjuttio år: vänbok till Krister Wahlbäck* (Stockholm: Hjalmarson & Högberg, 2007)

Zetterberg, Kent, 'Eftergifter och motstånd' in Andersson, Lars M. & Tydén, Mattias (eds), *Sverige och Nazityskland: skuldfrågor och moraldebatt* (Stockholm: Dialogos, 2007)

Åmark, Klas, 'Demokratin, neutraliteten och moralen: Sverige under andra världskriget' in Andersson, Lars M. & Tydén, Mattias (eds), *Sverige och Nazityskland: skuldfrågor och moraldebatt* (Stockholm: Dialogos, 2007)

Index

Note: Swedish letters ä, ö, å are ordered after z

Aalders and Wiebes, 278–9
ABC see American Bosch Company
Abwehr, 133, 145, 147, 152–3, 198
activists and activism, 22–3, 31, 37–40, 44, 55, 70, 110, 163–4, 285
  pressure on Radiotjanst, 65–6
Adler-Rudel, Salomon, 195–6
Advisory Council for Foreign Affairs see Utrikesnämnden
Agrarian Party, 10, 22–5, 69, 105, 164, 240–1, 243–4
agriculture see farming
AH (Active Housekeeping), 251
airforce, 102, 213
  attempted deception of, 138–9
  attitudes, 227
  equipment, 12–13, 216–17
  strength, 214–15
  operations, 223–4
Aktiv Hushållning see AH
Alien Property Custodian, 128–9
Aliens Office, 152, 256
Allmänna Säkerhetstjänsten (AS)
  British analysis of arrests, 146
  and Comintern, 134
  establishment of, 134
  legislation, 135
  links with Germany, criticism of, 146, 151
  Oxelösund sabotage, 140
  post-war inquiries, 152
  remit, 135
  structure, 135
  surveillance, 135, 256
  visit to Heydrich, 138
Allsvenskan, 266
Almqvist, Bertil, 257
Altmark incident, 42
American Bosch Company, 128–9
Andersson, Arne, 266
Andersson, Gustaf, 23–4, 26, 28, 69, 165, 272
Andersson, Lars, 281, 284
Andliga Befolkningsskydd, 175
Andolf, Göran, 203
Anglo-American trade memorandum, 82
Anglo-German Naval Agreement, 12
Anglo-Swedish WTA see WTA
anti-communism, 38, 92
  and camps, 144, 256
  and raids, 144, 146
anti-Semitism, 17, 20, 189–90
APC see Alien Property Custodian

Arbetaren, 163
Arbetsförmedlingar, 264
armed forces, 209–35
  capability, 228–9
  and disarmament, 10, 12
  invalids, 235
  leadership, 224–8
  strategy and deployment, 11, 209–11, 217
army
  attitudes, 212, 224–6, 234–5
  deployment, 217
  equipment, 209–10, 214–17
  leadership, 211, 225–6
  mobilisations, 212–13, 218–19
AS see Allmänna Säkerhetstjänsten
Assarsson, Vilhelm, 31, 272
Assessment Commission see Bedömningsnämnden
Assistance Committee for Finnish Children, 201
Atterberg, Kurt, 171–2

Babs, Alice, 262
Bagge, Gösta, 23, 25–8, 31, 66, 68–70, 76, 84, 123, 144, 173, 196, 226, 240–2
  and Coalition Cabinet 38–9
Baldwin, Stanley, 285
ball-bearings, 77, 82, 86
  agreements, 117, 124
  strategic importance in war of, 114
  Wallenbergs involvement, 125, 128
  Western Allied pressure on exports to Germany, 104–7, 124–5
Baltic Sea, 7, 11–12, 36–7, 41, 53
  iron ore route, 115, 126
  mining, 75, 222
  naval operations in, 12, 211–12, 220–2, 224, 227
Baltic states, 11, 15, 37, 92, 150–1, 153
Balts repatriation, 205
Bannister, Roger, 266
BBC, 19, 61, 159, 166, 174
Bedömningsnämnden, 153–4
Bengtsson, Frans G., 263
Beredskapsfilmer, 260

Beredskapstiden, 238
Berg, Bengt, 171
Bergendahl, Ragnar, 160
Bergman, Ingrid, 260
Bergman, Ingmar, 260
Bergman, Sten, 259
Bergquist, Mats, 281
Bergqvist, Torvald, 26
Bernadotte Count Folke, 108, 111, 192, 198–9, 202–4
Beskow, Nathanael, 19
Best, Werner, 100, 192, 195
Beurling, Arne, 150
Binney, Sir George, 76, 79–80, 138–9
Björkman, Jenny, 281
Björkman, Leif, 273
black market, 239, 248
blockade, 83
  British, 11, 36, 38, 57–8, 115, 196, 201, 246
  German, 45, 54, 64, 76, 79, 85, 92, 107, 117–19, 123, 138, 172, 201, 221, 241, 246–7
Boëthius, Maria-Pia, 274
Bofors, 215–16, 251
Boheman, Erik, 31–2, 39, 158, 162–3, 249, 271–2, 284
  and Allied demands, 104–5, 123–6,
  and Britain and United States 1942 visit, 82–4, 120–1
  and concessions, 68, 75, 87
  and Cripps, 67
  Jewish antecedents of, 197
  and Mallet, 77, 85, 172
  and Operation Performance, 139
  pre-war neutrality assessment by, 15, 286
  and Schnurre, 53
  and Soviet–Finnish mediation, 94, 96–7
  view of Munthe, 141, 155 n.33
  and Wallenbergs, 128
Bojerud, Stellan, 210
Bondeförbundet see Agrarian Party
Bornholm, Swedish invasion plans, 103, 220
Bosch Company, 114, 128–9

Boström, Wollmar, 31, 199
Boye, Karin, 262
Bramstorp, Axel Pehrsson-, 23–6, 28, 49
Branting, Hjalmar, 10, 188
Britain
　defeatism, 50–1, 271
　and Finland, 39–40, 42, 54, 82, 94, 212
　and Leave Traffic, 59, 88, 120
　MEW, 76, 83, 84, 196
　MOI, 172, 174
　and Norway, 11, 39, 42–3
　and Norwegian campaign, 44–6, 48–9, 51–2
　and Norwegian ships, 74, 79, 84, 121
　and propaganda, 136, 162, 172–4
　RAF, 223–4
　and raids, 65
　and Safe-Conduct Traffic, 58, 80, 82, 84–5
　and Swedish destroyers incident, 215
　trade agreements, 35–6, 57–8, 87–9, 96, 103–4, 113–18, 120, 124
　see also ball-bearings, blockade, iron ore, Binney, Mallet
British clandestine services
　MI6, 133, 137, 140, 149, 150
　SOE, 64, 79, 100, 101, 108, 115, 133, 136, 137, 139, 140, 141, 142, 143
British Council, 173–4
British Legation, 44, 64, 89, 128, 137–8, 140, 142, 146, 172–4
Brown Guard, 17
Buchenwald, 199
Buskis, 262
Butler, R. A., 50–1
Böök, Frederik, 158

Cadogan, Alexander, 44
Canaris Admiral, 145, 147
Caproni bombers, 217
Carlgren, Wilhelm, 40, 49, 273, 274, 281
Carlsson, Gunnar 'Spitfire', 115
censorship, 157–68
　Grey Slips, 161, 165

Central Finnish Relief (CFR), 201
Centralen, 134, 137, 142, 147–51, 153, 230
Chaplin, Charlie, 261
Christmas Møller, John, 64
Churchill, Winston, 21, 41–3, 50, 54, 57, 82–3, 109, 111, 120, 140, 228
cinemas, 259–61
Civil Defence, 254–6
civilian air service, Stockholm-Scotland, 82, 105
Civilian Security Service see *Allmänna Säkerhetstjänsten*
Clark, Sir Kenneth, 174
Clausen, Fritz, 64
coal and coke, 58, 71, 81, 106, 113, 115–16, 120, 123–6, 285
Coalition Government, 32
　Agrarian-Social Democrat, 10, 22–4
　all-party wartime, 22, 25, 27
　collapse of Agrarian-Social Democrat, 36–8
　Liberal-Social Democrat, 9
Coalition wartime Cabinet
　Boheman's description of, 28
　concessions granted to Germany, 45–54, 65–71
　concessions to Germany rescinded, 83–90, 103–7
　conduct, 27, 29, 33, 38–9
　formation of, 25, 26, 38
C-Office see *Centralen*
Comintern pre-war threat to Sweden, 134, 143, 146
Commandos (*jägartrupper*), 233–4
Commission for Economic Defence Preparation (RKE), 245
Commission on Jewish Assets, 278–9
Communists, 17, 19, 23, 76, 134–5, 143–4, 145, 146–7, 161, 163–4, 166, 180–1, 183, 244, 256, 265
communitarianism, 275–6, 280, 282
conscription, 144, 160, 177, 179, 183, 209, 212, 213, 218, 225, 227, 231, 232, 234, 235, 239, 244–6, 249–50, 251, 252, 256, 258, 263, 264, 266, 267

Conservatives, 10, 22, 23, 25–6, 38, 39, 69, 105, 239, 240–2, 243–4
Continuation War, 92, 94, 149, 201
Coordination Section for Counter-Propaganda see Propagandabyrån
cosmopolitanism, 275–6, 280, 282
Council of People's Commissars see NKVD
courier planes, 75, 77, 87, 224
cow-trade, 23–4
Cripps, Sir Stafford, 67

Dagens Eko, 19, 258
Dagens Nyheter, 19, 159, 226
Dagsposten, 167, 170, 181
Dahlerus, Birger, 47, 48
Danish Brigade, 101–2
Danish Freedom Council, 64, 101
Danish Jews, 100, 194–5
Danish resistance, 62, 63–4, 99–101
 Allied supplies through Sweden, 102
 German reprisals, 101
 Kontaktudvalg and Swedish authorities, 143
 Police deportations 1944, 101
 and SOE, 100
Danmarks National Socialistiske Arbejderparti (DNSAP), 64
defence expenditure, 7, 10, 12, 182, 209, 216, 234, 239–41, 243, 244
defence planning, 10, 11, 12, 55, 59, 209–11, 212, 213, 217–20, 233–5
defence procurement, 80, 211, 214–17
Den svenska livsformen, 181–2
Denham, Henry, 137, 142, 148
Denmark, 13, 18, 108, 149, 211, 230, 258, 259, 275
 and Britain, 11, 139
 collaboration, 57, 64
 Contact Committee in Stockholm, 143
 German surrender, 102, 109–11, 218, 220
 and Germany, 43, 45, 52, 59, 62–3, 64, 71, 83, 116, 212–13, 215, 220, 272
 and Jews, 194

 refugees, 136, 194–5, 199–200
 see also Danish resistance
Det brinner en eld, 260
Donau, 192, 194
Douglas, Archibald, 151, 211–12
Draeger, Dr, 168
Draken, 222
Dramaten, 262
Drottningholm, 204
Duckwitz, Georg, 100, 195
Dvärgen, 263
Dymling, Carl, 163–4, 166, 179, 258
Dömö, Fritiof, 26
Dönitz, Admiral Karl, 111

economic hardship, 239, 249, 253
Eden, Anthony, 172, 194
Ehrensvärd, Carl August, 151, 211–12, 226
Ekblad, N.-E., 173, 180–1
Ekman, Stig, 274, 279
elections, 8, 9, 17, 32, 33, 59, 64, 183, 242, 243–4, 280
Eliot, T. S., 174
employment, 10, 16, 18, 19, 20, 125, 183, 189, 190, 191, 232, 249, 250, 251, 263, 264
Engelbrecht Division, 67, 70, 71, 74, 75, 76, 94, 118, 165, 202, 219, 223, 225, 226
Engzell, Gösta, 192, 193
Enskilda Bank, 114, 127, 128, 129, 278
Ericsson, 216
Eriksson, Arvid, 178, 179, 180, 258
Eriksson, Hermann, 25, 26, 27, 28, 89, 129, 246
Erlander, Tage, 27, 152
Estonia, 11, 13, 15, 36, 49, 51, 92, 93, 104, 106, 150, 205, 287
Estonian Swedes, 205
Ewerlöf, Knut G., 27
Excellensen, 261

Faeroe Islands, 215
Fame is the Spur, 263
farming, 23, 246, 252–4, 258, 264
Festung Norwegen see Norway

INDEX   313

Fiat fighters, 217
films
  American, 260
  British, 260
  German, 260
  Swedish, 260–1
Finland Committee, 40
Finland
  Continuation War, 94–5, 97
  discussions in Moscow, 37
  German troop transit accord, 55, 93
  requests Swedish assistance, 37
  re-union with Sweden, 55, 93
  Russification, 7
  Soviet intentions, 54–5, 65, 82, 93
  Swedish arms shipments, 39–40
  Swedish humanitarian aid, 39, 40
  Swedish mediation, 39, 40, 41, 43, 96–7, 103
  Winter War, 37, 40–1
  see also activists and activism
Finnish Civil War, 147, 152, 212
Flyghed, Jan, 153, 161
Folkberedskap, 168, 175, 177, 178, 179, 180, 181, 182, 267
Folkhemmet, 10, 35, 183, 238, 240, 250, 267, 268, 275, 276
Folkhushållning i kristid exhibition, 247
Folkparken, 262
Folkpartiet see People's Party
Food Commission (Statens Livsmedelskommission), 245, 248
Football league see Allsvenskan
Foreign Affairs Committee (Riksdag) see Utrikesutskottet
Fortitude North deception, 106
FRA, 149, 150
free warfare see fria kriget
fria kriget, 233–4
Frit Danmark, 64
Fritz, Martin, 125, 273
Fru Lojal, 182–3
Frågebyrån (IFB) or 'Inquiry Office', 178
Furugård, Birger, 17
Fänrik Ståls sägner, 164

Garbo, Greta, 19
Gdańsk (Danzig), 7
Gegendruck, 105
GenGas, 248
George V, 115
Gerhardt, Karl, 259, 261
German clandestine services, 133, 138, 145–7, 150, 152–3
Germany, 12, 13, 29, 41, 56, 87
  and Denmark, 43, 62–64, 99–101, 220
  and Engelbrecht Division transit, 66, 67–71, 76
  and Finland, 14, 38, 56, 94–5, 219
  and First World War, 8–9, 12, 21, 127–8
  influence, 17, 23, 31, 75, 126, 153, 225, 226, 260, 265
  invasion plans, 43, 86, 229–30
  and Jews, 189, 191–200
  and Leave Traffic, 44, 45–54, 56, 64, 87, 89
  Norway, 43–4, 60–2, 78, 98–9, 220
  Norwegian campaign, 48
  and Norwegian ships, 76, 79–80, 84–6
  and Police Troops, 102
  and press, 19, 56, 76, 157–8, 162, 168
  propaganda, 168–172
  Safe-Conduct Traffic, 58, 64, 66, 107
  services to, 77, 202
  and Soviet Union, 37, 55, 65
  surrender, 108–11
  trade agreements, 35–6, 105–6, 115–18, 120–2, 123, 124, 216
  see also ball-bearings, blockade, iron ore
German Legation, 19, 31
Gesinungsneutralität, 158
Gestapo see German clandestine services
GHT, 19, 157, 159, 170, 176
Gifford, E. W., 188
Gjöres, Axel, 27, 246
Goebbels, Josef, 126, 162, 168, 170, 171, 260

Goerdeler, Carl, 114
Gotland, 66, 67, 150, 179, 222, 258
Grafström, Sven, 14, 30, 31, 49, 162, 174
Greater German Economic Area see Großraumwirtschaft
Greece, famine relief, 201
Grey Slips see censorship
Gripsholm, 204
Großraumwirtschaft, 117, 118, 126
Grundherr, Werner von, 87
Grupp Krilon, 262
G-Section see Centralen
Gulf of Bothnia, 11, 42, 113, 126, 217, 219, 221, 230
Gullberg, Hjalmar, 258, 259, 261, 262
Gullregn, 261
Gustav V
 appeal to Hungarians, 197
 messages to Hitler, 46, 77–8
 and Nazi leadership, 17
 resignation threat, 68–9
 role in politics, 8, 24–5, 32–3, 38, 40, 56, 69, 182, 261
Günther, Christian, 139, 214, 219, 243, 271, 273, 287
 appointment, 26, 27, 28, 30
 and Bagge, 39, 66
 and concessions, 49–51, 53, 64–5, 67–71, 75–6, 77, 79, 80, 81, 83, 84–6, 88–90, 121
 and Finland, 55, 66, 93–4, 97
 and humanitarian action, 100, 108, 191, 193, 195, 198–9
 manner, 30–1, 104
 and press, 56, 61, 81, 165, 166, 172
Gällivare, 113
Götaverken, 216
Göteborgs Handels-och Sjöfartstidning see GHT
Göteborgs Post, 280

Haakon VII, 44, 60
Hacha invitation, 93, 111 n.2
Hague Conventions, 8, 15, 202
Halifax, Lord Edward, 42, 44, 50
Hallgren, Eric, 134, 153, 154 n.3
Hambro, Carl J., 60

Hambro, Charles, 115, 118
Hammarskjöld, Hjalmar, 8–9, 25, 36, 123
Hanko (Hangö), 41
Hanneken, General Hermann von, 100
Hansson, Per Albin see Per Albin
Hansson, Sigfrid, 190
Heads of State meeting, Stockholm, 37
health, 247–8
Heder och samvete, 274
Hedin, Sven, 8, 158, 171
Heidenstam, Verner von, 158
Helsingborg, 102, 195, 223, 266
Hemingway, Ernest, 263
Hemvärnet, 231–2, 267
Heydrich, Reinhard, 138, 147, 192
Himmler, Heinrich, 111, 135, 192, 198–200, 202
Hird, 61, 99
Hitler, Adolf, 53, 55, 74, 93, 94, 111, 114, 121, 148, 198, 199, 258, 261, 265, 285
 admiration of 17, 19, 171, 226
 assurances to, 46, 77–8
 and Denmark, 62, 64, 101, 139
 and Norway, 43, 46, 71, 78, 139, 214, 219, 229
 and Swedish press, 19, 157, 158, 160, 163, 170
 view of Sweden, 66, 86
Holocaust, 19, 81, 188, 191, 192–4, 196–200
Home Front, 238–68
Home Guard see Hemvärnet
Household, Geoffrey, 261
Howard, Leslie, 174
HSFR, 279
Hugo, Yngve, 166, 179
Hull, 85, 105
Hull, Cordell, 105
Hungary, 196–7
Husqvarna, 216
Hägg, Gunder, 266
Hägglöf, Gunnar, 26, 27, 31, 46, 47, 81, 113, 114, 120, 121, 211, 272
 and 1943 London delegation, 87, 88, 90, 104, 106, 122, 123

INDEX

Högern see Conservatives
Hårsfjärden explosion, 140, 222

I. G. Farben, 128
Information Committees see
    Upplysningsnämnder
Inquiry Office see Frågebyrå (IFB)
International Committee of the Red
    Cross (ICRC), 200–1
internment
    King Haakon 44
    military, 111, 144, 202–5, 208
iron ore
    and British sabotage, 140
    defence of, 53, 133, 213, 228
    and Germany, 41, 43, 46, 77, 117,
        125–6, 169, 286
    pre-war threats by Britain, 115
    and trade negotiations, 35–6, 71,
        104, 105, 116, 123
    trading forecast, 15, 113
    transportation, 11, 39, 144–5, 221
    and Western Allies, 41–3, 44, 46, 82,
        124, 136, 182, 212
Italian destroyers incident, 215, 227

Jarring, Sven, 259
Jews see anti-Semitism, Danish Jews,
    Commission on Jewish Assets,
    Germany and Jews, Holocaust,
    Norway and Jews, refugees
Johansson, Alf, 273
Johansson, Ivar-Lo, 20, 259, 260
Johnson, Eyvind, 262
Joint Standing Commission, 104
Juberg, Ludde, 262
Jung, Helge, 218, 226
Jägartrupper see Commandos

Kallocain, 263
Karelia, 11, 41, 44
Karl XI, 7
Karl XII, 17, 226, 285
Karlskrona, 7
KBK, 251–2, 254
Keitel, Wilhelm, 43, 45, 46
Kellgren, Henry, 226, 272

Kempff, Curt, 151
Kenney, Rowland, 271–2
Kersten, Felix, 198–200
KGB, 133
Kiruna, 113
Koblik, Steve, 278
Kock, Karin, 252, 267
kohandeln see cow-trade
Kollontay, Mme. Alexandra, 40, 75, 94,
    96
Konstitutionsutskottet, 181
Kontaktudvalget see Danish resistance
Kornsjø, 53–4
Kriegsmarine, 215, 220, 230
Kristallnacht, 190
Kristidsnämnder see rationing
Kristidsstyrelserna see rationing
Krylbo, 140, 141
Kuusinen, Otto, 40
Kvinnoföreningarnas
    beredskapskommitté see KBK

Labour Offices see Arbetsförmedlingar
Lagerkrantz, Olof, 262
Lagerkvist, Pär, 259, 263
Lagerlöf, Selma, 19, 188, 262
Landqvist, Commodore Daniel, 137
Landstormen, 231, 232
Lapland, 40, 201
League of Nations, 12, 14, 42
Leander, Zarah, 260
Leave Traffic, 45–54
    agreement to end, 123
    Norwegian lobby and, 87, 98
    notice to end, 89
    Riksdag opposition to, 87
    trade negotiations, 88, 120, 121, 122
Lenin, V. I., 8
Levine, Paul, 192, 278
Lienhard, Dr Ludwig, 205
Lindal, Kurt, 176
Lindgren, Astrid, 263
Lindholm, Sven-Olof, 17
Lindsström, Claës, 227
Linkomies, Edwin, 96
Lionel and Dicto, 79, 83, 90, 122, 123,
    222

Günther's undertaking to Germany
  on, 87, 121, 139
Ljungquist, Seth, 159
Lofoten Islands, 219
Ivar-Lo see Johansson
London Tripartite Agreement (LTA)
  see LTA
Lotta Svärd see Lottor
Lottor, 232, 267
Lower Chamber Riksdagen, 32, 33, 70,
  240, 242, 243, 244
LTA, 104, 126
  negotiations, 123–4
  Swedish Cabinet reaction, 130
  Pentagon view, 106, 124
  agreement tonnages, 124
Luftskydd see Civil Defence
Luleå, 11, 39, 42, 77, 87, 113, 144
Lund, Ragnar, 182
Lundborg, Herman, 189
Lysekil and MTB exports, 85, 102, 105,
  165, 222
Länsarbetsnämnder, 264
Löfgren, Orvar, 249

Mallet, Sir Victor, 67, 149
  and Boheman, 77, 139, 172
  deception, 139
  defends supporting Sweden, 52, 54,
    103, 214
  and Günther, 110
  and Lionel and Dicto, 84–5
  propaganda, 173, 174, 179
  protest, 51
  and UD, 138, 166
Malmberg, Bertil, 259
Malmö, 151, 195, 223, 266
March Crisis, 65, 66, 221
Marionschaft coal mine, 127
Martinson, Harry, 20, 262
Maslow, Abraham, 275–7, 282
Masur, Norbert, 197, 200
Maycock, Richard, 203
Merchant of Venice, 262
MEW, 76, 82, 84, 196
MI6 see British clandestine services
Michael-Strandberg case, 145

Mikoyan, Anastas, 117
military mobilisation, 109, 165, 176,
  212–13, 218–19, 228, 234
Milorg, 98, 99
mining of Baltic, 37, 67, 75, 126, 145
mining of Norwegian waters, 41–3
mining of Swedish waters, 36
Ministry of Economic Warfare see
  MEW
Ministry of Information see MOI
Moberg, Vilhelm, 259, 261
MOI, 172, 174
Molotov, Vyacheslav, 41, 55, 202, 285
Molotov–Ribbentrop Pact, 15, 36, 45,
  147, 210, 220
Montague-Evans, Charles, 174
Montefiore, Simon Sebag, 285
Moscow Conference, 96
Mrs Loyalty campaign see Fru Lojal
Munck, Ebbe, 142
Munck, Kai, 259
Munthe, Malcolm, 140–1, 142
Murmansk, 78, 95, 217
Mustang fighter-bombers, 217
Myrdal, Alva, 16, 252
Myrdal, Gunnar, 16, 24, 252
Möller, Gustav, 10, 25, 26, 28, 38, 70,
  135, 136, 139, 143, 147, 152, 196

Narvik, 39, 42, 46, 47, 53, 65, 77, 78,
  113, 214, 217, 228
Narvik Plan, 48
Nasjonal Samling Party, 60, 61, 99
National Film Office see SBB
National Socialist Workers Party, 17
navy
  attitudes, 137, 144, 226, 227
  capability, 228
  equipment, 215, 216
  escorts, 82, 221
  leadership, 226–7
  losses, 140, 222
  mining, 75
  operations, 84, 85, 213, 217, 220,
    221, 222, 227
Nazis, Swedish, 17–18, 145, 153, 170–
  2, 190, 227

Nerman, Ture, 153, 158, 163, 189, 285
Neuengamme, 199–200
New Order, 54
Nicolson, Harold, 172
NKVD, 133
Nordenskiöld, Bengt, 227
Nordische Gesellschaft, 158
Norrköpings Tidningar, 159
Norrskenflamman, 144
Norway, 11, 13, 18, 29, 45, 46, 53, 54, 55, 83, 214
  and Britain, 41, 42, 43, 45, 51, 52, 65, 196, 202, 214, 219
  collaboration, 52, 60–1, 206, 256
  deportations, 99, 107, 147, 198–200
  German surrender, 99, 109–11
  government-in-exile, recognition by Sweden, 61
  and Jews, 81, 192–3
  Legation in Stockholm, assassination, 142
  refugees, 61, 264
  resistance to Germans, imprisonment and reprisals, 44, 48, 60–1, 62, 98–9, 133, 143, 148, 149, 164, 169, 220, 230
  volunteers for Finland, 40
  see also Norwegian merchant ships, Police Troops
Norwegian merchant ships 74, 76–7, 79, 83–4, 119, 121, 138, 222
Nothin, Torsten, 38
Ny Dag, 163
Ny Militär Tidskrift, 225
Nya Dagligt Allehanda, 159
Nyheter från Storbritannien, 172–4, 186 n.70
Nyström, Bror, 144
Någonstans i Sverige, 249

Ohlin, Bertil, 23
oil imports, 56, 221, 285
  from Romania, 117
  from USA, 58, 80, 82–3, 88, 103, 113, 118, 119, 120, 121, 123
  from USSR, 117
oil reserves, 120, 245, 248

Olsen, Iver, 197
Olsson, Jan Olof (Jolo), 249
Om det fanns telefon, 268
Om ett folk vill leva, 262
Onassis, Aristotle, 222
Operation Barbarossa, 64, 66, 118, 203, 221, 273
Operation Graffham, 106, 138–9
Operation Performance, 79, 138, 215
Operation Rubble, 76, 138
Operation 'Save Denmark', 220
Operation 'Save Norway', 220
Operation Tindall, 229
Operation Twinkle, 149
Operation Weserübung, 43–4, 213–14
OSS, 108, 129, 133, 149–51
osvensk propaganda, 180
Otter, Göran von, 191
over-flying, 75, 77, 87, 224
Overud, Johanna, 250
Oxelösund sabotage see iron ore and British sabotage

Palme, Olof, 273
Palme, Sven-Ulric, 273
Paulson, Robert, 151–3
Paulus, Field-Marshal Friedrich, 202
Pauly, Max, 200
Pehrsson-Bramstorp, Axel see Bramstorp, Axel
People's Party, 23, 25, 26, 69, 70, 240, 242
Per Albin Line, 212–13
Per Albin
  and Bagge, 23, 38
  and Balt repatriation, 205
  banning Communists, 76, 144
  and Coalition Cabinet, 24, 28, 29, 38, 39, 89, 244, 280
  and cow-trade, 23
  and Denmark, 143
  and Engelbrecht concession, 66, 68–70
  and elections, 59, 243–4
  ending concessions, 83, 84, 85, 86, 87, 88, 89, 90, 105, 122, 123
  and Finland, 94, 164, 211, 212

318 SWEDEN, THE SWASTIKA AND STALIN

Folkhem, 10, 35, 183, 238, 250, 267, 276
and foreign policy, 14, 30, 31, 37
forms wartime Coalition, 22, 25, 26, 27, 38
and German wounded, 202
and King Gustav, 24, 25, 38, 40, 68, 78, 265
and Jews, 100, 190, 193, 195, 196
and Police Troops, 101
and Leave Traffic concession, 47, 49, 50, 51, 52, 53, 58
in London, 21 n.18
and military, 210, 212, 219, 226
Minister of War, 10, 12, 20, 239
and Norway, 61, 98
and New Order, 57
and press, 158, 159, 160, 162
and Sandler, 14, 27, 30, 37, 38
speeches, 14, 44, 58, 59, 159, 177, 179, 209, 238, 245
staff talks with Western Allies, 110
and Wigforss, 27, 28, 37, 38
Pergament, Moses, 172
Persson, Edvard, 260
Persson, Göran, 279
Petersén, Carl, 137, 147–8, 149, 151
Petsamo (Pechanga), 41, 78, 97
  imports and exports, 126, 202
  nickel, 65, 93
Philby, 'Kim', 150
phoney war, 41, 163
Pilsnerfilmen, 19
Pippi Långstrump, 263
Police Troops
  Swedish policy 98, 101–2, 152, 165, 220
  German protests, 102, 286
Police Troops, Danish
  formation and training in Sweden, 101–2
Police Troops, Norwegian
  formation and training in Sweden, 102
  Allied support for, 99, 108, 149
  Operation Twinkle, 149
Poppe, Nils, 260, 262

Porkkala, 97, 219, 220
Posse, Amelie, 141
PoWs see prisoners of war
Pressnämnden, 161, 166
price control, 240–1, 242, 253, 265
Prince Carl, 202
prisoners of war, 203
  Dutch, 200
  exchanges, 202, 204, 206, 282
  Russian, 201
  see also internment
propaganda, 143
  British, 136, 162, 172–4
  German, 157, 162, 168–7
  and morale, 183–4
  policy, 160–1, 175–81
  Swedish, 181–3
Prytz, Björn, 31–2, 128, 272, 287 n.7
Prytz Telegram, 50–1, 271
public opinion, 18, 27, 29, 33, 42, 46, 58, 61, 62, 78, 81, 85, 87, 89, 90, 92, 94, 108, 111, 157, 159, 160, 163, 169, 171, 173, 174, 175–7, 193–4, 260, 265, 280
public transport, 248–9
PWE, 173

Quensel, Nils, 25, 26, 27, 28
Quisling, Vidkun CBE, 60–1, 62, 64, 98, 256, 266

Radiotjänst, 19, 60, 159, 160, 163–4, 166, 168, 179, 195, 254, 257–9, 261
RAF
  bombing, 100, 223
  internment, 202–4
  over-flying, 223–4
  in Sweden, 138–9, 151, 227
Rappe, Axel, 211–12
rationing, 165, 176, 177, 183, 239, 244–9, 253, 263, 267
  Emergency Boards (Kristidsstyrelserna), 245
  Emergency Committees (Kristidsnämnder), 245
Ravensbrück, 200
rearmament, 12, 54, 58, 71, 210, 228, 242

INDEX

Red Cross, 47, 61, 165, 188, 195, 198–9, 200–4
refugees, 18–9, 20, 39, 61–2, 97, 100, 102, 135, 136, 142, 147, 150, 151–3, 165, 179, 189–91, 193, 195, 201, 205, 232–3, 239, 256, 264, 279, 286
Reggiane fighters, 217
Reichsstelle für Aussenhandel, 191
Renault tanks, 211
Reuterskiöld, Gustaf, 168
RFSU, 16
Ribbentrop, Joachim von, 47, 48–9, 109, 171, 192, 198, 214
Richardson, Gunnar, 278
Richert, Arvid, 31, 46, 47, 48, 49, 51, 67, 78, 85, 158, 174, 193, 195, 198, 199, 212, 265
Rickman, Alfred, 140, 147
Ridd i natt!, 261
Riksdagen, 10, 12, 28, 29, 48, 50–1, 58–9, 68–70, 84, 87, 88, 89, 100, 110, 144, 160, 161, 166, 173, 181, 183, 188, 189, 190, 231, 241, 242, 243–4, 266, 267, 286
  secret sessions, 70, 77
  structure, 32–4
Riksföreningen Sverige-Tyskland, 171
Riksidrottsförbundet, 265
Riksmarschen, 266
Rinnan, Henry, 142
RKE see Commission for Economic Defence Preparation
Rogue Male, 261
Romania, 117, 120
Rosenberg, Alfred, 54, 171
Ross, Archibald, 146
RSHA, 192,
Runeberg, J. L., 164, 282
Russia (Tsarist), 7–9, 17, 18, 134, 164
Ryti, Risto, 40, 96, 97, 266
Röde Orm, 263

SAAB, 216–17
Safe-Conduct Traffic, 57
  belligerents and, 64, 80, 81, 82, 84–5, 87, 90, 104, 107, 118, 119, 120, 123–4
  importance of, 58, 84, 86, 103, 107, 118, 123, 125, 126, 165, 245, 247
Safehaven Programme, 129
SAK, 183, 251–2
Saltsjöbaden agreement, 24
Sandler Commission, 151–3
Sandler, Rickard, 10, 13, 14, 22, 26, 27, 28, 30, 34 n.11, 37–8, 47, 51, 55, 69, 151–2, 158, 191
Saturnus, 107
Scandinavian Pact, 75
Scavenius, Erik, 100
Schalberg Corps, 101
Schell, Adolf von, 229–30
Schellenberg, Walter, 111, 198–9
Schnurre, Karl, 53, 66, 67, 70, 75–6, 80, 123, 202
Schutz-Pass, 197, 199
SD, 133
SEB see Enskilda Banken
Secret Intelligence Service see MI6
Segerstedt, Torgny, 10, 19, 157, 158, 160, 280, 285
Sektionen för kulturell folkberedskap see Folkberedskap
Selborne, Earl Roundell Cecil Palmer, 122
shortages
  civilian, 8, 176, 239, 244, 245, 246, 247, 253, 263, 267
  military, 210, 221, 231
  skill and labour, 246, 264
Sicherheitsdienst see SD
Signal, 170
SIS, 160, 161, 165, 166, 168, 173, 175–82, 183, 193, 251, 257, 272; see also Folkberedskap
Sjöström, Victor, 19
SKBR, 232
SKF, 105–6, 113–14, 115, 125, 127, 128
Sköld, Per-Edvin, 24, 25, 26, 27, 28, 37, 38, 49, 50, 58, 70, 144, 178, 182, 205, 211, 212–14, 216, 221, 225, 227, 231
small-state realism, 270, 271, 272, 273, 274, 275, 277, 279
SNF Party, 170

Social Democratic Party, 8, 9, 10, 12, 14, 16, 17, 20, 22, 23, 24, 25, 28, 32, 37, 38, 46, 57, 59, 63, 69, 70, 71, 84, 89, 144, 166, 183, 188, 190, 205, 234, 239, 240, 242, 243–4, 244, 246
Socialstyrelsen, 190
SOE see British clandestine services
Soviet clandestine services, 133, 134, 135, 143–5, 146, 147, 149–51, 197–8
Soviet Union (Soviet Russia), 11, 13, 14, 15, 22, 29, 36–43, 49–57, 59, 63, 65, 66, 67, 68, 71, 74, 75, 79, 84, 92–9, 103, 106, 109, 110, 117, 118, 121, 129, 148, 153, 162, 163, 175, 184, 201, 202, 203–5, 209–12, 217–23, 225–8, 234, 240, 273, 281, 285
Special Operations Executive see British clandestine services
sport, 17, 265–266, 278
Spring, Howard, 263
Stalin, Joseph, 36, 40, 41, 59, 71, 82, 93, 94, 97, 126, 133, 174, 184, 202–3, 205, 258, 281, 285–6, 287
statare, 253
State Employment Commission see SAK
State Information Board see SIS
State Information Office (SIO), 159
Statens biografbyrå see SBB
Statens Informationsstyrelse see SIS
Statens reservförråd, 245
Stauning, Thorvald, 57, 64
Stephenson, Jill, 277
sterilisation, 16, 18
Stockholm Exhibition, 16
Stockholm Plan, 14, 37, 210
Stockholms Enskilda Bank see Enskilda Bank
Stolpe, Sven, 260
Storch, Gillel, 199
Storting, 60
Stridsberg, Gustaf, 19
Strindberg, August, 18
Strömbäck, Commodore Helge, 227

SUAV, 272–4, 279
surveillance see AS
Sutton-Pratt, Reggie, 138, 139, 140, 141, 151, 155 n.31
Svanberg, Ingvar and Tydén, Mattias, 278
Svensk historia, 270
Svensk Tiger, 257
Svenska Dagbladet, 19, 250
Svenska Kullagerfabriken see SKF
Svensk-tyska förening, 171
Sverige under andra världskriget see SUAV
Sveriges Lottakårer see Lottor
Svolvær raid, 65
Sweden, A Wartime Survey, 181, 182
Swedish Academy, 158
Swedish clandestine services see Allmänna Säkerhetstjänsten, Centralen
Swedish National Socialist Party, 17
Swedish Radio Service see Radiotjänst
Swedish Red Cross see Red Cross
Swedish State Institute for Race Biology, 188–9
Swedish Way of Life see Den svenska livsformen
Swedish–British–American London Tripartite Agreement see LTA
Söderblom, Staffan, 31

Tamm, Admiral Fabian, 46, 158, 226
Tamm, Viking, 233
Tanner, Väinö, 37
Taube, Evert, 20
taxation, 241–2
Tegnér, Esaias, 258
Teheran Conference, 103
Tennant, Sir Peter
  British Press Attaché, 169, 172–4, 283
  SOE officer, 136, 141, 14
Terboven, Josef, 60
Ternberg, Hellmuth, 147
Territorial Army see Landstorm
The Longships, 263
theatre, 257, 258, 261–2, 263

'A Theory of Human Motivation', 275–6
Thermaenius Edvard, 271, 272
Thomsen, Hans, 86, 87, 107, 169, 261
Thornton, Bill, 138, 139
Three-man Committee see Tremannanämnden
Thulstrup, Åke, 169, 272
Thörnell, Olof, 37, 47, 171, 179, 202, 209–13, 217, 219, 225–6, 234
Tisdagsklubben, 141
trade, 8, 15, 26, 27, 35, 113, 114, 115, 182, 245, 270, 272, 273, 274, 279
  with Britain, 35, 36, 115, 116
  with Finland, 88, 96, 97
  with Germany, 30, 36, 57, 66, 81, 82, 88, 90, 98, 104, 106, 108, 116, 117, 118, 120, 122, 123, 125, 126, 162, 190, 277, 282, 284, 285, 286, 287
  with other countries, 57, 58, 64, 71, 84, 116, 118
  with United States, 58, 81, 82, 104, 107
  with USSR, 117, 126
  with Western Allies, 82, 87, 88, 89, 103, 108, 120, 121, 124, 239
trades unions, 24, 60, 61
Trelleborg, 53, 205
Tremannanämnden, 159–60
Trojan Horse, 259
Trondheim, 53, 81, 230
Trots Allt!, 61, 153, 159, 161, 163
Trygve Lie, 83
TT, 158, 159, 160, 166, 168
Tunberg, Professor Sven, 175, 179, 180
Turnbull, Ronald, 142
Tänk, om jag gifter mig med prästen!, 263

UD (Swedish Foreign Ministry), 12, 14, 15, 30, 31, 32, 51, 53, 64, 68, 75, 76, 77, 82, 88, 95, 113, 128, 136, 140, 146, 147, 152, 153, 160, 161, 162, 163, 165, 166, 174, 182, 192, 193, 197, 199, 202, 203, 227, 257, 258, 259, 261, 262, 266, 272, 273, 274, 274, 279, 284, 287

Ulven, 222
Undén, Östen, 47, 85, 88, 205
United States (America), 74, 81, 82, 83, 90, 93, 94, 95, 96, 103, 104, 105, 106, 107, 113, 115, 119, 120, 121, 122, 124, 125, 128, 129, 190, 191, 197, 204, 211, 215, 217, 266
United States clandestine services see OSS
Upper Chamber Riksdagen, 32–3, 70, 243
Upplysningsnämnder, 176
USSR see Soviet Union
Uthmann, Bruno von, 179, 180, 226
Utrikesdepartementet see UD
Utrikesnämnden, 24, 25, 33, 38, 47, 53, 69, 85, 88, 89
Utrikesutskottet, 33, 50, 51, 68, 69, 84, 85, 88
Utrymningskommissionen, 254

Vassijaure, 223
Vennberg, Karl, 263
Volvo, 216
Vougt, Allan, 57
Västra Frölunda, 176

Waffen-SS, 200
Wahlbäck, Krister, 272, 278
Wallenberg, Jacob, 114
Wallenberg, Marcus Junior, 114, 116
  SVT interview, 129–30
Wallenberg, Marcus Senior, 114, 115, 128
Wallenberg, K. A., 8
Wallenberg, Raoul, 8, 174, 192, 197–8, 199, 279, 281
Wallenberg Brothers, 127, 128, 278
  blacklisting, 125, 129
  influence, 115, 129
War Refugee Board, 197
War Trade Agreement see WTA
Wechselmann, Maj, 278
Weserübung, 43, 44, 54
Westman, Karl-Gustav, 23, 25, 26, 28, 28, 35, 38, 49, 50, 71, 144, 213, 225, 225, 248, 254, 274
  and press, 161, 163, 164, 165, 166

White Buses, 108, 198–200, 206
Wied, Prince Viktor zu, 43, 51, 86, 163, 169, 193
Wigforss, Ernst, 10, 22, 24, 25, 26, 27, 28, 34 n.11, 37, 38, 49, 65, 69, 70, 76, 89, 130, 226, 240, 241, 242, 249, 251, 272
Winter War, 22, 36–41, 42, 44, 47, 59, 92, 93, 94, 97, 143, 163, 201, 211–12, 223, 231, 233, 259
Wollweber, Ernst, 146–7
women
  in employment, 181–3, 250–2, 264
  in politics, 32, 240, 242
  in services, 231–3
  in society, 9, 16, 249–52, 254, 267
Women's Employment Committee, 251
World Jewish Congress, 197, 199, 200
World Ski Championships, 265
WTA, 36, 41, 57, 83, 88, 116, 117, 118, 120, 122
Wägner, Elin, 262

Zetterberg, Kent, 279

Ådalen, 16
Åkerhielm, Samuel, 225–6
Åland Islands, 11, 14, 35, 36–7, 54–5, 97, 210, 217, 220, 222, 224
Åmark, Klaus, 279

EU representative:
Easy Access System Europe
Mustamäe tee 50, 10621 Tallinn, Estonia
Gpsr.requests@easproject.com

www.ingramcontent.com/pod-product-compliance
Lightning Source LLC
Chambersburg PA
CBHW070014010526
44117CB00011B/1560